"A truly engaging account of the Civil War through the lens of an important but now forgotten figure. Absalom Markland was a noted antebellum journalist who literally delivered the mail to General Grant's soldiers and then helped integrate the U.S. Postal Service after the war. This book brings to life so many aspects of the wartime experience that it should become a must-read for any devoted student of the Civil War."

—MATTHEW PINSKER, Pohanka Chair for
Civil War History, Dickinson College

"Although little known today, Absalom Markland made sure that the average Civil War soldier and leading generals received the latest mail from the home front and the battlefield. This important work kept Union morale high and . . . cannot be overemphasized. Candice Shy Hooper's new book only adds to her earlier study of the wives of Civil War generals and provides another important insight into the Civil War."

—JOHN F. MARSZALEK, executive director
of the Ulysses S. Grant Presidential Library

"*Delivered Under Fire* is the story of one man's efforts to keep soldiers and their families connected during the most divisive years in the nation's history. . . . Candice Shy Hooper has made us feel the importance of mail service as an expression of humanity juxtaposed with the cold-bloodedness of war."

—EDNA GREENE MEDFORD, historian
and author of *Lincoln and Emancipation*

DELIVERED UNDER FIRE

DELIVERED UNDER FIRE

ABSALOM MARKLAND
AND FREEDOM'S MAIL

CANDICE SHY HOOPER

Potomac Books

An imprint of the University of Nebraska Press

All rights reserved. Potomac Books is an imprint of the
University of Nebraska Press.
Manufactured in the United States of America.

Library of Congress Cataloging-in-Publication Data
Names: Hooper, Candice Shy, author.
Title: Delivered under fire: Absalom Markland and freedom's mail /
Candice Shy Hooper.
Description: Lincoln: Potomac Books, an imprint of the University of
Nebraska Press, [2023] | Includes bibliographical references and index.
Identifiers: LCCN 2022013783
ISBN 9781640124486 (hardback)
ISBN 9781640125759 (epub)
ISBN 9781640125766 (pdf)
Subjects: LCSH: Markland, Absalom H., –1888. | United States. Army—
Postal service. | United States. Post Office Department—Officials and
employees—Biography. | Letter carriers—United States—Biography. |
United States—History—Civil War, 1861–1865—Postal service.
Classification: LCC HE6385.M37 H66 2023 |
DDC 383/.492 [B]—dc23/eng/20220323
LC record available at https://lccn.loc.gov/2022013783

Set in Arno Pro by A. Shahan.

For Lindsay
again, and always

Contents

List of Illustrations . . ix

Preface . . xi

Prologue: April 14, 1865 . . 1

1. A Boy of the Buffalo Trace: 1825–55 . . 5

2. A Man in Search of a Mission: 1856–61 . . 23

3. Absalom Markland, Special Agent: 1861–62 . . 31

4. "An Honored & Favored Man":
February–September 1862 . . 47

5. "The Flood of Letters": September 1862–64 . . 73

6. "Twenty Tons of Mail": 1864 . . 105

7. "Trains Have Stopped Running, Except for the Mail":
January–April 1865 . . 135

8. "A Mark of Friendship and Esteem":
April 1865–November 1868 . . 155

9. "Our Continued Services Together": 1868–71 . . 173

10. The "Colonel" Becomes a "General": 1872–84 . . 205

11. A Man in Search of Himself: 1885–88 . . 233

Epilogue: 1889–Today . . 263

Acknowledgments . . 267

Notes . . 273

Bibliography . . 297

Index . . 305

Illustrations

Figures

Following page 154

1. Martha Louisa Simms Markland and Absalom Markland, ca. 1851

2. Markland's commission as special agent of the Post Office Department

3. Adversity cover

4. Gunboat attack on Fort Henry

5. Purported portrait of Grant after Fort Donelson

6. "Col. Absalom H. Markland, Superintendent of Mails"

7. Pittsburg Landing, ca. 1862

8. Memphis Post Office

9. Maj. Absalom Grimes

10. Civil War camp in winter

11. Soldiers writing letters and mending clothing

12. Markland's "All Points Pass"

13. Newspapers arriving in camp, ca. 1863

14. Poster announcing mail service

15. New Year's Day reception for the public at Sherman's headquarters

16. First Division, Ninth Corps, mail center, ca. 1864

17. "Murder of President Lincoln"

18. The Grimsley saddle

19. William H. Gibson Sr., 1897

20. Signing of the Ku Klux Klan Act of 1871

21. Interior of the Post Office and Custom House
after the Great Chicago Fire

22. Planked shad at Marshall Hall

23. Second and Market Streets, Maysville, 1884 flood

24. Absalom Hanks Markland, ca. 1885

Maps

1. Absalom Markland's world . . xiv

2. 1871 KKK attack on the railway mail . . 190

3. Maysville, Kentucky, ca. 1840 . . 244

Preface

Of heroes, history, grand events, premises, myths, poems,
The few drops known must stand for oceans of the unknown.
—WALT WHITMAN

More than seventy thousand volumes about the Civil War have been published in the 160 years since Confederates fired on Fort Sumter. Those books explore such a variety of topics that they often have little in common, except that most of them rely on letters written during the war. Whether in a biography of a famous general or an account of an enslaved woman seeking freedom, at least one letter written in the last half of the nineteenth century will be quoted as part of the tale. Indeed, the contents of letters written during those four bloody years have become so embedded in Civil War narratives that even historians give little thought to how millions of letters moved between the front lines and the home front—often faster than mail moves today.

This book tells the story of the courageous, innovative, self-made man who developed the infrastructure of the United States' military mail service, elements of which are still in use. Amid the unprecedented deployment of thousands of soldiers in defense of the United States, Absalom H. Markland managed the torrent of letters unleashed on the nation's postal system. By one count, Markland and his men handled nearly 250,000 soldiers' letters per day. It was an enormous undertaking, essential to the Union Army's morale. President Lincoln and his generals Ulysses S. Grant and William Tecumseh Sherman knew the value of mail to their soldiers' fighting spirit. Their respect for Markland's dedication and their enjoyment of his company forged bonds that lasted the rest of the men's lives.

From Cairo, Illinois, in 1861 to City Point, Virginia, in 1865, Markland traveled with (and often in advance of) Grant's armies, ensuring the swiftest possible delivery of mail, sometimes even as bullets whizzed overhead. He visited regularly with Lincoln and aided Sherman's March to the Sea. As Grant's responsibilities grew to embrace the entire Union Army, so did Markland's. Then, when Grant became president, he called on Markland again, to help him in the fight for civil rights. In doing so, Markland hired William H. Gibson as the first Black railroad mail agent in Kentucky. The remarkable Gibson courageously faced down the Ku Klux Klan, spurring passage of a major civil rights bill—a story told here for the first time.

I first encountered the name Absalom Markland in the Library of Congress in 2008. That name popped up again and again while I was researching my previous book, *Lincoln's Generals' Wives*, which relied heavily on letters exchanged by four famous couples during the war. The library's collection of Markland's papers gave me a tantalizing glimpse into his remarkable wartime mission and made me think for the first time about the debt owed to those who deliver the mail in wartime. I recalled just how important military mail was to my family when I was young, when my father, a U.S. Navy hospital corpsman, would disappear for months at a time on board a ship in the Pacific Ocean—no telephone, no email, no communication. I remember how my mother carefully wrapped and addressed our simple letters and homemade artwork to be sent through the FPO (Fleet Post Office) to ports where his ship would dock just long enough to take on supplies and mail from "the States." But it was only after reading letters to and from Civil War soldiers that I saw my childish expressions of love through my father's homesick eyes.

As the poet Walt Whitman wrote, the thousands of stories already written about the Civil War are but drops in the oceans of unknown tales of heroes and grand events that remain to be told. This book is my effort to bring deserved attention to a long-forgotten American hero, Absalom Markland.

Delivered Under Fire

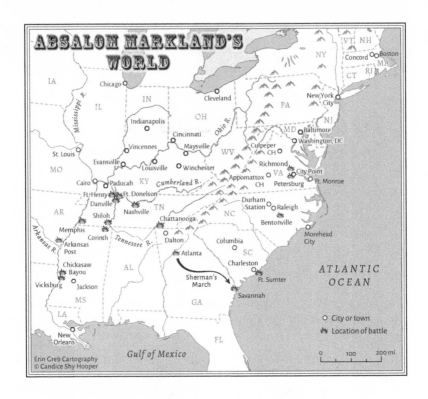

Map 1. Absalom Markland's world. Erin Greb Cartography.

Prologue

April 14, 1865

N ear midnight in the war-weary capital of the United States, the waning moon cast a pallid glow over the hushed crowd on Tenth Street between Ford's Theatre and the Petersen House, where Abraham Lincoln lay dying.

One hundred forty miles away, Lt. Gen. Ulysses Grant and his wife, Julia, who had declined the Lincolns' invitation to the theater that night, arrived in Philadelphia for a brief layover on their train journey home to New Jersey. At Bloodgood's Hotel, they ordered oysters for the general, who had not eaten since breakfast. Before the oysters were served, three telegrams were thrust into his hands in quick succession. Cautioning her not to exclaim, Grant told Julia in a low voice that the president had been shot. "I must go back at once," he said.[1]

Lincoln died, without ever regaining consciousness, at 7:22 the next morning, as Grant raced overnight to Washington on a private train, hastily arranged to ensure the general's safety. There, the search for Lincoln's killer—or killers, no one yet knew for sure—was spinning almost wildly out of control. Many witnesses saw the man who fled the theater after he shot the president, but no one could say definitively which way he went. Spurred by wild rumors, civilian and military authorities spread their resources widely, thinly—north toward Baltimore, even into Canada, and south toward Richmond.

Grant plunged back into the business of managing a war that seemed to have no end, one that now included a search for his commander in chief's elusive killer. Questions filled his—everyone's—

mind. Had the leadership of the Confederacy conspired to assassinate Lincoln and his cabinet in a final, desperate act to destroy the Union? How was the government to determine the full extent of the assassin's scheme?

Civil and military authorities moved swiftly to lock down the capital. In a wartime measure, the War Department had taken control of the telegraph lines, so treasonous messages carried by the assassin and any accomplices could still be intercepted. Roads and bridges out of the city were blocked, and no one was allowed to pass (galloping from the theater, John Wilkes Booth bluffed his way past the regular sentry before the city was placed on high alert). A rumor that the assassin was heading to Alexandria, Virginia, to take a train west to Fairfax, spurred Secretary of War Edwin Stanton's order that all trains be stopped and "all persons on train or on the road not known" arrested. Transportation and communications options in the middle of the nineteenth century, before invention of the telephone in 1876, were limited. One by one, all such means were suspended. "Boats can neither land at nor leave the wharf," wrote a volunteer nurse in Washington in her journal on April 15. "Trains have stopped running, except for the mail."[2]

Grant's thoughts turned to the mail. Immediately after the Union Army seized the Confederate capital of Richmond, Virginia, in early April, Grant had, as he had always done, ordered mail service restored to and from the newly Union-occupied city. Now he was having second thoughts, concerned about plotters who might be hiding in Richmond, conspiring in letters with assassins in Washington. He wondered if evidence of the plot could be found hiding in plain sight.

In that moment, Grant turned for help to the architect of the supremely efficient mail system that had connected the front lines to the home front throughout the war, the man who had traveled with his armies since his first great victory at the outset of the war, a civilian he called "colonel," known and beloved throughout the army, a self-made man from Kentucky whose integrity and resourcefulness he trusted implicitly. Grant turned to his childhood friend, Absalom Markland.

Headquarters Armies of the United States
Washington, D.C., April 17, 1865

Col. A. H. Markland

Special Agent of the P. O. Department, Washington City:

Colonel:

Lieutenant-General Grant directs that no mail matter be sent to Richmond addressed to citizens of that place until further orders. He further directs that you unseal and examine all letters in the mails addressed to citizens of Richmond and forward to these headquarters all such as contain contraband information.

Very respectfully, your obedient servant,

T. S. Bowers,
Assistant Adjutant-General.[3]

As he did every time Grant needed his help—from the triumph at Fort Donelson in 1862 to that darkest of days in Washington three years later—Markland delivered.

ONE

A Boy of the Buffalo Trace

1825–55

Kentucky was still considered the West when Absalom Markland was born in 1825. The land of bluegrass and bourbon, of bison and bears, was home to many Revolutionary War veterans who settled on "bounty land" cleaved from Virginia in 1792 and admitted as the fifteenth state in the Union. A determined, optimistic pioneer spirit—and backbreaking physical effort—enabled white men, women, and children to hew homes and farms out of the wilderness, while battling starvation, drought, and Native Americans.

Winchester, in the foothills of the mountains of eastern Kentucky, was Markland's first home. His father, Matthew, settled there in 1818 and married a daughter of one of its leading citizens. Less than four years after Absalom was born, Matthew Markland moved his family about sixty miles northeast, to Maysville. Thirty years earlier, Daniel Boone had helped to found Maysville at the point where bison forded the Ohio River and then pounded a trail southwest toward Lexington, seeking salt. This was the famous Buffalo Trace.[1]

From this river port, corn, tobacco, hemp, and whisky, largely produced by enslaved persons, were loaded aboard steamboats for transport up the Ohio River to Pittsburgh or down the Ohio to the Mississippi River and New Orleans. A visitor to Maysville in 1829 estimated it to be a town of three thousand citizens that "presents, from the river, an unbroken front of elegant brick buildings, the streets are well paved; has a good landing, and appears better from the water, than almost any town on the banks of the Ohio." He counted twenty-eight dry goods stores, one large "queensware [Wedgwood] and china store," four grocery stores, an iron foundry, a large paper mill, a stoneware manufacturer, and "three large churches, belonging to the Presbyterians, Baptists, and Methodists."[2]

The people of Maysville were strivers, achievers—and not just in business. Maysville Academy was a small but prestigious school founded in 1832 by John Brett Richeson and Jacob Rand, who challenged their pupils' minds beyond reading, writing, and sums. The academy was a training ground for teachers throughout Kentucky and gave Maysville a well-deserved reputation for educational excellence. Local newspapers flourished, and others arrived in the city by boat and by one of the earliest stage-mail routes, initiated by President Andrew Jackson's postmaster general in 1829.[3]

But Maysville was more than a bustling, literate, commercial junction high on the banks of the Ohio River. It was a community with a carefully concealed internal contradiction. Enslaved persons, who made up about one-quarter of Kentucky's population, were sold at auction on the front lawn of the courthouse. The searing memory of one of those slave auctions witnessed by Harriet Beecher Stowe in 1833 became a memorable scene in *Uncle Tom's Cabin*. At the same time, just down the street, the Bierbowers, a family of German immigrants, hid those running away from slavery under the floorboards of their house. It was one stop on the Underground Railroad to freedom across the river in Ohio, conducted by a system of secret volunteers operating in Kentucky since 1790. Decades before the Civil War, Maysville was a microcosm of the fatal flaw in American society, the "house divided."[4]

Matthew Markland, "a fine accountant & book keeper" who later studied the law, quickly found his footing in Maysville and became its justice of the peace soon after he arrived in 1828. He and his wife, Margaret, and their four children settled into life in the booming town that was second only to Louisville in commerce and trade in the state. Absalom was the fourth child and first son—daughters Adelia Ann, Rebecca, and Violinda preceded him. His brother, Matthew, the fifth and last child, was born in Maysville in 1837.[5]

The year before Matthew was born, eleven-year-old Absalom was enrolled in the Maysville Academy. There, he found friends and honed skills that launched the trajectory of his life. His fellow students included brothers Elijah and John Phister (the former became a member of Congress and the latter, a doctor), E. M. Richeson (son of the school's founder), future member of Congress William Henry Wadsworth, Walter Newman Haldeman (founder of the *Louisville Courier-Journal*), William H. "Bull" Nelson (who would later serve as both an admiral in the navy and a general in the army), Thomas Hill Nelson (an organizer of the Indiana Republican Party in the 1850s), and, boarding with his widowed aunt, a young man from Georgetown, Ohio, named Hiram Ulysses Grant (later known as Ulysses S. Grant). It is no stretch to say that Maysville, both the place and its people, stayed with Markland all his life.[6]

Recollections of those school days marked this circle of young men as determined and self-disciplined. In addition to their regular course of study, many of them were also active participants in a debating club called the Philomathean Society, the Greek term "philomathean" meaning "lover of learning." Records of the society reveal that the subjects they debated were weighty ones for the times—and often quite ironic, considering what their futures held. Among the topics they debated were these:

"*Resolved*, That females wield greater influence in society than males."

"*Resolved*, That it would not be just and politic to liberate the slaves at this time."

"*Resolved*, That intemperance is a greater evil than war."

"*Resolved*, That the writer deserves more praise than the orator."

"*Resolved*, That Columbus deserves more praise for discovering America than Washington did for defending it."

"*Resolved*, That America can boast of as great men as any other nation."[7]

Markland was designated judge for the last of the debates, and he pronounced the negative side the winner. He later confessed that he had fallen asleep during the debate and, upon being awakened, stammered his ruling based only on his unspoken rationale that America was the youngest country and that others had had more time to produce great men. Fortunately, he recalled, "I made no enemies by the decision and was congratulated on my astuteness."[8]

Along with Markland, Grant (called "Lyss" at school) was elected a member of the society's organizing committee and took that responsibility seriously. At one meeting, Grant proposed "that it be considered out of order for any member to speak on the opposite side to which he is placed." Each meeting featured an opening speech by one of the members and then a debate on the evening's chosen topic. Grant was an active debater, and his side of a question prevailed more often than not, but "he would rather pay six and a quarter cents fine than declaim," according to Professor Richeson, who also recalled that "he ranked high in all his classes, and his deportment was exceptionally good." Grant stayed only one year; his last record of attendance was in March 1838.[9]

Though Grant claims in his memoirs that the curriculum was repetitive and boring, he places blame for his departure on himself: "I was not studious in habit, and probably did not make progress enough to compensate for the outlay for board and tuition." The next year, at his father's insistence, he entered the U.S. Military Academy at West Point, where both board and tuition were free. Overall, though Grant's stay in Maysville was short, the friendships he forged there were strong and lasting, and his memories of Maysville were among the first and most poignant remembrances included in his memoirs, written nearly fifty years later.[10]

Markland's memories of Maysville stayed with him till the end of his life, too. Two years before he died, he wrote a series of letters to the *Maysville Republican* newspaper about his early life in that part of the country, which followed the rhythms of the seasons. As a young man, he fished and swam in the nearby rivers and ponds, rode horses over the countryside, learned to handle boats of all kinds, hunted berries and birds, attended church. He spent many Saturdays in Shultz's Mill, with "its wheels with their cogs, bands, shafts, pulleys and hoppers," and "never tired of watching its powerful motions."

A Boy of the Buffalo Trace

He recalled the historic flood of 1832 and a massive meteor shower in November 1833 that was "new, awful, and grand."[11]

After Maysville Academy, he attended Augusta College, the third Methodist university in the country and the first in Kentucky. Founded the same year Absalom was born, the college attracted teachers and students who vigorously opposed slavery, and the school was soon viewed as a breeding ground for abolitionists. As a result, not long after Markland left the college, Kentucky's legislature revoked Augusta College's charter, forcing the institution to close in 1849.[12]

Young Markland took a turn as schoolteacher in 1843 in Manchester, Ohio, but that did not suit his restless, independent personality. From 1843 until 1848, he worked as a freight clerk on steamboats between Cincinnati and New Orleans. Throughout his life he would recall his experience as "an old steamboatman," including a stint on an Arkansas mail boat. When he composed his résumé in later years, his consummate sense of self-marketing inflated that riverboat experience to read that he "became identified with the transportation interests on the Western lines." During his time on riverboats, Markland continued his program of self-improvement, studying the law and writing pieces for newspapers under his steamboat nickname, "Oily Buckshot." Among the newspapers to which he contributed was the recently established *Morning Courier and American Democrat* (predecessor to the *Louisville Courier*), started in 1844 by his fellow Maysville Academy classmate Walter Haldeman.[13]

Most of the January 17, 1845, edition of that newspaper—four pages of tiny, eye-watering type—was devoted to advertisements for the ever-proliferating array of goods and services in that era: "Lindsey's Liniment," lady's half gaiters, bagging and twine, borax, sugar, oysters (in the shell and canned), English carpets, passage on steamboats, books of all types, a "Negro Woman about 30 years of age, a good Cook and Washer, and her child, a girl 5 years of age," and just below a notice for a meeting of the Female Missionary Society, a relatively large advertisement for Markland's services as a "General Collector and Travelling Agent for the States of Ohio, Kentucky and Indiana." This was the first of hundreds of times Markland's name would appear in newspapers during his lifetime, though not the only time his name was misspelled. The advertisement read in full,

ABSOLEM H. MARKLAND,

General Collector and Travelling Agent for the States of Ohio, Kentucky and Indiana. Residence—Maysville, Ky.

Will attend faithfully to all business entrusted to his care. Collections remitted and accounts settled with dispatch. All letters addressed as above, *post paid*, will meet with immediate attention.

Refer to:

L. Collins
F. T. Hord   Maysville
R. H. Stanton
L. C. & H. T. Pearce

Shropshire & Ellmaker, New Orleans
Shults, Hadden & Leach

Frederick Vincent, Norfolk, Va.
Commodore Pendegrast, Philadelphia
W. N. Haldeman, Louisville[14]

In the nineteenth century, a "general collector and travelling agent" was an indispensable part of commerce, a sort of early independent courier who would reliably collect and deliver money, documents, and goods at a time when the post office mostly delivered newspapers and letters. The best agents were dependable, resourceful, and well acquainted with all the various modes of transportation. There was no formal bonding process for agents, so they relied on the reputation of their references to attract customers. Markland's references were impressive and appeared to be wide-ranging, from Philadelphia to New Orleans (though S. G. Shropshire and Commodore Pendegrast were both native Kentuckians—another deft marketing touch).

Despite the misspelling of his name, Markland's advertisement was a sober and professional appeal for customers in a time of financial and political turmoil. Considerable space in that same newspaper edition was devoted to detailed descriptions of widely circulated

A Boy of the Buffalo Trace

counterfeit bonds and paper money, all cautioning readers to examine carefully any that came their way. One of more than eighty fraudulent forms of payment described was a series of ten-dollar bills in which the legal version's prominent illustration was of a hunter on horseback, "while the counterfeits have for a vignette a view of a steamboat, ship, &c." Another article reported that a free Black man, arrested under the Fugitive Slave Act in St. Louis for aiding those running away from slavery, had subsequently been shot while trying to escape from jail. On page 2 the newspaper reprinted a desperate letter from dying former president Andrew Jackson to the publisher of the *Washington Globe* newspaper, Francis Preston Blair, urging Congress to annex the Republic of Texas. Above the letter, it was reported that the U.S. House of Representatives had just rejected the latest Texas annexation bill.

Annexation of Texas and its admission to the Union as a slave state occurred in December 1845, six months after Jackson's death. Conflicting claims between Mexico and the United States over the boundaries of the newest state were largely responsible for the almost immediate outbreak of war with Mexico, which lasted until 1848. Unlike Markland's friend Grant, who fought in some of that war's fiercest battles after graduating from West Point, his own life was relatively untouched by the turmoil. In 1848 he moved to the prosperous steamboat and rail town of Paducah, Kentucky, where he managed a wholesale trading operation and bought some property. Markland's parents also lived in Paducah at that time. The only definite record we have of his mother is that "Margaret Markland, consort of Matthew Markland," died in Paducah on December 13, 1848, possibly of cholera, at the age of fifty-three. She left behind a husband the same age, three grown daughters, and two sons. Young Matthew was eleven.[15]

That year, Absalom was twenty-three years old, a well-educated, ambitious, talented, and physically imposing young man. Standing six feet, two inches tall, he was seven inches taller than Grant at the same age, who at five feet, seven inches was average height for men of that era. Early in his life, Markland grew a beard, as did many men in those days. Physically strong, he was also described as "gentle in spirit and mild in bearing." Always alert to the humor in any situation, especially when the joke was on him, Markland easily made friends all his life. A daguerreotype of him, likely taken at age twenty-nine, shows a well-dressed, dark-haired, neatly groomed young man with a modest mustache and beard, kind eyes, and the hint of a smile.[16]

A year after his mother's death, Absalom and his father moved to Washington DC. The nation's capital needed men like Absalom and Matthew—honest, resourceful men who could write legibly, keep careful track of money, and handle paperwork by the ream. Thousands were hired to supply the ever-expanding bureaucracy's need for communication and records. In addition to the original executive departments established by the Constitution—Foreign Affairs (later renamed State), Treasury, and War—the Office of Attorney General (later Justice) demanded clerks, as did the Post Office Department, which predated creation of the United States. Benjamin Franklin, who had been colonial postmaster, established the postal system for the new nation, one that required lots of paper and lots of people to push it.

Expansion of the physical size of the nation, despite resistance from Native Americans who refused to step aside for land-hungry white settlers, compelled creation of a new executive department in December 1849. The Department of the Interior consolidated the General Land Office, Patent Office, Office of Indian Affairs, and the Bureau of Pensions. Absalom's father first appears in Washington in government records as a special agent of the Office of Indian Affairs in 1849. As such, he was entrusted to deliver documents, fancy medallions, and gold to army officials implementing the national policy begun with the Indian Removal Act, signed into law by President Jackson nearly two decades earlier.[17]

The policy originally involved the negotiation of treaties with Chickasaw, Choctaw, Seminole, Cherokee, and Creek groups in the United States, by which the U.S. government secured tribal lands wanted by white settlers for their fertile soil, prairie grass, or minerals. In exchange, the United States offered a payment (often in gold) and a promise to relocate the people to similarly productive lands in the Western Territories. But the land exchanged was never

A Boy of the Buffalo Trace

equivalent, nor did the money ever compensate for loss of their traditional way of life. Soon, tribes refused to deal at all. By 1849 the subsequent policy of forced removal had left only a small number of tenacious Seminoles in Florida. Paying them to move was Matthew Markland's assignment.

A special agent needed all the skills of a good office clerk—integrity, accountability, and dependability. In addition, the job required toughness, resourcefulness, resilience, and self-reliance. One of Matthew's early assignments sent him on a journey south from Washington, then to Arkansas, and finally to Oklahoma Territory in search of an army officer who was supposed to have been in Florida supervising the removal of a small band of Seminoles. A shorter and more direct mission began on February 9, 1850, when Markland left from New York "on the Southern steamer with $100,000 in gold" (worth more than $3 million today). Fifteen days later, in Tampa Bay, Florida, he delivered the gold to John C. Casey, "Capt. and Special Agent for removing Seminoles." Matthew Markland was commended for "having made great dispatch," and he returned to Washington with duplicate receipts for the funds he had delivered, which "arrived just in time to meet the payment of the first party of Indians consisting of 75 to 80 of all ages and both sexes."[18]

The military men who supervised these removals evicted most of the remaining Seminoles from their homes in the lush Florida Everglades, exiling them to the parched, windswept plains of Oklahoma. Even if they believed in the policy and their duty to execute it, it was a dirty business. Likewise, civilian special agents like Matthew Markland saw both the beloved forsaken homelands and the bleak conditions into which the hopeless, dispossessed men, women, and children were being delivered.

Matthew's son Absalom received his first mention in the Washington print media in the *Daily Republic* on April 6, 1850, when he was recorded as "A H Markland, Ky," and—in the tradition of the day—as having registered at the Brown's Hotel on Pennsylvania Avenue, between Sixth and Seventh Streets. Absalom was also employed as a clerk, first briefly in the Office of Indian Affairs and later in the Bureau of Pensions, responsible for military pensions, at an annual salary of $1,000. All the while, he continued to write articles for "the Western press." It would seem that the young man had little spare time for other pursuits, but in August of the next year, the *Daily Republic* reported the following news:

MARRIED,

On Sunday morning, the 24th instant, by Rev. L. F. Morgan, Mr. A. H. Markland of Kentucky, to Miss M. L. Simms, daughter of Mr. Sampson Simms, of this city.[19]

With his good looks, industrious demeanor, steady income, and engaging personality, Markland had swiftly wooed and wed the daughter of one of Washington's prominent men of business.

Sampson Simms was a carpenter whose own industriousness had built a small real estate empire. He began his enterprise in Baltimore in the mid-1840s, and by 1849 he had moved to the District of Columbia, where he accumulated land and erected buildings that he sold or rented. His high standing in the community is evident from the fact that he was one of nine trustees deeded land in Georgetown for construction of the Dumbarton Avenue Methodist Church, one of the earliest Methodist congregations in the area. Sampson and his wife, Harriet, had six children, of which Martha was the youngest girl. She was a dark-eyed, dark-haired beauty, and a photograph shows her wearing large hoop earrings and two bracelets, likely of gold, on one wrist. A large, intricately carved cameo brooch is pinned on an elaborate lace collar at her throat. The daguerreotype of the newly-wed Absalom and Martha shows a couple who look young but confident of their future. In the early years of their marriage, they lived in her father's house, which he operated as a boardinghouse, at 480 L Street Northwest.[20]

Less than a year after his marriage, Absalom resigned from the military pension office to practice law, thus continuing his long-term preference for being his own boss. He capitalized on his recent government employment to specialize in cases involving pensions and bounty land claims for veterans of the Revolutionary War and the War of 1812. Legal requirements to obtain pensions and bounty lands arising from service in those wars were strict and unforgiving, so Markland's pension office experience was a strong selling point. He likely also resumed his role as a general collector and traveling agent that fall, when he undertook an extended trip south to Georgia, Tennessee, and Ohio. On September 17 he wrote to "My beloved Wife," from Dalton, Georgia. In beautifully legible script and perfect grammar, this early letter to Martha set out themes that he repeated in the letters he wrote to her over the years:

> My beloved Wife,
>
> I am in perfect health—I pray God that you may be similarly blest. If I could be assured that you were well & in good spirits I would be comparatively happy but I fear, greatly fear that you will fret and become uneasy on account of my absence. You must not, you will not.
>
> If I ever get home again I will never undertake another trip without you.
>
> I am doing very well in business, yet, I am disturbed on your account. I have not heard from you since I left.
>
> I will be in Nashville, Tennessee in a few days & there I will get your letters. I am very anxious to hear from you. I have written to you regularly since I left, the letters were short but contained all you desired to know—that was that I was well. I will be at home if alive about the 10th Octo. Write to me at Cincinnati, Ohio care Barker Hart & Co. My love to all. May God bless you my affectionate wife.
>
> AHM
>
> P.S. I enclose you a draft for $50 which you will get your father to get cashed, with the money provide yourself with whatever you may want.[21]

Like most letters of the nineteenth century, it opens with a discussion of the health of the writer and of the reader. In Absalom's case, concern about his wife's state of mind in his absence is always present, and he reassures her of his health. A typical letter would then move to a status report on communication—how many or how regularly letters were mailed and received. Often the dates of letters mailed and those received are specified, so the correspondents could account for all their letters. Markland's emphasis on the regularity of his letter writing and his complaint about the lack of letters from Martha is another recurring theme in their correspondence. Absalom closes with a reference to finances, also a regular part of correspondence between husbands and wives.

On the other hand, two of Absalom's phrases, "If I ever get home again" and "I will be at home if alive," are not standard fare in peacetime correspondence. With no explanation of what threats he faced, we are left to assume that either Martha knew more than we do or that Absalom was regularly haunted by thoughts of death. The latter seems more likely, since his letters over the next thirty-five years—before, during, and after the Civil War—resonate with grim expressions of sorrow about illness and death, faint hopes of meeting loved ones again "in God," and emphatic demands that Martha "be cheerful" no matter the difficulties she is facing. In the face of high mortality rates, people in the mid- to late nineteenth century were preoccupied with death and practiced elaborate mourning rituals. But Markland's fixation on death and danger is a step beyond the norm, even for the Victorian era.

On this trip he would have traveled via several different modes of transportation—boat, horse and carriage, and railroad—all of which held their own dangers, to be sure, but those were not extraordinary for their time. In fact, his trip should have been an exciting one for someone with Markland's native curiosity and thirst for learning. The just-completed railroad tunnel at Dalton, Georgia, was a true feat of modern engineering. Nearly 1,500 feet long, it was the first tunnel through the Appalachian Mountains and the first railroad tunnel constructed in the South. As he journeyed through Georgia and Tennessee, Markland was unknowingly reconnoitering territory that would later be under his jurisdiction, areas that would feature in major military movements of the Civil War.[22]

Fortunately, no tragedy prevented Absalom's return to Washington from that trip, and he once again fully engaged in the life of the city. In 1853 he became a junior warden in Federal Lodge 1 of the Free and Accepted Masons, also known as the Pentalpha Lodge. Following his father-in-law's example, Markland invested in a vacant lot in northwest Washington. In addition, his legal practice would have gotten a boost that year through association with John A. Richardson, "Attorney at Law, and Agent for Pension and Bounty Land Claims" in North Carolina. In January 1853 Richardson posted an advertisement in the Fayetteville newspaper, touting his "associate Attorney, A. H. Markland, who was, for many years, a Clerk in the Pension office, and is therefore thoroughly acquainted with all the Pension and Bounty Land Laws, and the sources from which evidence can be obtained to establish such claims." Markland seems never to have relinquished his vocation as a traveling agent.[23]

How Martha spent her days is unfortunately not known. She may have assisted her mother, Harriet, who managed a grocery store near her parents' boardinghouse, or Martha may have worked in some capacity in the operation of that boardinghouse, where she and Markland made their home. Three years after their wedding, the couple had no children, nor would there ever be any. After the war there are reports of the Marklands attending "hops" at the Willard Hotel and of Martha attending fêtes at the White House, both activities indicating a lively social life that was probably evident from the start of their marriage. From all available evidence, they were a very happy couple.[24]

Markland's father was still clerking in Washington, though he had changed jobs. By July 1853 Matthew had moved from the Indian Office to the War Department, where he was listed as a "Class 2 Clerk" in the Office of the Quartermaster General at an annual salary of $1,000. The quartermaster general's department handled all the purchasing for the army, and even in peacetime it was often accused of being a hotbed of corruption, as crooked suppliers sought to sell inferior goods at inflated prices, bribing officials up and down the chain of command to line their pockets. At the same time, an honest mistake in the procurement of any one of thousands of items could subject a junior quartermaster to court-martial or a civilian clerk to criminal process. A man in Matthew's position would have been closely scrutinized by honest superiors and continually enticed by dishonest ones. While his new job with the army likely involved less travel, his move from the Indian Office to the army procurement office would not have been a stress-free trade-off.[25]

Matthew lived in another of the city's many boardinghouses, about six blocks from his son and daughter-in-law, knowledge that was available to anyone who paid $2 for the *Washington and Georgetown Directory: Strangers' Guide-Book for Washington*, published by Kirkwood and McGill in 1853. This "Congressional and Clerks' Register" contained priceless information, as vouchsafed by the epigram on its cover:

> He who steals my purse steals trash;
> But he who borrows my Directory
> Filches me most villainously.[26]

And then, on Sunday morning, September 2, 1855, Matthew Markland disappeared.

While his family and local authorities would have known earlier, the first public notice of his disappearance came six days later, on page 3 of the September 8 edition of the *Evening Star*. It announced that "Mr. Matthew Markland, one of our most respectable citizens, aged sixty years," left his boardinghouse the previous Sunday and had not yet been found. It referred readers to an advertisement on the same page for a detailed description of the missing man, noting, "It may readily be conceived that his relatives are much interested concerning him." Absalom had placed this advertisement. He described his father as six feet, two inches tall, with a "heavy frame and remarkably straight for one of his age," and wrote that Matthew had donned a "black dress coat, black pantaloons, black satin vest, white cravat with purple flower, a new pair calf skin boots" before he walked away from his boardinghouse at eight thirty in the morning.[27]

Two days later, on September 10, Absalom's distress about his father's absence had heightened, and he revised his advertisement to say that he would "cheerfully give" a $100 reward for information about his father. That would be about $3,000 today, a considerable sum for a man in his position.[28]

Newspapers all over the country began running articles about the missing man. A key part of the story, excerpted in newspapers in Washington, New York, Ohio, Kentucky, and Tennessee (among others), was that the elderly gentleman, who had left his boardinghouse early in the morning dressed in his Sunday best, had also left a letter for his family. Its doleful message presaged doom. It said, in part, "My mind is fully made up with all the affection I have for my family, and I yield to no man in the pride that I entertain; yet for their future good I choose to depart."[29]

Those articles were all headlined "SUICIDE OF MAJOR MARKLAND." They universally referred to Matthew as a major and "formerly an eminent Lawyer of Kentucky, and late a Clerk in the Quartermaster-General's office." The newspapers "supposed, from letters found in his secretary," that the sixty-year-old man had indeed committed suicide, averred that "old age and infirmity are the only reasons assigned," and reported, "his body has not been found." The *Louisville Courier* praised the missing man in the past tense: "We knew him well, and a more esteemable gentleman could not be found. He was respected and esteemed by all who knew him."[30] It is not hard to imagine the anguish—and, as so often in the case of possible suicide, the guilt—with which his father's letter was read by Absalom. Nor is it difficult to imagine the frantic nature of his search for his father—or his father's body.

Of course, Matthew had been missed at work. And in fact it was Matthew's employment by the Quartermaster General's Office that provides our only clues to the rest of his story. On the same day his suicide was announced in the newspapers, Deputy (and Acting) Quartermaster General Charles Thomas sent a brief memorandum to Secretary of War Jefferson Davis, revealing fears that the missing clerk, Mr. (not Maj.) Matthew Markland, had committed suicide. No response from Davis is noted in the files, but exactly one month later, on October 10, Thomas followed up with another internal communication to the secretary in which the demands of bureaucracy clearly trumped expressions of compassion:

Sir,

On the 10th of Sept. I reported that Mr. M. Markland, one of our Second Class Clerks, had then been absent about ten days, but as the cause was not known, I did not consider it necessary to report the situation as vacant. I have since heard from his son that he wandered off in a state of mental derangement and that it is doubtful whether he will ever be competent to fill the situation, and in fact that he [Absalom] does not wish him to do so. Under these circumstances I have to report the place vacant and respectfully recommend that James D. Nourse, now a first class clerk in the office be promoted to the vacancy. . . .

Chs. Thomas, Actg. Q. M. Genl[31]

Fortunately, Matthew had not committed suicide, but where or in what condition he was found is unknown. Unknown, too, is the cause of his sudden "derangement." Whether the demands of work simply overwhelmed him (there is no indication that he was accused of wrongdoing) or whether Matthew had a tendency toward depression that hardened into a resolve to escape all responsibilities, he did not recover from what appeared to be a nervous breakdown. Absalom's desire that his father not return to the Quartermaster General's Office signified his opinion that Matthew was not competent to return to work, and Matthew then departed from Washington altogether. That Matthew was perhaps not even competent to care for himself may be inferred from one of Absalom's letters in 1861, when he writes to Martha, "I got a letter from father today; Fletcher & Rebecca are at the Ridge." It appears that Absalom's sister Rebecca and brother-in-law Daniel Fletcher Barker were helping to care for Matthew, "the Ridge" being the house in Paducah, which Absalom owned for the rest of his life.[32]

In the wake of his father's very public affliction and exodus from Washington, Absalom soldiered on in the capital city, surely the object of pity and perhaps also of musings as to whether he might be similarly afflicted. Although a genetic link for depression was not found until 2003, for hundreds of years people suspected that depression, or "melancholia" as it was often called, could run in families. The physical description of his father sounds so much like his own that Absalom may well have worried that he had inherited his father's mental affliction.[33]

Markland displayed enormous moral strength as he industriously cobbled together a living from rental properties and the practice of law. Evidence of his representation of Revolutionary War veterans in the files of Virginia Revolutionary War pension applications reveals that the wheels of justice ground slowly, even for aged heroes. In one case, by the time Absalom Markland had received the verdict to secure a settlement in 1856, veteran Absalom Bostick had died. Transferring the funds to the man's son as executor must have been a bittersweet moment for Markland.[34]

That same year, tragedy struck the Simms boardinghouse. Little Mary Rebecca Powell, the seven-year-old adopted daughter of Frederick and Lucy Heffley, died on September 22 in their rented rooms. A Richmond newspaper carried a sad death notice and a lengthy, flowery poem about her death, which indicated that she died quite unexpectedly "at the residence of Sampson Simms." Coming, as it did, so near the anniversary of his father's disappearance and supposed suicide, Mary Rebecca's sudden passing would have fed Absalom's preoccupation with death.[35]

Also in 1856, Markland "demitted" from the Freemasons, a formal process for leaving the organization, although no reason was given in the lodge's records. He may have left because his father was no longer a fellow member. It is also possible that Markland, educated in a community of antislavery Methodists, had become increasingly uncomfortable with some Masonic lodges' stance in favor of slavery as political friction over the issue intensified, but that is speculation, based on his actions nearly two decades later.[36]

What is not to be doubted is that Markland, who debated weighty moral and political issues as a boy of the Buffalo Trace, became much more politically active in Washington as Kentucky became more central to national politics, beginning with the historic presidential election of 1856.

TWO

A Man in Search of a Mission

1856–61

The country was awash in political intrigue in the run-up to November 4. The presidential election of 1856 was the first time that an incumbent president (Franklin Pierce) had been denied renomination by his party. In his stead, the Democratic Party nominated Pierce's minister to Great Britain, James Buchanan, as its candidate. It was also the first time a candidate of the newly formed Republican Party ran for president: the famed western explorer John C. Frémont. It was also the first (and last) time that the memorably named Know-Nothing Party (or American Party) fielded a candidate: former president Millard Fillmore.[1]

And it was the first time that slavery was the paramount issue in a presidential election—specifically, whether slavery would be allowed to extend into the western territories, which were marching inexorably into statehood. The recent Kansas-Nebraska Act (1854), embodying the concept of popular sovereignty (allowing citizens in the territories to decide the issue themselves), had proven a disaster. Men on both sides of the slavery issue flooded into the territories, ostensibly to vote but equally ready to kill their opponents if necessary. The tragedy of "Bleeding Kansas" was the result. Notwithstanding the carnage, the Democratic Party emphasized popular choice for slave or free state status in its platform, warning that it was the best way to avoid secession by the South. Frémont, an ardent abolitionist, supported the Republican platform that did not endorse abolition but vowed to restrict slavery to those states where it currently existed. The Know-Nothings sought to focus voter anger against immigrants and Catholics, presenting the former president as one who could bridge the North-South divide.

Absalom Markland was then aligned with the Democratic Party, more specifically with the "Kentucky Democratic Association of Washington City." The purpose of the group was to "distribute throughout the State of Kentucky important political documents during the pending presidential canvass" and to encourage the establishment of similar organizations in every county in Kentucky. Markland was the group's secretary.[2]

Many voters who sympathized with Frémont's opposition to the extension of slavery into the territories nonetheless feared his election would outrage the South and lead to civil war. As a result, they reluctantly voted for Buchanan, who won the majority of popular and electoral votes over both of his rivals. Frémont carried eleven states, Fillmore one; Buchanan carried eighteen, including all the southern states.

Kentucky Democrats were elated at the results of the election, not least because one of their own, Kentucky senator John C. Breckinridge, became vice president. Several days after the election the *Evening Star* announced a meeting of the Kentucky Democratic Association to be held the next day. A follow-up story in the *Washington Union* revealed that at that meeting a committee was formed to confer with similar organizations in the city "as to the best manner of celebrating the late democratic victory."[3] Markland was one of six men chosen, and among the ways they celebrated was by paying a visit to the president-elect the next day.

Although the election results placed thirty-one-year-old Markland near the catbird seat in Washington, there is little evidence that his career profited from his proximity to power in the Buchanan/Breckinridge years. He continued to patch together a modest living from his writing, his law practice, his traveling agency, and his small real estate investments in Washington.

At the same time, misfortune pursued his wife's parents, with whom Absalom had become very close. In January 1857 the Washington Common Council reported a bill for the relief of Sampson Simms, and, though there are no details, the attempted sale of one

A Man in Search of a Mission

of his large buildings was then entering its third year. On November 21, 1857, Harriet Simms died at the age of fifty-seven. She was buried in Oak Hill Cemetery in Georgetown, near the church her husband had built. Two years later, the city posted a notice that two pieces of land owned by Sampson Simms would be sold at auction to satisfy unpaid taxes of $20.70. The fortunes of Sampson, who by this time was virtually a father figure to Absalom, had sunk very low.[4]

In yet another attempt to obtain a steady paycheck, Markland took a job in December 1857 that harked back to his first occupation in Washington a decade earlier. "At the request of Hon. Joshua H. Jewett (of Kentucky), chairman, and every member of the Committee on Invalid Pensions," he accepted a position as clerk of the committee, which at that time had jurisdiction over pensions for disabled veterans of the War of 1812. He retained the clerkship through the end of the Thirty-Fifth Congress, in March 1859. Hoping to retain that steady federal government paycheck, Markland ran for the office of doorkeeper of the U.S. House of Representatives early in 1860. Nominated by another Kentucky congressional representative, Samuel Peyton, Markland came in a distant third in a field of five candidates, garnering only 16 of the necessary 104 votes against a popular incumbent. He was gracious in defeat.[5]

Despite that loss, Markland maintained a foothold in the House. In 1860 he was listed in the *Congressional Directory* as a correspondent for the *Louisville Courier*, where he filed his observations under his steamboat nickname, "Oily Buckshot." That was the first year that reporters were officially recognized by the U.S. House of Representatives and assigned seats in the Correspondents Gallery, which gave Markland a ringside seat to the disintegration of civil society and to the oncoming war. On the floor of the House, members of Congress flayed each other with words as savagely as Representative Preston Brooks had beaten Senator Charles Sumner with his cane in the Senate chamber four years earlier. President Buchanan earned his well-deserved spot on historians' list of worst presidents during this time, when he did not merely abrogate his oath to "protect and defend the United States against all enemies foreign and domestic" but also in some instances aided southern governors' unconstitutional grab for federal arsenals, post offices, and forts as war appeared inevitable.[6]

The presidential election campaign of 1860 proved to be a complex, bitter affair. Lincoln—the quintessential come-from-behind candidate—was nominated by the Republican Party in its convention in Chicago, with a platform that echoed Frémont's in pledging not to disturb slavery in the states where it existed but to oppose its extension into new territories and states. The Democrats nominated Illinois senator Stephen A. Douglas on a platform of popular sovereignty. But southern Democrats, unhappy with any possible limitations on slavery, convened a separate convention, nominating Vice President Breckinridge. And the last surviving Whigs and Know-Nothings convened their own "Constitutional Union" party convention, in which they nominated Senator John Bell of Tennessee, whose platform attempted to sidestep the issue of slavery altogether.

In that crowded and confusing field, Lincoln won a plurality of the popular vote on November 6, 1860, which translated into a majority of the votes in the Electoral College. It was then that the dire warnings of secession, expressed four years earlier about the possible election of the first Republican Party presidential candidate, came to pass. On December 20 South Carolina seceded from the United States. Six more states seceded before Lincoln was inaugurated president the following March. By June 1861 eleven states had declared their independence: South Carolina, Mississippi, Florida, Alabama, Georgia, Louisiana, Texas, Virginia, Arkansas, North Carolina, and Tennessee. Missouri remained a slave state within the Union, and Kentucky announced its strict neutrality—and a pledge that it would align in opposition to whichever side violated it.

Markland underwent a striking evolution in his political life during the historic 1860 presidential election year, from Kentucky Democrat to Lincoln Republican. His allegiance at that time was to the "maintenance of the Union at whatever the cost," and, as a result, he did not leave the Democratic Party as much as it left him. Democrats in federal and state offices in the southern states led the South into the Confederacy; Democrats who remained in the North and opposed the war, known as "Copperheads," tried to sabotage the Union effort

A Man in Search of a Mission

at every turn. Even former Vice President John Breckinridge joined the Confederate Army once Kentucky's neutrality was broken. He was later appointed the Confederacy's secretary of war.[7]

Markland then became a member of a different "association" formed in Washington shortly after Lincoln's inauguration in March 1861. Its purpose was the gathering of information as to "the real condition of political affairs in the South with reference to threatened secession, and to organize for such remedies as might seem necessary." Markland was one of the younger participants in the gathering of influential and experienced graybeards, whose membership was largely southern, containing "men who had held prominent positions in the public service, and who were skilled in political diplomacy." He was deliberately vague about the group and its tactics, but he was clear on one point: "It was through this association that I became personally acquainted with Abraham Lincoln shortly after his inauguration."[8]

Less than a month later, on April 12, 1861, a mortar recently in the inventory of the United States fired a shell that burst like a "flash of lightning" above the small Federal force defending Fort Sumter in Charleston Harbor. That was the signal for the Confederate artillery on the shore: "Then the batteries opened on all sides, and shot and shell went screaming over Sumter as if an army of devils were swooping around it." If war was to come, Lincoln had wanted the Confederates to start it. They obliged.[9]

In the same way, according to Markland, if Kentucky's neutrality was to be broken, Lincoln wanted the Confederates to break it. "At a consultation between Mr. Lincoln and a number of Kentuckians then in Washington City" just after the Fort Sumter bombardment, Lincoln stressed, "Kentucky must not be precipitated into secession. She is the key to the situation." The Kentuckians' conference led to an immediate plan of action to keep their state in the Union, and "a pacific campaign it was." In addition to members of the Washington "association," the campaign on the ground in Kentucky was waged by close allies of Lincoln: Judge Joseph Holt, the Speeds (James, Joshua, and John), Cassius Clay, Judge William Clinton Goodloe, and William "Bull" Nelson, a navy lieutenant. Recruiting of U.S. soldiers to march into Kentucky should the Confederates invade was conducted in Cairo, Illinois, safely across the river from Kentucky.[10]

In the fall it appeared that Kentucky's delicate balancing act could hold no longer. Events in other parts of the country roiled the "pacific campaign." The disastrous defeat of the Union Army at Bull Run in July gave a boost to Confederate fortunes, and Gen. John Frémont's emancipation order in Missouri in late August put neighboring Kentucky Unionists on edge. The latter development was particularly perilous. Just days after Lincoln read Frémont's emancipation order in a newspaper (Frémont had not bothered to consult Lincoln before issuing it), the president's closest friend and Kentucky confidant Joshua Speed warned him of the danger: "Frémont's order will hurt us in Ky. . . . If a Military Commander can turn [enslaved persons] loose by the thousands by mere proclamation, it will be a most difficult matter. . . . [Frémont's proclamation] will crush out every vestige of a union party in the state." The president's subsequent command to Frémont to withdraw his order was spurned by the general, and on September 10 newspapers around the country announced that the president himself had revoked the ill-timed emancipation order. In a letter to a staunch abolitionist friend who had criticized the revocation, Lincoln later wrote, "I took my course on the proclamation *because* of Kentucky."[11]

During those days of national political and military agitation, Markland continued his own local efforts in Washington as part of Lincoln's Kentucky inner circle and continued (under his pseudonym, Oily Buckshot) to comment on Washington and the war by writing articles for publication. Unlike his brother, Matthew, who joined the Twenty-Second Kentucky Infantry early in the war and who had a distinguished military career for thirty years, it does not appear that Absalom ever contemplated enlisting in the military. However, he angled for a day job a bit closer to the real action. In the fall of 1861, Absalom sought an appointment as a paymaster for the army.[12]

On September 1 he drafted a personal letter to Lincoln, which began, "To the President of the U.S., Dear Sir, I ask at your hand the appointment of Paymaster to the Army." Markland succinctly offered six cleverly crafted substantive and political arguments for

A Man in Search of a Mission

his appointment as a military paymaster in the War Department, then riven with corruption under its soon-to-be-replaced secretary, Simon Cameron:

> 1st, I am a native born, loyal citizen of the state of Kentucky, a resident of the first congressional district, where but few men are now found who are willing to battle for the Constitution & the Enforcement of the laws. 2nd My qualification for the office will be readily admitted by all who know me. 3rd My integrity & moral character have never been questioned. 4th I can procure any number of recommendations. . . . 5th, I am not aware that any one else in that end of the state desires the office, and I feel that some one should be appointed from that locality as a rebuke to the disloyalty of the people thereabouts.[13]

To ensure that Lincoln would see his letter, Markland arranged for it to be endorsed by several prominent Kentuckians, including three men who wrote a note supporting "the appointment of A. H. Markland (Oily Buckshot of the Louisville Democrat)," and by Judge Allan A. Burton, who had been a delegate to the 1860 Republican convention. Burton's endorsement read, "I know Mr. Markland personally, and well, and concur most cordially in the opinion and request of Mr. Dunlap [a Congressman from Kentucky] and others. Allan A. Burton."[14]

That endorsement, in turn, was supported by President Lincoln, who wrote on the letter: "The within brief note of Judge Burton shows that Absalom H. Markland is a worthy man. I believe I have before endorsed a letter sent to the Department for him as Paymaster. As a Kentucky appointment, I think it would be a good one. A. Lincoln Sept. 6, 1861." Five days later, no action had been taken, and Burton must have repeated his request to Lincoln. On September 11 Lincoln reiterated his support for Markland in another note to Cameron, this one with a testier tone: "I have before said, and now repeat, that by the within, and other sources of information, I have no doubt of the fitness and worthiness of Mr. Markland to be a Paymaster, and I desire his appointment if it can consist[ent]ly be made. A. Lincoln."[15]

Many times in his presidency, Lincoln humorously professed to office seekers that he had little influence over the workings of his own administration. This time it was true. Markland never received the appointment that Lincoln requested at least three times. But in one of the most serendipitous twists of fate in the Civil War, the president's failure to secure Markland the army paymaster job resulted in the young man receiving a government post that benefited Lincoln's war effort far beyond either man's imagination.

THREE

Absalom Markland, Special Agent

1861–62

One of Lincoln's first cabinet appointees was Montgomery Blair, a graduate of West Point, a formidable attorney, and a Kentuckian. Lincoln named Blair postmaster general, which was at that time a cabinet-level position. Even as Secretary Simon Cameron at the War Department was snubbing the president's requests on Markland's behalf, Blair was at work bringing the talented fellow Kentuckian into his operation. He appointed Markland to be special agent of the U.S. Post Office for western Kentucky in late September at an annual salary of $1,600 (about $46,000 today).[1]

Special agents still operate as an internal investigative and police force against financial fraud, contract fraud, internal mail theft, and official misconduct, although they are now called postal inspectors. As conflict over slavery escalated, opportunities for malice and disruption—or "depredations," in official Post Office Department jargon—in the mails were rampant. When the war began, the prospect of large numbers of soldiers moving around the country presaged additional issues unique to wartime mail service. To address those issues, the number of special agents increased from sixteen to twenty-one in the first year of the war. Although there was already a special agent for Kentucky, that man was actually a Virginian. The need for a *special* special agent, a trusted Lincoln ally, and a native of Kentucky in that post in western Kentucky became apparent in early September when Kentucky's neutrality was suddenly breached by the Confederate Army.[2]

On September 3 the Confederate Army's Gen. Leonidas Polk ordered Gen. Gideon Pillow to occupy Columbus, Kentucky. In that stroke, the Confederates had done just what Lincoln hoped they would do—provide an opening for the United States to gain Kentucky's loyalty. Responding to a scout's report that Pillow's troops were eyeing Paducah as their next target, recently minted Brig. Gen. Ulysses S. Grant ordered his troops aboard gunboats and steamboats for the forty-five-mile trip from his headquarters in Cairo, Illinois, to Paducah in western Kentucky. His sudden appearance surprised the townspeople, who were awaiting the arrival of Pillow's Confederates with eager anticipation. Grant cleverly blunted their incipient rebellion. He reported the following to his commanding officer, General Frémont:

> Arrived at Paducah at 8.30 this morning. Found numerous secession flags flying over the city, and the citizens in anticipation of the approach of the rebel army, which was reliably reported 3,800 strong 16 miles distant. . . . I landed the troops and took possession of the city without firing a gun. . . . I also took possession of the telegraph office, and seized some letters and dispatches, which I herewith transmit. . . . I distributed the troops so as best to command the city and least annoy peaceable citizens, and published a proclamation to the citizens, a copy of which will be handed you by Captain Foote.[3]

In stark contrast to Frémont's recent order to strip rebels of their enslaved laborers in Missouri, Grant's proclamation was a model of how to deal with a potentially hostile situation in a valuable, sensitive border state. "I have come among you," Grant's announcement stated, "not as an enemy, but as your friend and fellow-citizen" and as one who would not interfere with their rights, including (by implication) their right to own slaves. Aligning their interests with his, he gave local residents no opportunity to rebuff him. He proclaimed that "an enemy in rebellion against our common Government has . . . fired upon our flag." Their common enemy, Grant warned, was on the way to Paducah, so he had come to defend his fellow Americans against that enemy. "I have nothing to do with opinions," he wrote. "I shall deal only with armed rebellion and its aiders and abettors."[4]

It was at this delicate juncture that Lincoln wrote to Senator Orville Browning, telling his friend, "I think to lose Kentucky is nearly the same as to lose the whole game." Lincoln had need of the best possible representatives of his government in dealing with the Kentucky situation, and in Grant and Markland he had two of the very best. As Markland prepared to head toward that politically sensitive area to deal with the always sensitive issue of the integrity of the mail system, he "saw Mr. Lincoln quite frequently up to the time I left Washington City in October 1861." On one of those occasions, Lincoln commented to Markland on Grant's recent proclamation. "The modesty and brevity of that address to the citizens of Paducah," said the president, "show that the officer issuing it understands the situation, and is a proper man to command there at this time."[5]

Markland's journey to his new posting took him on a winding route by river and rail, and he probably handled several special agent tasks along the way. He wrote to Martha nearly every day between October 9 and November 7 as he traveled through Indiana and Kentucky, writing from Louisville (several times), Vincennes, Henderson, and Evansville, and he noted side trips to the Kentucky towns of Owensboro and Frankfort and to Seymour, Indiana. His letter of October 11, written from "Steamer Commercial, Ohio River," began, "My dear Wife, I am now on my way down the Ohio River towards Paducah." A visit by "Oily Buckshot" to Louisville was humorously announced in the *Louisville Democrat* on October 17.[6]

His final destination was Cairo, Illinois, where he was charged with imposing order on the postal chaos in that fast-growing military encampment. The existing post office, "about fourteen feet square, was full to the ceiling with mail, the station platform was stacked with bags, and . . . at one time there were forty carloads of mail on sidings. The service was at a standstill." Soon, the office was moved to a larger building, and Markland began to tackle the disarray. It was then that he "was thrown in with Gen. Grant at Cairo at about the time he took command." Markland had not seen him since Maysville Academy in 1838. "Here," Markland wrote, "I got my first glimpse of him as a man. As an instance of his remarkable memory of features, though he could not have known I was coming to Cairo, he recognized me at once one day when I was passing the window of his headquarters. I did not recognize him. It did not take us long to revive our old school fellowship, and we became great friends."[7]

Both men's physical appearance had changed considerably in twenty-three years. Markland's hairline had receded somewhat, and his beard had grown well beyond the modest version seen in his wedding photograph. Grant, too, had worn a trimmed, short beard until he assumed command in Cairo and grew a uniquely ugly one. It was a sort of beard on top of a beard—a three-dimensional affair that featured a neatly trimmed mustache and a pointed beard carved from a waterfall of wavy whiskers that reached to his chest, where it was roughly trimmed straight across. It is no surprise that Markland did not recognize in this hirsute, martial character the slim, almost feminine features of the young man he had known more than two decades earlier. Indeed, Grant's wife, Julia, who saw the new beard when she arrived in Cairo in early November, was appalled by it. Their son Fred recalled, "One of the first things that my mother said to him was, that she did not like the length of his beard." Though Grant had just recently sent his sister what he termed a "handsome" photograph of himself in his new brigadier general's uniform and new beard, he would soon bow to Julia's demand and trim his whiskers.[8]

In Cairo the two men bonded over their shared school experiences and remembrances of mutual friends. They might also have bonded over the behavior of their wives. Both men had married women they adored but who frustrated them mightily by not writing regularly. Markland's complaints about Martha's failure to write to him were faint echoes of Grant's persistent complaints to Julia. For nearly twenty years, from the war with Mexico to the bleak landscape of Washington Territory to the camps and battlefields of the Civil War, Grant pleaded to Julia to write to him, repeating that plea in every letter he wrote to her—and he wrote regularly, often twice a week. He fell into depression and turned to alcohol more than once from her lack of communication. Beginning with his command at Cairo, the Grants tried to address her seeming inability to write to him (which may have been the result of a congenital eye problem now known as strabismus) by having Julia visit him in camp, often with the children, as much as possible. Markland, whose letters speak of the same longing and homesickness for Martha, had no similar solution available for her lack of letters early in the war. He was on the move more often than even Grant, and it was not feasible for Martha to travel with him.[9]

Martha was also kept from Markland's side by her father's serious illness at that time. In his October 1861 letters to her, Markland refers again and again to "your afflicted father," though there is no hint in any of his letters about the nature of Sampson Simms's affliction. Shortly after Markland left Martha's side in early October, he wrote that he regretted leaving when he did, feeling that "in the ordinary course of nature I might not see [your father] again this side of the dark valley that separates us from the land of Hereafter." So imminent was that prospect, in Markland's opinion, that he admonished Martha to "do all in your power to make the few days that remain to him on this earth pleasant and happy." Letter after letter that month expressed his fear of Simms's death, often in the most vivid language, reminiscent of his earlier talk of his own possible death and indicative of his close relationship with his father-in-law. His fears about her father multiplied, no doubt, in the absence of letters from Martha, but in his own letters, he continually charged her to be cheerful for her father's sake—and her own.[10]

In other respects, Markland's letters mirrored those of so many others during that time. Reassuring his wife of his love and longing for her, he reminded her of his duty to his country and his pride in his work: "You cannot imagine how I miss you, yet I owed it to you, myself and all our relations to accept this office. It is one of great dignity and as little danger as any I could have gotten in Washington." She was not to worry about him, but she was put on notice that his patriotism was paramount: "I will not fall into the hands of the Secessionists if I can help it, yet I should be with the Star-Spangled Banner and if it falls, I may go with it. Your husband will not desert his country." Danger appeared ever present, and yet, fewer than six months into the war, he was also—like so many other men in service to the country at that time—already bored: "The same old story of no news, 'the everlasting war is all the cry,' nobody traveling but soldiers and myself," he wrote from the Ohio River port town of Evansville, Indiana, on October 24.[11]

His next letter, on November 2, began with an apology: "I have not written you for one week owing to the fact that I have been in no one place long enough to write. Never since I commenced transacting business have I been as pressed for time, nor have I had greater anxiety as to the result of my labors." With the increasing tempo of the war, demands on the U.S. Post Office Department and its special agents were growing, and the importance of their work was growing, too.[12]

Markland was initially tasked, as were the twenty other regional special agents, with uncorking mail bottlenecks and sniffing out corruption in some of the major postal service hubs. Such work required excellent administrative skills, keen powers of observation, rock-solid integrity, and a tenacious personality. This was a job tailor-made for Markland. His original jurisdiction was limited to western Kentucky, but he was almost immediately directed by the postmaster general to also "observe every postmaster, route agent, and mail contractor who appeared to be a secessionist," and if he found definite proof of disloyalty, he was to dismiss the postmaster and provide mail service until "a suitable replacement could be found." Treasonous postmasters cost the United States dearly.[13]

Mail delivery between the loyal and rebel states was halted by Montgomery Blair, the U.S. postmaster general, on June 1, 1861, and two wholly independent mail systems began operating—one within the United States and the other within the self-proclaimed Confederate States of America. But even before the firing on Fort Sumter two months earlier, Confederate postmaster general John H. Reagan (a former congressional representative from Texas) had successfully wooed many postmasters in the South to defect to the Confederacy, and they had taken with them the expensive tools of their trade—stamps, forms, scales, mailbags, and locks. The Texan did the same with most of the heads of the various administrative bureaus of the Post Office Department in Washington. According to historian William C. Davis, "Reagan in effect had stolen the U.S. Post Office."[14]

The position of Confederate postmaster general, also established as a cabinet-level post in the first Confederate constitution (or Provisional Constitution), adopted February 1861, was a particularly challenging position in the newly organized breakaway nation, and Reagan refused it three times before President Jefferson Davis prevailed upon him to accept it on March 1. The major challenge—and major difference from the U.S. Post Office Department—was that the Confederate Post Office was constitutionally required to pay for itself. Indeed, it was hoped that it would turn a profit. From the first, Reagan knew that would be difficult (the U.S. Post Office had never posted a profit), hence his strategy of appropriating as many human and material assets of the U.S. Post Office as possible. Even so, throughout the war the Confederate postal service suffered, as did the Confederacy as a whole, from shortages of items that were still readily available in the North. Some shortages, though, hit Reagan's department particularly hard.[15]

Mail service in the United States during the nineteenth century (as in the rest of the Western world) was undergoing rapid evolution as improvements in printing, transportation, and communication proliferated. Custom presses for printing and folding envelopes and for printing counterfeit-proof adhesive stamps, railway cars specially outfitted for transporting the mail, and myriad other sophisticated products for the postal service (plus metallic components of telegraph systems) were not manufactured in the South, and their importation was forbidden—indeed, blockaded—by the North. Without access to professionally printed stamps, some Confederate postmasters made crude (provisional) versions or simply marked letters with their own unique symbol to note they were postpaid. As the war wore on, Southerners' inventiveness in dealing with shortages led to distinctive homemade envelopes, constructed one at a time from wallpaper, newspapers, ledger sheets, and old magazines. In the jargon of stamp collectors, envelopes with postmarks on them are called "covers," and the rarer they are, the more eagerly they are sought. An entire cottage industry has arisen around the one-off envelopes called "adversity covers," lovingly crafted for use during the Confederacy's short history and commanding a high price from collectors.[16]

Adversity covers were but one indication of the importance of mail during the war, as well as of the lengths to which civilians and soldiers, from both North and South, went to send and receive letters. It is no understatement to say that from the very beginning of the war, letters were nearly as important as ammunition to men fighting in the field.

The value of communication in wartime between the front lines and the home front is impossible to overstate. Such communication reminds the husband and wife, the son and mother, the brother and sister why each is sacrificing. It lifts spirits, provides reassurance, makes each feel a part of the other's very different day-to-day existence. It is a major component of one of the most valuable factors in military victory—morale. Senior military commanders and government leaders have always recognized the value of such communication; through history and across continents, they have sought to enable their warriors to communicate with home and vice versa.[17]

"I can always fight best after a rousing letter from home," one Union soldier told his companions in 1863. The periodical that contained his quotation admonished its readers, "Let us then who cannot fight write, and help on the good cause by sending to the field cheerful, courageous, patriotic letters." Mothers and wives were told that they held "the power to lead a soldier into battle."[18]

Civil War soldiers were eager to get mail. "Oh! Ye wives, sisters, mothers, &c. If ye could only sometimes witness the ecstatic delight your affectionate letters create, you would never neglect to send so cheap a boon to those who are doating on your affectionate breathings with almost idol worship, and watching with intense zeal its seasonable return, at the arrival of every mail," wrote George Sharland, a private of the Sixty-Fourth Illinois Volunteer Infantry who marched through Georgia with General Sherman.[19]

The high literacy rate among the white population in the nineteenth century, particularly in the North, was reflected in the hundreds of thousands of letters and diaries written during the war and the many postwar reminiscences by men, women, and even children that have survived. But even if a person could not write or a recipient could not read, correspondence flourished with the aid of comrades and neighbors. The Union Army's Gen. Clinton Fisk, who arrived in Helena, Arkansas, in February 1863, after "one of the fruitless expeditions to climb up some other way into Vicksburg (Mississippi)," later recalled,

> We had been removed for a month from our lines of communication and had received no letters from home. Of course, when the way was re-opened, our first thought was of the mail. I went to the post-office tent and received my precious budget from home—from wife and children, pastor and Sunday-school children. . . . I sat down on a log by my tent to peruse the messages of love. I had read them through and through, and was about to rise, when an old soldier, seated near me on the same log, accosted me with—
>
> "Old fellow, I want you to read my letter for me."
>
> I had nothing on to indicate my rank. I turned and looked at the man, and then reached for the letter. It was directed to "John Shearer, Helena, Arkansas." The address began at the top of the envelope and ran diagonally across to the lower corner.
>
> "Can't you read it yourself, John?"
>
> "No."
>
> "Then I will, of course; but why don't you know how to read? The fellows that don't know how to read ought by rights to be found only on Jeff Davis' side."
>
> I learned that he had been born in a slave State, though he was an Iowa soldier, and that might have helped to excuse him.[20]

Letters were written for the illiterate in camps by their comrades and for the disabled in hospitals by nurses or volunteers. One of the many things that Walt Whitman did as a nurse in Washington DC was to "encourage the men to write, and myself, when call'd upon, write all sorts of letters for them, (including love letters, very tender ones)." On February 4, 1863, Whitman was at the Armory Square Hospital, where, he noted, he "supplied paper and envelopes to all who wish'd—as usual, found plenty of the men who needed these articles. Wrote letters." Another author, Louisa May Alcott, whose novel *Little Women* was set during the Civil War, also nursed soldiers and delighted in penning letters for them.[21] Mary Todd Lincoln wrote letters for soldiers in the hospitals around Washington during the war. On her second visit to sixteen-year-old soldier James Agen, she wrote his mother in New York,

Dear Mrs. Agen:

I am sitting by the side of your soldier boy. He has been quite sick, but is getting well. He tells me to say to you that he is all right. With respect for the mother of the young soldier, Mrs. Abraham Lincoln.[22]

Many regiments prided themselves on the number of letters they mailed and on the number they received. Regimental surgeon James A. Mowris recalled the reaction of a rebel landowner near the camp of his New York regiment in Virginia in December 1862, when the local man saw the large amount of mail that was being posted one day. "He did not attempt to conceal his surprise, when assured that the 117th Regiment alone, furnished nearly 300 letters per day for the mail, nor was he quite ready to hear that more than 90 per cent. of our organization, wrote and directed their own letters."[23]

According to John Wesley Hanson, the Sixth Massachusetts Volunteers "were known in Suffolk as the 'writing regiment.' The mailbag we regularly received was a wonder to other soldiers, for it often contained several hundred letters at a time." During the unit's three years of active duty, he noticed that the "habits and character of the men improved during the campaign." He concluded, "This was largely due to the great number of letters constantly received from home."[24]

"I take up my pen to write to you" and "I received your welcome letter today" were introductory phrases to thousands of soldiers' letters. At one point in the war, 180,000 letters per day were processed by the Union military mail service. On a rough per capita basis, that meant that nearly one-third of U.S. service members mailed or received a letter every day. Indeed, even in the Union Army stamps became scarce because so many letters were sent home. To ease the problem, Congress passed a law in early 1862 that letters could be sent, postage due, with just the phrase "soldiers letter" written on the envelope where a stamp would otherwise be found. Politicians were keen to facilitate the soldiers' mail—and get the soldiers' votes.[25]

In the early days of the war, in the frenzied run-up to major battles involving thousands of men serving hundreds of miles from their homes, chaos overwhelmed the mail system, corruption flourished, and morale of the fighting troops sagged. Special agents of the Post Office Department were charged with improving the efficiency and integrity of the military mail, and Markland's jack-of-all-trades experience as traveling agent, "steamboatman," lawyer, government clerk, attorney, and even debater made him successful in ferreting out and fixing problems. At the same time, the lack of letters from Martha made him lonesome. He thought briefly about quitting his position in early November to return to Washington to be with his wife and her dying father. "I am tempted to give up my place and return to you," he wrote, "with the hope that good fortune will provide a place for me somewhere where I can have your company." But he was conflicted: "When I see the thousands of soldiers who have left their homes, and who in all probability will be prevented by the misfortunes of war from ever returning, I feel that I should not grumble or be dissatisfied."[26]

It was during this time that Markland probably shared with Grant the compliment about the general's Paducah proclamation that President Lincoln had made before Markland left Washington. Markland later wrote that from the time he became a special agent, he "returned to Washington at monthly intervals and always called on Mr. Lincoln at such times." Markland established a pattern of carrying messages between the president and the general during the war. There would have been an immediate bond between Markland and Lincoln, who had served for three years as the postmaster of New Salem, Illinois, in the 1830s.[27]

Markland was then cooperating with Brigadier General Grant in a non–postal service capacity, as evidenced by a claim that Markland submitted in 1867 for $2,799.60 for "lumber &c. furnished for barracks at Paducah, Ky. In November 1861." Two years after the end of the war, Grant (who by then was the army's sole lieutenant general) endorsed that claim, stating, "I am personally cognizant of the application to public uses, viz: the construction of temporary shelter, for officers and men of the U.S. forces of Paducah, of the materials of Mr.

Markland's house—referred to in the accompanying papers—and believe the account to be just." Markland may have allowed parts of his house to be sacrificed for the Union Army's use, to avoid potential blowback on the Union cause if a Southern-leaning resident's home were similarly appropriated, in keeping with Grant's pledge not to "injure or annoy" the citizens of Paducah and Lincoln's desire to keep Kentucky mollified and in the Union.[28]

January 1862 found Markland lonesome in Louisville. "How very lonely to feel that you are a stranger even when among friends," he wrote to his "Beloved Martha" on the seventeenth of the month. "I am sure our friends in the hotel must have thought me pitiful. I know I feel so," he lamented. "Contrary to my usual custom I strolled into the parlor, took a seat in the far corner, as distant from the company as I could get." One of his many Kentucky acquaintances soon came to his aid, however. "Dr. Speed like a good Samaritan gave me a good Cigar and for a while I puffed away the cares and anxieties of the world. The Dr. sat awhile with me." Dr. John J. Speed, brother of Lincoln's best friend Joshua Speed, was postmaster at Louisville. Absalom enclosed a Bible for Martha that he had promised her earlier. He closed the letter somberly: "May you & I profit by its teachings is the prayer of Your Affectionate husband, A H Markland."[29]

While Markland's thoughts were nine hundred miles away in Washington, his friend Grant's full attention was focused just ninety miles away, on the poorly sited and lightly defended Fort Henry in northwestern Tennessee. Capture of Fort Henry on the Tennessee River and nearby Fort Donelson on the Cumberland River would bring a great swath of Tennessee under Union control and open a path to the South. In January, Grant traveled to St. Louis to propose that plan to his new superior officer, Maj. Gen. Henry W. Halleck, who had succeeded Frémont in command of the Western Department. Vain, fussy, and just plain odd, Halleck proceeded to rebuff Grant's scheme brusquely, almost rudely. Grant returned to Cairo dejected—but, to Julia's relief, beardless. His son Fred later recalled vividly, "During that visit, he was shaved—the first time in my recollection that he was ever shaved."[30]

Absalom Markland, Special Agent

But Halleck did not long prevent Grant's move on Fort Henry. Larger forces were at work in Washington. As a result of an order by President Lincoln that all military forces move simultaneously against the Confederacy, Halleck soon approved a renewed joint proposal by Grant and U.S. Navy flag officer Andrew Foote to capture Fort Henry. There, nearly three thousand rebels, some armed with flintlocks last used in the War of 1812, huddled together against a cold rain that puddled at their ankles. The Confederate Army's Brig. Gen. Lloyd Tilghman began to dispatch some of his men toward Fort Donelson, a more robust fortress (and Grant's next target), keeping a small force at Fort Henry to cover their retreat.

As Foote led the way from Cairo with his flotilla of gunboats, Grant's troops marched toward Fort Henry. They "were delayed for want of roads, as well as by the dense forest and the high water," Grant wrote in his memoirs, but "this delay made no difference in the result." Foote arrived first, and after bombarding the fort with his naval guns at close range, Tilghman and what was left of his army surrendered to the U.S. Navy on February 6, even before Grant arrived aboard the steamer *New Uncle Sam*. When Grant did reach the fort, he was entirely gratified by Foote's accomplishment, recognizing it for what it was—the first major Union victory of the Civil War.[31]

What Grant's planning had accomplished at Fort Henry was just one of the two highly successful plans he set in motion on the Tennessee River that day. Absalom Markland was with him on that journey and later recalled that "Gen. Grant asked me if I did not want to see a fight, and invited me to go to Fort Henry with him." Grant revealed the other plan to Markland:

> On the way to Fort Henry, on the headquarters steamer *New Uncle Sam*, knowing that I was an officer of the Post Office Department, he suggested to me, or rather inquired if it were not possible, to keep the mail up to the army and to take the soldiers' letters home. On my answering that I thought that this could be done, he gave me that branch of the service, and from that beginning sprang the great army mail service of the war, and to Gen. Grant the credit of originating that service belongs.[32]

Grant, too, recalled that moment but gave the credit for the idea—and its superb execution—to Markland. In a letter to historian Benson J. Lossing after the war, Grant wrote,

Dear Sir:

Among the subjects that occupied my mind when I assumed command at Cairo, in the fall of 1861, was the regular supply of mails to and from the troops; not only those in garrison, but those on march when active movements should begin. When I commenced the movement on Fort Henry on [February] 7, 1862, a plan was proposed by which the mails should promptly follow, and as promptly be sent from the army. . . .

It is a source of congratulation that the postal service was so conducted, that officers and men were in constant communication with kindred and friends at home, and with as much regularity as the most favored in the large cities of the Union. The postal system of the army, so far as I know was not attended with any additional expense to the service.

The system adopted by me was suggested and ably superintended by A. H. Markland, special agent of the Post-office Department.

Respectfully, &c., (signed) U. S. Grant, General.[33]

When Markland later saw this letter, he protested to his friend that credit for the plan was really Grant's. No matter which man deserves credit—in fact, both do—in the official military record there is irrefutable evidence of the importance of this plan to the young brigadier general, who always longed for mail from his wife. This was the first order Grant issued on the day Fort Henry fell:

SPECIAL FIELD ORDERS
No. 1
Hdqrs, District of Cairo,
Camp near Fort Henry, Tenn., Feb. 6, 1862

A. H. Markland, esq. special U.S. mail agent, will take charge of all mail matter from and to the troops composing the present expedition, and make such arrangements as he may be authorized by the Department to make to forward the same.

All Government boats are commanded to carry all mail matter, and such persons as may have charge of the same under the direction of Mr. Markland, free of charge to and from all points to which said boats may be plying.

By order of Brig. Gen. U.S. Grant:

Jno. A. Rawlins,
Assistant Adjutant-General.[34]

One of the great partnerships of the Civil War had begun.

FOUR

"An Honored & Favored Man"

February–September 1862

With Grant's order that he head up the military mail service, Markland's life changed completely. He remained a special agent of the Post Office Department, paid by and accountable to the postmaster general in Washington, but he also immediately assumed the mantle of military duty and took direction from Grant. It was probably at this time that Grant bestowed the honorary title of "Colonel" on Markland to establish his authority within the military hierarchy, although no paperwork to confirm this has been found. Both the mantle and the title fit him well.

Everything Markland had learned in the years before the war perfectly prepared him for the novel and monumental task that Grant's request would prove to be. For the next four years, cloaked in Grant's authority and carried along with his army, Markland labored tirelessly to provide regular, reliable mail service for soldiers and their families and thereby helped to bridge the anxious and lonely gap between the front line and the home front. Where Grant's army went, there went Markland. For the rest of his life, he was identified as "Col. Markland" in correspondence with military veterans and in newspapers around the country. Indeed, Markland became so identified with the U.S. Army during the Civil War that ten years after his death, the first assistant postmaster requested a full, formal report on the question of whether Absalom H. Markland had ever served in the army. The report's conclusion? No, he did not.[1]

After the victory at Fort Henry on February 6, Grant turned his full attention to the capture of Fort Donelson. Situated twelve miles east of Fort Henry on the left bank of the Cumberland River, Fort Donelson bore the promise of Union control of middle Tennessee and direct access to the heart of the South. Union Army reconnaissance parties began flushing rebel forces from the woods surrounding Fort Donelson, and on February 9 Grant and his staff scouted to within four miles of the fort.

On that same day, a reporter for the *Chicago Tribune* identified Markland in his new capacity for the first time. "Col. A. H. Markland . . . the military mail agent accompanying the army . . . by order of Gen. Grant, took possession of eleven bags of mail matter at Danville [Tennessee] and closed the office yesterday." Danville, on the Tennessee River just above Fort Henry, had been occupied by Confederates before the fort fell. When Markland made a second trip to Danville with Grant's staff the next day, they saw in the trove of hastily abandoned Confederate supplies, unfinished meals, scattered furnishings, and discarded personal letters that "confusion, and terror and dismay seem to have filled the breasts of the occupants."[2]

From that and other reports, the challenge facing Grant became clearer. More than two thousand Confederate soldiers had evacuated Fort Henry as the Union gunboats approached, swelling the numbers at Donelson, and more rebel reinforcements were on the way. Fort Donelson itself was much stronger than Fort Henry. Atop high bluffs above the Cumberland River, the fort had two batteries of nine cannons to threaten Union gunboats, while a three-mile line of engineered breastworks protected it on the landward side. Though conventional military doctrine dictated a three-to-one ratio for an assault against an entrenched foe, Grant's eventual force of twenty-seven thousand men would face approximately twenty-one thousand Confederate soldiers. In addition, according to his intelligence reports, four of the Confederacy's generals were waiting for him. Despite the odds, Grant was not fearful. Rather, he was genuinely excited, and it showed in a message he sent to Markland before the battle began.

"Imperturbable" is a word often used by historians to describe Grant. He was a man of few words and even fewer outwardly expressed emotions. The elegant, spare, direct style of writing he displayed at the end of his life in his masterful *Personal Memoirs* was

"An Honored & Favored Man"

first appreciated by those who read his military orders. One of his aides, Gen. Horace Porter, wrote that the hallmarks of Grant's orders were "correctness and clarity. No one ever has the slightest doubt as to their meaning or ever has to read them over a second time."[3] There was, however, an exception to that rule. In the midst of his battle preparations for Fort Donelson, Grant took a pencil and hastily scrawled this order to Markland, who was then at Fort Henry:

Headquarters, &c.

Markland, Special Mail Agt.

Send the Mail steamer as soon as possible after receiving this.

All is well here but we have a powerful force. Johns[t]on, Buckner Floyd and Pillow are all said to be here.

U. S. Grant.[4]

After the war, when Markland showed Grant the message, which he had saved, Grant wrote on it,

This was written from the front of Fort Donelson on the 13th or 14th of Feb.y/62.

After the words "powerful force" the words "in front of us" should have followed.

U.S. Grant
General
May 3rd 1867[5]

Not only did Grant omit the date (possibly for the only time in his military career), but he also omitted key words in the second sentence that clouded its meaning. Grant's excitement is obvious when you realize that the only information Markland needed to do Grant's bidding was in the first sentence. The rest was pure adrenaline applied to paper. Grant was sharing with a friend his excitement at the prospect of engaging the rebel army.

And it was excitement, not apprehension. Though he was wrong about Gen. Albert Sidney Johnston being in the fort, he was right about the three others, whom he knew. He disdained the competence of the two most senior officers, John Floyd and Gideon Pillow. Grant also judged that they were more concerned about their own fates than that of their fort or their men and would not put up a determined, effective defense. In addition, Grant believed the disarray Markland and his aides had seen at Danville revealed that his Fort Henry victory had dampened the Confederates' morale. Grant believed another assault by Flag Officer Foote's mighty gunboat flotilla could tip the unfavorable balance of force in his favor. As Union forces approached Fort Donelson, a Louisville newspaper reported that "Colonel A. H. Markland alias Oily Buckshot is attached to this expedition and will perfect his arrangements for the regular forwarding of the mails from the advance of the army."[6]

Two days of fierce fighting on water and land began on February 14, as bitterly cold weather amplified the usual human misery of war. Wounded soldiers suffered icy temperatures that froze their hair and clothing to the ground. The lucky wounded were cut or ripped from the earth by medical teams. The unlucky were literally immobilized on the battlefield, where they could not escape their neighbors' cries for help, nor their dead comrades who lay next to them, nor scavengers (mostly fleeing rebels) who crept about silently to strip clothing and possessions from the dead and the helpless wounded alike. That night, as Grant and his staff rode over the ground, "their horses shied constantly at the many dead men and horses on the ground. 'Let's get away from this dreadful place,'" he told his aide.[7]

In the end, Grant and his army prevailed, though there were several times over the two days of the battle when the outcome was in doubt. But Grant and some of his subordinate generals displayed calm, firm leadership during the crises that motivated their men to heroic effort. When the certainty of defeat prompted Floyd and Pillow to skedaddle, Gen. Simon Bolivar Buckner was left with the humiliating duty of asking his former West Point classmate for a meeting to discuss terms of surrender. Grant's written reply remains one of the most famous statements in military history: "No terms except an unconditional and immediate surrender can be accepted." That statement cemented his fame as "Unconditional Surrender" Grant, the general who captured the largest enemy army in U.S. history since George Washington's feat at Yorktown.[8]

"An Honored & Favored Man"

Markland, too, rose to the unprecedented challenge facing him. "For want of proper facilities to handle the immense mail going to the army, the floor and tables on steamboats were used in assorting and distributing," recalled one of the military mail agents, and "wagons and ambulances were likewise used in the field." Within an hour of the Union occupation of Fort Donelson on February 16, Markland's mail wagons had arrived, and letters and packages were being distributed to the troops. "As the Union soldiers marched into the fort on one side, messengers started to meet them from the other with letters from home," Markland later recalled. Confederates had thrown much of their mail into the Cumberland River, but "Col. Markland, postal director, however, succeeded in seizing a number of mail bags and some outside letters, supposed to contain important information," according to a newspaper in Buffalo, New York.[9]

Those discarded Confederate mailbags Markland retrieved in mid-February—as well as the Union ones he carried into Fort Donelson—would have also contained numerous Valentine's Day cards, sent with affection from men and women to their loved ones. Mass-produced valentines were first made in the United States in the mid-1800s under the direction of Esther Howland, the daughter of a Massachusetts printer, who had earlier encountered valentines from Great Britain. While those sent from the home front might well have been purchased, those from soldiers in the field were often handmade, woven from scraps of newspapers and other paper at hand. Most valentines (as well as other greeting cards) sent during the war were tender and poignant, but a peculiarly humorous, often insulting category of valentines developed during this era.[10] Called "vinegar valentines," many spoofed military life and were most often sent anonymously. One version, addressed "To the Surgeon," rhymed,

> Ho! Ho! old saw bones, here you come,
> Yes, when the rebels whack us,
> You are always ready with your traps,
> To mangle, saw, and hack us.[11]

Sweet or sour, valentines were in high demand throughout the Civil War.

Like Grant's excitement before the battle, Markland's excitement in its aftermath was palpable. A letter to Martha written at Fort Donelson and dated February 18, 1862, began on a buoyant note: "I am in most excellent health. . . . I was never prouder of a position than that which I have held during the terrific battles through which I have just [passed]." But like Grant, he could not get the scenes of carnage out of his mind: "I will not pretend now to give you a description of what war is. The theory of war is horrid enough, but the reality is far more terrible. I rode over the battle field here after the surrender and the sight was such as I never want to see again."[12]

Martha was staying in Louisville, and he promised to return to her as soon as he could "arrange some business of importance intrusted to me by Genl Grant." That "business of importance" was made official on February 20, when First Assistant Postmaster John Kasson sent Markland a lengthy letter from Washington DC indicating approval of his role as General Grant's army mail supervisor and greatly enlarging his responsibilities on behalf of the Post Office Department: "In view of the advance of the army into Tennessee it is deemed important that the mail service shall keep pace, to a reasonable extent, with its movements, in order to afford the facilities necessary to its efficiency, as well as to the communications between it and the Headquarters at Washington and elsewhere."[13]

In the letter, Kasson also directed him to restart mail service—halted nearly a year earlier by Postmaster General Blair—in those parts of Tennessee under Union control. He gave Markland "discretion to re-establish post offices and appoint postmasters" but only "so far as our occupation will be permanent and the mails permanently secure." Markland was also responsible for ensuring that the postmasters he appointed were "unconditional Union men . . . willing to take the necessary oath of allegiance to the Government of the United States." Conveniently, "to save delay, a package of blank letters of appointments, bonds, and affidavits" was enclosed. The forms were to be signed by the appointee, countersigned by Markland, and returned to Washington. This was a significant expansion of the usual role of a special agent of the Post Office Department, one that required excellent judgment (if not precognition about the

"An Honored & Favored Man"

army's success) and the highest integrity, and one that imposed great responsibility. Kasson also took the occasion "to add my testimony to the efficiency, energy, and zeal manifested in the discharge of the important duties devolved upon you."[14]

Such recognition from Post Office headquarters was heady stuff, and Markland wasted no time reporting to Martha that he had received "a very flattering letter from Mr. Kasson at Washington" the day before. "I am entirely satisfied with the change made in the Special Agency," he wrote, adding that he hoped to see her soon, when he would tell her "more than I have time to write about."[15]

What a difference Markland's chance encounter with Grant in Cairo had made in his life! Just a month earlier, he had lamented in a letter that he had nothing to write to Martha. Now, he was too busy to write long letters. He no longer felt lonely or bored. His service at Fort Donelson "accomplished all that I expected to when I left Louisville; that was to show that I was willing to test my love of country in another manner than by holding a civil office." With a bit of pardonable exaggeration about his role, he told her, "I participated in the greatest & bloodiest battle ever fought on this continent." But it was no exaggeration to say that he now held a position of importance and responsibility in the fight to save the Union, at the right hand of the army's rising officer. After the victory, Lincoln promoted Grant to the grade of "Major General of Volunteers," retroactive to the date of the Confederate surrender at Fort Donelson.[16]

The United States rejoiced in the decisive victory. In Boston the news "created a perfect *furore* of patriotic jubilation." Indianapolis held citywide celebrations at the same time citizens met to plan for "taking care of the wounded that will be sent here." In Chicago "the people heard nothing, saw nothing, knew nothing except that our boys had taken Fort Donelson and maintained the honor of the dear old flag," and one newspaper article listed eight cities in which one-hundred-gun salutes were planned.[17]

Back in Tennessee, Grant and Markland moved on. The next logical target was Nashville, first Confederate state capital of Tennessee and a strategically important industrial center on the Cumberland River, fewer than one hundred miles upriver from Fort Donelson.

The city was in a state of justifiable panic at news of the fall of Forts Henry and Donelson. Gen. Don Carlos Buell, commander of the Army of the Ohio, had ordered Gen. William "Bull" Nelson to the city, where it was hoped he and Nelson would join up and attack the Confederate force there. As it happened, no attack was necessary. According to the *Nashville Banner*, the Confederate generals virtually surrendered the city to Nelson before Buell got there by "declining [to remain] long enough to go through the necessary formalities." It was the first Confederate capital to fall to the Union Army in the war. The city was in U.S. hands on February 28, when Markland joined Grant and his staff for a trip aboard the *W. H. Brown* to Nashville. While Grant soon returned to the Army of the Tennessee at his Fort Henry headquarters, Markland telegraphed Kasson on March 1: "The United States flag is floating over the post office here. I am in charge of the office, and will retain it until relieved." Until Markland could find a suitable, loyal replacement, per Kasson's charge to him, it was Markland's responsibility to act as postmaster of Nashville himself.[18]

In the torrent of tales of the occupation of Nashville that poured from the front lines, newspaper readers in the North soon learned that "the first Federal civil officer to enter Tennessee and begin the discharge of his duties since the rebellion, is Col. A. H. Markland ... agent of the Post Office Department." The *Nashville Banner* also reported on Markland's arrival in the most favorable, albeit not always accurate, terms as "a native Kentuckian, fully identified by education, association, and interests with the South." Several northern newspapers familiar with Markland's politics pushed back on that characterization. One Indiana newspaper editorialized, "For our part we are getting tired of this kind of talk. . . . We know Mr. Markland personally, and know him to be excellently qualified. . . . We do not know that he is any better for being a Kentuckian, fully identified ... with the South." It concluded, "Col. Markland belongs to the side of the Union, and not where the traitorous Banner would insinuatingly place him." Within a week, Markland traveled to Clarksville, Tennessee, "for the purpose of restoring mail facilities." A widely reprinted article observed, "Col. M. seems only anxious to extend the mail facilities in his power to the people in the most agreeable and polite manner."[19]

The value of those mail facilities to the people was enormous. The U.S. Post Office was an engine of commerce and community that touched nearly every citizen, both on the battlefield and off. Under the leadership of Postmaster General Montgomery Blair, significant improvements were made in the postal service during the Civil War. At the outset of the conflict, the department was hemorrhaging cash. In 1862, the first full year of the Lincoln administration, it lost $6 million on a revenue base of $8 million. By June 1865 it was showing a small profit of $861,431 on a revenue base of $14.5 million. Yes, it benefited during the war years by not having the expense of serving long, sparsely populated rural mail routes in the seceded states. But the enormous increase in the sale of postage stamps prompted by the blizzard of mail that swept across the nation also funded a host of costly but important innovations.

On the home front, the most significant development was "free city delivery," credit for which often goes to Joseph Briggs, a mail clerk in Cleveland. Briggs empathized with soldiers' families (mostly women), who had to wait in long lines at the post office, often to receive terrible news of the wounding or death of a loved one in a letter passed across the crowded counter or in a newspaper death roll tacked to the post office wall. According to one historian, "Briggs's excruciating experience of handing officers' notes of condolence and bundles of returned letters to the suddenly bereaved . . . convinced him that post offices should not be public stages for personal heartbreak." With his supervisor's approval, he and other clerks began delivering mail to homes in the winter of 1862. Once Postmaster General Blair learned of the experiment, he convinced Congress to authorize "a new, peaceful army to march through the Union," one that was welcomed everywhere it went. By July 1863 forty-nine cities were enjoying home delivery by uniformed letter carriers who averaged twenty miles a day, five miles more per day than Sherman's men did on the March to the Sea the next year.[20]

As city delivery expanded, so did a host of related changes that we often take for granted. In order for a city to qualify for the new service, streets had to be named and labeled (sometimes for the first time), homes and buildings had to be numbered, mailboxes had to be manufactured and installed, and regulations regarding maintenance of sidewalks (including clearing snow) enacted and enforced. While the impulse for home delivery was to make receipt of letters more private and convenient, locked "collection boxes," often attached to lampposts, also proliferated in cities to enable citizens to mail or "post" their letters without having to brave the throngs at the post office.[21]

An exponential increase in international mail because of the war prompted First Assistant Postmaster John Kasson to propose that an "international postal congress" be convened. At that time, postal rates for international mail varied with each country and seemed to change on a whim. It was a daunting matter for a local postmaster to assure a customer of the correct international postage. Once again, Postmaster General Blair seized upon a subordinate's good idea and promptly agreed, giving Kasson public credit for it. At Blair's request, Secretary of State William Henry Seward sent letters to a host of countries, and in May 1863 representatives of twelve nations meeting in Paris created the predecessor to the Universal Postal Union. Its thirty-one articles established rules governing international mail matters, including uniform postage rates.[22]

The earliest steps toward what became the Railway Mail Service were taken during the Civil War period in the region west of the Appalachians. While mailbags had been transported by rail for decades, a temporary foray into sorting letters en route was made during the brief existence of the privately owned Pony Express. Mail to be carried by swift riders to California was sorted inside a car specifically constructed for that purpose and then transferred to the Pony Express saddlebags at St. Joseph, Missouri. But that enterprise lasted only from April 1860 to October 1861, when the Pony Express ceased due to a combination of completion of the transcontinental telegraph line and bankruptcy of the parent company. By early 1862, however, the flood of letters to and from soldiers scattered far from home inspired the army to take another look at the idea of dedicating a railcar, outfitting it with counters and walls of cubbyholes, and assigning clerks to work on board around the clock sorting mail for distribution at each stop. According to Absalom Markland, the "railway mail system originated in February 1862, within the lines of the Army of the Tennessee."[23]

Performing that work required all the skills of a good clerk, plus steady nerves, since "at many stations trains did not even stop— clerks readied the mail pouches and threw them out of the open car door while simultaneously snagging pouches of outgoing mail that hung trackside." According to the official history of the U.S. Postal Service, "Working elbow-to-elbow in fast-moving railcars, they needed brains and brawn to memorize complicated mail sorting schemes and accurately sort mail in transit."[24]

In Nashville, Markland encountered for the first time—but certainly not the last—the hallmark of fleeing Confederate postmasters. "When the Rebels left they did not forget, in their panic, to carry off every letter and paper from their post office," reported the *Philadelphia Inquirer*. "No new postage stamps or envelopes have been received yet; and as the citizens have nothing but the stamps with Jeff. Davis' phiz [face] on them, which won't carry letters through the United States, they are compelled to pay postage for the present in specie."[25]

The opening of Nashville's post office released the pent-up demand of nearly twenty thousand residents for mail to and from the North. "Not an hour passes, that scores of ladies and gentlemen do not call to inquire when the first mail from the North may be expected," reported an observer in the city. "Swarms of persons crowd up with letters, nearly every one of which is directed to some one in the Northern States." Here was a firsthand glimpse of the daily price of the Confederacy less than a year into the war: the severing of precious communication between families and friends North and South.[26]

"The Southern feeling continued strong and reliant" in Nashville, as one newspaper reported from Mobile, Alabama, but Markland was at that moment the face of the United States in its most benign personification to the citizens. He was the man who could put them back in touch with their loved ones. A Philadelphia reporter wrote that "mothers come in with letters to sons, from whom they have not heard for eight months . . . [a young lady was] 'so glad I can write home once more!' . . . a piteous appeal to a long unheard-of mother to come down and comfort her [daughter].' Some postal customers asked for reassurance that their mail would indeed go through: "'Are you quite sure you can get a letter all the way to Philadelphia without some Lincolnite's destroying it?'" Others were concerned about censorship, though there was none: "'Will you look over this, sir, so as to be sure there's nothing wrong in it, that it may go on as fast as possible?' asks a young lady dressed in deep mourning. 'It isn't necessary at all, madam,' replies the officer. 'They'll go just as speedily without examination.'"[27]

The first shipment of mail left Nashville "for the North" on February 28, and a second departed on March 1. The *Chicago Tribune* gave credit to "Col. Markland [who thereby] conferred another benefit on the undeserving nephews of Uncle Sam."[28]

But restoring civilian mail service was only half of Markland's job. In addition to supervising mail services for Grant and the Army of the Tennessee, he was ordered to supervise military mail service for General Buell's Army of the Ohio, which garrisoned Nashville and prepared for further operations southward. At least ten thousand Union soldiers were writing and receiving mail that, after it was collected in camp, went through the Nashville post office, too—and in record numbers. One close observer of military mail estimated twenty thousand letters per day were mailed from the Nashville post office over a two-month period, "besides two or three bushels of photographs, daguerreotypes, &c." Once stamps were available, he reckoned that more than a thousand dollars per day were spent on them, mostly at one or three cents per stamp. On March 4 an order from Buell assigned additional brigade postmasters for "special duty in this city with Col. A. H. Markland, mail agent Post-Office Department, for ten days."[29]

Markland's supreme difficulty was keeping track of hundreds of thousands of men among the volunteer and regular army divisions, brigades, and regiments to ensure mail delivery. That problem was compounded by the addition of other essential military units, such as "pioneers, engineers, the signal corps, sharpshooters, artillery bat-

"An Honored & Favored Man"

teries, scouts, hospitals, convalescent camps, &c. &c.," all of whose ranks changed frequently through reorganization or attrition and who were often on the move. In Markland's papers in the Library of Congress is a ten-page order of battle for the Army of the Ohio in early 1862, in beautiful penmanship (not Markland's), detailing divisions, brigades, and regiments. Requiring constant updating due to changes in command, reassignment of units, and casualties, such lists were necessary to performing the duties of a mail supervisor. At the same time, they give insight into the complexities of getting mail to the thousands of soldiers in motion across the western theater. Letter writers on the home front were constantly counseled on how best to address their letters and packages to ensure delivery to those traveling service members: "the name, the title (if any there be), the company, the regiment, the State from which it comes, the arm of service to which it belongs, and the army or corps of which it is a part." Before or after a big battle, "postmasters near Army camps often found themselves suddenly called upon to serve 100,000 soldiers," and additional help for the beleaguered military mail staff had to be secured.[30]

Markland's logistical skills enhanced the military's natural penchant for organization. When mail arrived in Nashville by train from the western postal hub in Louisville (the eastern hub was Washington DC), the mail for soldiers was separated from the rest and then sent by rail and/or boat and/or mail wagon to division, then to brigade, then to regimental headquarters. It was sorted at each step of the way and then distributed to the men by soldiers specially detailed for that service. Grant specified that no civilians (other than Markland, of course) were to handle his army's mail. In camp, each regiment had its own post office—often a tent—which struggled to supply sufficient stamps to troops eager to write letters. In a tribute to Markland, one of his military comrades later wrote about the efficiency of his operations, "These field Postmasters became wonderfully expert. The apparent intricacies of army advances or retreats gave them little trouble. They kept lines of march and company places in view, and when the column halted its mails were seldom delayed."[31] Even if the address were correct, however, the letter might go astray; the bane of every postmaster was (and remains) illegible handwriting. Between bad addresses and poor handwriting, thousands of priceless messages from home ended up in the Dead Letter Office in Washington every year of the war.

And priceless they were. "The letters and papers . . . which came by mail . . . were inexpressibly welcome, and were devoured with even more avidity than our rations at the close of a day's march," wrote one Union soldier. Another soldier wrote, "I have seen a good many of the boys sell their rations for stamps." A chaplain in the Indiana Volunteer Infantry wrote at length about the positive effects of letters upon the soldiers, observing that "the presence of loved ones is denied him, and his only solace is in the silent messenger borne to him by the coming mail." A Confederate echoed the sentiment of all soldiers when he wrote that a mail carrier who did not bring long-awaited letters was often showered with curses.[32]

It was at this vital, demanding intersection of the front lines and the home front that Markland found his true calling. He was busy and healthy and happy. "I am in good health and spirits," he wrote Martha from Nashville on March 3. "As the Postmaster of this city I am regarded as an honored & favored man." He had received a letter from the postmaster general, which "gave me the largest powers & jurisdiction ever given to an agent of the Dept." There was only one cloud on his horizon. He had not yet received some new clothing Martha had sent him. "They are certainly needed," he wrote, referring to his "shabby appearance," though he cautioned wryly that, "in time of war, as in peace, appearances are deceitful." He closed, "In camp, on the march & everywhere, under all circumstances, I have thought affectionately of you."[33]

Though they were separated for much of the next month, Grant and Markland were united on March 8 in a most peculiar manner. On that date, the most widely read periodical in the country, *Harper's Weekly*, carried on its cover a full-page engraving of "Major-General Ulysses S. Grant, U.S.A.—The Hero of Fort Donelson." Historians and biographers have often criticized the image, since so many of its details are just plain wrong.

The image of a fully buttoned formal uniform, massive epaulets dripping over his shoulders, and shiny brass buckle on a belt straining to hold in a paunch that Grant didn't acquire until after the war are puzzling enough. But the head is wrong, too. Grant had a high forehead, though not the hairline that has retreated as precipitously as this one. Grant's eyebrows are evenly set in the engraving, although in nearly all photographs his left eyebrow is lower than his right. And if you look carefully, you will see that the body and uniform were drawn, not photographed—the sketch marks are obvious—but the head has fine detail: it looks more like a photograph. This image of Grant is a composite—and not even a good one. The head is not aligned with the neck and body, and there is the faintest light edging around the bottom of the beard, also indicative of a bad cut-and-paste job. Most disconcerting, though, is that long wavy beard—Grant had shaved off his beard when he visited General Halleck in St. Louis in January, as Fred Grant had remembered so well.

The caption on the cover illustration says the image is "From a Photograph," but that begs the question, "Whose photograph?" The head on this engraving has been attributed by several writers to a butcher named William Grant, who is said to have had his photograph taken in Cairo at the same time as the general, but neither that daguerreotype nor a contemporaneous source for the story has surfaced.[34] Another answer to the question appeared in the *Chicago Journal* in April 1866, in an entertaining article about mislabeled photographs of war heroes:

> We remember another blunder of this sort. Harper's Weekly had an enterprising sketcher at Fort Donelson, just after its fall, who "took" its hero, Gen. Grant, as he supposed, and sent it on to the Weekly, which published it with a toot or two on its trumpet, and the consequence was that the first portrait of Gen. Grant, which went all over the land was copied in every imaginable size and shape, was nothing more nor less than the head of Col. Markland, the United States post office agent, with Gen. Grant's stars upon his pictorial shoulders.[35]

While we do not know if Markland had his photograph taken or a sketch produced in Cairo, we do have a photograph of him taken in 1862, and the similarity to the *Harper's* engraving is remarkable, particularly in the hairline and the eyes. While photographs of Grant are numerous, there are only three extant of Markland, so the *Harper's* magazine's mistakenly labeled composite engraving of the childhood friends is a great accidental treasure.[36]

Per Grant's orders, Markland was temporarily under Buell's jurisdiction as postmaster of Nashville and direct supervisor of the Army of the Ohio's mail just as Grant fell into serious disfavor with his commander. As Grant had foreseen, his victories in Tennessee opened the way to deeper Federal penetration into the South. Eager to take advantage of the momentum, Grant pushed for a rapid attack on the strategic Confederate railroad hub of Corinth, Mississippi, about 150 miles south of Fort Henry. However, General Halleck, commander of the Department of the West, was not a man of action. He ordered the armies south, but with explicit instructions not to bring on a fight before he could get there and lead the troops into battle at Corinth. In addition to his meticulous battle plans, he had other priorities to address.

Since Fort Henry, Halleck had sought to leverage Grant's stunning victories into an expansion of his own command. He also wanted to replace Grant with a subordinate more attentive to Halleck's beloved army regulations. In early March, Halleck seized upon what he thought was another of Grant's failures and sent a dispatch fairly bursting with rage: "You will place Maj. Gen. C. F. Smith in command of expedition and remain yourself at Fort Henry. Why do you not obey my orders to report strength and positions of your command?" Stunned, Grant only later learned that a treasonous telegraph operator had intercepted his regular cables to Halleck for more than a month, leaving his superior in the dark about his movements. However, the damage was done. As the Army of the Tennessee readied for a major engagement at Corinth, Mississippi, in Grant's words, he was "virtually in arrest and without command."[37]

As the Union forces moved toward Corinth, so did Jefferson Davis's favorite general, Albert Sidney Johnston, with a substantial rebel force. While his initial aim was to confront the Federals at Corinth, he sought to destroy one of the armies before the two could combine their numbers against him. Looking at the maps and assessing reports of Federal troop movements, Johnston set his sights on the Union forces camped on the west bank of the Tennessee River near a small church called Shiloh. When his soldiers burst like an explosion from the nearby woods early one morning, they had the element of surprise on their side. But the Union force had Grant on its side after all. Because of an injury to General Smith and because of Grant's rising fame in the wake of Fort Donelson, Halleck had been forced to restore Grant to command three weeks earlier.

After a day of fierce fighting, the night of Sunday, April 6, foretold bitter defeat for the Union Army the next day. Confederate officers, dining in what had been Gen. William Tecumseh Sherman's tent (which had been overrun early in the attack), telegraphed to Richmond that their victory was complete. Less than a mile to the southeast was an old log cabin perched above the river at Pittsburg Landing. It served as Grant's temporary headquarters in the days before the battle but had been commandeered by Union surgeons during the fight. Inside the cabin, away from the driving April rain, they industriously amputated arms and legs. Repulsed by the blood and cries of pain, Grant sought shelter instead under a nearby oak.

Searching for Grant in order to advise him to retreat in the face of the next day's certain carnage, Sherman came upon him in the dark under the tree outside the cabin. Something in Grant's aspect made Sherman decide not to press him. Instead, as rain dripped off Grant's hat brim, Sherman laconically observed, "We've had the devil's own day." Grant was not ready to give up. "Lick 'em tomorrow," he replied.[38]

And they did. Immortalized by the Battle of Shiloh, the log cabin did more than double duty as headquarters before the battle and as hospital during the fighting; it was also Absalom Markland's military post office (post office functions were moved into a hospital tent on the night of April 6). After a careful search for a postmaster to replace himself in Nashville, Markland had found John Lellyet, a Tennessee Unionist (and sometimes spy). After signing the required loyalty oath, Lellyet took office on March 20, and Markland raced south to Pittsburg Landing to make sure the mail moved expeditiously to and from the troops. Gen. Lew Wallace later recalled that he and "Colonel A. H. Markland, the very successful postal-agent for the army," together met with General Grant at Pittsburg Landing in the last week of March. According to a nurse who later arrived on the scene, on just one day of the week before the battle, "there were sold to the soldiers, from the Pittsburg post-office, seven hundred dollars' worth of postage stamps." Assuming the usual rate of three cents per letter, soldiers apparently bought stamps for more than twenty-one thousand letters that day.[39]

What Markland saw at the Battle of Shiloh stayed with him until the end of his life. In April 1888 Markland wrote to his best friend and brother-in-law, Fletcher, "This night twenty-six years ago the army of Gen. Grant lay at Pittsburg Landing all unconscious of danger. What the rising and setting sun of the day following looked upon in that neighborhood the world knows." And then, using "ideal" in the nineteenth-century sense of "existing in the idea or in fancy," he continued, "It seems now as if it were among the things I had dreamed in some ideal panoramic vision. . . . I think of the days when battles went on and the horrors of war were on every side—when the living went to death as the rivers go to the sea."[40]

Shiloh was a significant victory for the United States, but it might have gone the other way, and everyone in the Union forces' high command knew it. Halleck, who arrived at Pittsburg Landing after the fighting was over, looked with disdain upon Grant's untidy camp and lack of attention to bureaucratic minutiae, and again—for all practical purposes—removed Grant from active command. All the while, Halleck patiently groomed his massive army for a march to Corinth, Mississippi, convinced the Confederates would await his arrival.

By the end of April, more than one hundred thousand Union soldiers had arrived in the vicinity of Pittsburg Landing and made camp. In the aftermath of battle, the dead were buried, the wounded shipped out, and the missing and captured accounted for. New arrivals replaced casualties, and the enormous army was poised to march toward Corinth. There was also "a general complaint at home and in camp" of delays in the mail. When asked about these shortcomings by a newspaper correspondent from Indiana, Markland explained, "The Post Office at Pittsburg is located in a miserable old log cabin—

the only house to be had." It was wholly inadequate as a post office, he said, and the staff of three was insufficient to process the "letters [that] come in here by tens of thousands." Markland always had a knack for dealing with journalists, and in an inspired move he placed that reporter "in charge of ten sacks of letters—nearly twenty bushels—to go to Cairo for distribution." The overwhelmed correspondent was quick to report that "Col. Markland will soon regulate these affairs . . . and there will be an improvement."[41]

On May 3 Halleck had telegraphed Washington that his army would be at the outskirts of Corinth on May 4, about twenty miles from Shiloh, but the man of inaction and his massive army did not arrive until May 30. By that time, the Confederates had leisurely departed the city ahead of Halleck's snail-like advance. A major Confederate army had abandoned that field to fight elsewhere, to Grant's and many others' dismay.

As usual, Markland hurried to set up business in the latest captured city. In a testament to the amount of time the rebels had to manage their escape, he told a reporter that the place "was left by the enemy barren of everything of value." Markland was only one of many observers to comment on the Confederates' departure and Halleck's hollow victory: "No revelation of the mysterious disappearance of the rebel army is made. There was Generalship displayed in conducting that retreat such as the world has seldom or never seen. It will go upon record as one of the most remarkable achievements in military history. It astonishes everyone."[42]

A week later the *Chicago Tribune* reported that Markland was "*en route* to Memphis, and mail arrangements with that city will be made undoubtedly." Like Nashville and Corinth, Memphis had been quickly abandoned by its Confederate generals and their soldiers; a fierce naval battle on the morning of June 6 settled the question of who would control the city. Thousands of Memphis residents thronged the riverbank to witness a decisive win for the U.S. gunboat fleet. According to a historical marker that stands today at the site of the post office, "The only resistance by citizens occurred here as a shot fired at the soldiers hoisting the U.S. flag over the post office." Memphis was a strategic prize for the Federals; its capture opened the Mississippi River to traffic north of the Mississippi state line.[43]

Once again, Markland took control of the post office in a major rebel city with Kasson's full endorsement. On June 12 Kasson sent a message to Markland noting that authorities in Washington were already planning to change "the transit of military supplies and mails from the Tennessee River to the Mississippi, and via Memphis and Charleston Railroad." Kasson continued, "In this expectation, as well as for the immediate accommodation of the troops and citizens at Memphis and vicinity, it will be desirable to reopen that office at an early date. . . . Your experience will indicate the further action to be taken for the proper re-establishment of mail service to Memphis." He closed by saying, "Your past action has been generally warmly approved by the Department."[44]

The only thing that could warm Absalom's heart more than those words from Washington was the letter he received from Martha on June 20, in which she reported that her health and her spirits were good. In return, he wrote that he was healthy and "as cheerful as the nature of circumstances will admit" and that his work was filling his time and his mind. "It is at just such places as Memphis that genuine work is to be done—a large city with a population full of anxiety to correspond with friends & relations from whom they have not heard for months, with no other office facilities than such as can be picked up here and there is not a place for comfort, especially when the mercury in the thermometer is far beyond 90 degrees."[45]

His concern about the lack of comfort in the sweltering city was not just for himself; Martha's letter had expressed her desire to go to Memphis to be with Absalom. Martha's housing situation was complicated and continually changing, like that of other wives who wanted to be near husbands who had left for the war. Most military wives remained in their hometowns, but a number followed their husbands into the camps between major battles, though only when the commanding generals tolerated the presence of women. Some, like William Tecumseh Sherman, did not. Others, like Ulysses Grant, did, and Julia Grant traveled more than ten thousand miles to be with her husband in camps from Cairo in 1861 to City Point, Virginia, in

1865. The Marklands were fortunate that the Grants wanted to be near each other whenever possible, because the general's acceptance of women's presence in camp meant that Markland's wife could visit him from time to time.[46]

By this time in the war, Martha had already moved at least twice—from Washington DC to Louisville and then to Nashville—as Markland followed Grant's army south. Both cities had excellent rail and river transportation, which meant that Absalom could easily visit Martha when he had spare time or had business in either of those two postal hubs. Where hotels were good and available, Absalom had shown a preference to stay in them; where they were not, the couple sought accommodations in private homes, renting a room from homeowners trying to supplement their incomes, hoping the hosts and fellow lodgers were agreeable. Interestingly, he avoided boardinghouses, such as the one that Sampson and Louisa Simms operated. Absalom wanted to be sure that Martha was comfortable in his absence and that he would be comfortable when he visited.

His letter from Memphis continued, "I am boarding at the hotel, a place where you could not be comfortable; boarding houses I will not live in; and private families are cold and formal." He all but ordered her to "remain in Nashville until you are advised by me to join me unless you find that our friends are incommoded. . . . Do not impose on such kindness as you have received at their hands." But if she did leave, he wrote, "do not forget that the girls in the dining room & kitchen have been very attentive," reminding her to give them a gratuity. He told her he hoped that he would not be in Memphis long, but in that hope he would prove sadly mistaken.[47]

In fact, Markland was busier than ever in a city struggling to adapt to seismic changes in its governance. He continued to share his views on the rebels and Federals alike with correspondents and government officials. In late June, he reported to Tennessee's military governor, Andrew Johnson, "Memphis is beginning to assume a healthy loyal appearance—business is reviving and the people look more cheerful." For those residents not lining up under the Stars and Stripes (and there were many Memphians hostile to the Union Army's control), Markland assured Johnson, "[Provost Marshal] Colonel [James R.]

Slack who is in command of the city knows how, and when, to turn the screws so as to make loyalty set well on the unruly." Demands of the soldiers for mail never slowed; in fact, they expanded as U.S. military efforts to pressure the Confederacy along all its borders increased. On June 19 Col. J. B. Fry, chief of staff to General Buell, telegraphed Markland from Huntsville, Alabama, to ask what arrangements he was making "for establishing [post] offices for Buell's army on this line," more than two hundred miles from Memphis.[48]

Despite the increased responsibilities, Markland's hard work was paying off. The *Memphis Avalanche* reported that the post office "under the popular management of Colonel Markland is now a useful institution," that "the mails come and go regularly," and that "about the establishment there is an air of energy, life, and activity." The correspondent claimed that there were forty men vying to be postmaster of Memphis but averred that "the Government could not be more efficiently served than by continuing the invaluable services of Col. Markland." Sadly, such hard work in the steamy, stifling confines of the Memphis Post Office building finally took its toll. On July 5, just as *Harper's Weekly* regaled its readers with an engraving of the Stars and Stripes being hoisted over the Memphis Post Office a month earlier, Markland's health failed.[49]

"I was taken suddenly ill in the office and for three days I could not be moved to the hotel," he wrote Martha on July 8. "The families living in the neighborhood sent in and did all they could to make me comfortable," even though "some of them were secession families." He assured her he was doing better but that he had "lost confidence in the mercury in the thermometers about here." As much as he missed her, he forbade her to visit him—"Memphis is no place for you in such weather as this"—and promised to "be along in a few days."[50]

There is nothing in the letter to indicate the nature of his illness, but disease was rampant in the middle of the nineteenth century, before science revealed the relationship of germs and insects to disease. Two-thirds of the deaths during the Civil War were from disease, not from the battlefield. Cholera, typhoid, and smallpox swept through Memphis before and after the war, but there is no record of those diseases during the war years. Markland's continual references to the hot temperatures in Memphis that July are indicative of the nineteenth-century public's association of hot, humid weather with yellow fever and malaria that flourished in those conditions, although no one at the time knew the specific cause of the illnesses. One of the military hospitals in Memphis reported a large number of malaria cases in the summer of 1862, so it may have been widespread in the region. Perhaps Markland contracted malaria, as he exhibited the rapid onset of chills, fever, and debilitating weakness that are its most striking symptoms.[51]

This is one of his most affectionate letters to Martha; his near-death experience prompted him to reassure her of his love. He began the letter "My Martha" instead of his usual "Dearest Martha," saying, "How could I address you more affectionately and when did I so much miss your kind affection," and closed, "Home is where you are." Two days later he wrote again, to assure her that he was "still improving," and he told her to "give yourself no fear. I am out of all danger." A week later, the *Nashville Daily Union* said, "We are glad to learn from the Memphis papers that [Markland] is again able to walk about."[52]

While Markland recovered, major changes were taking place in the Union Army's high command. Halleck was named general in chief of all U.S. armies, and as he left for duty in Washington, he grudgingly promoted Grant to commander of the Army of the Tennessee and the Army of the Mississippi. Buell still led the Army of the Ohio, so command remained fractured in the West, but Grant's expanded command signaled an attempt at better coordination in the trans-Mississippi theater. In the eastern theater, Gen. George McClellan failed to capture Richmond despite a massive investment of men and matériel over three months, and he was in nearly open revolt against the president, his cabinet, and Congress. Soon thereafter, President Lincoln presented to his cabinet a draft of the Emancipation Proclamation he intended to issue, which would change the purpose of the war from one solely fought to reunite the United States to one also fought to free the enslaved. Secretary of State Seward convinced him to delay publication of this momentous pronouncement until U.S. forces could point to a military success.

Late summer found Markland recovered and in Washington on one of his regular visits to tend to postal business and probably—though there is no record this time—to report to President Lincoln, as he regularly did. It is not clear where he stayed; the Simms boardinghouse was no longer in the family. Sampson Simms had finally succumbed to his health problems in early May. With his death, Martha was orphaned and Absalom lost the man who had become a father figure to him after his own father's mental breakdown. A simple, dignified obelisk would soon mark Sampson's and his wife's gravesite in the family plot in Oak Hill Cemetery, near the church he had founded in Georgetown. Of her five siblings, Martha had only one sister and one brother still living. Sometime during the year, one of Absalom's older sisters, Rebecca, had also died, leaving three children and a bereaved widower, Absalom's best friend, Fletcher.[53]

As Martha and Absalom grieved the deaths of Sampson and Rebecca, their sorrow mirrored the national mood of despondency at the Union Army's dismal progress in the war through the summer of 1862. An aggressive Confederate push north from eastern Tennessee toward Louisville, Kentucky, scrambled Union forces into battle near Bowling Green. In the East, the Second Battle of Bull Run, on August 26, saw a reprise of the First Battle of Bull Run in the defeat of Federal forces and consequent boost to Confederate morale. As September opened, rebel forces under Gen. Robert E. Lee moved north into Maryland. On September 16 Gen. George McClellan forced Lee to retreat after the Battle of Antietam, giving Lincoln the thinnest of victories to justify publishing his preliminary Emancipation Proclamation less than a week later. In declaring enslaved persons in the rebel states free and setting the stage for Black men to serve in the Union Army (as the final proclamation did), it was an instrument of war as much as it was a promise of freedom.

Nearly a decade earlier, the Reverend Theodore Parker of Boston had spoken of the moral force animating Lincoln's executive order when he delivered a sermon in which he famously said, "I do not pretend to understand the moral universe; the arc is a long one, my eye reaches but little ways; I cannot calculate the curve and complete the figure by the experience of sight; I can divine it by conscience.

"An Honored & Favored Man"

And from what I see I am sure it bends towards justice." What Reverend Parker, who died a year before the Civil War began, said next has been less noted but was truly prophetic: "Things refuse to be mismanaged long. Jefferson trembled when he thought of slavery and remembered that God is just. Ere long America will tremble."[54]

At Shiloh, more than twenty-three thousand soldiers on both sides became casualties; more Americans fell on that battlefield than in any of America's wars to that point. Grant later wrote, "Up to the battle of Shiloh, I, as well as thousands of other citizens believed that the rebellion against the Government would collapse suddenly and soon, if a decisive victory could be gained over any of its armies." But after the decisive victories at Forts Henry and Donelson, the loss of most of Kentucky and Tennessee, and the carnage at Shiloh failed to stop Confederate aggression, "I gave up all idea of saving the Union except by complete conquest."[55]

As America trembled, Lincoln and Grant pressed on.

FIVE

"The Flood of Letters"

September 1862–64

L incoln had undergone a sea change since his election regarding the authority of a president to end slavery. He had run and won on a political platform that promised to allow slavery to remain in the states where it was already legal but vowed to stop admission of new slave states. However, the rapid secession of slave states immediately after his election, followed by the attack on Fort Sumter, proved that policy worthless in avoiding war. As the war progressed, the importance of enslaved labor in supporting the rebel army in the field and the Southern economy on the home front persuaded him that ending slavery was essential to defeating the Confederacy. Lincoln's legal analysis convinced him that as commander in chief he could take steps to deprive the Confederacy of the valuable military asset that the enslaved people represented. The president's September 22, 1862, preliminary Emancipation Proclamation announcement that on January 1, 1863, he would free all enslaved persons in the states and those parts of states still fighting the United States signaled a new chapter in the war. The war would thereafter be fought not only to reunite the Union but also to end the institution of slavery in it. Lincoln's political and military strategy finally aligned with the moral stance he had always taken: "If slavery is not wrong, nothing is wrong." The evolution of Lincoln's thinking was reflected in soldiers' correspondence, too.[1]

Soldiers' earliest letters home in 1861 regularly spoke about the novelty of their new way of life, such as ill-fitting army-issued clothing, new routines, inedible food, and travel beyond their home states.

They wrote about the things they needed from home, including clothing, food, coffee, tobacco, and—in almost every missive—a heartfelt plea for more letters from their friends and families and more stationery and stamps. They wrote about the boredom of camp life and the shocking, overwhelming introduction to combat. They were homesick, and in writing these letters to their families they sought to justify their voluntary enlistment; their statements often sounded like they were trying to convince themselves they had made the right decision in leaving home to fight.

Duty, writ large and small, was a moral obligation that weighed heavily upon a man's conscience in that era. One volunteer from Kentucky wrote to his sister in December 1861 that "an all-absorbing, all-engrossing sense of duty, alike to country and family, impelled me [to enlist]." Though the surge of patriotism in the wake of the firing on Fort Sumter and the promise of a steady paycheck also compelled many to join up, thoughtful letter writers reflected upon the bond between the nation and the citizen. A former student at Harvard argued to his father, "What is the worth of this man's life or that man's education if this great and glorious fabric of our Union . . . is to be shattered to pieces by traitorous hands."[2]

In those early days of the war, relatively few volunteer soldiers in the Union Army mentioned ending slavery or helping enslaved persons find freedom as a spur to enlistment. As 1862 neared its end and more Northern soldiers had been exposed firsthand to slavery, however, that experience began to filter into their motivation for fighting and into their letters home. "Any country that allows the curse of Slavery and Amalgamation as this has done, should be cursed, and I believe in my soul that God allowed this war for the very purpose of clearing out evil and punishing us as a nation for allowing it," wrote an Illinois soldier to his sister and brother-in-law. "Amalgamation," which became known as miscegenation, was particularly odious to Union Army soldiers, who commented on it in their letters, finding "the sight of mixed-race children unsettling" and the fact that a master would sell his own child horrific.[3]

When the president's preliminary Emancipation Proclamation became known to the troops, a Kansas regiment "rejoiced to learn that Abraham has, at last begun at the bottom of the difficulty to solve it," one of its soldiers wrote home.[4] This sentiment was by no means unanimous, and hostility toward the proclamation and the policy it embodied remained widespread. But soldiers in the field saw firsthand what Lincoln had grasped from afar—how valuable slaves were to the Confederate Army in camp and on the march and to rebel families and the economy on the Southern home front. That realization prodded many to believe that slavery's demise was essential to ending the war. Soldiers' letters increasingly argued for the freeing of enslaved people, insisting that "since slavery had caused the war, only the destruction of slavery could end it."[5] As the war wore on, more and more of the mail carried by Markland's organization between the front lines and the home front spoke of the need to free enslaved persons.

On October 3, according to a newspaper report, Markland arrived in Louisville with "two wagonloads of mails from Nashville." By November 1862 Markland and the resources at his disposal had been stretched very thin by what Louisville's assistant postmaster called "the flood of letters." So thin, in fact, that Markland telegraphed Grant for assistance in finding "good, reliable" military men to replace postmasters in Corinth, Mississippi, and Jackson, Missouri. At the same time, Markland was on the receiving end of wrath from the quartermaster's office in St. Louis over the high cost of paying private contractors to transport the massive quantity of mail for the armies. According to one well-informed contemporary source, "The average number of letters sent to the Army on the Atlantic coast was forty-five thousand daily. An equally large number was sent through the mails by the soldiers, making an aggregate of ninety thousand daily letters that passed through the post-office at Washington. About the same number were carried by the mails to and from Louisville, these two cities being the gateways to the army during the war. One hundred and eighty thousand daily letters received and answered."[6]

If all those letters were equally spread across the six hundred thousand men in the Union Army in mid-1863 (which of course they were not), one in three sent or received a letter on any given day. Another indication of the mail volume can be seen in a letter from the Finance Office of the Post Office Department advising Markland that "there will be sent to you at Louisville, Ky. one hundred thousand (100,000) three cent Postage stamps, for sale to the Army," along with detailed instructions on depositing the proceeds of the sale and assurances that more would be forthcoming, as needed.[7]

Under Markland's supervision, according to Grant, mail service between the front lines and the home front became as regular as civilian mail service. "The postal service was so conducted, that officers and men were in constant communication with kindred and friends at home, and with as much regularity as the most favored in the large cities," he wrote after the war. While it might take up to two weeks for a letter to reach a soldier in camp, letters were often received within a week of posting or less. One soldier camped near Memphis wrote that letters from central Ohio "are about four or five days reaching us." Some letters were written in hopes they might never be mailed: before battle, soldiers often placed a letter in a pocket to be sent by a comrade if they did not survive combat.[8]

So much mail was chasing so many soldiers through so much territory that in early November, Markland had to remind Grant and three other generals to please advise the postmasters in Cairo and Louisville of changes in the locations of their divisions, brigades, and regiments, "when not incompatible with the public service." The latter point was crucial, since troop movements were of keen interest to the Confederate Army, which used secret agents, including treasonous and sometimes even fake postmasters, to obtain military intelligence. Special agents were critical to preventing treasonous use of the mails. The postmaster general commended Markland on November 6 for "breaking up the bogus military mail agency carried on at Cairo Ills. by one F. W. Flanner."[9]

At the same time, the Confederate Post Office was having its own problems. Although Postmaster General Reagan's department did show a profit early in the war, that profit masked systemic problems. The gain was due to high rates for postage, low costs for contract carriers who were exempted from military service (in order to evade the draft, one contractor offered to charge "one ten-millionth of a cent" to transport mail through most of what is now Oklahoma),

"The Flood of Letters"

and deliberately curtailed frequency of mail collection and distribution. In 1861 the cost to mail a letter up to three thousand miles in the United States was three cents; the cost in the Confederacy was five cents for up to five hundred miles.[10]

But the most intractable problem existed even before the Union Army began dismantling the Confederacy's infrastructure. The South lacked an extensive and reliable rail system, and the small, fragile one it had was overwhelmed by the need to transport military supplies throughout the war. To Reagan's frustration, movement of mail by rail was "so irregular, as to make it an accident, now, instead of the rule, to have regular connections between any distant and important points." Even though the Confederate Army—like the Union Army—operated its own mail collection and distribution system within its lines, those letters became part of Reagan's unreliable enterprise when they traveled beyond the army's camps. As a result, many of the Confederacy's citizens relied on unofficial methods for getting their letters to the ones they loved. Indeed, according to one historian, it is likely that "most Confederate correspondence was delivered by hand" and thus outside Reagan's postal system.[11]

Private express companies, though legally prohibited from carrying correspondence, filled some of the gap. Soldiers who left camp for home because of furloughs, illness, or injury often carried mail from fellow soldiers who lived in the same town or county. This informal service worked in reverse, too, as wives and mothers entrusted letters to neighbors who were returning to the front. In addition, some daring men assumed the role of "mail runners," often with essential help from a network of women. The most famous of the Confederate mail runners was—in one of the many coincidences to be found in Civil War history—like Markland, also a former "steamboatman," also originally from Kentucky, and also named Absalom.

Indeed, other than Montgomery Blair and John Reagan, Absalom Grimes is probably the most famous person now associated with mail delivery during the Civil War. Because he operated as both a spy and a mail courier across enemy lines, he took enormous risks and was captured, imprisoned, and escaped numerous times. Grimes and his exploits received far less attention from newspapers during the war than did Absalom Markland, but because of his detailed and dramatic autobiography—*Absalom Grimes, Confederate Mail Runner*, published posthumously in 1926—Grimes has since become something of a folk hero. He is the subject of everything from a reenactor's video to a children's book.[12]

Absalom Carlisle Grimes, born near Louisville, Kentucky, learned his trade as a steamboat pilot from his father and worked on the Mississippi River between St. Paul, Minnesota, and St. Louis, Missouri, for nearly a decade. That job ended for him in May 1861, when he was told by a "diminutive, beer-soaked German" federal inspector that to renew his pilot's license he had to take an oath of loyalty to the United States. Grimes's latent Southern sympathies, combined with an aggressive anti-immigrant bent, led him to declare loudly that he "had no objection to taking the oath but when I did, it would not be from an alien." In his decision to leave the inspector's office, he was joined by two other pilots also awaiting their license renewal appointments—Sam Bowen and Samuel L. Clemens.

Not long thereafter, the three men enlisted in a Confederate Army unit organized near Hannibal, Missouri. Clemens and Bowen soon exited the service: Clemens deserted and headed to Nevada, where he began his career as the writer Mark Twain; Bowen was captured, jailed, and released upon taking an oath of loyalty to the United States. Grimes remained in the Confederate Army, and in December 1861, while a member of the First Missouri Cavalry, he was on a foraging mission near Springfield, Missouri, when he was captured and imprisoned. That was but the first of his many prison stints in Missouri. He succeeded in escaping each time, according to his narrative, because of ingenuity on his part and the incompetence of the Federals. Inspired by his ease of movement through enemy territory, in April 1862 Grimes "conceived the idea of gathering up all the letters I could and carrying them south to the Missouri boys in the army."

As part of his scheme, he organized a network of equally ingenious and fearless women who gathered mail for Grimes to smuggle through enemy lines and then, in turn, distributed the letters he brought back with him. Grimes's "grapevine," as he called it, was an efficient service. On his first mission, he left St. Louis on April 6 and arrived in Rienzi, Mississippi, via Centralia and Cairo, Illinois, and Memphis, Tennessee, on April 12. There, the "Rebel soldiers were about the happiest set of men in America when I delivered the letters, the first they had received since they had left their homes many months previous." They called him an "angel without wings." The soldiers were so eager to correspond with their families that Grimes stayed in camp for several days while "every log, stump, box, keg, and other available place was used as a writing desk." Loaded with those precious letters, he began his return trip on April 15, taking a train first to Holly Springs, Mississippi (to avoid General Halleck's army in the vicinity of Corinth), and arriving in St. Louis on April 21. Despite the extra days in camp and time-consuming maneuvers to evade Federal authorities, Grimes completed the nearly eight-hundred-mile round-trip in about two weeks. Once back in St. Louis, "I required two or three days to get my lady assistants out with the mail, as much sorting and changing of envelopes had to be done. The ladies went in various directions to different towns and gave the letters to trustworthy persons for delivery to the addressees.... In order to facilitate the work they arranged with some corset and hosiery houses to act as drummers [traveling sales agents] for them so that if they were questioned by the Federal authorities they could refer them to the business houses."

The women who aided Grimes (on at least one occasion a woman was carrying up to a thousand letters concealed in "double hoop skirts" that the mail-carrying women had designed for this purpose) knew they were taking great risks. The authorities followed up with the corset and hosiery houses as part of their effort to ferret out disloyal citizens of St. Louis. And after Lincoln authorized the removal of residents "whose public sympathies were too comforting to the rebel cause" in the spring of 1863, several of his "lady assistants" were forcibly removed from the city (something Grimes never mentioned in his book). In June 1863 Mrs. Marion Wall Vail, whom Grimes praises several times in his book, was one of seventeen citizens put aboard the steamer *City of Alton* and shipped south. The *Memphis Bulletin* labeled them all "St. Louis Rebel Emigrants" and noted that "Mrs. W. Vail, of St. Louis, was deemed unduly outspoken in her avowals of disloyalty. She is also alleged to have aided in the escape of the rebel spy Absalom Grimes, and to have been actively engaged in the rebel mail enterprises . . . and also held to have corresponded in cypher with the enemy."[13]

After his first successful round-trip mail mission, Grimes decided to combine delivering a large quantity of mail with "some private investigating of the Union forces so I could make an important report when I reached headquarters." From that point on, spying for the Confederates became a regular part of his mission. Gen. Sterling Price recognized Grimes's value by awarding him a commission as major along with the position of "official mail-carrier for the Confederate army." Unlike Absalom Markland, who never enlisted in the army, Absalom Grimes was entitled to wear an officer's uniform and proudly had his photograph taken in one. As his fellow officers congratulated him, the chaplain warned that he would be "in constant danger of being arrested and hanged as a spy." The chaplain was right. In September 1862, he was captured with three thousand letters on him, charged with the crimes of being a rebel mail courier and a spy, and sentenced to be shot to death in December of that year. His previous successful escapes led the authorities to place Grimes in solitary confinement in the formidable Gratiot Prison in St. Louis, with a thirty-two-pound cannonball shackled to his ankles. Prison officials scoffed at his repeated vows to escape, but within a month—aided by several male and female accomplices and his legendary ingenuity—Grimes broke out of the prison.

Grimes remained at large for nearly two more years, running mail and gathering secrets, until he once again became a "guest" of the United States in Gratiot Prison. There he witnessed the hanging of several fellow inmates before he learned in July 1864 that President Lincoln had commuted his own death sentence to life in prison, upon petition by several prominent friends and in line with Lincoln's tendency toward leniency in nonviolent cases. In December of that year, after intercession by the Catholic archbishop, the president pardoned him and he was set free.

In 1865 Grimes returned to his first career as a steamboat pilot and married the woman who had waited for him through the war.

Thirteen years later, he took his wife and children to Gratiot Prison, where he unsuccessfully searched for the ball and chain he had buried during his escape. Grimes lived into the twentieth century; he died in 1911 at the age of seventy-six. According to his obituary, he spent his later years in St. Louis as operator of "a moving-picture show, next a shooting gallery, and lately has worked for the General Compressed-Air Vacuum Cleaning Company." Grimes's life spanned two centuries of mind-boggling events and inventions, but his gravestone in the New London, Missouri, cemetery celebrates the parts of his life most important to him. It reads,

MAJOR A.C. GRIMES

OFFICIAL CONFEDERATE MAIL CARRIER

1861–1865

STEAMBOAT PILOT CAPTAIN

1852–1884[14]

Rebel spies and disloyal postmasters were not the only source of concern in the Union Army about leaks regarding military movements. There was always tension between the army high command and Northern newspapers, which sought to print any bit of information about the war that its eager correspondents could pry loose. Senior military and civilian authorities were rightly concerned about the amount of military information carried in newspapers and sought to contain it. During the Civil War, newspapers were censored at the urging of President Lincoln, who even condoned the jailing of two newspaper publishers during the war. Some military commanders accused publishers of aiding the enemy, and some even attempted to prevent distribution of newspapers, which arrived in military encampments via the mail. General Sherman, who at that time was the military commander of Memphis, had a well-known antipathy toward correspondents who were relentless in their efforts to obtain information on where armies were headed. The antagonism was mutual, and reporters played out their frustrations with him in newspapers across the North for the duration of the war.

As 1862 drew to a close, Grant organized several strategies aimed at seizing Vicksburg, Mississippi, which both Lincoln and Jefferson

Davis recognized as the key to controlling the vital Mississippi River. At that time, Vicksburg sat on a bluff high above the main channel of the river. Several batteries of Confederate cannons waited on the bluff, poised to destroy any Union assault that might cross the river from the west; a nearly impenetrable swamp guarded Vicksburg's northern frontier. In December, Grant conceived of a plan to mount a three-pronged attack against the Confederate stronghold. He would lead his forces to a position northeast of the city to prevent any Confederate reinforcements from reaching Vicksburg. Sherman, then still in Memphis, would move his army south on the river to strike the enemy from the north, through nearly treacherous swamps and bayous and up steep hills to Vicksburg. And it was hoped that Gen. Nathaniel Banks, newly installed in Louisiana, would promptly move north to attack from the south.

Sherman hurried to his mission, after issuing a stern warning on December 18 to reporters not to infiltrate any of the fifty-plus transports carrying troops, horses, and supplies downriver. Those transports and seven gunboats were under the command of Rear Adm. David Dixon Porter, on his flagship *Black Hawk*. Sherman and his aides traveled to Chickasaw Bayou aboard his headquarters boat, *Forest Queen*, along with Absalom Markland, who had been directed by Grant to "go with Sherman by the rivers and remain under his orders." Markland's travel with Sherman got off on the wrong foot when the tall, rangy, redheaded general failed to recognize Markland and, thinking he was a reporter, threatened to shoot him if he boarded. Markland quickly resolved the mistake and safely embarked with Sherman. He remained aboard *Forest Queen* for the duration of the fighting, his sense of gloom amplified by a "great pile of ready made coffins [that] loomed up on the levee."[15]

The Battle of Chickasaw Bayou did indeed prove a disaster for the Union Army. Sherman was the only one of the three commanders who arrived at his appointed place at the appointed time. Sherman did not know that Grant's initiative had been derailed by a Confederate raid on his supply depot, nor did he know that Banks was slow to start. More important, he did not confirm that the two other generals were where they were meant to be to support him before he launched a series of frontal assaults over three days through the marsh against the enemy entrenched in the hills. His army suffered nearly two thousand casualties to the enemy's two hundred. It was a tactical disaster, which stymied Grant's strategy for moving on Vicksburg, Mississippi.

For Sherman, however, the stunning defeat was also a prelude to public humiliation. In direct defiance of his stern General Order No. 8, forbidding any nonmilitary citizens to accompany his expedition and specifically warning that anyone who made "reports for publication, which might reach the enemy, giving them information, aid and comfort, will be arrested and treated as spies," several reporters had secreted themselves aboard the flotilla to Chickasaw Bayou and shared in the misery and confusion of the conflict.[16]

One of those was Thomas W. Knox, correspondent for the *New York Herald*, who wrote a report of the battle based mostly on inaccurate secondhand accounts, addressed it to a private citizen (pointedly not to his newspaper, to avoid Sherman's strictures), sealed it, and placed it "in the military mail at Sherman's headquarters." One of Knox's fellow journalists, Albert D. Richardson, later recalled that "one 'Col.' A. H. Markland, of Kentucky, U.S. Postal Agent, on mere surmise about its contents took the letter from the mail and permitted it to be opened." The contents of the letter laid the blame for the military disaster directly at Sherman's feet (as did later accounts by Knox). In Richardson's dramatic book, *The Secret Service, the Field, the Dungeon, and the Escape*, he claimed that Markland said Sherman commanded him to open it, which Sherman denied, though Sherman did not criticize Markland's actions.[17]

"Markland should have been arrested for robbing the Government mails, which he was sworn to protect," Richardson declared. Instead, it was Knox who was arrested and court-martialed, on Sherman's orders. After hearing witnesses (Sherman was the only witness for the prosecution) and deliberating for four days, the tribunal found Knox guilty of the least serious of the three charges that had been preferred. It ordered him "outside Army lines under threat of arrest," making Knox the only accredited reporter in U.S. history ever tried and convicted by a military court. But what of Markland?

Although the mails were not routinely examined and censored during the Civil War—other than letters from prisoners of war and those who traveled across enemy lines under a "flag of truce"—a special agent of the Post Office Department was "by virtue of his commission, authorized to open and examine the mails whenever and wherever warranted." The whole episode was widely publicized and even reached the White House when Knox unsuccessfully sought a pardon from Lincoln, but Markland was never disciplined for his part in the mail imbroglio.[18]

Markland did, however, suffer a loss during that time—his brother, Matthew, was taken prisoner during the battle. That was actually good news; the initial news had been that Corporal Markland of the Twenty-Second Kentucky Infantry had been killed. Matthew was apparently released in a prisoner exchange later in 1863.[19]

After the disastrous battle at Chickasaw Bayou, Markland remained aboard *Forest Queen*, where he was witness to yet another of the many uncomfortable episodes in Sherman's Civil War career. After much political pressure—but without formally notifying either Grant or Sherman—Lincoln had reluctantly allowed Gen. John McClernand, a vain, self-serving, ambitious Illinois politician, to raise troops for a Vicksburg operation that McClernand was sure would lead to glory for himself and for the United States. It was just at the time of the Chickasaw Bayou dénouement that McClernand approached *Forest Queen* on his own headquarters boat, *Tigress*, carrying orders to take over Sherman's command. Newspaper correspondents gleefully hailed this as a rebuke of Sherman because of his recent defeat, but it was not. It was just an unfortunate combination of Lincoln's inability to deal forthrightly with McClernand and bad timing for Sherman, but it reinforced the public perception that Sherman was in serious disfavor.

By all accounts, including Markland's, Sherman was uncharacteristically composed in the face of the unexpected demotion when McClernand arrived on the scene, eager to make his mark but "with apparently no idea of what to do with the command." According to Markland, Sherman then offered McClernand a plan to assault Fort Hindman, commonly called Arkansas Post, about one hundred miles to the north at the confluence of the Arkansas and White Rivers. On the last day of 1861, rebels had seized the steamboat *Blue Wing* on the Mississippi River and towed it to Arkansas Post, where they burned it and stole sixteen bags of "an important mail onboard," which had been purloined from the Memphis Post Office "by a man who was in no business connected with the army mail service." This was merely the latest depredation launched from Arkansas Post, and Sherman believed the rebel fort posed a continuing threat to U.S. operations in the region and thus should be removed.[20]

At their request, Markland accompanied the two generals and their aides to Admiral Porter's headquarters boat, *Black Hawk*, where the exuberant Porter enthusiastically endorsed the plan. He promised to lead his flotilla in the combined forces' effort but loudly proclaimed he would do so only if Sherman were part of the expedition. Although Sherman was embarrassed by Porter's pointed rudeness to McClernand, the battle plan was agreed upon, and on January 6 preparations began for the assault on Arkansas Post.

It seems highly unusual that a civilian should be part of what was essentially a council of war, and yet Markland was there, as his detailed memorandum of the event, penned in 1887 but never published, clearly shows. Indeed, throughout the war Markland moved easily among the highest councils of military and civilian decision-makers, never wearing a uniform yet always called "Colonel." Those who knew Markland used the words "trusted," "liked," or "faithful" to describe him; these were qualities prized by military and civilian authorities alike, and the logistics of mail handling were a proper subject of discussion as the Union Army continued its drive against the enemy. There is no evidence that Markland's opinion on military matters was ever requested, but he and his work were greatly valued by the armies, up and down the chain of command, and he was known to be a confidant of General Grant.

It is not surprising, then, that McClernand quickly recognized that Markland could be a valuable asset to him in his new command. Right after that meeting aboard the *Black Hawk*, Markland received an order from McClernand to report "without delay at the Head Quarters of the Genl. Commanding the Army on board the

Steamer Tigress." However, Markland was an equally good judge of his own interests. His temporary service with Buell in Nashville and Memphis and with Sherman on the Mississippi River had been at Grant's specific direction, but neither man commanded an army anymore. It was time for him to return to Grant. Taking advantage of the confusion surrounding battle preparations, Markland wrote that he "obeyed [the order] promptly by putting it in my pocket . . . and taking a boat at once for Memphis where Genl. Grant then was."[21]

Markland did not actually directly disobey McClernand's order, however. Delivering mail was always Markland's trump card, and there was always mail to be transported, even when a general called. At Markland's request, McClernand's aide de camp ordered the captain of the steamer *Henry von Phul* to "transport free from this point to Cairo Col. Markland special agent of P.O. Dept & his mail matter, also his orderly." Any boat to Cairo from Arkansas Post would stop in Memphis along the way.[22]

It was snowing in Memphis when Markland disembarked the *Henry von Phul*, which continued its mail delivery route. There, according to his account, Markland briefed Grant on what he had heard and seen. Grant recalled in his memoirs, "From [Arkansas] I received messages from both Sherman and Admiral Porter, urging me to come and take command in person, and expressing their distrust of McClernand's ability and fitness for so important and intricate an expedition." No contemporaneous written message from either man to Grant has ever been found, so it is plausible that "trusted" Markland could have been trusted with verbal messages of concern about McClernand that Porter and Sherman may not have wished to commit to paper. Indeed, that may have been the reason Porter and Sherman included him in their deliberations.[23]

Alarmed that McClernand was leading troops in combat on a mission he had not authorized, Grant immediately proceeded to Arkansas Post to sort out chain-of-command issues there. By the time he arrived, the battle had been fought and won by the Union forces. Although Grant initially took a dim view of the value of the battle, once he learned it was actually Sherman's plan he accepted its tactical contribution to the overall Vicksburg strategy. Happily, soon after he

"The Flood of Letters"

arrived, Grant received authority from Washington to relieve McClernand from command of the Army of the Mississippi. Not wanting to embarrass the proud, political general by putting someone more junior (like Sherman) over him, Grant assumed command of McClernand and his troops himself, and, as he wrote in his memoirs, "the real work of the campaign and siege of Vicksburg now began."[24]

"What a lot of land these fellows hold, of which Vicksburg is the key," Lincoln famously said. "The war can never be brought to a close until that key is in our pocket." For nearly six months more, Grant labored relentlessly to put that key into his commander in chief's pocket. Grant's multiple efforts at capturing the Confederate stronghold were not all textbook military strategy or tactics, as military historians have attested for the past century and a half. Some were disparaged by reporters, military experts, and even by his wife when she visited him in early 1863. Grant would continue to improvise as he went along—like the very best military commanders have always done—remembering what he had learned at West Point and on the battlefields of Mexico and his own country, applying those lessons to the challenge in front of him, thinking ahead and out of the box. Though we often look upon Grant's campaign from January to July 4, 1863, as a relentless march toward an inevitable victory at Vicksburg, his success was never guaranteed.[25]

While Grant struggled in the swamps and bayous of Mississippi, Markland traveled between Memphis, Louisville, Cairo, and Washington during the first half of 1863, putting out postal fires and resolving bureaucratic snafus. He succeeded in getting the mail through to Corinth, where encamped Illinois soldiers had not seen shipments of rations or mail for three weeks, according to Cpl. John Newton Prentice of the Fifty-Seventh Illinois. He wrote in his diary on January 5, "To-day we received a mail from the north, and a smile lights up the faces of the boys of the 57th. . . . Though the mail came it brought us no provisions, and we are still on half rations."[26]

In addition to dealing with the ever-increasing volume of military mail, smaller issues demanded Markland's attention. Before city delivery was widespread, newspapers would publish lists of unclaimed letters reported by the post office, and when the Memphis Post Office changed the day of the week that it released the names of those who had "letters remaining in the office," a firestorm erupted. The new day conflicted with the publication date of the German-language newspaper in the city, so the notices were delayed to German residents of Memphis, who were furious. The German newspaper "complain[ed] of the serious injury their paper has received." Markland referred that problem to headquarters in Washington for resolution. At the same time, he sent a plea on behalf of a mail clerk in Memphis who had not been paid to Special Agent R. C. Gist in that city. The clerk's name was C. S. S. Todd, whom Markland pointedly noted was from Kentucky. Markland was in Louisville, Kentucky, when he applied to Gist to correct the situation, so it is possible that Todd's Kentucky relatives (perhaps related to First Lady Mary Todd Lincoln) petitioned Markland for help in the matter. Markland was always alive to any opportunity to serve Lincoln. Markland also had time to tell the *Louisville Daily Democrat* that he had a work in progress titled "The War, and What I Saw of It," an account of his fifteen months with the army. The newspaper promised that the "racy and original style" of "the famous 'Oily Buckshot'" would make for good reading.[27]

Because he worked closely with military officials and military contractors, Markland had plenty of opportunities to observe waste and corruption on an even larger scale than the Post Office Department offered. In a letter to Martha in mid-1863, he complained, "There are a number of persons in government employ who are there to steal, or for consummate rascality of some kind. . . . The schemes by which they rob the Government are too apparent to be overlooked."[28] Markland's rising confidence in solving problems for the military mail service and his perpetual desire to be in the midst of the action led him to volunteer to tackle problems outside his jurisdiction. In the spring of 1863, he wrote a lengthy letter to one of President Lincoln's personal secretaries, John J. Nicolay, in which he sought to offer his services:

Dear Sir:

If the President or the Secretary of War will give me authority to teach divers and sundry Quarter-Masters in this section of the country a little economy I will save millions of money to the public treasury and at the same time will facilitate the legitimate operations of that department.... That frauds are being daily practiced cannot be denied.... I am slightly known to you personally which will, I trust be sufficient apology for addressing you this hasty note.[29]

He assured Nicolay that he did not want to leave the Post Office Department but would accept a temporary transfer from the post-master general's authority to the War Department for "a month or two as an Agent to look after QMrs [quartermasters]." Nicolay forwarded the letter to Quartermaster General Montgomery Meigs, who expressed a willingness to take Markland on in this capacity, "but as I know nothing of the writer—his fitness should be ascertained before making the appt."[30]

There is no record of any follow-up by either Nicolay or Meigs. However, one cannot help but imagine the negative reaction on the part of the Quartermaster Corps if Markland's proposal had been sent down the chain of command. Having a civilian postal agent supervise military mail distribution was one thing; having a civilian micromanage army officers in charge of acquisition and distribution of all military stores and supplies would have been quite another. Nothing ever came from Markland's offer, so he doubled down on his postal duties, taking possession of thousands of dollars' worth of stamps for the troops and contracting additional steamboat companies to carry the mail. He also suggested to Grant a change he felt would be an improvement in the military mail system—having the mail for the Department of the Tennessee distributed from Cairo instead of from Memphis—but the general rejected it as unnecessary to "the present satisfactory postal arrangement."[31]

While spring turned to summer, the Union Army made uneven progress against the enemy. In Virginia, the Battle of Chancellorsville proved a major defeat for Gen. Joseph Hooker, Lincoln's third commander of the Army of the Potomac in two years. At about the same time, in a brilliant strategic operation, Grant moved his army down the western bank of the Mississippi River and across the river onto Mississippi soil more than thirty miles south of Vicksburg. He was finally on the same side of the river as his target, and the land campaign could begin at last. By the end of May, he had made two unsuccessful assaults against Vicksburg. He then resolved upon a siege of the city, where the isolated residents were subsisting on mule meat in caves they had dug in the bluffs to avoid the constant bombardment of the city from Admiral Porter's naval guns.

By this time, Black soldiers were serving in the Union Army both in the East and in the West, including in the Vicksburg campaign. Once the Emancipation Proclamation took effect on January 1, 1863, recruiting of Black soldiers began. In some places, like Kentucky and Missouri, recruiters encountered hostile opposition, but Black volunteers from South Carolina, Tennessee, and Massachusetts served in the first regiments, and the army inducted Black men by the thousands. In all, nearly two hundred thousand Black troops served in the army and navy on the Union side. In the army, men served in the U.S. Colored Troops, the Fifty-Fourth and Fifty-Fifth Massachusetts Infantry, and the Louisiana Native Guards, but always under white commanding officers. Once mustered into a company, the men were subject to the racism of their white officers, who most often deployed them as laborers or cooks. But some white commanders sent them into the fight, beginning with the siege of Port Hudson, Louisiana, which was part of the Vicksburg campaign.[32]

On May 27, 1863, Brig. Gen. William Dwight ordered the First and Third Louisiana Native Guard to attack a well-defended Confederate position. Dwight had previously confined his Black troops to building a pontoon bridge and had not contemplated sending them into battle, but the men proved courageous, determined, and effective, although the strength of the Confederate defenses ultimately forced them to retreat. According to one of the white officers, "One thing I am glad to say, that is that the black troops at P. Hudson fought & acted superbly. The theory of negro inefficiency is, I am very thankful at last thoroughly exploded by facts."[33]

Though they were often ill-equipped, underpaid, and subject to death or enslavement if captured, Black soldiers displayed courage at the Battle of Milliken's Bend, Mississippi, in June of that year and later on in battles at South Carolina's Fort Wagner, Florida's Olustee,

Tennessee's Fort Pillow, and at the Crater at Petersburg, Virginia. As the number of Black soldiers increased, their letters swelled the mail-bags that Markland's team handled. While they often wrote about the usual camp topics—food, homesickness, and mail—Black soldiers had concerns unknown to white soldiers, and those concerns were reflected in some of the most poignant of all Civil War letters.

Perhaps the most famous in this regard are two letters composed by Pvt. Spotswood Rice, of the Sixty-Seventh U.S. Colored Infantry Regiment, while he was ill in the Benton Barracks Hospital in St. Louis, Missouri. Both were written on the same day in 1864. One was addressed to his children, the other to the white woman who owned them.

My Children

I take my pen in hand to rite you A few lines to let you know that I have not forgot you and that I want to see you as bad as ever. . . . Miss Kaitty said that I tried to steal you But I'll let her know that god never intended for man to steal his own flesh and blood. . . . Oh! My Dear children how I do want to see you

Spotswood Rice

[to Kittey Diggs]

I want you to understand kittey diggs that were ever you and I meet we are enmays to each othere. . . . My Children is my own and I expect to get them and when I come after [my wife] I will have bout a powrer and authority to bring [her] away and to execute vengencens on them that holds my Child. . . .

Spotswood Rice[34]

Another unforgettable letter was penned by a formerly enslaved man who served in Company B of the 123rd U.S. Colored Infantry. It is a letter from George Washington to Abraham Lincoln:

December 4, 1864

Taylors Barracks, Louisville, KY

Mr. Abrham Lincoln

I have one recest to make to you that is I ask you to dis Charge me for I have a wife and she has four children thay have a hard master . . . and if you will free me and [her] and [her] children with me I Can take Cair of them. . . .

I ask this to your [honor] . . .

George Washington[35]

After the Battle of Fort Wagner in October 1863, in which Cpl. Henry S. Harmon and "the gallant 3d Regiment of United States Colored Troops" participated, that soldier wrote, "When you hear of a white family that has lost father, husband, or brother, you can say of the colored man, we too have . . . suffered and died in defense of that starry banner which floats only over free men."[36]

Lincoln was besieged by Black civilians on the home front, too, in letters that often never made it to his desk. Jane Welcome of Carlisle, Pennsylvania, begged the president to relieve her son of duty because "he is all the subport I have now[.] his father is Dead and his brother wase all the help that I had. . . . Mart Welcom is his name he is a sarjent." A reply sent promptly to Mrs. Welcome from the Bureau of Colored Troops told her that "the interest of the service will not permit that your request be granted."[37]

As June 1863 unfolded, the attention of the nation was riveted on the major military campaigns unfolding in the two significant theaters of the war. In an effort to take the offensive in the East, Gen. Robert E. Lee and his army began to move north from Virginia toward Pennsylvania. A thousand miles west, Grant began his siege of Vicksburg. Following the textbooks he had studied at West Point, his siege was not a static military operation. The encirclement of the Confederate Army was but the initial casting of the noose around the enemy's neck; the real work lay in the constant inching of men and fortifications and tunnels ever closer, to tighten the noose. Sporadic fighting against rebel troops under the command of Gen. John C. Pemberton continually erupted along the siege lines around Vicksburg as the city's weary and underfed women, children, and old men became increasingly desperate.

The monthslong campaign against Vicksburg tried the patience of the military and civilians alike, but it created an opportunity for wives of some of the U.S. Army officers to visit their husbands in the field. On April 16 Julia Grant, Minerva McClernand, and Belle Reynolds had joined General Grant aboard the *Henry von Phul* to witness the successful running of the Confederate blockade of Vicksburg, which enabled Grant's move onto Mississippi soil. Sometime after that, Martha Markland joined her husband there for a visit. In a letter from him to her on June 22, datelined Chickasaw Bayou (where he was likely quartered aboard a steamboat near Grant's headquarters boat, the *Magnolia*), he lamented that he had little news to tell her because "we are just now where we were when you left." This is the first evidence we have that Martha visited Absalom in the field during the war. No doubt General Grant's example of sending for Julia and his children at every opportunity inspired and enabled Markland to invite his wife to visit. It appears that Martha was as willing as Grant's wife to risk danger and suffer inconvenience to be with her husband, even if, like Julia, she sometimes was the only woman present in the company of officers. In that same letter, Markland told Martha, "I see no greater prospect of occupying the city than when I first arrived, yet I dislike to leave for the reason that at any moment the army might take possession of it." He closed the letter, "I will leave for Memphis on, or about the 4th of July, if the Post Office is not opened in Vicksburg before that time."[38]

Military storm clouds gathered in late June in the East as General Lee and Gen. George Gordon Meade, Lincoln's fourth commander of the Army of the Potomac, marched toward each other in southern Pennsylvania. In the West, the Confederacy's Gen. Joseph E. Johnston pondered sending reinforcements to General Pemberton, then besieged by Grant in Vicksburg. When the metaphorical storm broke on the Fourth of July, the United States had defeated the Confederates in both places. Lee hastily retreated from Gettysburg (without Meade at his heels), while Pemberton reluctantly and irritably surrendered his army to Grant. The news from Gettysburg reached the major media outlets much more quickly than that from the swamps and bluffs of Mississippi, so it was known sooner, but the latter was more important and gave Lincoln the most satisfaction. The president wrote letters to both of his generals but did not send the one seething with disappointment he had penned to Meade; he put it away in a drawer.

In the letter he sent to Grant, whom he had not yet met in person, Lincoln's appreciation was effusive. He offered "a grateful acknowledgement for the almost inestimable service you have done the country," and he proclaimed to the nation that "the Father of Waters goes unvexed to the Sea," figuratively putting the Vicksburg "key" in his pocket.[39] Grant had cleaved the Confederacy in half. Henceforth, it would no longer have access to much-needed beef from Texas or rice from Arkansas; its communications with the West and its armed forces there were severely compromised; and the morale of the rebels plummeted. Once again the United States controlled the major waterway—the major internal means of north-south transportation—on the continent.

Markland had vowed to Martha that he would leave for Memphis on July 4 if the post office in Vicksburg did not open by then. Instead, he entered Vicksburg that day and telegraphed Washington that he would open the post office the next. Readers of the *Detroit Free Press* learned on July 9 that "not long after formal possession had been taken of the city, Col. Markland made his entrance, took charge of the post office and agreed to establish Federal mail routes with the rest of the world." While Grant's army paroled more than thirty thousand prisoners, fed them and starving citizens, and assumed control of the local government, the job of opening communication to the wider world was taken on by Absalom Markland. Amid all his other military priorities, the chief quartermaster, Lt. Col. J. D. Bingham, ordered a subordinate to "furnish a team [of horses] for the Post Master until one can be supplied by the P.O. Dept. Hire a good driver . . . and place him under the order of the Post Master temporarily."[40] As news of the major victory spread eastward, newspapers from Wisconsin to South Carolina reported to anxious parents and wives of soldiers in Grant's army that Colonel Markland had reopened the Vicksburg Post Office. Once again he received the thanks of Post Office Department senior officials: "Your promptness in taking charge and opening the post office immediately upon the occupation of that place [by] our troops merit and receive the commendation of the department." Markland assumed the role of postmaster in Vicksburg until Benjamin Johnson, who had just been named special agent for Vicksburg, could take charge of the mail there.[41]

Markland also advised Washington that it was now safe (and thus would be quicker) to send mail to and from New Orleans via the Mississippi River rather than overland. He was told that the matter would be referred to the Contract Office, "where it will receive due consideration." Without waiting for a response, Markland sought passage to New Orleans to conduct his own inspection. Grant asked one of his subordinates, Maj. Gen. Francis Herron, "as a personal favor to myself," to allow Colonel and Mrs. Markland to accompany the general on the *Ocean Steamer* to New Orleans, to enable Markland to transact "business connected with his Dept." Once again, Martha joined Absalom in the field. Their return trip was with Gen. Nathaniel Banks and a sizable military entourage aboard the steamer *Crescent*, with Martha being the sole woman among the passengers on board.[42]

Grant's momentous Vicksburg victory landed him on the cover of *Harper's Weekly* again near the end of July. Engraved from "a new photograph just received," this image was far different from the one published after the Battle of Fort Donelson. Grant now had on his uniform and sported a modest beard. "We publish . . . a new portrait of Major-General Grant, the hero of Vicksburg," writes the editor, with faint acknowledgment of the earlier error. "Most of the portraits in existence represent him as he was at the commencement of the war, with a flowing beard. He has since trimmed this hirsute appendage, and now looks as he is shown in our picture." Thanks to his wife, Grant's beard would never again reach the proportions of Markland's "hirsute appendage."[43]

The machinery of the U.S. Post Office Department was now fully operational in the newly occupied city of Vicksburg. In Markland's papers at the Library of Congress there is an order from General Grant at Vicksburg on July 30 commanding that "all steamboats will carry authorized Military Mail Messengers, furnish them subsistence at seventy five cents per day, and assign a stateroom with a lock and key for their exclusive use." A "double-circle" postmark was created for U.S. mail from Vicksburg, and an officer and three clerks under the command of Maj. Gen. James McPherson were detailed to Markland on August 3. The exponential increase in the amount of mail going to and from the city was acknowledged when the chief quartermaster of the Department of the Tennessee assigned a larger downtown building to the Post Office Department in Vicksburg because the current one was "too small for the transaction of business." And Markland was aided in dealing with all mail south of Memphis through detailed directives issued by Grant in August in his Special Orders No. 217. Grant's orders to military authorities collecting and distributing the mail in each "department, corps, division, and post headquarters" included a specific prohibition against forwarding "letters from any citizen in any insurrectionary State in this department, without first examining the same and marking their approval thereon."[44]

Markland and his military colleagues sought to create a semblance of civilized society in the battered city. During the months before Vicksburg fell, they carefully saved "small stores" of luxury items. When the victory came, they celebrated with "two baskets of champagne wine, plenty of crackers, some canteens of whisky, a box or two of cigars, and a few more baskets of whisky." And with a bevy of speeches. Commodore George Washington "Wash" Graham opened the celebration and in his speech, which Markland remembered more than twenty years later, said, "'Boys, when we get to be old men, seventy-five or eighty years old, we will be meeting each other, and forgetting the names of those we have not recently met. We will say, in the shrill voice of age, What ever became of that fellow—Oh, you know his name—Oh, that fellow who used to be about with us, and kept the post-office? The name will be gone but the fellow, with all his fun and folic, will be remembered.'" Markland himself recalled "how that matchless soldier and genial comrade McPherson, then in command of that city, laid aside the emblems of command and the pomp and circumstance of war, to become a troubadour under the windows of the fair ladies of that stricken city."[45]

On one of his many trips between Vicksburg and Cairo, he visited the Ridge, the Markland family home in Paducah, Kentucky, where Martha and his brother-in-law Fletcher (and perhaps other Markland family members) were staying, but he was in Cairo without Martha on the thirteenth anniversary of their marriage. He had written her a letter on August 23 but wrote another the next day "because it is the 24th day of August." He was feeling physically well but was saddened by news of the death of "Mr. Johnson the P.M. [postmaster] at Vicksburg on the 19th inst.," who had died just before he formally assumed the office. "Poor man, he risked his life for the office and it was worse than a bubble when he got it." But he had cheerful news, too. "Mrs. Grant & family came up when I did," and two of his other friends in the army were to arrive soon.[46]

The very next day, his plans changed. A telegram arrived from the Post Office Department, ordering him to return to Vicksburg. "How long I will be detained there I cannot say, or what my instructions will be when I receive them at that point," he wrote to Martha. "I hope, however, that I will [be] ordered North, or to the Pacific Coast." But he seems to have had an intimation he would be in Vicksburg for a while, since he included detailed directives for Martha in the event he had to stay. He wanted her to return to Vicksburg in that case and said he would notify Chief Commissary Officer Robert MacFeely to bring Martha along with MacFeely's wife. He also wrote that, if she did come, she should bring "some bedding"—about which he would write "full instructions from Vicksburg." And he wanted her to bring along Fletcher, saying, "This trip would be beneficial to him." Perhaps Markland thought his brother-in-law and best friend was still grieving a year after his wife's death and could use a change of scenery. (As it happened, Fletcher found consolation closer to home—he soon married another of Absalom's sisters, Violinda Hanks Markland.) In his letter, Markland also advised Martha to get some money from Mr. Kelly in Louisville to bring with her. He wrote that he had some bank drafts he could send her to redeem, but ironically for a special agent of the Post Office Department (or perhaps knowingly), he was "afraid to trust them by the mail."[47]

Absalom was correct about his extended stay in Vicksburg. With the death of Benjamin Johnson, he was forced to resume direct supervision of the enormous volume of mail that passed through Vicksburg until a skilled, loyal replacement could be found. Although he would receive an additional per diem of $2 during the time he served as Vicksburg postmaster, disappointment in his situation was clear in the prickly tone of the opening of his letter to Martha on September 17. "I cannot but think you are sick, too sick to write," he wrote. "It is two weeks to-day since your last letter was written and we have mails from Cincinnati to the last six days, still there is nothing from you." He threatened to leave his position and head to the Ridge if he did not hear from her soon. However, Markland quickly dropped his complaining tone to tell her that a "badly injured" Grant had arrived from New Orleans the night before. "Will be confined to his bed for some weeks. Mrs. Grant & family are expected every boat." Grant had fallen off a borrowed horse that had spooked on the streets of New Orleans, a mishap so rare for the supremely talented horseman that rumors abounded it was the result of alcohol. Markland ended the letter to Martha as affectionately as ever: "God & His Providence watch over & protect you."[48]

The Grant family's return to Vicksburg coincided with a rare, extended visit by General Sherman's large family. Although summer months in the South posed high risk of typhoid fever, malaria, and yellow fever, Grant and Sherman had judged their camp to be safe when they approved their families' travel. Nonetheless, young Jesse Grant fell ill toward the end of the month, prompting Grant to seek a supply of milk for him from the provisions of Sherman, who in turn urged him to write to Gen. Giles Smith, "doubtless in possession of many cows," and say, "your boy is sick & needs milk." No milk materialized from that source, so two days later the worried father sent a message to Absalom Markland: "Having exhausted every other resource for procuring a cow I now send to you to get one of those at the Quarter Master & Commissary's quarters." Markland was clearly Grant's go-to man, and no doubt he was pleased to be of service.[49]

According to a reporter who later wrote about the milk request, "It is needless to add that the children were provided for," since

Markland was well known for his resourcefulness. We know that Jesse Grant recovered from his illness, but tragedy struck the Shermans less than a week later. As they were leaving Vicksburg, they realized that young Willy Sherman had fallen ill with typhoid. The nine-year-old boy died just after their boat arrived in Memphis.[50]

While Grant and the grieving Sherman headed to Tennessee to relieve Union troops pinned at Chattanooga after the rebel victory at Chickamauga, Markland was being touted by newspapers around the country as a candidate for military governor of Mississippi. The *Nashville Daily Union* said Markland was "spoken of as most likely to fill the gubernatorial chair. . . . [He] is very favorably known in this department while acting as General Mail agent for the Government in the rebellious States. He is a gentleman of fine business tact, and extraordinary energy, and thoroughly liberal in his views."[51] At the same time, Markland was also being touted for a prestigious (though unspecified) federal position in glowing terms by the most praiseworthy Union general of the recent defeat, the "Rock of Chickamauga" himself, Gen. George H. Thomas. The letter was written to the postmaster general on October 11 aboard the steamer *Metropolitan*:

> My Dear Blair
>
> It has been my pleasure to journey with Mr. Markland on several occasions on the Mississippi River, and I not only speak the sentiments of myself, but also of General Grant and those connected with him when I say he is an elegant gentleman, and a first rate officer. I should like to see him in a high position civil or military.
>
> Very truly yours,
>
> G. Thomas
> Major General[52]

A beautiful copy of the letter in another's handwriting (perhaps that of the general's aide) can be found today in Markland's papers in the Library of Congress. It is possible that Markland solicited the letter with an eye to delivering it himself, as an aid in requesting a more lucrative position, and Thomas gladly assented. We do know that two weeks after the letter was written Markland was in Washington DC for one of his regular meetings at Post Office Department headquarters. Though rumors of the possible military governorship persisted in the newspapers, it was still as special agent of the Post Office Department that Markland left Washington on October 29 for Chattanooga. There, Grant had opened a supply line to the besieged troops, who were as anxious for mail as for food. The late November battles of Lookout Mountain and Missionary Ridge proved decisive victories for Union Army troops, who won revenge for their earlier stunning defeat by taunting beaten Confederate soldiers with cries of "Chickamauga! Chickamauga!"[53]

Shortly after the Battle of Missionary Ridge, Markland was part of an elaborate prank played upon the quartermaster of the venerable XI Corps, which had only recently come from the eastern theater. Markland left Chattanooga with a group of military officers, but they became stranded in Stevenson, Alabama, awaiting a train north. When told it would be more than twelve hours before the train would arrive, they sought shelter, rest, and something to eat, but there were no accommodations to be had in the small town.[54]

Spying the quartermaster's snug office in the railway station, they conspired to designate one of their group "Major General Clark" (reason: "there was no officer of that grade and that name in the army"). Another officer then informed the quartermaster of the major general's presence and his desire for "a stimulant to brace him up." Alive to the honor of accommodating the high-ranking officer, the quartermaster offered "Major General Clark" dinner and drink, only to be told by "Clark" that "he had made it a rule since he had been in the army never to take a glass of whisky without having his staff join him." Of course, the quartermaster was then obliged to include the staff in the whisky.

And so it went, from whisky for all, to cold snacks for all, to dinner for all, to more whisky for all, until at the end of a well-lubricated evening and in a rush of gratitude, "General Clark" promised to secure from General Grant a promotion to the grade of colonel for the quartermaster. The old soldier was beside himself as a bogus telegram was prepared, sent, and another returned with his "commission." The officers' train finally arrived at 2:00 a.m., when "General

Clark" and all but one of his party of officers left with the troops. The one who missed the train took out his frustration in curses in the station, revealing the prank that had been played upon the quartermaster. The venerable quartermaster complained to army headquarters about the nonexistent general but was admonished for his naïveté. Soon thereafter, "General Clark" and the quartermaster met again, laughed at the incident together, "were good friends and remained so." It takes little imagination to envision Markland as "General Clark."

When Markland's story was published more than twenty years later, the *Louisville Courier* headlined it "How Army Officers of High Rank Euchred a Quartermaster Out of a Good Dinner and Made Him a Colonel While Eating It." It was one of many such tales that Markland would later publish in newspapers, in keeping with his ebullient personality and love of camaraderie. "Colonel Markland was one of the leaders in the mischief of the camp," according to Frank A. Burr, a war correspondent for the *New York Herald*, who was often in the field.[55]

Markland was never made military governor of Mississippi (in fact, no military governor was appointed until after the war, during Reconstruction), but he was given the post of "Aid[e] to the Governor of Kentucky," Thomas E. Bramlette. That position came with the honorary rank of "Colonel in the Kentucky Volunteer Militia." An engraved certificate, with the governor's seal, can be found in Markland's papers in the Tennessee State Library and Archives.

Yes, Markland—like Harlan Sanders and Shirley Temple in later years—became a "Kentucky Colonel." Unlike today, however, during Bramlette's era this was not an honor bestowed often or lightly or without responsibility. It was a sign of respect and imposed an obligation upon the recipient to assist the governor if requested. First awarded after the War of 1812, there were fewer than 650 such titles awarded over the next one hundred years. Its use for publicity and political advantage exploded during the term of Governor Ruby Laffoon, who appointed thousands in the 1930s. There are currently more than 200,000 active Kentucky Colonels, who are for the most part noted for their civic involvement.[56]

Col. Marcellus Mundy of the Kentucky militia, a Union loyalist (and slaveowner), sought the commission for Markland as a means of preventing the replacement of the commander of the Kentucky militia with "some pure fanatical partizan." In a letter to Governor Bramlette on November 17, 1863, Mundy wrote, "To counteract the evil purposes of some bad men . . . I desire to have Col. A. H. Markland general Post office agent appointed an aid[e] on your staff." Mundy sought Markland as a back channel to Grant. "Markland has the confidence of General Grant and can certainly make the truth predominate over the rascalities of men who seek personal advancement and revenge. . . . Col. Markland goes to Chattanooga tomorrow and I hope you will forward him a Commission as Col. on your staff." Markland's commission as a Kentucky colonel was dated the next day.[57]

Although no commission from Grant for an honorary U.S. Army colonelship during the war has ever been found, by the end of 1863 Markland had been named an honorary colonel of his native state militia, with a proper paper commission to show for it.[58]

For much of the rest of 1863, Markland attended to his myriad post office duties, traveling between Nashville, Memphis, Louisville, St. Louis, and Washington. He supervised other military mail agents, such as Grant's cousin Orlando H. Ross. As the volume of letters and the length of supply lines increased, postal supplies ran short, and Markland went on the figurative warpath to "prevent the accumulation or detention of mail bags or locks in post offices (not mail bag depositories) where they are not actually needed." After the New Orleans postmaster wrote to the postmaster general proposing a change in operations between Louisiana and Louisville, he was advised that headquarters "would be pleased to have [Markland's] views on the subject before any further proposed arrangements are submitted to the Postmaster General for his consideration." The Contract Office in Washington rubber-stamped many of the decisions Markland made in awarding high-dollar contracts to private carriers a thousand miles away. "Relying entirely upon your judgement and discretion in this matter" was a phrase seen time and again in correspondence from headquarters to Markland.[59]

As Markland's influence within the Post Office Department grew, his friend Grant's military authority also expanded. Vicksburg riveted the attention of the nation on the brilliant, unpretentious commander, whom Lincoln commissioned a major general in the regular U.S. Army after the victory (he retained his grade as major general of volunteers). In mid-October, Halleck had combined the Armies of the Tennessee, the Cumberland, and the Ohio into a newly created Military Division of the Mississippi, and Grant was given full command. November saw striking victories at Lookout Mountain and Missionary Ridge. Grant's dogged resolve steadily brought more and more former Confederate territory under Federal control. By the end of the year, the contrast between the progress and the commanding general west of the Appalachians and the lack of progress and the shortcomings of a succession of generals in the East became too stark to ignore.

Once again, Congress, the president, and the secretary of war eyed a change in the leadership of the Union Army in the East. This time, though, they would not merely replace one commander of the Army of the Potomac with another. This time, they looked back in history and decided to revive the grade of lieutenant general of the army, last held by George Washington. They would put into that uniform a man who would bring to bear all the military resources of the United States in a coordinated strategy to crush the rebellion. Even before the necessary legislation was passed and signed into law, it was no secret who that new lieutenant general would be. As 1864 dawned, important changes were in store for Ulysses Grant—and for his indispensable special agent, Absalom Markland.

SIX

"Twenty Tons of Mail"

1864

Soldiers huddled in tents and makeshift huts during the winter of 1863–64 as bitterly cold temperatures swept across the North and into the South. Frozen roads and extreme weather hampered movements of large armies, so there were no major military campaigns from December through mid-March. But where opposing armies camped in proximity to each other, skirmishes punctuated the winter quiet. Confined to camp for months at a time, soldiers played cards, attended religious services, read newspapers, suffered from diseases (often fatal) caused by crowded conditions and poor sanitation, and—always—wrote letters. Mary Livermore, who worked as a nurse in many Union camps, observed, "There never was an army so intent on corresponding with the kindred and friends left behind. If you went into any camp at any time, you would see dozens and sometimes hundreds, of soldiers writing letters. Some would be stretched at full length on the ground, with a book or a knapsack for a table—some sitting upright against the trunks of trees, with the paper resting on their drawn-up knees—others would stand and write."[1]

Those letters carried precious messages of love and hope, instructions for handling financial matters, and even much-needed cash from the paymaster. They also carried pleas for mail from home, and those pleas were answered by the bushel. The valuable missives entrusted to Absalom Markland were crucial to supporting the morale of the troops and their families as the war entered its fourth calendar year with no end in sight.

Markland embraced the responsibility assigned to him by Postmaster General Montgomery Blair and by Maj. Gen. Ulysses Grant. He was determined to deliver the soldiers' mail, no matter the obstacles. Distributing letters to troops in camp was the easiest aspect of military mail delivery, even with an expanding army and widely scattered locations. Letters to Grant's armies moved from postal hubs by rail, boat, and carriage to camp post offices, where soldiers assigned to Markland distributed them. When an army was on the move, delivering mail was more difficult, but he and his military aides rose to the challenge. After Fort Donelson, the postmaster general sent Markland "his thanks and the thanks of my Government for the energy & ability displayed in the management of the mails whilst the Army of Genl Grant was on its march."[2]

But Markland did not believe his duty ended when the marching stopped and the fighting started. "It was no unusual matter to have letters distributed along the very lines of battle and even among the skirmishers," according to the *New York Times*. Gen. Henry Van Ness Boynton later waxed eloquent on the supreme dedication of Markland and his assistants: "Colonel Markland was well known throughout the armies which Grant commanded as the originator of the army mail system. It was more wonderful in its regular workings, when the obstacles are considered, than the railway mail service of to-day. Those faithful servants of the public, the letter-carriers, do their work in the face of storm, and heat, and bitter cold. But under General Markland's system letters were often collected and delivered under fire."[3]

Such earnest praise came unsolicited to Markland throughout the war. In 1864 Markland was at the top of his game—thirty-nine years old, healthy, happily married, and wholeheartedly engaged in work essential to his nation's welfare. He was the epitome of the nineteenth century's self-made man. Markland had reinvented himself many times in less than four decades—schoolteacher, steamboatman, newspaper reporter, express agent, clerk, political activist, lawyer—until the reunion with a childhood friend led to his reinvention as a one-of-a-kind special agent of the Post Office Department for General Grant's armies.

No other special agent in the United States was addressed in official and unofficial correspondence as "Colonel" by graduates of West Point, who jealously guarded the sanctity and exclusivity of military grades. No other postal agent met regularly with President Lincoln or carried messages from him to senior commanders or between senior commanders in the field. And though they rarely used "Colonel" in their correspondence with him, high-ranking officials of the U.S. Post Office Department regularly deferred to him in matters involving large sums of money and major postal policy. In the middle of the Civil War, Markland was operating simultaneously at a senior level in two worlds—the civilian world that paid his salary and the military world that commanded his energy, expertise, and dedication. He navigated both worlds with ease, making friends and increasing his authority in each as time went on.

In the United States, the nineteenth century itself was marked by a dichotomy, in a broad philosophical sense. Leading philosophers of the age, mostly resident in the Northeast, were by and large contemplative romanticists; some were called Transcendentalists. Ralph Waldo Emerson, Henry David Thoreau, and Henry Adams all preached and practiced lives of quiet introspection to guide themselves and others toward a meaningful existence. They paid attention to the crises of their age but called attention to injustice in their own way. Thoreau advocated for abolition of enslavement through civil disobedience; Emerson lectured against slavery. Adams spent the Civil Wars years in London as secretary to his father, the U.S. minister to Great Britain, where sympathy for the Confederacy was rampant. None of them saw the war up close.

In places a thousand miles west of Boston and Concord, men like Lincoln, Grant, Sherman, and Markland employed a more active approach to shaping their individual worlds, a more muscular form of character building. Even if they read Thoreau's *Walden*, they neither could have nor would have withdrawn from society for two years to "find" themselves. From the time they left home, they found themselves in precarious, unstable circumstances, and success—if not survival—demanded their full attention and all their mental and physical energies. This is not to say they lacked the capacity for inner reflection or the ability to look beyond themselves to the complex, shifting political landscape and decide where they should make their stand. Indeed, each of them left behind letters, speeches, articles, and, in the case of Grant and Sherman, memoirs that reveal the line of internal reasoning that led each to be an active participant in the bloody central contest of the age. But it was the riskiness and contingency of life and their vigorous approach to it that shaped their character.

Markland's character was well defined by this third year of the war. The letters he wrote, the correspondence sent to him, official orders, and newspaper accounts all paint a picture of a man of intelligence, honesty, integrity, resilience, curiosity, perseverance, loyalty, self-reliance. Other men—often very important men—trusted him with great responsibilities and highly confidential information. He had shown leadership qualities early in his life, but at the same time he was diligent in executing assignments from superiors. He always craved independence, however, and even in a staff role more often than not he controlled the way tasks were accomplished and found ways to elude orders he did not judge appropriate. He was not a yes-man, but he was a can-do man. If you wanted to reopen a post office the day after a major battle or find milk for a sick child, Absalom Markland was your man.

His personality, too, was perfectly suited to his job—or, rather, it appears he molded the job to fit his personality. The same handbook stipulating that a special agent could open a letter if necessary also dictated that "he should, when travelling, attract as little attention as possible, and conceal his official character from observation as much as possible." To the contrary, Markland used his title as his calling card; everyone knew Markland was a special agent of the Post Office Department—and that he was Grant's man, too. He was conspicuous not only by his title, his important friends, and his considerable size; he was also a hale fellow well met, one who smoked cigars, drank whisky, and told tales with the best of them. Markland was a man's man in an era that prized "manly" qualities and recognized separate social "spheres" (and thus separate standards of behavior) for men and women. Markland's sense of humor came through in the pranks he helped perpetrate and in the self-deprecating tales he told about them. But he was sincere in his dealings with soldiers and civilians, as well as fair in those dealings.[4]

Ambition was another hallmark of the nineteenth-century self-made man, according to the formerly enslaved and famously self-made orator and activist Frederick Douglass. Markland was always ambitious. Like Abraham Lincoln, Markland was a man whose "ambition was a little engine that knew no rest," and that engine drove his lifelong efforts to improve himself and his situation. But it does not appear that his ambition was so overweening that it alienated those around him. In fact, as seen in the letter by Gen. George Thomas quoted earlier, men who knew him were eager to help Markland advance.[5]

As 1864 began, the handwriting seemed to be on the wall with respect to Grant's immediate future: as soon as Congress passed legislation reinstituting the position of lieutenant general of the army, it appeared almost certain the president would award him the commission. (There was faint speculation that Halleck would get the nod, but most of the focus was on Grant.) It was widely assumed Grant would take up that command in Washington and work in proximity to the president and his cabinet.

In that scenario, Markland's future was unclear. His unique position within the postal world was predicated on his original assignment as a special agent of the Post Office Department for Kentucky; his unique position within the military world as "colonel" and military mail supervisor was predicated on Grant commanding armies in the field. There was no precedent for his dual position, so he had no idea what the future held for him. What Markland wanted was a responsible position where he was in charge, in a location where he and Martha could live together. As the new year dawned, it seemed possible that he would remain what he was, where he was—special agent and military mail supervisor at the beck and call of Grant's successor in the western theater. If that successor were to be Sherman, as appeared likely, the general's preference not to have women in camp was well known, so the chances for Martha to be with her husband as often as before would be severely, if not completely, diminished.[6]

Predictably, Markland did not wait to have his fate decided for him. On January 26, 1864, before Congress approved the bill creating the position of lieutenant general, he took pen in hand and wrote to Grant:

> Can you consistently write the President recommending me for a position in the revolted states, or rather the late revolted states. I desire to locate permanently in some one of them with the hope that I may, as a citizen, and an officer of some experience be of service to the Federal Govt. Having followed your fortunes for the past two years, and having been more prominently identified with the Army in the West than any other civil officer it is reasonable to presume that you are somewhat acquainted with my qualifications to do good for the administration and the government. My conduct as an officer of the P. O. Dept since the beginning of the rebellion are well known at Washington. My reputation as a gentleman of integrity &c is known to all who have been so unfortunate as to cultivate my acquaintance. Since the rebellion this is the first personal favor I have asked of any one.[7]

While the position Markland described may have been truly his desire, the letter may also have been his way of simply prodding Grant to decide whether he wanted to retain Markland's services when Grant moved back East. Markland's dry reference to his relationship with Grant ("it is reasonable to presume you are somewhat acquainted with my qualifications") and to his circle of friends ("all who have been so unfortunate as to cultivate my acquaintance") seem to be almost inside jokes, designed to provoke a response from Grant, even if not necessarily the one spelled out in the letter. There is no record of a reply from Grant to Markland, written or otherwise, nor of any letter from Grant to Lincoln about Markland.

As Markland waited, winter turned to spring, and he handled military mail issues that ranged from personnel matters to major policy initiatives. In mid-January he appointed Pvt. Henry A. Russell of the Seventeenth Illinois Volunteer Infantry as "Assistant and Special Agent" for the Military Division of the Mississippi. Grant's adjutant, Thomas S. Bowers, had earlier proposed to Markland a quicker mail

"Twenty Tons of Mail"

route from Nashville to Knoxville, based on his own travels between the two cities, and it appears Markland adopted his suggestion. The Post Office Department's Contract Office in Washington issued a notice in mid-January that, contrary to its own authority and practice, it would "not make contracts for the conveyance of mails with the lines of the military division of the Mississippi," thus leaving to Markland "the management of all necessary service to that end." The provost marshal general of eastern Tennessee, who had requested additional mail routes in that region, was told by postal headquarters in Washington that Markland "has been invested with full control of that matter of furnishing mails to that section," and he was "advised to correspond with [Markland] upon the subject."[8]

Because mail transports were given privileged access to roads and to waterways crowded with military vehicles and vessels, some enterprising operators sported signs indicating they were carrying mail, even when they were not, to expedite their shipments. Markland raised a red flag about this practice with the Post Office Department's Contract Office, and on January 14 he was informed that the Senate Post Office Committee chair had drafted a bill "prohibiting by law the use of the words 'U.S. Mail' painted or printed upon coaches or steamboats of persons not actually carrying the mails." Also in January, Brig. Gen. Robert W. Allen, chief quartermaster of all military operations in the western theater, sent Markland a quarrelsome letter disputing Markland's criticisms of the man handling the military mail in Chattanooga. Despite that disagreement, Allen concluded with an endorsement that read, "The Quarter Masters at Cairo and Memphis will not interfere with any steam boats that Col. Markland Special Agent of the Post Office Dept. may require for the transportation of the mails."[9]

That spring, headquarters chastised the postmaster of New Orleans for his allegation that Markland had improperly undertaken a visit to his city. "The Postmaster General desires it to be understood that [Mr. Markland's visit] to New Orleans was by the direction of this Dept. and consequently not a pleasure trip <u>as unnecessarily stated in your letter</u>" (emphasis in the original). The letter to the New Orleans postmaster also contained this extraordinary, definitive endorsement of Markland: "The Postmaster General has instructed me . . . to inform you that the entire control and management of the mails on the Mississippi River is under the direction of A. H. Markland Esq. Special Agent of the P.O. Department whose experience and service has saved the government a large amount of money, and given entire satisfaction to this Department."[10] For all practical purposes, Markland had more authority over mail west of the Appalachians than the U.S. postmaster general.

By the end of February, Congress had passed legislation restoring the grade of lieutenant general of the army, and Lincoln signed it into law on February 29. The next day the president sent Grant's nomination for the position to the Senate, which took barely twenty-four hours to confirm the appointment. A week later, Grant—who had not yet met President Lincoln—arrived in Washington DC with his thirteen-year-old son, Fred, who accompanied him to the White House. There, Ulysses S. Grant received his commission as the highest-ranking officer in the Union Army from the president in the presence of the cabinet, Gen. Henry Halleck, and several of Grant's staff. As predicted, Grant placed Sherman in command of the Military Division of the Mississippi, roughly all the troops between the Mississippi River and the Appalachian Mountains. In his memoirs, Grant wrote that he gave Sherman his orders: "[Gen. Joseph] Johnston's army was the first objective, and that important railroad centre, Atlanta, the second."[11]

The next day Grant headed west to Culpeper County, Virginia, along with his staff officers and Markland, who would henceforth supervise the mail for all the armies of the United States, now consolidated under Grant's command. That decision had been made. The next decision Grant had to make was whether to replace the commander of the Army of the Potomac, Gen. George Meade, called "Old Snapping Turtle" by his troops. To the surprise of almost everyone, especially Old Snapping Turtle himself, Grant decided to leave Meade where he was. And in a wholly unexpected turn of events, Grant also decided that his headquarters would be in the field with Meade and the Army of the Potomac. Grant had been favorably impressed by Meade in their meeting but felt he could best prose-

"Twenty Tons of Mail"

cute the war if he were with the Army of the Potomac as it pursued its prime objective, Confederate general Robert E. Lee's Army of Northern Virginia.[12]

Some twenty years later, Markland recalled the return trip from Grant's headquarters, located near Meade's at Culpeper Court House.[13] Grant traveled in a special passenger car attached to a train carrying sick and wounded soldiers back to Washington. The car was reserved for Grant and several aides, leaving many empty seats on a train otherwise destined to be overcrowded. Inquiring about some sharp remarks he overheard by the guard posted outside his car, Grant was told that a soldier had attempted to enter the "special car for General Grant and his staff." Grant quickly replied, "Let him come in. I only occupy one seat in this car." Grant then inquired about the many men he saw crowded on the platform and was told they were all seeking transportation to Washington. "'Let all who can crowd in get in,' [Grant] said to the guard. The car was soon filled, one private soldier taking a seat beside the General and engaging him in conversation nearly all the way to Alexandria, not knowing with whom he was talking."[14]

Shortly thereafter, several newspapers reported that William M. Reilly, Esq., a former assistant postmaster at Louisville, was appointed a special agent of the Post Office Department, "in place of Col. Markland, transferred to a higher sphere of duty at Washington City, in connection with Grant's army." Grant and Markland would both be playing on a much bigger stage and for much bigger stakes. A front-page story in the *Evening Star* on May 16 elaborated on Markland's new duties. Reporting from Washington DC on the war in Virginia, it included the news that Col. A. H. Markland, who had been "so efficiently overlooking the postal arrangements" with Grant in the West, was now also "permanently establishing the postal facilities for the army" in the East.[15]

Five days later, Markland returned from the front and briefed a newspaper reporter extensively about what he had seen. He described Lee's position at Spotsylvania Court House as "fortified all around . . . his camp is a perfect fortress" and also said that Grant had "made almost an entire circuit of the enemy's position in the various assaults made upon it," all without forcing Lee out of his fortifications. Markland said there were "several reasons why little else than these demonstrations have been made within the last few days," the most important being the roads were "never in worse condition for the movement of artillery, cavalry, or even infantry." Markland thus became the latest in a long line of men during the Civil War to complain about Virginia's legendary "mud season." According to the article, "Col. Markland says that Virginia cannot be beat for mud. When he was with the Western army he thought the cry of 'mud in Virginia' was more talk than anything else, but he says he is satisfied to the contrary." Even Vicksburg "during the muddiest times" did not match Virginia, Markland avowed.[16]

Reminding his readers that Markland had been with Grant and his armies "in the Southwestern campaigns" for the past two years, the correspondent quoted Markland as saying that "he never saw the army in better condition and finer spirits, and never in his life did he witness such enthusiasm manifested toward a General as the army of the Potomac manifests toward Gen. Grant whenever and wherever he goes." Indeed, he said, corps commanders were compelled to "request the soldiers not to be so demonstrative." Markland also commented upon General Meade's wholly cooperative attitude toward Grant and concluded by saying that when he left headquarters to return to Washington, "General Grant was in the very best spirits, and evidently felt that he was master of the situation." Markland's remarks, reprinted in a number of newspapers around the country, served to reassure the home front that the Army of the Potomac welcomed Grant as its leader, that its soldiers would enthusiastically fight under him, and that there would be no cross-purposes between Grant and Meade.[17]

Most important, newspapers published this positive message about Grant to readers on the home front during a series of battles that became known as Grant's Overland Campaign, which stretched from early May to mid-June. These were battles so fierce and so bloody that Lincoln groaned in despair over the death toll, and the new lieutenant general was called "butcher" by many, including First Lady Mary Todd Lincoln. Beginning roughly seventy miles south-

"Twenty Tons of Mail"

west of Washington in a dense, tangled forest simply but ominously called the Wilderness, the campaign between the two armies ended after a succession of stalemates at the horrifically bloody but inconclusive Battle of Cold Harbor in early June. Despite outcries in the Northern press at the loss of life at Cold Harbor, Grant persevered, pursuing Lee in retreat southward toward Petersburg. There, in mid-June, Lee's army once again withdrew behind a series of extensive earthworks less than thirty miles from the capital of the Confederacy, Richmond.

During those six weeks of near constant bloody combat, four of the men most intimately involved in the military survival of the United States and in the political survival of the Lincoln administration took time to sort out a disagreement over the handling of military mail.

Although Markland was already acting as Grant's military mail supervisor in the East, Postmaster General Blair wanted to have the arrangement formalized in writing. According to Markland, when Grant learned of this, he "suggested that the proper orders ought to be issued by the secretary of war, Mr. Stanton." Grant arranged for the orders to be drafted by staff at the War Department, and, along with a cover letter, they were sent to Blair's office. Blair then deputized Markland to carry the draft orders back to the War Department and request that they be issued. But Stanton refused to issue them, there being, according to Markland, "a little official jealousy between the two cabinet members."[18] That was putting it mildly; the two men despised each other. When Blair learned that Stanton had declined to issue the orders, Blair wrote a letter to the president, which he directed Markland to deliver along with the draft order. In the letter, Blair claimed credit for bringing Markland back from the western theater but noted Grant's approval:

> I would respectfully ask the president's attention to the within
> communication. While the mail communications with the army
> of the west have been satisfactory, those with the army here have
> not been. To remedy this I brought Col. Markland here. He had
> been with Gen. Grant and had his confidence. The general, you will

perceive, prepared the requisite orders, but they remain unacted on in the war department.

M. Blair, P.M.G.

June 9, [18]64[19]

Markland delivered the letter to President Lincoln on the same day, and he recorded Lincoln's analysis and commonsense resolution of the spat between his cabinet members: "If I understand the case, Gen. Grant wants the orders issued, and Blair wants them issued, and you want them issued, and Stanton won't issue them. Now, don't you see what kind of a fix I'll be in if I interfere? I'll tell you what to do. If you and Gen. Grant understand one another, suppose you try to get along without the orders, and if Blair or Stanton makes a fuss I may be called in as a referee, and I may decide in your favor." Markland noted that the orders, though never issued, were informally followed, "and pleasant relations were maintained on that score all around."[20]

Markland's visit with the president was on the same day that a delegation from the Baltimore convention of the Republican Party (carrying the temporary name "National Union Party"), led by former Ohio governor William Dennison, met with Lincoln to formally inform him he had just been nominated as its candidate in the presidential election in November. One of Lincoln's former major generals (and Grant's former superior officer), John Charles Frémont, had already been nominated by a Republican splinter party of fervent abolitionists who were disappointed with Lincoln's emancipation efforts; that group called itself the Radical Democracy Party. Another of Lincoln's former generals, George Brinton McClellan, was all but certain to get the Democratic Party's nomination at its convention in August and run on a platform seeking peace at any cost, including maintaining slavery. Progress in the war was vital to Lincoln's success at the polls in just five months, particularly considering that Frémont's third-party candidacy would draw voters who would otherwise support Lincoln over McClellan. Although the president grieved over the death toll in Grant's Overland Campaign, he knew he finally had a general who would relentlessly press

"Twenty Tons of Mail"

the war on all fronts. Despite the cries of "butcher" in the press, Lincoln doggedly supported Grant. The president knew that he and his lieutenant general desperately needed victories.

On June 15, in preparation for his siege of Petersburg, Grant established his headquarters on an abandoned plantation at the confluence of the James and Appomattox Rivers, near what is today Hopewell, Virginia. Union Army quartermaster Rufus Ingalls had already set up a massive supply depot at that location, then called City Point. Grant's arrival prompted Ingalls to offer the plantation's elegant house, known as Appomattox Manor, to the general for his lodging. Grant refused, choosing instead to live in a tent on the grounds.[21] Five days later, Grant issued Special Orders No. 39. If Secretary of War Stanton would not formally place Markland in charge of his army's mail, Grant would do it himself:

> To further facilitate the transmission of the mails to and from the Armies operating from the James river, the following regulations are published.
>
> 1st—A. H. Markland, an authorized Agent of the Post Office Department at City Point VA, will receive and forward all Army mails to their destination. Commanders of Armies or Departments will, on his application detail from the ranks to report to him such assistants as may be necessary to enable him promptly to discharge his duties.[22]

The news was hailed by the Army of the Potomac. The *Soldiers' Journal*, a newspaper that circulated widely in military hospitals and convalescent camps around Washington DC, reported that the order "will be read with interest by the many friends and families of the soldiers" and that "under this arrangement correspondence with the army will be more regularly and safely transmitted than it has ever heretofore." Soldiers were advised to address any future mail complaints to Col. A. H. Markland, in whose hands they "will meet with prompt attention."[23]

What Blair had referenced in his letter to Lincoln about the unsatisfactory state of military mail in the eastern theater of the war had been obvious since 1861. Under the mail system in the West, Grant said, soldiers "received letters from home with as much regularity as if they had been residents of a large city." But according to Benson J. Lossing, a historian with whom Grant cooperated after the war in the preparation of a three-volume history of the Civil War, "that system was not introduced into the Army of the Potomac while McClellan commanded it." Instead, "one much less perfect and efficient" continued until Grant and Markland arrived.[24]

At the outset of the war in Virginia, "the chaplain of each regiment was recognized as 'regimental post-master,' and he usually called at the Washington City Post-office for the army mail." The rapid growth of the army in that region and the many battles fought in the relatively small geographic area meant that "much of the time there was very little regularity in the delivery of the mails."[25] One chaplain, who wrote about his service during McClellan's Peninsula Campaign in early 1862, found his duties distasteful beyond description, especially those regarding the mail. After a lengthy bill of complaints about how poorly he was treated by officers and how few soldiers ever attended his services, Rev. James Junius Marks of the Sixty-Third Pennsylvania Regiment then grumbled,

> If after all this he still hangs on, degrade him by making him post-master and mail-boy. If he has no horse on which to carry the mail-bag, put him as a nurse into a hospital. If postmaster, take a pound of flesh; make him turn out with the mail in thunder-storms, struggle through sloughs deep enough to engulf armies. If he demurs at conveying the mail on Sundays, let him know most distinctly that no officer has any business with a conscience in the United States service; but if he still refuses to go, take as a matter of compromise the most drunken, furious soldier in the camp, borrow for him the ferocious spurs of the quartermaster, mount him on the chaplain's horse, send him with the mail-bag; and if the animal returns wind-broken and blind of an eye, pity the horse, curse the chaplain, and reward the soldier. . . . This only faintly hints at the indignities that many chaplains have had to endure.[26]

Understandably, such an attitude may have in and of itself impeded distribution of mail in some camps (not to mention attendance at religious services), but fortunately not all chaplains regarded mail duty in the same light. The Reverend Jonathan Pinkney Hammond, whose *Army Chaplain's Manual* was published in 1863, described how a chaplain's handling of the mail, including personal assistance in writing letters for soldiers, "increased opportunities afforded him of becoming acquainted with them individually, and of exchanging with them words of kindness, and perhaps of instruction." He also pointed out that if the chaplain also provided, as was generally the case in the Army of the Potomac, the service of officially marking "soldiers mail" on letters (which would substitute for a stamp), that could also "be the means of bringing the soldiers frequently to his office, and of causing them to connect his position with their temporal, as well as spiritual welfare." But it was inefficient to burden chaplains with such a responsibility. Whether the chaplains in the East embraced the Marks or the Hammond mind-set about their mail duties, the system needed to change, and under Grant it did.[27]

According to historian Lossing, "The peculiar army mail-service organized under the auspices of General Grant was finally extended to all Departments, and was managed by Colonel Markland, who was made the general superintendent of the mails of the armies of the Republic." In a letter to Lossing in 1866, Grant recalled how his soldiers had received mail "within one hour after the troops began to march into Fort Donelson." He further asserted that "the same promptness was always observed in the armies under my command, up to the period of the final disbandment." It was in this letter that Grant gave public credit to his childhood friend: "The system adopted by me was suggested and ably superintended by A. H. Markland, special agent of the Post-office Department."[28]

With City Point established as Grant's headquarters for the foreseeable future, Julia soon joined him, and the Marklands took up residence there as well. In her memoirs, Julia Grant recalled that her husband "used to send for me to visit him and that was pleasant. He always sent a ship or boat to meet me and allowed me to invite friends to accompany me. He would come down the James river in his own boat and meet us at Fortress Monroe, and taking the party on his boat, we would arrive at City Point the next morning." We do not know if Martha Markland accompanied Julia on any of these trips, but on June 19 Grant personally wrote, on letterhead from "Head-Quarters Armies of the United States," the instruction to "pass Mrs. A. H. Markland to Fortress Monroe, Va." Other wives soon followed, and soon "Julia was the reigning queen, due to her husband's status, of a small but merry society of officers' wives," which included Mary Mercer Ord, Margaretta Meade, and Sallie Griffin.[29]

Officers at City Point had their own diversions, many of which took place at a spot called "The Rialto," named for the bustling marketplace and its bridge in Italy, made famous by Shakespeare in *The Merchant of Venice*. Markland described City Point's Rialto as a "changeable kind of place" in camp, one "where the officers would wish to lay aside all thought of the cares and burdens of military life and to entertain one another and their guests with stories of the silver linings of war. At the meeting leather medals would be presented to such officers as deserved them. Speeches of rare humorous mirth would be made and it is only the truth to say that the speeches of Col. Horace Porter at the meetings never failed to instruct and enliven."[30]

Markland elaborated on the gatherings at the Rialto more than twenty years later, when he shared a tale of a medal ceremony, scheduled late one evening when Grant was presumed to be asleep and would not "know of the proposed merriment." After a particularly enjoyable gathering, the officers retired late in the evening, congratulating themselves that they had not disturbed their commander. At breakfast the next morning, Grant "startled his military family at the table with the question: 'Why did you not ask me to the presentation last night?'" The famously speech-averse general joked, "I might have made a speech."[31]

A day after Grant's order placing Markland in charge of all mails, Markland was informed that the postmaster general had confirmed Grant's military mail arrangements in a letter that expressed Blair's pleasure in Grant's full cooperation with his department:

> The Postmaster General directs that you report to Lieutenant General Grant for duty, as Special Agent of the Department, in the supervision of the mail service to and from the Army.

"Twenty Tons of Mail"

Your experience with the armies in the West, and especially those under the command of General Grant, makes it unnecessary to enter into details as to the duties of the position to which you are now assigned.

The cheerful and effective cooperation of General Grant with the Post Office Dept. in affording postal facilities to our troops in the field is an evidence that you need but to carry out such arrangements and details as experience has shown to be effective in accomplishing beneficial results elsewhere to produce the same desirable ends in your new sphere of actions.

You will please communicate this order to Lieutenant General Grant, and place yourself at his disposal in accordance therewith.[32]

With this, Markland had achieved what he had hoped for when he wrote Grant in January: a position in a "revolted" state (Virginia), with Martha by his side, managing the largest postal challenge in the nation's history alongside his now-famous childhood friend.

Less than a month later, Markland also received a pass from Grant, but this one was of particular note. In later years, it was reported, "excepting President Lincoln and General Grant himself, Col. Markland . . . is believed to be the only person in the United States whoever [sic] held authority to pass to all points within the lines of the Union Armies without hindrance." If that is accurate, it is very likely that he was the only civilian aside from the president and secretary of war who not only could pass "to and from all points" within the Union Army lines but who was also provided transportation by the army's quartermaster department. He would soon make frequent use of the pass as he moved between Grant's field of operations and Sherman's.[33]

While Grant battled Lee in Virginia, Sherman fought and maneuvered Gen. Joseph E. Johnston toward Atlanta from May through mid-July, when impatient Confederate president Jefferson Davis replaced Johnston with John Bell Hood because Johnston had "failed to arrest the advance of the enemy to the vicinity of Atlanta." Sherman pressed on and within six weeks forced Hood and his army to evacuate Atlanta. On September 2 Sherman entered the city. The next day he telegraphed to Washington the welcome news: "Atlanta is ours and fairly won."[34]

Capture of the Confederacy's vital southern rail hub thrilled the North; newspapers across the country trumpeted the glorious news, even those that had consistently criticized Sherman since the beginning of the war. In addition to its immense strategic value in the military contest, Sherman's victory immediately boosted Lincoln's political prospects, which had appeared utterly dismal less than two weeks earlier. The president had asked his cabinet to sign—unseen—a memorandum that read, "It seems exceedingly probable that this Administration will not be re-elected," and it also called on them to pledge their cooperation with the president-elect from the day he was elected.[35] It was an unprecedented act by a sitting president, a solemn, tangible commitment by a man dedicated to the welfare of his country through a peaceful transition of the office if he lost. Mid-August was the low point of Lincoln's bid for reelection; the dramatic change in the Union's war fortunes wrought by the fall of Atlanta prompted President Lincoln to call for a national day of celebration on September 5. It also prompted Lincoln's reenergized political backers to ramp up their efforts to reelect him.

One of the most active Lincoln supporters in early September was also one of the newest—the powerful, capricious founder and publisher of the *New York Tribune*, Horace Greeley. Greeley's relationship with Lincoln had been problematic since at least 1860. In 1864 Greeley initially championed Frémont, then plotted to remove Lincoln from the ballot and replace him with Grant. Upon hearing the news from Atlanta, however, the publisher jumped into the Lincoln camp with both feet. On September 6 the *Tribune* carried a stunning announcement that "henceforth we fly the banner of Abraham Lincoln for the next President. . . . We MUST re-elect him, and, God helping us, we WILL." To several in Lincoln's inner circle, Greeley broached a brash and self-serving plan to aid Lincoln's reelection: he proposed to deliver massive quantities of newspapers to soldiers in the field.[36]

Newspapers were a staple of army camps, eagerly sought and eagerly read, passed from soldier to soldier until they literally fell apart. In the East, large newspapers sometimes circulated their wares in camp themselves or through distributors, but most newspapers arrived in camp via the mail, as they did in the western theater. In the nineteenth century, newspaper publishers did not try to hide their political preferences, and there was no separation or even labeling of an item as news or opinion. In an election year especially, publishers wore their politics on their pages in black and white; newspapers were transparent weapons of propaganda. Greeley sought to wield those weapons to attract the soldiers' vote for Lincoln. Greeley's scheme was not merely to ensure that more soldiers got more newspapers; it was to ensure that they got the "right" ones, the Republican ones that endorsed Lincoln for president, like his *Tribune* and the *New York Times*.

As it happened, the head of the National Union Party in 1864 was not only a staunch Republican but also the publisher of the *Times*. Henry Jarvis Raymond was a brilliant, politically active man whose first experience in newspapers had been as a young correspondent for Greeley's *Tribune*. When Greeley approached him with his idea, Raymond quickly agreed. With Raymond's blessing, Greeley outlined his plan to Lincoln's personal secretary, John Nicolay. Nicolay then contacted Postmaster General Blair, who reached into his vast network of postal employees and chose the man he thought would best implement this important political effort on behalf of Lincoln and thus help the Union survive—his fellow Kentuckian, and now military mail supervisor for all the armies, Special Agent Absalom Markland. Markland leaped at the chance to once again aid Lincoln's political prospects.

Barely a week after Greeley first endorsed Lincoln, what had been a germ of an idea became manifest. On September 14 Markland wrote to Blair:

Sir:

I have arranged with Henry T. Davis to receive at City Point Va, all papers documents &c that are sent gratuitously to the officers and soldiers in the Army operating against Richmond. . . . Col. Pitkin the Quarter Master of the Post of City Point will give to Mr. Davis all needful assistance. The Mail Agents will take charge of the packages from Washington to City Point.

I am sir, Very Respectfully Your Obt Srvt

A. H. Markland[37]

And then, because even the postmaster general might need a gentle reminder about properly addressing mail, Markland appended, "Packages should be plainly marked Henry T. Davis City Point."[38]

Blair quickly forwarded to Nicolay "the letter of Col. Markland for whom I sent to make the desired arrangements for distributing the papers &c which Mr. Greeley proposed. . . . The arrangement is complete." Nicolay, in turn, wrote Greeley a letter marked "Private" in which he said, "In furtherance of the idea you suggested to me when in New York, I send you enclosed a copy of the letter of Col. Markland Special Mail Agent, who has under Mr. Blair's instructions, made arrangements for the distribution of such newspapers, or other political matter, as the National Committee may determine to circulate in the Army of the Potomac. Will you please show it to Mr. Raymond and confer with him further on the subject?"[39]

According to historian Harold Holzer, Greeley's scheme gave an effective "monopoly of the sale of the papers in General Grant's and Sheridan's armies" to Republican-leaning newspapers. In addition to getting the "right" newspapers into the hands of soldiers—and perhaps as the result of Greeley's and Raymond's "further" discussions—the new newspaper regime also resulted in far fewer "wrong," or Democratic, newspapers available in the field. One of the Democratic newspapers that supported George McClellan for president, the *New York World*, shortly thereafter complained that the administration's "opposition papers are suppressed outright within the military lines."[40]

Markland's implementation of Blair's request was possibly the last time the two men communicated in their official capacities. On September 22 Abraham Lincoln asked for Blair's resignation. The open enmity between Blair and Stanton had made managing the country and the war impossibly difficult; for example, Stanton would not attend cabinet meetings that Blair attended. Two days later, Lincoln nominated William Dennison, former governor of Ohio, to be postmaster general.[41]

One of the first things Dennison did was to write to Grant: "I have requested Col. Markland to express to you my earnest purpose of promptly furnishing you, and the army at all times, all the assistance in my power connected with the postal service in the army." Dennison continued, "Your experience in the Military postal service having been greater than that of any other Army Officer, you will greatly oblige me by communicating to me any views you may have on that subject."[42] Grant quickly replied:

I . . . am glad to be able to inform you, that so far as my knowledge extends the Army is well and satisfactorily supplied with mails. . . .

When the expedition started from Cairo in February 1862 against Fort Henry Col. A. H. Markland voluntarily joined me and was assigned to the duty of keeping up the mails to and from the Army in the field. . . . A system of receiving and forwarding mails was adopted and enlisted men detailed for the purpose of carrying into effect, which they did under Col. Markland's supervision, with signal fidelity and acceptance, and without any expense to the Post Office Department, that I am aware of.

The policy I then adopted of prohibiting civilians from having anything to do the with the mails within the lines of the Army, and of detailing intelligent, reliable enlisted men for the purpose, my subsequent experience has confirmed.[43]

As the country celebrated Sherman's capture of Atlanta, the general was planning his next move. Hood's army remained at large around Atlanta, and Sherman knew it had to be defeated. But he also believed that fighting that army might not be the most useful service he could provide his country at the moment. His subordinate officer Gen. George Thomas could handle Hood, he believed. Instead, Sherman proposed to march. He reasoned, "If we can march a well-appointed Army right through [enemy] territory, it is a demonstration to the world, foreign and domestic, that we have a power which [Jefferson] Davis cannot resist." Sherman took great care in planning the march. He chose only the healthiest of his soldiers to make the trek; he consulted census records for information on crops and forage and livestock that would be available along the way to feed his troops and horses; he stripped down the supplies to be drawn by wagon trains to a bare minimum; and he thought about his soldiers' mail.[44]

Like Grant, Sherman knew the value of reliable mail service to his army. In the portion of his memoirs titled "Military Lessons of the War," he wrote, "Mail facilities should be kept up with an army if possible, that Officers and men may receive and send letters to their friends, thus maintaining the home influence of infinite assistance to discipline." But he knew the mail could not keep up on this march through enemy territory, and mail deliveries could not be planned. Indeed, Sherman's intention was to keep the Confederates guessing as to his destination and his route to it—he even kept it a secret from his troops.[45]

Sherman wrote to Grant numerous times during September and October. He reasoned that he could not keep his army crouched on the defensive in Atlanta; he tamped down doubts that Grant, Halleck, and Lincoln shared about such a march and about Thomas's ability to handle Hood; and he enlarged upon the advantages of his plan to take the offensive. In early November, Grant gave his approval. "On the 6th of November, at Kingston [Georgia]," Sherman recalled in his memoirs, "I wrote and telegraphed to General Grant, reviewing the whole situation, gave him my full plan of action, stated that I was ready to march as soon as the election was over."[46]

Lincoln's victory in the November 8 election was a runaway 212–12 vote in the Electoral College. McClellan took 45 percent of the popular vote to Lincoln's 55 percent, though some state results were close (Frémont had withdrawn). What was not close were the votes cast by soldiers in the field, whose ballots were sent by mail. After three and a half years of bitter, bloody war, soldiers voted for Lincoln—the man who wanted them to keep fighting—by more than 75 percent over the former general whose platform pledged peace through appeasement. The extent to which the Greeley-Nicolay-Blair-Markland newspaper caper influenced the race cannot be known, but it is unlikely that receiving more Republican newspapers made a major difference to soldiers who did not want their service—or that of their fallen fellow troops—to be in vain.

Sherman's army stepped off on the cool, cloudy morning of November 15. Many of the men assumed they were headed to Richmond to meet Grant. Sherman, however, wrote that he "had no purpose to march direct for Richmond . . . but always designed to reach the sea-coast first at Savannah or Port Royal, South Carolina, and even kept in mind the alternative of Pensacola." Spending much of his time at Grant's City Point headquarters and visiting Atlanta more than once, Markland would have been privy to Sherman's evolving plan. As the outlines of Sherman's strategy became clear, Markland grasped how the mail could be used to help deceive the enemy about Sherman's route.[47]

Years later, Markland wrote a four-page narrative (never published) about his plan for the marchers' mail. "When the army was gone the question arose 'Where shall we send Sherman's mail?'" he wrote. Markland decided that if mail for the soldiers continued to be sent via the Louisville & Nashville Railroad, as it had been during the occupation of Atlanta, the enemy "might be misled into supposing that the movement was a feint and think the army might unexpectedly come back." That was done for fifteen days, by which time the Confederates suspected that Sherman and his army were headed to the coast. At that point, Markland proposed to have all the mail for the army directed to Baltimore, which "might confuse (the enemy) into the belief that Sherman did not intend to go to the Coast but to turn to the north and get in the rear of Lee's Army. At all events," he wrote, "the mail was as handy at Baltimore as anywhere else."[48] Markland asked Col. Horace Porter to seek Grant's approval of his plan, and on November 24, Porter sent a note to Markland from City Point:

Dear Markland—

I spoke to the General about Sherman's mails and he thinks it a Capital idea to have them collected at Baltimore, or such points as you see fit. All hands here send regards and beg you to meet us on the Rialto at nine.

Yours tenderly,

Horace Porter[49]

Markland soon proceeded to Baltimore to make the appropriate arrangements, and three days later he sent a telegram in cipher to the Nashville postmaster to forward to Baltimore "all mail for Maj Genl W. T. Sherman & the Army now on the march with him."[50]

For nearly a month, sixty thousand U.S. soldiers marched through Georgia, as cut off from friends and family as if they were marching on the moon. Confederate newspapers reported only rumors of the Union Army's invasion plans, and even Lincoln admitted he did not know where Sherman and his army were. The soldiers traveled in two wings of infantry and artillery, plus cavalry, carving a sixty-mile-wide swath through nearly three hundred miles, creating more terror than actual damage (though there was plenty of that) to the women, old men, and children in their path. Some greeted the Yankees' arrival joyously, however. Estimates of the number of enslaved persons who followed Sherman's army to freedom range from ten thousand to nineteen thousand. By December 10 the army had reached the outskirts of Savannah and surrounded the city in semicircle, anchoring the Savannah River at each end. In military terms, Sherman's forces had invested the city, and the siege could commence. At the same time, Sherman sought to eliminate the threat from Fort McAllister, about twelve miles southwest on the Ogeechee River, which guarded Savannah's southeast approach.[51]

First, however, Sherman needed to contact the Union Navy, which would resupply needed provisions (mostly bread, sugar, and coffee, unavailable in the South) and open communications to the North. In hopes of contacting Sherman's forces, the navy had sent the gunboat USS *Flag* to scout Ossabaw Sound, the large bay into which the Ogeechee River empties. That contact was made on December 11, and the army and navy soon cooperated in the capture of Fort McAllister. By December 13 the river had been made fully accessible for Union Navy operations.

One of the very first steamboats to navigate upriver to Sherman's headquarters was the U.S. transport *Fulton*, carrying several of General Grant's aides and Absalom Markland—with twenty tons of mail.

According to Markland, Sherman went to great pains to ensure that the mail was in the first boat that would reach his men surrounding Savannah. "I will signal over to the rice mill [the highest point in the vicinity] that you are here with the mail," Sherman told him, "and they will signal to the army, and everybody will be on the lookout for you." He directed that Markland and the mail be transferred to a smaller boat, the *Island City*. It could navigate the obstacles in the river to King's Bridge, Markland further recalled,

> where more than twenty thousand troops were assembled to give me welcome. No man so humble as I ever received so cordial and enthusiastic a welcome. I was again with the soldiers I had known at forts Henry and Donelson, Nashville and Memphis, at Vicksburg, Shiloh, and Chattanooga. I had been with them on the Mississippi River from Cairo to New Orleans, and along the railroad from Louisville to Atlanta. . . .
>
> The mail messengers who had been associated with me in all of the campaigns of the valley of the Mississippi, and who had shouldered their muskets for the march to the sea, reported to me and the more than three hundred sacks of mail matter was soon ready for distribution. We had it so arranged that it could be distributed as easily and as quickly as the mail of a city is distributed by carrier.[52]

Carl Sandburg captured the scene in his biography of Abraham Lincoln: "Men and officers whooped with glee over the first letters from home in many weeks." An Illinois soldier wrote of the windfall, "What a scene our camp presents as the boys are scattered here and there, perusing the letters just received from loved ones a thousand miles or more away and talking over with each other the news from home." According to a Wisconsin soldier, "This last trip through Rebeldom had made letters a priceless boon." Samuel H. Hurst, commander of the Seventy-Third Ohio Volunteer Infantry, which had fought from western Virginia to Gettysburg to Lookout Mountain to Savannah, exulted, "How glad we were to get letters from home!" In his memoirs, Sherman noted that the letters for his army had arrived "under charge of Colonel A. H. Markland . . . [and] were most welcome to all the officers and soldiers of the army, which had been cut off from friends and the world for two months."[53]

While Markland supervised the collection, storage, sorting, transporting, and distributing of hundreds of mailbags for Sherman's troops, General Grant had issued the orders that made it all happen. On December 3 he issued Special Orders No. 142 from City Point, which read in part, "The Quarter Masters Department, at New York City, will furnish transportation to Colonel A. H. Markland, Special Agent of the Post Office Department, and 1st Lieut. Wm. K. Dunn, Acting Aid-de-Camp, and Mails for Maj. Gen. W. T. Sherman's Army from New York to Blockading Fleet off Savannah." The Quartermaster's Office in New York endorsed the order five days later, noting "Transportation Furnished to Hilton Head." On the same day, Grant had written a letter to Sherman, which he gave to his aide, Lieutenant Dunn, to deliver. Its first sentence read, "The little information gleaned from the Southern press indicating no great obstacle to your progress, I have directed your mails, which had previously been collected in Baltimore by Col. Markland, Spl. Agt. of the P.O. Dept., to be sent as far as the Blockading Squadron off Savannah to be forwarded to you as soon as heard from on the Coast."[54]

Sherman welcomed this letter from Grant that expressed confidence in Sherman's ultimate success at Savannah, but Sherman appreciated even more a very special message from his commander in chief that Markland personally delivered to him. Markland had traveled to Savannah from New York City via Washington DC. There, on December 5, after he visited with Postmaster General Dennison, he met with Abraham Lincoln at the White House. He had visited with Lincoln nearly every month from the time he began working with Grant in the West until March 1864, when the postal agent came East with Grant and Markland began weekly visits. Of course, Markland could not know at the time that the December visit would be his last, but he later wrote,

> My last interview with Mr. Lincoln had a touch of pathos I can never forget. . . . I remember his words well, but the expression of his coun-

"Twenty Tons of Mail"

tenance and the modulation of his voice is far beyond any description I could give. . . . Extending his hand to me, he said:

"Well, Colonel. I got word from General Grant that you were going to find Sherman, and that you would take any message I might have. I know you will find him, because we always get good news from you. Say to General Sherman, for me, whenever and wherever you see him, 'God bless him and god bless his army.' That is as much as I can say, and more than I can write."

He held my hand during the delivery of this message . . . and his voice faltered. He gave evidence of being greatly affected. He shook my hand, bade me good-by, and I proceeded to the door, when he called to me. When I looked back he was standing like a statue where I had left him. "Now, remember what I say . . ."[55]

When he finally caught up with Sherman, Markland recalled, "as soon as I could strike hands with him I delivered him the message, and by its language he was visibly affected." Markland later elaborated, "When I delivered that message to General Sherman, [it] was the only time that I ever saw him affected or moved by anything."[56]

Now that Fort McAllister had been seized and communications with the North opened, Sherman's attention returned to the city of Savannah, still in Confederate hands. He sent a letter to Gen. William J. Hardee offering "liberal terms to the inhabitants and garrison" if the Confederate general would surrender but promising "the harshest measures" should he be obliged to resort to force of arms to take the city. Neither came to pass; Hardee and his men slipped out of Savannah on the night of December 20. The Union Army entered the next morning. Two days later, Charles R. Green, who had made his fortune in cotton and shipping in Savannah after emigrating from England, offered his home to Sherman for his headquarters and lodging. The house, one of the most grand and expensive in the city, "was so spacious, so convenient, with a large yard and stabling," according to Sherman, that after initially hesitating, he accepted the offer.[57]

While Sherman attended to the myriad issues inherent in occupying a major city—including telegraphing the president, "I beg to present you as a Christmas-gift the city of Savannah"—Markland collected the thousands of letters Sherman's soldiers had written during the march. He reported selling $2,100 worth of stamps (enough for at least seventy thousand letters) and could, "had [he] brought more, sold double that amount."[58]

Markland wasted no time in carrying the soldiers' mail northward. He disembarked from the *Fulton* at City Point on December 20, while Savannah was still in enemy hands; the *Fulton* carried more than ten thousand letters on to New York for distribution. The Evansville, Indiana, newspaper reported on Markland's travels, saying, "We may be looking for a perfect avalanche from the boys in Sherman's army in a day or two." Based on the number of letters Markland had brought back, the reporter calculated, "one soldier in every four or five sent letters home in the first mail from the army."[59]

Almost immediately, Grant asked Markland to take on another assignment, and this time Martha was included. "I would be pleased to have you obtain the authority from the Postmaster-General to go to Savannah and arrange for the regular transmission and distribution of the mails for General Sherman's army," he wrote. "I understand Mrs. Markland desires to accompany you; if so, she has permission to go." Three days later, Markland got the go-ahead from the Postmaster General's Office to "proceed immediately to the headquarters of Gen. Sherman. . . . You will have the entire and exclusive control of these mails, subject only to the orders and directions of Sherman." The postmaster general had also directed that all letters and packages for Sherman's army be collected in New York until further notice. On December 24 Absalom and Martha Markland left New York City for Savannah with another load of mail—and lots of stamps.[60]

That day, General Sherman wrote a lengthy letter to Major General Halleck, the Union Army chief of staff, outlining his daring plan to march his soldiers north through the Carolinas to try to trap Lee between his army and Grant's. As he concluded the letter, Sherman asked Halleck, "Please say to the President that I have received his kind message through Colonel Markland, and feel thankful for his high favor."[61]

As 1864 closed, the Savannah Post Office reopened under the control of the United States of America. On December 31 the *Savannah*

Republican reported, "Col. A. H. Markland, Superintendent of the Mails of the United States Army, arrived yesterday from the North, and has taken possession of the Post-office. He has made arrangements to open the office for general business in a few days; yet meanwhile none but soldier's letters will be received. Postage stamps in any quantity can be obtained at the office windows to-day." As in the other captured Confederate cities where Markland had reopened the mail, the newspaper was full of praise and hope: "Col. Markland, whose experience and energy are already well known in this army, as in others, has taken hold of his work with a determination to offer to us the best mail facility possible, and we shall hereafter be placed in reliable and regular communication with the North."[62]

SEVEN

"Trains Have Stopped Running, Except for the Mail"

January–April 1865

Ceneral Sherman's spacious and gracious headquarters held several noteworthy social events over the course of his month-long stay in Savannah, including a Christmas dinner for his top officers, a New Year's Day reception for the public, and a reception hosted by the Union Army's most celebrated general to honor one of the navy's most celebrated admirals. On January 3, 1865, the Marklands received an invitation relaying "Major Gen'l Sherman's compliments to Col. Markland and Lady, and requests the pleasure of their presence at a Social Gathering on Thursday evening at 8 o'clock at Head Quarters house of Mr. Green."[1]

The "social gathering" the evening of January 5 was designated a "Reception for Admiral Dahlgren and Naval Officers." According to Gen. Green B. Raum's memoirs, it was "the first social gathering of this kind that had occurred with the officers of the army, and it was made all the more interesting to have present officers of the navy with their great Admiral." Raum recalled that among the long list of generals and the array of brigade commanders "there was one lady present with her husband, namely, Mrs. A. H. Markland, wife of Col. A. H. Markland, who, at Gen. Grant's request, had been assigned to duty by the Post office Department as Special Agent of Mails for Sherman's Army. Mrs. Markland was a handsome and spirited woman; was beautifully attired, and added interest and grace to the occasion. She was the first and only loyal woman from the North that we had seen since the campaign began, and it can well be understood that great respect was shown her."[2]

Other than the daguerreotype taken shortly after the Marklands' wedding, Raum's delightful recollection of Martha is the only depiction of any type that we have of her, and it is a revealing one. Even if we take for granted the chivalry of a nineteenth-century man commenting upon the only woman in a room (and of course, he did not have to comment upon her at all), she comes to life as a "handsome," graceful, and "spirited" woman who clearly held her own in the company of war-hardened men who had fought to Savannah on land and water and claimed it as a prize for the Union. The fact that she was there at Sherman's specific invitation is a notable tribute to Martha by the man who had famously banned wives (including his own) from his camps since the beginning of the war. To all the men gathered in Green's house, separated from their families for months at a time, the vivacious dark-haired, dark-eyed Martha brought a welcome touch of home.

Her husband may have brought something equally welcome to the dinner party. In Markland's slim file in the Library of Congress is a scrap of paper dated January 5, 1865, on which the chief quartermaster of the Fifteenth Army Corps scrawled in pencil, "I send you a little wood tonight according to promise." *Harper's Weekly* reported on the "scarcity of wood" for home and business fires in the vicinity of Savannah during the month of January, so the wood may have been requested for Markland's own quarters or for the post office. But it also may have been destined for the comfort of General Sherman's dinner party. The man who had procured scarce cow's milk for Grant might well have procured scarce wood for Sherman.[3]

It may have also been Markland's way of atoning for a slight to General Sherman that Markland had unwittingly committed on that first trip to Savannah to deliver those twenty tons of mail—one that Sherman probably never knew happened until Markland talked about it to a reporter twenty years later.

"It was when I went to meet Sherman at the close of his march to the sea to give his army their mail," Markland related. "Before we left New York Capt. Dunn's grandfather . . . gave him a box of very fine cigars to present to Gen. Sherman." Markland told the newspaper correspondent that Dunn, Markland's cabin mate who was

"Trains Have Stopped Running"

carrying a letter from Grant to Sherman, had quickly come down with seasickness "and took to his berth, which he did not leave until we reached Hilton head." Markland, on the other hand, "was proof against seasickness. . . . I was also a very great smoker." Since Markland's own cigars had been "stowed away with my luggage below, I thought it would make no difference to the captain if I used the cigars from his box." Not knowing they were destined for the famous general, Markland "opened the box and began to smoke. . . . They were even better than those smoked by Gen. Grant, and I wondered at their quality, which was far superior to the cigars which I had formerly smoked with Capt. Dunn." By the time the ship arrived at Hilton Head, to transfer its passengers and mail to another vessel, "the box was empty."[4]

As the shaky Captain Dunn prepared to disembark, he realized to his consternation that the cigars were missing. Learning that Markland had smoked them and tossed the box "to the fishes," Dunn panicked. He moaned to Markland that the cigars "were a choice brand" he had pledged to present to Sherman on behalf of his grandfather, who would "want to know what Gen. Sherman says about the cigars." Markland reassured him, based on his familiarity with Sherman and cigars, "That is easily fixed. Gen. Sherman chews a cigar more than he smokes it. I don't believe he knows a good cigar from a bad one . . . go and buy a box from the sutler and give that to him in the place of the other. Tell him they are extraordinary cigars, and he will make a great deal of them and think them just what you call them."

Markland recalled, "This was the last I heard of the matter. I don't suppose that his grandfather or Gen. Sherman ever knew but what the cigars sent were smoked as they were intended"—at least not until that article was published in 1885.

While Sherman plotted his army's move from Savannah and chewed the substitute cigars, Grant maintained pressure on Petersburg and Richmond from his City Point headquarters. He also made an important decision on behalf of his approximately one hundred thousand soldiers bivouacking in the area: he endorsed Markland's proposal to establish a "Money Post Office" there.

Postal money orders had first been used in Great Britain in 1838;

their popularity and usefulness had garnered Postmaster General Blair's attention because of the significant theft of cash sent through the mail in the United States. In 1855 alone, it was estimated that an amount between $500,000 and $1 million was lost or stolen from the regular mail. Express companies, like Adams Express and American Express, provided more safety but at a high—often prohibitive—cost. In his annual report in 1862, Blair recommended starting a system like Great Britain's in U.S. post offices; he reiterated his proposal the next year. Congress finally responded on May 17, 1864, with "An Act to establish a Postal Money-order System," yet another of Blair's Civil War–era postal innovations. By the end of 1864, 141 post offices in the United States could issue money orders for between $1 and $30, at a cost of ten cents to twenty cents.[5]

If sending money by mail in peacetime risked losses, sending funds safely home from thousands of soldiers in camps in wartime was even more of a challenge. In December 1863, for example, there were reports of military mail robberies in Nashville and Chattanooga, but as 1865 began, no money order offices had yet been approved in any military encampment. Markland proposed in December 1864 to establish a money order service at City Point, where it would be accessible to Grant's army. Grant immediately grasped its value to his men: "I fully approve the system and I believe that it will be highly advantageous to the soldier in the transmission of his money to his family or relations." That was one of the most important developments in military mail history and one that remains part of the global U.S. military postal service.[6]

The law required that money order operations be supervised by a duly appointed postmaster, so Dennison solicited Grant's recommendation for one at City Point. Shortly thereafter, a recently appointed special agent of the Post Office Department, Lt. David B. Parker, was named postmaster of the City Point Post Office and commenced implementation of the money order program. Parker "had several interviews with the zealous Superintendent of the Money Order System at the Department at Washington, who had objected to extending the service to the army . . . he was extremely anxious as to its success." But backed by Grant and Markland, Parker persevered, expanding the City Point post office building to accommodate a "money order room" and displaying notices with "full information as to how money orders could be obtained and how they were paid, etc. . . . at every camp." The posters were also read "on dress parade by the adjutants of the regiments." As the army prepared for its move on Petersburg, Parker recalled in his memoirs, "we found a long line of officers and soldiers at the office desiring to purchase money orders." Markland's proposal that City Point become the first military money order center enabled Grant's men to send their pay home more easily and cheaply, relieving them of at least some portion of worry as they prepared to march into battle.[7]

In Savannah, Sherman's soldiers were also preparing to march—north this time, through the Carolinas. They would encounter terrain and citizens so hostile that once again Grant initially urged Sherman not to march and instead move his men by boat up the coast. But Sherman believed that his soldiers, who had arrived in Savannah generally healthy and well fed after the March to the Sea, would be better off marching and foraging their way to Virginia than crowding aboard unsanitary transports and eating hardtack on rolling seas. Sherman also believed that his mission "to whip the rebels, to humble their pride, to follow them to their inmost recesses, and make them fear and dread us" would not be complete until South Carolina, where secession began, had experienced the same sense of helpless terror his men had inflicted upon Georgia. As Grant's men prepared for their coming battle by buying money orders, Sherman's prepared to be incommunicado once again by writing letters.[8]

On January 16 the *Buffalo (NY) Commercial* reported that in Savannah "the rush for postage stamps has been unparalleled. Over $10,000 worth have been sold since the arrival of Col. Markland in the city." That sum would have bought more than three hundred thousand three-cent stamps. The reporter asserted that "excepting the army itself, [the post office] is the great feature and institution of the city." Later that month, Markland was sent $10,000 more in stamps.[9] *Harper's Weekly* even carried a poem titled "Letters from Sherman's Army," which provided poetic insight into how the avalanche of soldiers' letters was being greeted on the home front. It opened and closed with the following lines:

> Five hundred thousand evangels
> Sent to a million hearts
> With the messages of triumph
> In the strength which love imparts. . . .
>
> The volumes of sage and scholar
> Grow lifeless and dim beside
> The life of these wingèd letters
> And their meaning glorified.[10]

While Markland took pride in the fact that he was bringing families closer together, the work was exhausting in the extreme. "The past three weeks have been the most trying I have had since I have been in the Service," he wrote to Postmaster General Dennison on January 23, using stationery imprinted "Headquarters, Military Division of the Mississippi, In the Field" (the only example that exists of Markland using official army letterhead). Markland was clearly overwhelmed by the workload, and with this letter he hoped to impress upon Dennison (who had not been in office even six months) his superhuman dedication to the postal service.[11]

He opened by telling Dennison about the lengthy letter he was enclosing from Savannah's former Confederate postmaster, an unreconstructed rebel named Solomon Cohen whose financial accounts Markland was trying to validate. While that was the ostensible purpose of writing directly to the postmaster general, Markland had an ulterior motive. He laid the groundwork for it carefully.

After discussing Cohen's claims, Markland described in detail the frenzied mail situation in Savannah since the arrival of Sherman's troops: "The fact that the whole command has been encamped in a radius of four miles and having, as it has been, out of the world on their march through this state, made them more eager for mails than usual." He depicted the post office as a "besieged institution," with too much mail and too few dedicated, experienced clerks. Markland spelled out the enormous challenges he faced even after delivering the initial twenty tons of mail in mid-December: "To give you an idea of the business done in this office since the 19th [of January], I would state that there have been received in this office One Hundred and Ninety-Three of the largest size pouches & sacks of mail, the greater portion of which was letters, every one of which had to be re-handled and properly distributed to an impatient army and a clamorous crowd of citizens." He and his few clerks had to work by candlelight, he wrote, because the price of oil for lamps was exorbitant. But, he declared, "I have sent off all the Northern mail in the best shape I could. The office has been kept open night and day."

Markland then referred to the second letter he enclosed: "I take the liberty of enclosing a copy of a letter from Maj Genl Sherman to the Secy of War," the original of which had been mailed to Washington by Sherman more than a week earlier.

Headquarters, Military Division of the Mississippi
In the Field, Savannah Jan 14 1865

[To] Hon. E. M. Stanton
Secretary of War

Sir—

As our mail facilities form an important link in the chain of events now transpiring, it gives me pleasure to note the peculiar energy which characterizes the Agents of the Department under the charge of Col. A. H. Markland.

Col. Markland has managed this Dept in connection with my Army to my entire satisfaction and with a kindly interest that shows a devotion to our cause that takes him with the advance of our Army, has won its respect, and my confidence.

I am Very Respectfully
Your Obedient Servant

[signed] W. T. Sherman
Major General[12]

Markland had received written praise from important military men—most notably Generals Grant and Thomas—in the past, but this apparently unsolicited letter from the Union's hero of the hour to the secretary of war triggered within the beleaguered Markland a yearning for greater recognition of his service: "This voluntary consideration of my services by Gen. Sherman I cannot too highly prize." He pointedly noted to Dennison, "The Rail Road representative & recruiting agents in the lines of the Army have been brevetted Brig[adier] Genls." Then he dropped his bombshell request: "Why cannot the P. O. Special Agent be a brevet Brig. Genl.?" Markland argued his case for a generalship to Dennison, a man relatively new to the reins of power in the Lincoln cabinet. "I am sure that every officer & soldier who knows him would recommend it," he wrote, awkwardly referring to himself in the third person.[13]

A "brevet" grade in the military was a promotion awarded for meritorious service or to assign a special task above a soldier's current grade. It was a promotion that came with a new title but no corresponding increase in pay. The process for brevet promotions in the volunteer or regular army of the United States during the Civil War began with a soldier's superior officer making a recommendation to the secretary of war. If the request for a brevet rank received approval, the secretary (on behalf of the president) would send the nomination to the U.S. Senate for confirmation. The candidate would be required to take an oath and report to the appropriate office and officer while awaiting the arrival of the signed and sealed commission, the final step in the process. Over the course of the Civil War, more than 1,500 lieutenant colonels and colonels were breveted brigadier generals, but the course of Markland's petition was anything but straightforward.[14]

We know that his petition was forwarded to the War Department because the documents Markland sent to Dennison are in the files of the U.S. Army in the National Archives. Chronologically, Sherman's letter to Stanton was the first in the file. As was the custom, the letter was folded in thirds and was "endorsed," or dated and summarized, by a clerk in the Adjutant General's Office (AGO), who wrote on it that it was from General Sherman, who "notes the peculiar energy which characterizes the Mail Agents of this Department under the charge of Col. A. H. Markland" (emphasis in the original). This would indicate that Stanton or a senior aide had seen the letter and that no further action was required.[15]

The next entry in the AGO files relating to Markland was logged in on February 13 and includes his three-page letter to Dennison, the four-page letter from Confederate postmaster Cohen, and a one-page copy of the letter from Sherman to Stanton. Enfolding those eight pages is a cover page that says, in a different and beautifully clear hand: "A. H. Markland, Special Agent, P. O. Dept., Brigadier Genl Vols, by Brevet, Recommended by Maj. Genl W. T. Sherman."[16]

Reading the papers in the order they would now be unfolded—like peeling an onion—Markland's petition for a brevet brigadier generalship transforms from one recommended by Sherman to one requested by Markland. The package is a historian's dream, since this request, fueled by Sherman's praise, gives insight into Markland's ambition, his sense of worth, and his desire for recognition at this point in his life. It is also a historian's nightmare, since in the end, it poses more questions than it answers. Reconstructing the papers' journey from Markland through the Post Office Department, the U.S. Army, and into the National Archives is akin to searching for the exit from a perfectly designed bureaucratic maze. Based on documents available online in the AGO files in the National Archives, no action was ever taken on Markland's petition. If it had been approved, there would be some evidence of a brevet brigadier general commission somewhere in the U.S. Army records; if it had been denied, there should be some indication of that. There is none. There is, in fact, no evidence that any decision was made at all. While that sort of gap in the official record is not common in the army—with its bureaucratic imperative to dot every *i* and cross every *t*—there are several possible reasons for this nonresult.

One possibility is that Stanton, having read the original letter from Sherman two weeks earlier, recognized that it was neither a request nor a recommendation (as required) for a brevet brigadier generalship for Markland, and he therefore simply ignored the petition. Or Stanton, whose ability to hold a grudge was legendary, may have remembered (from the "newspapers-for-soldiers" election gambit) that Markland had been Blair's man before he was Dennison's and so refused to approve the petition out of his implacable hatred of Blair. But when confronted with a puzzle, it is always best to consider the simplest solution. And that would be that Markland's file was simply lost among the thousands of similar petitions during that very busy time in the Civil War. Things like that do happen, even in the most efficient bureaucracy.[17]

The best argument for the lost-in-the-army-files answer can be found in another government department's files. Ten years after Markland's death, the Post Office Department asked the U.S. Army for "the military record of Col. A. H. Markland." The chief of the army's Record and Pension Office replied, "I have the honor to inform you that nothing has been found of record to show that Colonel Markland was ever appointed or commissioned as an officer of the Army, or that he was ever mustered into the United States military service as of any grade." The detailed report was published as part of the postmaster general's annual report in 1898. It included dozens of documents from official records of the U.S. Army and the U.S. Post Office, but not one of the documents relating to Markland's brevet general request was part of that report.[18]

It is not hard to understand Markland's desire to gain the genuine military designation of general (albeit brevet) at this late date in the war. It would confer a title that would carry respect and open doors for the rest of his life. And, at least in the short run, it would pay more than his post office salary. Beyond simply seeking possible financial rewards, the gregarious Markland's pursuit of the brevet rank may have reflected a desire to in some way remain part of the "band of brothers" that war has always forged among men in the field. As he wrote to Dennison, since the autumn of 1861 in Cairo, Illinois, he had spent far more time in military camps and on battlefields in the company of officers and soldiers than he ever had with his postal colleagues. Indeed, though special agents of the Post Office Department had been appointed to expedite military mail in other commands, he had little communication with them and certainly no real peers among them. The friends he had made over four years were military men with whom he saw the horror of war firsthand and with whom he shared victories and setbacks, tents and

"Trains Have Stopped Running"

hardtack, pranks and funerals, letters containing good news and bad. If he remained part of the Post Office Department after the war, Markland would return to a world that knew little of what he had experienced.[19]

No doubt he was disappointed not to be made a brevet brigadier general—who wouldn't be? But the lack of any additional supporting letters in this file could also indicate that Markland himself backed away from pursuing the honorary rank. There is no evidence of any additional lobbying by him or any allies after he sent the one-paragraph plea to Dennison. In contrast, less than three years earlier, Markland had submitted or orchestrated the sending of eight letters to the president and the secretary of war in his bid to become an army paymaster.[20]

The lack of supporting letters in the file may indicate that Markland quickly recognized the incongruity (perhaps the embarrassment) of a civilian asking to be made a general—even one who had been with the armies throughout the war. Sherman's letter had gone to his head, and his ambition had overtaken his good judgment. He was acting far too aggressively on his own behalf—behavior that was generally frowned upon in the nineteenth century. Asking his superior, Dennison, to propose him for a higher office was one thing (and he may well have regretted even that). But asking Grant for a letter of recommendation? Or Buell? Or Thomas? Or asking Sherman to rewrite his letter in the form of a nomination? While those West Pointers were all comfortable calling him "Colonel," it is hard to imagine they would propose a civilian (even an "honorary" colonel) for brevet brigadier general in the U.S. Army as the bloody war was grinding to a close.

And it was. The sense of an ending was palpable. The Confederacy was on its last legs; its citizens and its high command knew it. In the capital of the Confederacy, First Lady Varina Davis later recalled, "every one felt the cataclysm which impended." Grant's siege of Petersburg—the last bulwark against the fall of Richmond, just twenty-three miles away—was entering its seventh month. The once-mighty hosts of Lee and Johnston that had ranged from Virginia to Arkansas were now corralled by Grant and Sherman within a stretch of territory from Savannah to Richmond. Though the end was near, they knew the marching and killing were not yet finished.[21]

Sherman prepared to tighten the vise.

He planned to push off from Savannah in mid-January, but incessant rain kept his men in camp for an additional week. That meant more letters could be written, and they were. By the time Sherman's soldiers began heading north in a series of waves on January 19, the volume of mail in Savannah destined for the North had surpassed all previous records. While Markland had enough stamps for the soldiers' letters, he and his few clerks were unable to individually cancel the avalanche of missives that descended on the candlelit post office. When the last batch of soldiers' letters arrived in New York City in late January, the event was noteworthy enough to be reported widely, even across the Atlantic. The *Illustrated London News* informed its readers,

> The mail from Sherman's army, by the [steamship] *Arago*, reached the New York post-office at half-past six o'clock on Friday night, and the last of more than 200,000 letters was dispatched by the Erie line [railroad] at a quarter past four the next afternoon. The stamps not having been cancelled, this labour was necessarily performed in the New York post-office, and employed fifteen men throughout the night and up to noon on Saturday. Twenty men were required to sort the letters. This is the largest mail that the New York post office ever received.[22]

Markland continued to oversee the Savannah Post Office and supervise overall army mail operations from City Point through mid-February, as Sherman's troops advanced toward the capital of South Carolina, Columbia. On February 17 the Union Army captured that city—news that panicked the Confederate commander at Charleston. By evening Charleston's guard had fled and Columbia was in flames. Sherman denied he had instigated the burning of Columbia, but he was pleased that Charleston—the site of the Confederate attack on Fort Sumter in April 1861 that sparked the bloody war—would surrender without a fight. Again, Markland was one of the first officials of the U.S. government to enter a captured city.

On February 22 the *Charleston Courier*, under management of the Union Army since February 20, announced, "Once more the people of Charleston, under the protection of the Old Flag, can have uninterrupted communication with the whole world, as may be seen by the order of Col. Markland, the Special Agent of the Post-office Department."[23]

Barely a week later, Markland moved on again, to keep the mail in advance of Sherman's army as it entered North Carolina. Markland transferred first to Wilmington, North Carolina, and then to the port of New Bern, which the quartermaster corps deemed a better site for a supply base. Shortly thereafter, Markland was reported to be in the coastal town of Morehead City, "with a large mail for Sherman's army, which he is waiting to deliver by way of Newbern." If Markland saw that article in the *Charleston Daily Courier*, he might have been amused (or gratified), since it referred to the military's mail agent as "General Markland."[24]

Sherman's men had captured Fayetteville on March 11, but he was keeping the Confederates guessing as to his exact route. According to the same Charleston newspaper article, "The enemy is much alarmed and mystified regarding Sherman's movements. We expect to hear from him in a day or two." On March 16 Sherman's forces attacked Confederates near the town of Averasboro, where a spirited battle resulted in losses on both sides before the rebels retreated northeastward. They had not marched far when they turned and attacked the pursuing Federals near the town of Bentonville. The three-day battle, which ended in Gen. Joseph E. Johnston's retreat on March 21, proved to be the Confederates' final major effort to stop the relentless progress of Sherman's army. Once again, Markland was ready. "After the hard fought battle of Bentonville, [Sherman] met the mail for his army on the evening of the day of that battle," an Indiana newspaper later reported.[25]

A week later, Sherman established his headquarters near Goldsboro, North Carolina, ending the four-hundred-mile march from Savannah. Almost immediately, he issued a detailed "circular" about the subject on every soldier's mind: "Colonel A. H. Markland has the full authority for the distribution of mail matter for this army . . .

he will for the present receive mail at Newbern, and there distribute it in packages for regiments, brigades, divisions and corps, and from there forward it to Goldsboro, by messengers of the Military Mail Department, at which point he will deliver it only to such persons as corps commanders may designate, viz: one (1) postmaster for each corps."[26]

Separately, Sherman's aide, L. M. Dayton, who was an assistant adjutant general, alerted Maj. Gen. Oliver O. Howard that "there is now at New Berne, in the hands of Colonel Markland, a large mail for your command, which you had better send your army messenger for."[27]

In his most recent dispatch to Sherman, Grant had described obvious signs of demoralization in Lee's army, including an increase in desertions, but admitted he did not understand "what the rebels intend to do." As a result, Sherman recalled in his memoirs, "I deemed it of great importance that I should have a personal interview with the general, and determined to go in person to City Point." So, on the same day his mail circular was published, Sherman began the 150-mile journey north to City Point to better understand Grant's thoughts about how their armies would end the war. That trip was serendipitous in the extreme; President Lincoln had arrived at City Point three days earlier.[28]

On the morning of March 28, Sherman, Grant, and Adm. David Porter assembled in a stateroom aboard the paddlewheel steamer *River Queen* for what would prove to be a momentous meeting with the president. Written firsthand recollections of the conversation, one by Porter that evening and one in Sherman's 1875 memoirs, stress Lincoln's desire that the rebel soldiers go "back to their homes, at work on their farms and in their shops," at the conclusion of hostilities. The president asked if further bloodshed could be avoided and was told by Grant that that was entirely in Lee's hands. The military men came away from the meeting convinced that Lincoln wanted the hard war to end in a soft peace.[29]

More than once, Lincoln voiced his unease that Sherman was so far from his command. Though the general tried to reassure him that the military situation in Goldsboro was well in hand, the president was clearly relieved when Sherman, along with his brother, Senator John Sherman, and the secretary of war's son (also named Edwin Stanton), boarded a fast boat and headed south as soon as the talks concluded. The morning after Sherman returned to New Bern, according to Markland, "at the breakfast table were seated General Sherman, Mr. Stanton, Captain Kimball and wife, and Mrs. Markland, my wife, and myself." Sherman related some of the highlights of his time at City Point and fielded questions from the group, a conversation that would become extraordinarily important in the coming days.[30]

As March came to a close, Grant's 125,000 soldiers were positioned along an extended line around Petersburg and Richmond that Lee's diminished army could not match. With each passing day, the likelihood faded that Lee and Johnston could unite their armies before facing a combined Grant-Sherman force. On April 1 Union cavalry commander Philip Sheridan emerged the hero of a battle at a vital crossroads southeast of Richmond called Five Forks, which Lee had ordered Gen. George Pickett to "hold at all costs" that morning. With that loss, Lee realized the fate of Richmond was sealed. The next morning—a beautiful spring Sunday morning—he sent a telegram to his commander in chief. Jefferson Davis received it while sitting in his pew at St. Paul's church. "I think it is absolutely necessary that we should abandon our position tonight," Lee warned. "I advise that all preparation be made for leaving Richmond tonight." An ashen-faced Davis quickly made his way out of the church alone; he had sent his wife and children away from the city days earlier.[31]

The next day, soldiers of the Union Army entered the capital of the Confederacy, which fleeing rebel soldiers had set ablaze and abandoned in smoking ruins. For the first time in the war, Absalom Markland was not the man who reopened the U.S. Post Office in a major rebel city that Grant's army had captured. Instead, Special Agent David Parker was temporarily dispatched from City Point. On April 4, as President Lincoln and his son Tad visited Richmond, Parker telegraphed Washington that he had entered the city. When Parker arrived, "the lower part of the city was burning . . . [and the post office] was being ransacked by some of our soldiers." After placing a guard on the premises, the next morning he "opened the post-office and sent a mail to City Point in the afternoon." George McLellan, second assistant postmaster, commended Parker on April 6, saying, "It is desirable that the Richmond post office should be put in operation as soon as possible, and upon the return of the Postmaster General from Ohio the last of this week, some one will probably be appointed to relieve you of your duties at that point."[32]

Markland was still in New Bern, dealing with the never-ending flow of mail to and from Sherman's army. Testifying to the importance of the mail even as the collapsing Confederacy escalated the Union's logistical challenges, the chief quartermaster of the Army of the Tennessee notified Markland, "I sent you one horse last night— the only one that has been sent to me." The same day Parker opened the Richmond Post Office, Markland telegraphed Sherman about the magnitude of the amount of mail awaiting delivery: "If the mails are to be distributed to the army from this point three (3) steamers will be required . . . the public service demands it. I have had but one (1) mail this week." Later that day, he sent another telegram to Sherman: "The mail of to-day will be delivered to the army to-morrow. No further mails will be sent to the army until after I reach Fortress Monroe. They could not reach here in time to distribute." Sherman replied that day with Special Field Orders No. 55, naming eight enlisted men "detailed for duty in the Military Post Office Department of the Army and will report to Col. A. H. Markland Supt. Mil. Mails for instruction."[33]

On April 7 Sherman addressed the bigger picture in a detailed letter to Markland, which began, "I have thought over mail matters." He proposed a plan for how the mails should be transported to reach his men no matter what route his army would take in its march north to meet with Grant and defeat Johnston. He reassured Markland, "Mail matter and carriers to have preference of carriage and all citizens or goods debarred the privilege." He closed by inviting Markland to send him any suggestions. Markland promptly replied, "Your views in reference to the mails are all that could be wished. . . . I have now all the facilities in the way of clerks. I will . . . carry out your views." Also on April 7 Markland received "several tons of mail matter" at

New Bern and forwarded them to Goldsboro, according to the recollections of Maj. George Ward Nichols, a staff aide to Sherman.[34]

On that same day, Grant assessed Lee's military position as hopeless. Lee had fewer than fifteen thousand effectives, all in desperate need of food and ammunition. They had only the slimmest chance of getting either without risking battle against the much stronger Union force. And so, on April 8, Grant sent a message to his opponent through enemy lines, expressing his hope that Lee would surrender his army to avoid further bloodshed. Lee pushed back on Grant's grim assessment, but Grant stood firm, promising only that he would impose but one condition, "that the men and officers surrendered be disqualified for taking up arms again, against the Government of the United States."[35]

A day later, Absalom and Martha left North Carolina, courtesy of transportation provided by the quartermaster department, departing from Morehead City and traveling to Fort Monroe and then on to City Point. That was April 9, the momentous day that Robert E. Lee agreed to surrender terms from Ulysses S. Grant at a hastily improvised meeting in a private home in the town of Appomattox Court House. The small company assembled in Wilmer McLean's sitting room that afternoon included an impeccably outfitted white-haired general with a jewel-hilted sword, a "brown-bearded little man in a mud-spattered uniform," and a Seneca Indian, Col. Ely S. Parker, who was Grant's prewar friend and military aide and who penned the final surrender document. That iconic tableau is now a fixed part of our historical memory. At the time, though, because of the collapse of the Confederacy's transportation and communication systems, news of Lee's surrender lagged far behind the event. Even when Confederates heard of it, they initially refused to believe it.[36]

President and Mrs. Lincoln had left for Washington the day before, but Julia Grant remained at City Point until her husband and his staff returned on April 12. The next day Grant's entire entourage steamed to a rousing reception in the nation's capital, while three hundred miles away Sherman's men marched into North Carolina's capital city. Although Lee and his army had quit the fight, the war was not over. There were still Confederate forces under arms in the far West, in the trans-Mississippi region, and in the East under Joseph Johnston. But Sherman was poised to force Johnston's quick surrender. On April 14 Johnston applied to Sherman for a "temporary suspension" of hostilities so that "arrangements to terminate the existing war" could be negotiated. It appeared that the final act of this four-year national tragedy would open in the gently rolling green hills surrounding Raleigh.[37]

Sadly, the real tragedy was about to unfold in Ford's Theatre in Washington.

We have lived so long with the story of the assassination of President Lincoln that it now seems less like a contingency and more like a preordained event. It takes as much effort for us in the twenty-first century to imagine John Wilkes Booth unsuccessful as it did for men and women in 1865 to accept that he succeeded.

"A stroke from Heaven laying the whole of the city in instant ruins could not have startled us as did the word that broke from Ford's Theatre a half hour ago that the President had been shot," reported the *New York Times* in a story datelined Washington, 11:15 p.m. Another newspaper reported that "the entire city last night presented a scene of wild excitement, accompanied by violent expressions of indignation, and the profoundest sorrow."[38]

The Grants—who had declined the Lincolns' invitation to join them at the theater that evening—were traveling to their home in New Jersey when, during a layover in Philadelphia, they learned of the attack on the president. Stanton's telegram demanded the general return right away. Grant first accompanied Julia home, then immediately boarded a hastily arranged and heavily guarded private train for the return journey. He arrived shortly after Lincoln was pronounced dead at 7:22 a.m., April 15, 1865.

By then rumor and panic were rampant in the nation's capital and mounting across the country. People were arrested for speaking "disrespectfully of the President and lightly of his sad death." When news of Lincoln's assassination reached New Orleans, four men were murdered in the streets by a frenzied mob "for rejoicing over his death." The editor of the *Westminster (MD) Democrat* saw his offices mobbed and his equipment wrecked; when he fired upon the throng and wounded one of them, an Alexandria newspaper reported that "the enraged crowd killed [him] on the spot." At noon on April 15, Vice President Andrew Johnson was sworn into office by the chief justice of the Supreme Court. A cabinet meeting was then held, and Grant attended it in an attempt to calm the nation by a swift, peaceful transition of power in that chaotic moment.[39]

As the city pivoted from celebrating the victory over Lee to mourning the murder of Lincoln, a grieving Markland and other prominent Kentuckians convened in the Willard Hotel to prepare a proper tribute to the slain president. Markland was one of five men appointed to draft a resolution, which was unanimously approved and published: "As Kentuckians we feel deeply the loss to our citizens of one who, born on their soil, acquainted with their people . . . was eminently fitted to temper severity with mercy. . . . We heartily condole with Mrs. Lincoln, and her household, in their affliction and grief, assuring the esteemed wife of our late honored President (like him, a native of Kentucky) of our sympathy, and that of every loyal Kentuckian."[40]

The real business of the hour was the apprehension of the assassin, or assassins—no one knew how many were involved in the plot to kill Lincoln, Seward, Johnson, Stanton, Grant, and . . . who else? Did Booth act alone or were Confederate government officials involved? The possible options seemed endless. Rumors were rife, and they led to a scatter-shot, poorly managed search at first, one in which everyone and no one seemed to be in charge. Stanton lashed out with orders to pursue possible assassins in all directions from the capital, north to Canada, south to Richmond. He leaned on Grant to find the assassin(s) and to ensure that the capital was safe. Military orders flew to and from the War Department like lightning, day and night. It was grueling work for the few men who held the reins of power.

That evening, Washington buildings that had been illuminated in celebration a night earlier were draped in black crape to signify mourning. A clerk who had helped hang crape at the windows of the White House walked to the War Department to perform the same service. As he entered a room on the third floor, he realized there was a man hunched over a desk in the semidarkness. "Pardon me," apologized Charles Jones, who began to back out. When the man raised his head, Jones realized with a shock that it was General Grant, who looked "haggard and utterly exhausted." Grant waved him in, saying, "Don't mind me. Carry out your orders."[41]

Among the many orders issued from the War Department were those to prevent persons from leaving Washington-area wharves and ports by boat. The military still controlled the telegraph lines, eliminating that method of communication between possible conspirators. Stanton forbade trains running west toward Fairfax, Virginia, where the assassin was reported to be heading. Army nurse Julia Wheelock Freeman wrote in her diary on the evening of April 16, "The trains have stopped running, except for the mail."[42]

Grant remembered with a start that the Richmond Post Office had reopened nine days earlier and that mail was still being transported between Washington and Richmond. It was then that he sent an urgent message to Markland, whom he knew was in Washington, ordering him to ensure "that no mail matter be sent to Richmond addressed to citizens of that place until further orders." Grant also directed Markland to search the Washington Post Office and "unseal and examine all letters in the mails addressed to citizens of Richmond and forward to these headquarters all such as contain contraband information."[43]

If any evidence of a larger plot against the U.S. government could be obtained through the mail, Grant knew he could rely on Markland to find it.

1. Martha Louisa Simms Markland and Absalom Markland, ca. 1851.
Heritage Auctions.

2. Absalom H. Markland's commission as special agent
of the Post Office Department. Heritage Auctions.

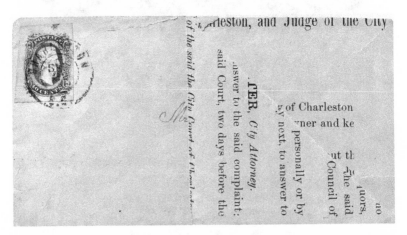

3. An adversity cover was an envelope or stationery improvised from whatever
used paper products could be found during the shortages experienced in the
Confederacy during the war. This adversity cover was made from "a Charleston
city attorney summons concerning sales of liquor to Negros," ca.
September 1863. Courtesy Paul Dessau.

4. Gunboat attack on Fort Henry. From *Harper's Weekly*, February 22, 1862.

5. Purported portrait of Grant after Fort Donelson.
From *Harper's Weekly*, March 8, 1862.

6. "Col. Absalom H. Markland, Superintendent of Mails," 1862. MOLLUS Mass Photograph Collection, U.S. Army Heritage and Education Center, Carlisle PA.

7. Log cabin at Pittsburg Landing, located on the Tennessee River, ca. 1862. The fighting there is often referred to as the Battle of Shiloh and was the first major military clash in the western theater of the Civil War. From *Battles and Leaders of the Civil War*, vol. 1 (New York, 1887).

8. Triumphant Union troops at the Memphis Post Office, where Markland fell ill. From *Harper's Weekly*, July 5, 1862.

9. Maj. Absalom Grimes, Confederate spy and mail courier. This is likely a postwar photograph, since he has gray in his hair and beard. Missouri History Museum, Wikimedia Commons.

10. Civil War camp in winter. Library of Congress, Morgan collection of
Civil War drawings, LC-DIG-ppmsca-20642. Created by Edwin Forbes.

11. (*opposite top*) Soldiers writing letters and mending clothing in camp.
Library of Congress, Civil War photographs collection, LC-DIG-cwpb-02194.

12. (*opposite bottom*) Markland's "All Points Pass," issued July 4, 1864,
at City Point. Heritage Auctions.

13. Newspapers arriving in camp, ca. 1863. Library of Congress, Civil War photographs collection, LC-DIG-cwpb-01140. Photograph by Alexander Gardner.

NOTICE.

The United States Mail will leave Savannah for the North at five o'clock this day. Citizens can avail themselves of all postal facilities.

A. H. MARKLAND,
Superintendent of Mails
For the Armies of the United States.
Dec'r 31, 1864.

14. Poster announcing mail service, Savannah, Georgia. Heritage Auctions.

15. New Year's Day reception for the public at General Sherman's headquarters, home of Charles Green. From *Harper's Weekly*, January 28, 1865.

16. First Division, Ninth Corps, mail center near Petersburg, ca. 1864.
U.S. Army Heritage and Education Center, Carlisle PA.

17. "Murder of President Lincoln." From *Philadelphia Inquirer*, April 17, 1865.

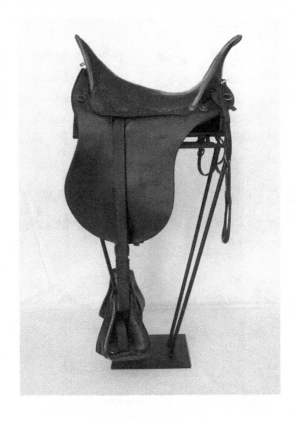

18. The Grimsley saddle Grant gave to Markland after the Civil War.
U.S. Army Quartermaster Museum.

19. (*opposite top*) William H. Gibson Sr., 1897. Wikimedia Commons.

20. (*opposite bottom*) Signing of the Ku Klux Klan Act of 1871.
At the table: President Grant, Navy Secretary George M. Robeson,
and Gen. Horace Porter, personal secretary to the president.
Library of Congress, LC-USZ62-87440.

21. Interior of the Post Office and Custom House building after the Great Chicago Fire. Library of Congress, LC-USZ62-57053. Created by P. B. Greene.

22. Planked shad at Marshall Hall, nineteenth century. Library of Congress, Brady-Handy photograph collection, LC-DIG-cwpbh-03334. Photograph by William Cruikshank.

23. Second and Market Streets, Maysville, 1884 flood. Kentucky Gateway Museum Center.

24. Absalom Hanks Markland, ca. 1885, age sixty.
Kentucky Gateway Museum Center.

EIGHT

"A Mark of Friendship and Esteem"

April 1865–November 1868

There is no indication that Markland found anything incriminating in his search of the mail at the post office in Washington in the wake of Lincoln's assassination. Though rumors of the involvement of Jefferson Davis and his cabinet in the assassination swirled around the nation's capital for weeks, no evidence has ever surfaced of a Confederate government connection to Booth's scheme. Nonetheless, it would have given Grant some peace of mind to know that Markland had that base covered.[1]

On the same day Grant sent that order to Markland—April 17—Sherman first learned of Lincoln's death through an encrypted telegram from Secretary Stanton. He read it just as he was leaving Raleigh to meet with Joseph Johnston about terms of surrender. Arriving at Durham Station, Sherman mounted a horse and, after a brief ride with a cavalry escort, encountered Johnston. The two men had served in the U.S. Army for thirteen years before the Civil War and had fought on opposite sides from Bull Run in July 1861 to Bentonville in April 1865, but they had never met face to face until this day. They rode to a small farmhouse, whose owners agreed to step outside. While their escorts waited in the yard, the two generals entered, and, according to Sherman,

> As soon as we were alone together I showed him the dispatch announcing Mr. Lincoln's assassination, and watched him closely. The perspiration came out in large drops on his forehead, and he did not attempt to conceal his distress. He denounced the act as a dis-

grace to the age, and hoped I did not charge it to the Confederate Government. I told him I could not believe that he or General Lee, or the officers of the Confederate army could possibly be privy to acts of assassination, but I would not say as much for Jeff. Davis . . . and men of that stripe.[2]

Both men recognized that negotiating the surrender of all Confederate armies, not just Johnston's, would be in the best interests of a lasting peace. In short order, they decided to meet again the next day with that end in mind, if Johnston could secure permission from his president to do so in the interim. And so on the afternoon of April 18, Sherman later wrote, "recalling the conversation of Mr. Lincoln, at City Point, I sat down at the table, and wrote off the terms, which I thought concisely expressed his views and wishes." Sherman's terms not only encompassed the surrender of all the remaining Confederate armies but also provided for conditional recognition of the seceded states' legislative, judicial, and executive branches. As Johnston signed the document, Sherman made it clear that nothing was final until he submitted the proposed surrender terms for President Andrew Johnson's approval. Accordingly, the document went by private courier to Grant in Washington for that purpose the next day. Both generals pledged to observe a truce until a response was received.[3]

Sherman was supremely confident his actions had finally and fully ended the war, but there were two things he did not know that were about to blindside him. First, Sherman had not been told that, in early March, President Lincoln explicitly forbade Grant from discussing nonmilitary issues in any surrender talks with General Lee. Second, Sherman's isolation in North Carolina, where news of Lincoln's assassination had not yet arrived, prevented him from knowing the violent anti-Confederate responses to the murder throughout the North, especially in Washington. Consequently, Sherman's surrender terms—crafted with Lincoln's "hard war" and "soft peace" guidance in mind—landed with a distinct thud on Grant's desk, followed by the most extreme vitriol on the part of several cabinet members

　　　　　　　　"A Mark of Friendship and Esteem"

when Grant took them to the White House for review. Grant knew that the nonmilitary terms were unacceptable, but even that did not prepare him for the backlash—from Stanton, in particular. The secretary of war accused Sherman of disobedience if not outright treason, alleging that Sherman had enabled Jefferson Davis to escape with millions of dollars, some of which, Stanton implied, had probably stuck to Sherman's fingers.

Grant left immediately for North Carolina, arriving unannounced (for security reasons) in Raleigh on April 24. He quickly brought Sherman up to date on both the volatile atmosphere in Washington and the telegram that Lincoln or Stanton should have copied him on much earlier. Grant then quietly returned to Washington. Always the obedient soldier, Sherman stifled his frustration and notified Johnston that the only terms he could offer to his army were those that Lee had accepted. On April 26—the same day federal agents cornered and killed John Wilkes Booth in a tobacco barn in Maryland—the two generals met again in the farmhouse belonging to the Bennett family. There they signed a document surrendering the largest Confederate army still in the field.

The death of Lincoln's assassin and the surrender of Johnston's army were tremendously good news for the Union, but the latter event was immediately overshadowed by universal declarations of outrage by Northern newspapers over Sherman's first surrender terms, which Stanton had leaked to the press. In fact, other than Lincoln's assassination, Sherman's first surrender terms garnered more press attention than any other event in the Civil War, and the reaction was negative in the extreme. The *New York Times* opined that "one is at a loss to know which side agreed to surrender." Words like "traitor" and "treason" were sprinkled through the reports of Sherman's actions, and Stanton also leaked the Lincoln telegram to newspapers without noting that Sherman had not seen it before negotiating with Johnston. Even Sherman's sanity was questioned. By the time he and his army marched from Raleigh to the outskirts of Washington to prepare for a grand review of the victorious troops, Sherman's fury at Stanton and other critical politicians who had profited from his many victories boiled over. "The Vandal Sherman is encamped near . . . Alexandria," Sherman grimly informed Grant's chief of staff on May 14.[4]

Those who knew Sherman well were furious at the slurs on his character, too. Even though they could not endorse Sherman's generosity toward the Confederacy, his Sherman brothers and Ewing foster brothers sought to tamp down his anger when he was called to defend his actions before the Committee on the Conduct of the War. In advance of that hearing, Absalom Markland sought to set the record straight by making public his knowledge of Lincoln's influence on Sherman's first surrender terms. As Markland recalled, "When General Sherman reached Washington City, or rather the south bank of the Potomac, with his army, and established his camp and headquarters there, I, in company with my wife and General O. O. Howard, went over to the headquarters to make a social call on General Sherman and his staff officers. My real object in making that call was to get General Sherman's permission to make the conversation we had had at the breakfast table in Newberne, N.C., public."[5]

However, Markland recalled, "General Sherman was in no mood to take up the subject, and very clearly intimated to me, that I should be silent concerning it."[6]

In that volatile atmosphere, Sherman did not want to lay blame for the highly unpopular surrender terms on the grave of the dead president. Markland, of course, acceded to Sherman's request. "It would not only have been idle, but the extreme of folly for me to have publicly repeated the conversation then," Markland wrote twenty years later. "The people of the North were frenzied, and would not have listened to anything short of an abrogation of the terms, even though General Grant himself had *known* that the terms would have been satisfactory to President Lincoln."[7]

Through all the chaos and confusion following the assassination, Grant—the undisputed hero of the war and of the hour—toiled on in the War Department. The famously quiet and speech-averse general was besieged for appearances around the country; he refused nearly all. After the final surrender of the Confederacy, dismantling the enormous Union Army (from nearly a million troops in 1865 to about twenty-five thousand by the end of 1866) was a Herculean task of logistics and paperwork, with detail upon detail requiring attention. In addition, the military—essentially the army under Grant—was charged with responsibility for safety, security, and governance in the devastated and unstable former Confederate states that had not yet returned to the Union, requiring an unprecedented use of armed forces in the United States.[8]

And yet, little more than a month after he had accepted Lee's surrender, and in the midst of all the claims on him, Grant took the time to send Markland a very special gift.

Washington, D.C. May 19, 1865

Col. A. H. Markland
Spl. Agt. P.O. Dept.

Colonel,

I take great pleasure in presenting you the "Grimsley Saddle" which I have used in all the battles from Fort Henry, Tenn, in Feb. 1862, to the battles about Petersburg, Va. ending in the surrender of Lee's Army at Appomattox C. H. Va. on the 9th of Apl. 1865.

I present this saddle not for any intrinsic value it possesses but as a mark of friendship and esteem after continued service with you through the Great Rebellion, our services commencing together at Cairo, Ill. in the Fall of 1861 and continuing to the present day. I hope our friendship, if not our continued services together, will continue as heretofore.

Yours Truly,

U. S. Grant
Lt. Gn.[9]

Grant's choice of a Grimsley saddle during the Civil War, as opposed to the army's standard McClellan saddle, was likely the result of his exposure to it during the Mexican War in the late 1840s. The Grimsley model was considered especially comfortable, durable, and—importantly for Grant, whose love of horses is legendary—easy on a horse's back. The saddle gift was reported widely in the press at the time, as so many actions by the famous general were. The saddle continued to garner notice from the press well into the twentieth century as Absalom and then his heirs lent it to a series of organizations for the public to view, from the National Soldiers' Home in Dayton, Ohio, to the Smithsonian, to the museum at City Point. It now resides in the U.S. Army Quartermaster Museum in Fort Lee, Virginia. There is no record of a similarly cherished memento of the war from Grant to any other person. Indeed, there is little evidence that Grant gave many gifts outside his family. This saddle, representing the entire span of the Grant-Markland Civil War partnership, remains a powerful symbol of their friendship.[10]

The gift of the saddle was not the only kindness that Grant showed Markland in the immediate aftermath of the war. On May 9 Grant wrote to Postmaster General Dennison, "Now that [Col. Markland] is about settling with the Govt. for his past service, I beg to state that from my knowledge of the nature of his duties a sum less than Five dollars ($5.00) per day would not remunerate him for his extra expenses." Clearly, Markland had approached Grant to assist him in obtaining more than the statutory $2 per diem for his tireless service to the army, and Grant generously did so. The letter produced a positive result, though not at all what Markland or Grant had sought. Barely a week later, Markland received a letter from the Post Office Department saying, "The Postmaster General has this day made an order that you be allowed and paid the sum of $4.00 per day for your necessary travelling and incidental expenses while actually employed from and after the first day of July 1865." He would not receive the increase retroactively, but, going forward, Markland would be paid double the regular per diem for a special agent. It is unlikely that he was happy with that decision, which was proof that Post Office Department bureaucrats knew little of his hazardous work during the war.[11]

Until he received other assignments, Markland continued reopening post offices—in Richmond, Petersburg, Charlottesville, and Yorktown, and other towns in Virginia—as authorized by military authorities in the region who certified they were under Federal control. He was advised that "garrisons will shortly be established at Lynchburg, Staunton, Gordonsville, and Danville," and he should prepare to transmit mail to and from those towns. When he was not traveling to those sites to supervise their operations, he lived in Washington, where he and Martha shared a house with Gen. Oliver Otis Howard, who after the Battle of Atlanta had commanded the Army of the Tennessee, which became the right wing of Sherman's troops as they marched through Georgia and the Carolinas.[12]

On one occasion, the location of the Markland/Howard residence led him "very near to getting the United States and England into a difficulty by answering a polite question asked by a British diplomat." Pierre L'Enfant's original plan for Washington included broad avenues named for states that ran diagonally through the city, creating many confusing, pie-shaped, three-street intersections. The Markland/Howard house stood at the three-way intersection of Twenty-Fifth Street, L Street, and Pennsylvania Avenue. The British minister to the United States, Sir Frederick Bruce, resided across the street at the corner of Twenty-Fifth and L Street. One day, one of the British attachés approached Markland, who was sitting on the verandah of his house, and with great politeness asked for the name of the street that faced the minister's building. According to Markland, he replied in kind: "Give my compliments to the minister and say to him that the legation is on L street, sir." The young diplomat rushed off in a huff, reporting to Sir Frederick that the "officer sent his compliments and said, 'Go to hell, sir.'" Sir Frederick, of course, took offense at the comment and sought an explanation. After several more round-trips by the attaché, Markland rightfully attributed the mistake to the common language that separates the United States and England (in this case, the pronunciation of the letter *l* versus "[h]ell"). Good humor won in the end, and the neighbors became good friends, according to Markland's account twenty years later.[13]

While in Washington, Markland secured one of the most sought-after tickets in the city—entry to the trial of the Lincoln conspirators. Of the more than one hundred people arrested by federal authorities after the president's assassination, seven men and one woman were charged with conspiracy to murder the president, a plot that had been organized by John Wilkes Booth, whose death put him beyond the reach of temporal justice. The record of passes issued for spectators shows Markland was present on May 17 in the court-room in the Washington Arsenal penitentiary (now Fort McNair) in southeast Washington. That was five days after the start of the military tribunal that conducted the trial, and it was the day that Dr. Samuel Mudd testified he had set the broken leg of a stranger very early on the morning of April 15. Nine presiding officers took seven weeks to hear testimony from more than three hundred witnesses before voting all the defendants guilty. Four were sentenced to death by hanging (including Mary Surratt, the first woman executed by the U.S. government), three were sentenced to life in prison (including Dr. Mudd), and one received a sentence of six years in prison.[14]

Toward the end of May, General Howard was appointed head of the Bureau of Refugees, Freedmen, and Abandoned Lands, commonly known as the Freedmen's Bureau. Never sufficiently funded and roiled by the politics of Reconstruction, the Freedmen's Bureau would struggle mightily to assist millions of formerly enslaved Black and poor white Americans with food, housing, education, and legal aid. It also sought to settle its charges on land, formerly owned by Confederates, that had come under U.S. jurisdiction by abandonment or confiscation. Howard's empathy, piety, and organizational skills made him an excellent choice for the unprecedented societal challenge. As he was about to be relieved of his military command to take up his new duties, Howard took the time to address a lengthy letter of thanks to Colonel Markland in recognition of the debt his army owed the special agent. It read in part,

> During all the weary marching from Chattanooga to Atlanta from Atlanta to Savannah, in the homeward campaign through the quicksands and marshes of the Carolinas, you, my dear colonel, have received from the officers and soldiers of the army the warmest thanks for the interest you have taken, the energy you have displayed and for the successful manner in which the immense mail accumulating has been, through your agency alone, forwarded by sea and land and distributed . . . and when our march was finally finished, and the troops encamped in sight of the dome of the Capitol, you were still in the advance of us, and the letters were waiting.[15]

"A Mark of Friendship and Esteem"

The next month, Markland's commission as special agent was renewed, and his area of responsibility changed. He was designated general superintendent of steamboat mail transportation, and George Armstrong of Chicago was made superintendent of railroad transportation. Together, they managed the two main methods of transporting mail between major and minor postal hubs. These appointments were in line with Postmaster General Dennison's desire that "the great through mails between Baltimore and Washington and the West taken from the line during the war, shall be at once fully restored." Dennison noted that "western travel, especially by tourists over this route, is now very large." With the war over, steamboats and railroads were once again owned by and under the authority of private companies. In keeping with its traditional role as a key subsidizer and utilizer of innovative transportation and communication technology, the Post Office Department negotiated sizable contracts with them to carry the mail. Such contracts were magnets for corruption, so special agents were particularly qualified to manage them.[16]

In October 1865 the scope of Markland's assignment and his continuing fame were apparent in a paragraph that appeared in the *New York Herald* and a number of other newspapers: "Colonel A. H. Markland, special, traveling, working and a little of everything agent of the United States Postal Department sails today on the *New York* for California, for the purpose, we believe, of regulating the overland mail, and establishing a weekly China mail to and from the Pacific Coast." Martha accompanied him on the long journey, during which they had the companionship of Richard McCormick, who was secretary of Arizona Territory, and his new bride, whose wedding the Marklands had attended at the Astor House in New York just prior to the voyage.[17]

Once in California, the Marklands were given free passage on all vessels of the California Steam Navigation Company by one of its founders, Capt. James Whitney, in order to facilitate his job (and no doubt to gain favor with him). Markland also received the assistance of California governor Frederick F. Low in contacting William Parks, a western transportation magnate who effected a merger of steam lines on the Sacramento River. Whether or not he had a hand in establishing a mail route to China, Markland did travel to Oregon in November on an inspection tour. There, he was greeted by newspaper articles pressing him to deal with numerous postal problems in the state, especially the delays caused by what one newspaper identified as "sending the mails from the States by the way of Great Salt Lake City, Sacramento and Portland, to be distributed in 'a portion of Idaho and Montana.'" Another newspaper, the *Daily Mountaineer* (published in The Dalles, a town in Oregon) went on to editorialize, "In advance, it is proper to give Col. Markland credit for some knowledge of the business upon which he comes to this country. Up to this time, we have not heard of his delivering temperance lectures, or theorizing on reconstruction, and other bewildering questions. These are good signs. We hope for further favorable developments of his ability and character."[18]

However, before Markland had an opportunity to accomplish much in the West, he was summoned back East by the postmaster general. Indeed, the *Daily Mountaineer* reported that Markland had returned "without having visited the Columbia River interior." Although we do not know on what ship the Marklands traveled from San Francisco to Panama, they embarked on January 19, 1866, for the trip from Panama to New York City on the ss *Chauncey* of the Pacific Coast Steamship Line, whose passenger manifest mistakenly lists Absalom as forty-four years old (he was forty-one) and Martha as twenty-eight (she was thirty-three).[19]

It is not clear why the postmaster general asked Markland to return, but in mid-March the Cincinnati City Council passed a resolution thanking Markland for assisting the council president "while on his mission to Washington City, to collect the claims of this city against the General Government." In the aftermath of the war, claims and counterclaims by individuals, companies, cities, and states against the federal government for its wartime emergency use of private and public property consumed an enormous amount of time and energy across the country. Former Ohio governor Dennison, who was in the state just prior to requesting Markland's return, may have sought Markland's help for his state's "Queen City."[20]

Around this time, Markland received a letter from Grant requesting a favor. "Lt. Col. P[eter] Hudson of the Volunteer service, and now a member of my Staff, purposes [sic] crossing the Plains to the Pacific this Spring," Grant wrote on April 11. He said Hudson would gladly perform any business for the Post Office Department, and "I can recommend him for such service and would feel glad to see him receive an appointment which will secure him a passage." It is likely that Markland jumped at the chance to return a favor to his patron.[21]

The next month, Markland received an important assignment— reorganization of the mail service in the Mississippi valley—and the news was widely reported, including in the German-language newspaper in Nashville, the *Tennessee Staatszeitung*. Rapidly increasing population and demand for mail services from Cairo to New Orleans required more steamboat landings than the thirty that were then operating, and there were the usual claims of corruption and inefficiencies that needed investigation. Markland was "empowered to make new contracts, to divide the service from point to point on the river where it can be done advantageously, and to appoint loyal men who will act in post offices as if appointed from the Department." In short order, Markland traveled the length of the route, making contracts and changes as needed, ending in New Orleans at the St. Charles Hotel. Barely two weeks later, Markland returned to Washington, "having succeeded," according to a Columbus, Ohio, newspaper, "in correcting the abuses in the mail service and adjusting the difficulties among the mail contractors on the routes from Cairo to New Orleans." The journey may have reminded him of the many battles he had witnessed in the region since he first encountered Grant in Cairo in the fall of 1861.[22]

Shortly after his return to Washington in June 1874, newspapers reported that Colonel Markland had resigned from the Post Office Department "to engage in the practice of law and as an advocate in the Departments in this city." There is no other insight into his decision. Perhaps he scorned to accept the higher postal per diem rate for work that was far less challenging than what he had done during the war; perhaps he saw the opportunity for a lucrative new career by representing claimants and lobbying government departments; perhaps he wanted to stop traveling so much and settle down again with Martha. Or perhaps it was all the above, plus the chance to do some of the wheeling and dealing he had always enjoyed.[23]

The political chaos that followed Lincoln's assassination had not calmed, despite—or rather, because of—the peaceful transfer of presidential power to Andrew Johnson. The dead president and his successor had begun their lives with much in common: childhood poverty, hardscrabble frontier surroundings, and little formal schooling. That background forced them both to make their own way in the world at an early age, and they were both lifelong voracious readers. But where Lincoln's arduous early life had softened and humbled him, Johnson's had embittered him, making him forever envious of those above his social status and forever disdainful of those beneath him, especially those whose skin was a different color. At the age of ten, Johnson's widowed mother bound him over as an indentured servant to a tailor in North Carolina; he ran away five years later. He scraped along for several years in the Carolinas and Tennessee before he set up his own tailoring business in Greeneville, Tennessee. There he prospered, ultimately owning ten slaves. Johnson's oratorical skills led him into politics, and he rose in the ranks, becoming governor of Tennessee and later a U.S. senator; as mentioned earlier, he served as military governor of the state during the war. Lincoln's political operatives chose him to replace Hannibal Hamlin as vice president in the election of 1864 for political reasons: he was a loyal Union man from a seceded state, "a southern war Democrat." He was expected to do virtually nothing in Lincoln's second term, as was the tradition with vice presidents, so Lincoln's men had not worried much about Johnson's personality or character before they selected him.[24]

If only they had. Johnson's lack of a coherent vision for reuniting the nation and his "almost unconquerable prejudices against the African race" guided his actions during the difficult and disheartening immediate postwar period, often called Presidential Reconstruction. Reconstruction—the process of readmitting the seceded Confederate states into the Union with appropriate safeguards for the rights of free Black men and women—actually began in December 1863, when Lincoln issued his Proclamation of Amnesty and Reconstruction. If Confederates swore an oath of loyalty to the United States and accepted the abolition of slavery, they would receive a pardon. When 10 percent of a state's voters from the 1860 election did so and the state adopted a new constitution that did not permit slavery, then the state could reenter the Union. Congressional Republicans opposed the measure, first because they believed only Congress had the authority to admit states to the Union and second because they believed Lincoln's criteria were far too lenient. Congress passed a bill setting a higher bar for reentry in 1864, but Lincoln refused to sign it, and it never became law.[25]

As Lincoln's successor, Johnson also believed he had sole authority to dictate the terms to the Confederacy. Johnson granted amnesty to former Confederates whose assets totaled less than $20,000, and he dispensed pardons liberally to those who requested them. As far as the seceded states were concerned, they needed only to adopt new constitutions that abolished slavery, recant their secession decrees, and repudiate their war debts. With such a low bar, six former rebel states were readmitted in 1868: Alabama, Arkansas, Florida, Louisiana, North Carolina, and South Carolina. Although Johnson declared the United States reunited, Congress rejected his declaration and his attempts to take charge of the process of Reconstruction.[26]

The subsequent "Congressional," or "Military," Reconstruction fared no better with Johnson in the White House, where he sought to obstruct and limit congressional Republicans' power. Johnson overruled Freedmen's Bureau chief Howard and allowed former Confederates he had pardoned to reclaim their lands. Shortly thereafter, the bureau was effectively disbanded without a whimper from the president, who also vetoed the first civil rights bill.

The president's lack of support for Black suffrage enabled the planter class to reclaim its prewar political advantages in many southern states by enacting "Black Codes" or "Black Laws," which first appeared in Mississippi in 1865. Among other extreme measures, those laws prevented Black residents from renting land, from hunting, fishing, or free grazing of livestock, and from working as anything other than a farmer or servant without paying a tax of up to $100. Police in the South were often former Confederate soldiers who wore their gray uniforms on duty, and white persons were rarely prosecuted for crimes against their Black neighbors. The latter were routinely jailed on the thinnest of excuses and then leased out as farmhands. White northerners were appalled, and Black Americans across the country were universally outraged. In an "Application of the Colored People of Shelbyville [Kentucky]," a former sergeant major of the U.S. Colored Cavalry, Henry Mars, asked Secretary Stanton in May 1866, "If you call this Freedom, what do you call Slavery?"[27]

In the fourteen years between Lincoln's proclamation in 1863 and 1877, when Reconstruction was "officially" deemed at an end, four successive presidents and six Congresses battled over the best way to achieve their evolving vision of how the states should attempt to live in harmony. There were many fits and starts, but there never really was an end; many of the issues Reconstruction sought to resolve are still with us today.[28]

With so many decisions about former Confederates and former Confederate property to be made by public servants, the rocky road through Reconstruction dangled numerous money-making opportunities before a lobbyist with extensive political connections and a thorough understanding of the Washington bureaucracy. Markland fit that bill, and along with a host of lawyers and agents in the nation's capital, he represented an assortment of aggrieved parties. Among his clients were a southern railroad owner, "Samuel Tate, a rebel," who received a pardon from President Johnson after taking the loyalty oath, and several southern railroad companies that Markland helped to bring back into service to improve the nation's transportation network. And Markland claimed money for damages to his own property in Paducah, Kentucky. Perhaps surprisingly, he also numbered among his clients one of the most famous former Confederate generals, Pierre Gustave Toutant Beauregard, who sought Markland's help to reclaim his land in Memphis that had been confiscated by the Freedmen's Bureau.[29]

A native of Louisiana who grew up on a prosperous sugar plantation south of New Orleans, Beauregard attended the U.S. Military Academy at West Point with Sherman and later supported Sherman's successful application for the top position at the Louisiana Military Academy on the eve of the Civil War. Small in stature but outsized in personal presence, he was formal and reserved; those around him said he could "go for months without smiling." After fighting in the Mexican War and managing some major projects as an army engineer, Beauregard was appointed superintendent of West Point. He began his tenure there on January 23, 1861. Three days later, Louisiana voted to secede from the Union, and two days after that, the U.S. secretary of war ordered Beauregard to leave the academy. He protested his removal, but once he returned to New Orleans he resigned his U.S. Army commission and began to rise in the Confederate ranks. One of only eight men who became full generals in the rebel army, Beauregard was present at the beginning (Fort Sumter) and the end (Raleigh) of the war. He was also nearly everywhere during it, including occupying Sherman's tent at Shiloh as his headquarters on the evening of the first day of the battle there, when Beauregard ordered his troops to halt action in the late afternoon, providing an opening for Grant's victory the next day. By 1865 he had become a better judge of battlefield situations—in April of that year, he urged a reluctant Jefferson Davis to allow General Johnston to negotiate surrender terms with Sherman.[30]

There is no evidence of a connection between Beauregard and Markland during or after the war other than the general's letter to the "colonel" in 1867, requesting help with the three lots in Memphis he wanted to regain. While many Confederates were aided in their postwar careers by loyal Union men who acted as lawyers and lobbyists, it would have been unlikely for Markland to have assisted Beauregard if he were anathema to either Sherman or Grant. But Beauregard was one of the earliest senior Confederate officers to take the required pledge of loyalty to the United States, the first step in securing the presidential pardon that was necessary to regain confiscated land and to obtain certain jobs (rank-and-file soldiers were granted general amnesty). He was also a rare former rebel in that he supported schools to teach newly freed Black Americans to read, and he made a major speech supporting Black suffrage, to the disgust of some of his former Confederate comrades. It was not unusual for former combatants, especially West Point alumni, to resume friendships after the war, so it is even possible that Beauregard was referred to Markland for help by Sherman or Thomas or Grant. Indeed, in addition to writing to Markland for help, Beauregard traveled to Washington and met with Grant, as well as with Johnson and his attorney general. But it was not until July 4, 1868, when Johnson enlarged the pool of former Confederates who could receive general amnesty, that Beauregard got his land back.[31]

In December 1867 Markland was called upon to organize and escort members of Congress on an "excursion to New Orleans." The bipartisan but largely Republican delegation of six senators and five representatives included the powerful former chair of the Committee on the Conduct of the War, Senator Benjamin Wade, and a future president, Representative Rutherford B. Hayes. Called the "Raid on New Orleans" by a sly headline writer for the *Detroit Free Press*, the visiting assembly of Congress members also included General Howard, Senate Sergeant at Arms George T. Brown, and Stanton's son, Edwin Stanton Jr. Several wives, including Martha Markland, accompanied the party. The delegation stopped along the way to visit Lookout Mountain and scenes of other Civil War battles. In Nashville, Howard addressed a group of freedmen at the state capitol, and the group was fêted by governors and mayors in the cities through which they traveled. When they reached New Orleans, courtesy of railroad passes secured by Markland, they were rained out of a river trip, but a grand banquet took place at the St. Louis Hotel. Once Markland shepherded his congressional charges back to Washington, the members of Congress presented Martha with two beautifully embossed silver goblets, engraved "Mrs. A. H. Markland."[32]

At the same time the Markland delegation was dining in the St. Louis Hotel—which still contained a slave auction block under its beautiful Beaux-Arts rotunda—a three-member U.S. House of Representatives select committee was there to hold hearings on the two days of rioting that had occurred in the city the previous July. A white mob, assisted by the local police, had attacked a convention considering the issue of Black voting rights. The mob burned Black residents' homes and businesses, raped Black women, and murdered forty Black persons in New Orleans before troops were called in. It

"A Mark of Friendship and Esteem"

was the second of two horrific racially motivated riots in 1867. The first, in Memphis in May, was also sparked by white anger at the city's Black population, particularly Black veterans, whose very existence incensed white Memphians.

The rising tide of unrest and Johnson's constant disagreements with Grant on issues from prosecution of Robert E. Lee to military management of the states spurred even more interest in nominating the former Union Army general to oppose Johnson as a candidate for president in 1868. Although Markland had a good relationship with Johnson in Memphis while the latter was military governor of Tennessee, there was no question about whom he would support: Grant was his man. Markland briefly allied himself with a group of former Union soldiers who were organizing a national "Soldiers' and Sailors' Convention." Along with former generals George Custer, George Crook, and Darius Couch, Colonel Markland was named to the Committee of Arrangements for the September gathering in Cleveland, Ohio. Many years later, Markland wrote that the original purpose of the convention was to show support for Grant as a Union Democrat in opposition "to the views of what was known as Copperhead Democracy."[33] But, he wrote, "like many another well-intended thing, it got astray," and since Johnson supporters showed up, "it was suspected as being a copperhead affair itself." Indeed it was, since the convention voted to support nearly all of Johnson's measures on Reconstruction.[34]

As 1867 neared its end, Johnson tried many elaborate schemes to quell opposition within his cabinet and within the hierarchy of the military. However, his political world came crashing down when, in defiance of a recently passed law requiring Senate approval to remove certain cabinet members, Johnson fired Secretary of War Stanton, briefly maneuvering a reluctant Grant into his place. Although threats of impeachment had surfaced earlier in his tenure, this time a resolution of impeachment was swiftly drafted and overwhelmingly passed, 126–47, by the House on February 24, 1868. A week later, the House had approved eleven articles of impeachment, and the Senate trial began two days after that. Markland's recent traveling companion, Senate Sergeant at Arms George Brown, delivered the summons for the trial to the president on March 7. For nearly three months, the trial captured the attention of the country. It ended in dramatic fashion. Though a clear majority of senators voted to convict on three of the eleven articles, successive roll calls failed to achieve the necessary two-thirds majority on May 26 by a single vote.

Nearly a week earlier, the Republican Party had nominated Ulysses S. Grant as its candidate, after serious soul-searching on his part and—according to Markland—after Grant had been approached by each party to run under its banner. In a meeting at Grant's home in Washington that Markland attended, Grant "was earnest in his desire that the nomination should go to some other person." He urged Republican leaders to nominate Sherman because "Sherman had a more statesmanlike view of the secession and the rebellion than any of us." They rejected his advice, and Grant agreed to have his name put forward by the Republican Party. He was nominated by acclamation.[35]

Johnson had survived the impeachment trial, but he was politically damaged goods. Though he received some early support at the Democratic convention in New York in July, former New York governor Horatio Seymour was nominated on the twenty-second ballot. The campaign was marked by vicious attacks on the proposed Reconstruction policies of each party and by slurs against all the candidates. In the end, Grant won the popular vote by a slim margin and overwhelmed Seymour in the Electoral College. Alone among the four presidential and vice presidential candidates, the forty-five-year-old lieutenant general did not campaign, nor did he make any speeches.[36]

Grant let his one-sentence remark when accepting the Republican nomination stand as his platform and his rallying cry: "Let us have peace."[37]

But Grant was to have no peace as president.

NINE

"Our Continued Services Together"

1868–71

Major national and international problems would plague Grant's White House tenure. Even before he became president—during the four months between his election in November and his inauguration on March 4—he was besieged by office seekers and importuned by lobbyists who offered their sage advice to the man they viewed as a political novice. In the interim, he continued in his post as lieutenant general of the U.S. Army, both to keep his salary and to prevent President Johnson from choosing his successor. Indeed, his first significant act as president would be to nominate William Tecumseh Sherman to be lieutenant general of the U.S. Army.

Grant's disenchantment with Johnson had grown exponentially since Lincoln's death, as Johnson repeatedly tried to use the general's popularity for his own political purposes. Johnson increasingly favored pardoning and elevating "unreconstructed" Confederates to power over newly freed Black residents in the South, which Grant viewed as reversing the hard-won fruits of victory that had cost so many of his soldiers' lives—and Lincoln's, too. On December 12, 1868, President-Elect Grant was working in his army headquarters across from the White House, preparing to leave the next day for Chicago "to attend the reunion of the societies of the Western armies." According to a DC newspaper reporter, he was accompanied by Generals Thomas, Dent, and Porter, Col. Ely Parker and Col. "A. M. [*sic*] Markland," and several other military men "*via* the Northern and Pennsylvania Central railroads" in a private car provided by the Baltimore and Ohio Railroad.[1]

As lieutenant general, Grant continued to play a significant role in the Reconstruction process in former Confederate states, often by issuing orders to his generals that conflicted with Johnson's policies and by providing security to Black residents of those states and their white Republican allies, to protect them from the rising tide of violence in the South. Grant's actions signaled his increasing dedication to guaranteeing civil rights for all Americans. By the time of his inauguration as president on March 4, 1869, hostility between Johnson and Grant had become so implacable that Johnson did not attend Grant's swearing-in ceremony on the Capitol steps.

The incoming president had previewed some of his policies to the public, but Grant held his cabinet choices close to his vest. So close, in fact, that almost none of his advisors knew his selections in advance. Even some of the men he intended to nominate did not receive notice of his favor until just before the announcement. The day after his inauguration, Grant's former chief of staff and soon to be his secretary of war, John Rawlins, entered the Senate chamber in executive session, submitted the names of Grant's cabinet to the presiding officer to read, and then walked out the door. Senators at their desks and visitors waiting outside the door to the Senate were astounded when they heard the names; many of the men had no political background and were barely known to the senatorial audience, much less the general public. Almost immediately, several prominent men who believed they were owed nominations or at least prior consultation regarding them—including Senator Charles Sumner, Boston Brahmin Henry Adams, and Charles Dana, assistant secretary of war to Stanton—bitterly and openly denounced Grant's cabinet picks as second rate or worse. Despite the criticism, the Senate unanimously approved the entire slate the same day.[2]

While some selections were less than ideal, two of Grant's early choices still stand the test of time. Hamilton Fish of New York, who succeeded Elihu Washburne's brief turn at the State Department in 1869, is even today considered one of best secretaries of state. He and Grant had come to know each other in 1867 through their service together as trustees of the Peabody Education Fund, an organization whose original goal was to promote education for the poor residents of the South regardless of race. One of the wealthiest men in Washington, Fish had a calm, reserved demeanor that mirrored Grant's. The two men genuinely liked each other, which was apparent when Grant talked him out of resigning numerous times over eight years. From a historian's viewpoint, one of Fish's most valuable legacies is his diary, which gives an insider's account of Grant's cabinet meetings. During his tenure, Fish dealt with several knotty international problems, including resolving politically sensitive claims against Great Britain for damages to Union ships during the Civil War, avoiding war with Spain over Cuba, and shepherding Grant's multiyear effort to annex Santo Domingo.[3]

Santo Domingo, also referred to as Dominica and now the Dominican Republic, occupies roughly two-thirds of the island of Hispaniola, the other third being Haiti. Various factions in the United States had long coveted Caribbean islands as potential targets of annexation because they could be sources of valuable sugar and coffee. Before the Civil War, the South saw them as future slave states, while some in the North imagined them as "ideal" places for freed Black persons to settle. After the war, interest in the islands remained high, and conflict between the two independent nations on Hispaniola led to overtures from Santo Domingo to President Johnson for protection and annexation. Secretary of State Seward was an early and enthusiastic proponent of annexation. According to one of Grant's aides who questioned him about the topic before his inauguration, the president-elect was "in favor of the proposition" and "preferred that the question should be submitted to Congress without delay." There was a great effort to accomplish that, but Johnson's term ended without final action on annexation.[4]

Historians' accounts of Grant's direct engagement with the annexation question credit Joseph Warren Fabens, the U.S. commercial agent in Santo Domingo, with reviving the issue soon after Grant's inauguration. In April 1869 Fabens presented a report on the island's valuable natural resources and political situation to the State Department. Secretary Fish greeted it unenthusiastically, but he nonetheless presented it to Grant and the other department heads in a cabinet meeting later that month. However, a heretofore unpublished letter written in 1885 to Absalom Markland describes an earlier meeting he had had with President-Elect Grant on the subject, a meeting that took place shortly after the election.

"In compliance with your request I take pleasure in giving you the following statement of facts concerning the origin of the movement that was made in the early days of Grant's Administration for the acquisition of Sto. Domingo," wrote Alexander R. Boteler from his room at the Metropolitan Hotel in Washington on November 23, 1885.[5] Boteler, a prewar U.S. representative and former Confederate soldier, was a wealthy lawyer, businessman, artist, and innovative farmer in Shepherdstown, West Virginia. With his neatly trimmed beard, gray hair, conservative tailoring, and pince-nez, Boteler looked the part of a professor. His handwriting is clear and bold, and the seven-page letter to Markland is full of details that corroborate the timing of the meeting and key people involved, though his spelling of proper names is often not quite accurate.

No doubt the request to Boteler for a narrative of the annexation effort was one of Markland's many late-in-life efforts to assemble material for the memoir he often mentioned he was writing. In this letter to Markland, Boteler wrote that "sometime after the election but before the inauguration" he had been in contact, through two other men, "with a Mr. Angena[rd] who was a confidential friend of General Biaz [Báez] the President of Sto. Domingo." Boteler said Angenard was "desirous to have it known that President [Báez] was anxious for some arrangement to be made for the acquisition of Sto. Domingo by the United States Government." So Boteler contacted Markland, since "you had been on terms of intimacy with [Grant] ever since you and he had been school-mates."

Boteler continued: "You kindly consented to see Genl Grant at once. . . . After you had been at Army Head Quarters you told me that both Genl Grant and his accomplished adjutant General Rawlings [Rawlins], had evinced much interest in the matter and wanted the whole correspondence." Boteler gave it to Markland to provide to Rawlins "and to the President Elect."

After the initial meeting and exchange of papers, there is no evidence of any further involvement of Markland or Boteler in the

"Our Continued Services Together"

lengthy, convoluted, politically divisive, and ultimately unsuccessful effort by Grant to annex the Santo Domingo portion of Hispaniola. Considering the many charges of self-dealing and corruption surrounding the multiyear diplomatic and legislative effort, it is notable that Boteler also reminded Markland that Grant had asked him in that first meeting whether there was a "ring" (i.e., group of men) who would obtain government funds from the proposed deal. "For if there is," the president-elect told Markland, "I'll put my foot on it and smash the egg before it is hatched." Grant forever believed there were strong economic and national defense reasons for annexing the island, in addition to the prospect of adding a territory and eventually a state where he believed free Black persons could relocate in friendly surroundings. Secretary of State Fish, though cool to the idea of annexation from the beginning, was an honest broker for Grant throughout the difficult process.

Another of Grant's stellar cabinet appointments was one of his first—John A. J. Creswell as postmaster general. Creswell was born into a wealthy and prominent family from Maryland's Eastern Shore, and while he was practicing law, he married a beautiful and wealthy woman from the same area. Creswell, described as "burly" but also as "debonair," wore finely tailored suits and sported a full salt-and-pepper beard on a face with kindly eyes and a receding hairline. The well-educated and hardworking Creswell's intellectual and political journey from Whig to Democrat to unabashed and enthusiastic antislavery Republican officeholder made him a close ally of Lincoln in efforts to keep Maryland in the Union. Maryland's geographic location alone made it indispensable. All land transportation and communication between Washington and points north crossed through the state, so if it had seceded, the capital of the United States would have been surrounded by hostile Confederate states. Lincoln corresponded several times with Creswell, who was in the state legislature as the war began. The president encouraged Creswell's efforts to keep the state from seceding and to free enslaved persons in the state. Creswell was pivotal in passage of the Maryland constitution that ended slavery in that state on November 1, 1864.[6]

Two months later, on January 5, 1865, as a new member of the U.S.

House of Representatives, Creswell was given the singular honor of delivering the first speech in the House in favor of passage of the Thirteenth Amendment, which abolished slavery. Creswell held the floor for more than an hour, and in a memorable passage he recalled riding through his district in rural Maryland late on the night before the new state constitution took effect: "The negroes had assembled at midnight, in their rude churches, hastily built by the roadside, in the woods, or down at the marshes, to watch for the advent of their day of jubilee, in order that they might receive their earliest experience of Heaven's priceless gift to man—thrice-blessed liberty— while on their knees before the Father of all. Surely, a people who will thus dedicate the first moments of their freedom to God are worthy to be free."[7]

The day after his speech, the *New York Tribune* reported how, in describing "the poor negroes . . . at midnight prayer meetings in the cabins of the Eastern shore," Creswell "rose to a pitch of genuine eloquence that secured undivided attention and unbroken silence. . . . The effort was on all hands pronounced one of the most successful ever made in that Hall by a new member. From that day he rapidly rose to a commanding position in State and National politics." His oratory in support of the amendment was considered significant enough to have him prominently featured in a sketch on the front page of *Harper's Weekly*, clasping hands with jubilant Pennsylvania Republican representatives Thaddeus Stevens and William D. Kelley. Creswell was appointed to fill a vacant seat in the U.S. Senate later that year and was one of the last people to meet with Lincoln on the day of his assassination, April 14, 1865. Two years later, at the end of his Senate term, he left Washington to practice law in his home state. That lasted but a year before Grant requested that he join his administration.[8]

Grant's decision to award a cabinet spot to Creswell is consistently viewed by historians as a concession to southerners, who pleaded for at least one cabinet member from the South or from a border state, such as Maryland. But a closer look reveals it was far more than a mere political balancing act. In one stroke, Grant's choice of forty-six-year-old Creswell as postmaster general put the largest repository

"Our Continued Services Together"

of patronage jobs in the U.S. government into the hands of one of the most avid prewar abolitionists. Grant knew what he was doing. Creswell appointed male and female African Americans to prominent post office positions around the country, making it the most integrated cabinet department of its day. Among Creswell's historic postal firsts were the first African American postmistress, mail route agent, mail carrier, railway mail agent, and postal inspector. It was in this era that the Post Office Department became a reliable path to the middle class for Black Americans.[9]

In addition, under Creswell's skilled management, the Post Office Department cut waste, increased revenue, and launched the popular, profitable use of one-cent or "penny" postcards, printed by the government and sold at post offices. He also led a successful fight to repeal the costly franking privilege, which at that time enabled nearly thirty-two thousand government employees to send mail free of charge—and many thousand more scofflaws to easily counterfeit their own franks.[10]

The Grants and the Creswells formed a close friendship. Early in his presidency, Ulysses and Julia Grant traveled to Elkton, Maryland, to visit John and Hannah Creswell, and they socialized in Washington and at the Grants' summer home in Long Branch, New Jersey. The Creswells were with the Grants in the cabin at Mount McGregor in New York State, on July 23, 1885, when the former president died of throat cancer. For decades, Grant was considered a failed president, until historians examined more closely his commitment to and actions on behalf of poor Black Americans, many of them formerly enslaved. The appointment of Creswell as postmaster general is still considered one of Grant's major contributions to civil rights.[11]

Loyalty to friends was a hallmark of Grant (and one of the reasons he often got into trouble), and his rise to the presidency opened doors for Markland. But Grant's efforts to secure a higher position for his friend within the Post Office Department did not go smoothly. On April 16, 1869, Grant sent a batch of nominations to the Senate. Among those was "A. H. Markland to be Third Assistant Postmaster-General." That position would take advantage of Markland's record for efficiency and integrity as a special agent, since it oversaw all of the financial and accounting responsibilities of the department, including collecting revenue from all sources, disbursing payments to all contractors (including builders, railroads, and steamship lines), and managing the dead letter office, the registered mail service, and the money order system. It would also place him near the top of the hierarchy of the largest employer in the United States and would enable the Marklands to put down roots in Washington again.[12]

The nomination drew a significant amount of press attention. Most of it was positive, recalling Markland's service with Grant and "his energetic superintendency" of the mails during and after the war. But there were early signs of opposition from the radical antislavery wing of the Republican Party. Much of it centered on Markland's participation in the Cleveland Soldiers' and Sailors' Convention, which as Markland had admitted was interpreted as a pro-Johnson gathering. Indeed, a Memphis newspaper observed shortly after Markland's nomination that although he had served as "Grant's mail agent," he had been a delegate to that convention and "was a Johnson man." Shortly thereafter, the *Baltimore Sun* reported, "a strong effort is being made, it is said, to get the Senate to reject Col. Markland." His approval was considered "doubtful" by the *Cincinnati Enquirer*, which also reported that "Pomeroy and other Republican Senators are opposing his nomination." And then, on April 23, the *Evening Star* (Washington DC) published a list of nominations that had expired because the Senate adjourned the day before without acting on them. Among them was Markland's. There was speculation that Grant would renominate him when the Senate reconvened later that year.[13]

According to a newspaper columnist, Markland saw the president at the White House shortly after his nomination expired. Writing under the pseudonym "Olivia," Emily Edson Briggs was one of the first women journalists in the United States with a national reputation and also the first to be admitted to the House and Senate press galleries. For decades she published in Washington newspapers a column bursting with purple prose and mischievous wit that gave readers a peek inside Congress and the White House. On April 27, 1869, her column was titled "Awaiting Audience at the White House," and its third paragraph began with a mention of Frederick Dent, Grant's West Point roommate and his brother-in-law:

> President Grant has a grand vizier. It is General Dent, late of the Union Army. It is the business of General Dent to receive all who seek the presence of the President. . . . [In the waiting room,] the doors of the inner temple tremble on their hinges, and the form of a ponderous senator emerges from the presence of the sun of day. It is Henry Wilson, of Massachusetts. He strides to a centre table and shakes hands with a distinguished group of men, composed of Cole of California, Carpenter of Wisconsin, irrepressible General Butler, and General Markland, the personal friend of General Grant, who was nominated for Third Assistant Postmaster-General.[14]

We do not know for certain what Markland discussed with the president when it came time for his meeting that day, but barely a week later Grant nominated Gen. William Henry Harrison Terrell of Indiana to be third assistant postmaster. In reporting the news, a couple of accounts referred to Markland as having been "thrown overboard" by Grant. However, the *National Republican* in Washington soon reported, "We have the highest authority for saying that there has been no feeling between the friends of Gen. Markland and those of Gen. Terrell in regard to the office of Third Assistant Postmaster-General. . . . The nomination of Gen. M. was without consultation with him, and made by the President and Postmaster General as a fitting tribute to his faithful services as superintendent of mails during the war, and unyielding integrity as an officer of the Post Office Department after the war and during the reorganization of the postal service in the late insurrectionary states."[15]

Later in his life, Markland used the unsought nomination to illustrate how Grant was "specially thoughtful" about taking care of his wartime staff before he left the army and became president. He recalled the private train car in which he rode to the Chicago "Grand Reunion" in December 1868, when Grant sat next to him. On that journey, Markland wrote, Grant asked me if there was any office I had thought I would like to have.... I told him that I could not possibly enter upon the duties of any office before a specified time, because of the business arrangements I was then bound by.... [However, after Grant's inauguration, he,] without any intimation whatever, sent my name to the Senate for confirmation to an office he had not before alluded to, and gave me, as a reason for it, that the office required a disbursement of $30,000,000 a year, and that he wanted an officer in it who would see that it was properly disbursed. The compliment was more valuable than the office.[16]

On May 20, 1869, Postmaster General Creswell announced a reorganization of special agents within the department. The new scheme divided the country into six divisions, each of which was further subdivided into districts. At the same time, he named Colonel Markland "superintendent" of the Third District of the Fourth Division. His district encompassed Kentucky and Tennessee. By area and population, it was one of the smallest of the newly created jurisdictions.[17]

Judging from newspaper accounts alone, it appeared that Markland's postal career had simply traced a circle, from the job that Montgomery Blair had given him in 1861 (special agent for Kentucky) to the one Grant had created for him (supervising mail for hundreds of thousands of soldiers and families across the nation), to the one Creswell offered him (superintendent of Kentucky, with the addition of Tennessee, perhaps as a sop). It does not seem to be the kind of position that a man who so recently thought he should be a brevet brigadier general would accept.

In the past, when Markland was unhappy with his situation, he had struck out on his own, resuming the practice of law and lobbying, taking advantage of his experience and connections to build a lucrative and enjoyable livelihood. Indeed, from his youngest days, he had always forged his own path and felt most comfortable when he was in charge of his destiny. He did not do so this time. Markland's acceptance of this apparently subordinate post at this point in his life seems so out of character that it makes one wonder why he took it. Noting Grant's ability to talk Fish out of resigning so many times, it may have been yet another example of the enduring loyalty that Grant inspired throughout Markland's life. Whatever the reasoning behind his decision to accept the job, within a week of the announcement the Marklands left Washington for Kentucky.

Louisville was headquarters of the Third District of the Fourth Division of the U.S. Post Office Department. There, Martha and Absalom would begin again in a city and a region of the country that was at once both familiar and new. Louisville was Kentucky's largest city and a major postal hub. During the four years Markland had traveled to the city during the war, it had grown by almost 50 percent. Its nearly one hundred thousand white residents outnumbered free Black residents ten to one in the 1870 census. Though their numbers were relatively small, free Black Kentuckians were the focus of white residents' animosity and unrelenting efforts to limit their political and economic freedom. While Kentucky had remained in the Union during the Civil War (to Lincoln's everlasting gratitude), white bitterness over their free Black neighbors' hard-won civil rights have led many to observe that "Kentucky did not join the Confederacy until *after* the Civil War." Like many northern cities that avoided significant damage from the war, Louisville was booming, as was much of Kentucky. Louisville was always a key inland port important for shipping from the industrialized North and the more agricultural South, it produced nearly a third of all bourbon made in the United States, and the city was also headquarters for major tobacco companies.[18]

In contrast, the numerous battles fought on Tennessee soil damaged or destroyed many homes and businesses, and wartime occupation by Federal troops embittered its white residents. Still largely agricultural, the state was left mostly a wasteland after the war, with few economic opportunities for any of its residents, no matter their race. After the war, the large population of free Black persons in Memphis, including veteran U.S. Colored Troops, was the target of white officials and businessmen who in May 1866 killed forty-six and destroyed more than one hundred houses, churches, and schools over a two-day period. The blatantly racist and horrifically vicious rampage shook the country. Despite the turmoil, however, investment in industrial capacity in Tennessee—including iron works, furniture factories, sawmills, and wool mills—began to increase and by 1870 exceeded the antebellum level. While Markland's postal duties were not new to him, he faced enormous challenges in both Kentucky and Tennessee as their growing economies accelerated the volume of mail to be processed and the number of problems to resolve.

If Markland's career appeared to have slipped, his social status had not. He and Martha were back in Washington only a month after their move to Louisville. While in the nation's capital, they participated in "one of the most pleasant affairs of the season . . . the moonlight excursion of the Analostan boat club to Glymont." Now known as Indian Head, Maryland, Glymont is a stubby peninsula on the eastern shore of the Potomac River, approximately twenty miles southeast of the capital by boat. With its shade trees, freshwater springs, and breezes off the bay, it was a favorite place for Washingtonians to escape summer's brutal heat. Among the nearly 250 "leading citizens" who ate and danced until midnight under starry June skies were "Col. Markland and lady," Gen. and Mrs. Ely S. Parker (he was head of Indian Affairs by Grant's appointment), an assistant judge advocate and his wife, an assistant commissioner of internal revenue, a sprinkling of other judges and generals, and a Russian count. The Marklands also attended an event identified as "Mrs. President Grant's Tuesday reception" that spring. There were many other well-dressed, well-known guests who passed through the Red, Green, East, and Blue Rooms of the White House that Tuesday afternoon, including the journalist "Olivia." In February 1870 the Marklands enjoyed "one of the most brilliant enjoyable entertainments . . . attended by the beauty and *elite* of the city," which was "The Hop at Willard's" hotel in Washington. There, they joined Postmaster General John and Hannah Creswell, as well as General Sherman and his daughter Minnie, "among the large number of distinguished guests" who dined and danced the night away. And in a city where politics and society reinforced each other, the Marklands' attendance was also noted in a newspaper account of House Speaker James Blaine's weekly reception for "prominent statesmen and high officials" in the same month.[19]

Markland's new role also didn't prevent his maintaining connections to his wartime comrades. As reported in national newspapers, he was named to the Executive Committee of Arrangements for a reunion of the Society of the Army of the Tennessee to be held in Louisville in November 1869. He attended a meeting of that planning committee in Memphis in September, and the next month it was Markland who announced that both President Grant and General Sherman would attend the gathering in Louisville.[20]

Most public accounts of Markland's activities in 1869 and 1870, however, are found in local Kentucky and Tennessee newspapers and relate to his work in those states. He was reported to be inspecting the Railway Mail Service on a trip from Nashville to Chattanooga, and he visited Memphis and Nashville on several occasions, where his assistance in resolving mail problems was earnestly requested. One Memphis newspaper queried, "Complaints of failure of the mails are so frequent that we are again constrained to call the attention of the Postoffice authorities thereto in the hope that some radical change will be effected, insuring the citizens of this section greater regularity in mail distribution. Will Colonel Markland give this his attention?"[21]

But there were much bigger problems in Markland's district than substandard mail service, and the whole country knew what they were. Tennessee was the home of the first Ku Klux Klan "fraternal society," organized by former Confederate soldiers in Pulaski, Tennessee, in 1865. The secretive society swiftly gathered steam across the South as a means of playing out white Americans' grievances against newly freed Black Americans and those who supported them through savage murders, lynchings, beatings, and organized intimidation. White authorities rarely intervened or investigated. Fear of the Klan was so great—and so justified—that Klan members who perpetrated crimes were almost never identified, nor were witnesses willing to testify against them. By 1871 accounts of Klan violence in the Carolinas had become legion, but Kentucky and Tennessee were also roiled by the Klan's increasingly audacious savagery.[22]

For the most part, the KKK focused its murderous terror on poor, illiterate, isolated Black residents in areas where officials were unlikely to prosecute such crime. Sometimes, however, the KKK erred in identifying a soft target. That was the case in January 1871, when Mark-land replaced a white railway mail route agent in Kentucky with a Black agent who was not poor, illiterate, or isolated.

Born in Baltimore in 1829 to a free Black couple, William H. Gibson was educated in "the select schools of those days" and learned to play the violin as a child. Small in stature, he always dressed neatly and expressed himself with impeccable diction. His modest demeanor, however, belied a fierce, lifelong determination to better himself and other members of his race. According to the autobiography that he penned in 1897 as part of a history of the United Brothers of Friendship (a national Black fraternal society he helped to found), he moved to Louisville in 1847 to work as a teacher for the purpose of "benefiting his race." Just eighteen years old, the intrepid Gibson traveled from Maryland by stagecoach to Pittsburgh, "changing horses every ten miles," by steamer to Cincinnati, then on to Louisville. After a brief internship, he opened a school for Black students in the heart of the city but was forbidden to teach any enslaved persons "without a written permit from their master or mistress." That did not prove to be a great impediment to attracting students, he recalled, "for amid the strictures of the laws and prejudices of the slaveholders to negroes learning to read and write, there were other Christians (white) who did not object, and would give those permits."[23]

Gibson's energy in teaching and organizing raised his profile and brought him into contact with prominent individuals of both races among the clergy, the business world, and politics. On a trip to Pittsburgh in 1852 as an observer of the Free Soil Party's convention to nominate candidates for office, Gibson first saw and heard Frederick Douglass. Although free from birth, Gibson witnessed many evils of the slave system, but it was not until 1848 that he viewed a slave auction. After watching a family tearfully separated and sold to different buyers on Market Street in Louisville, he left, "praying God that we might be saved from another such scene."

At the outset of the war, Gibson was commissioned a recruiting sergeant for the Fifty-Fifth Massachusetts Regiment. He determined to recruit Kentucky men and did indeed attract "hundreds of applicants, but, through the interference of the officials at headquarters . . . failed to get a man enrolled at Louisville." His efforts in Indiana proved more successful, resulting in the enrollment of one hundred men. At war's end, Gibson moved to Kansas and taught in the public schools for more than a year, after which his friends prevailed upon him to return, as he put it, to his "Old Kentucky Home." Back in Louisville, he taught in one of the schools organized by the Freedmen's Bureau, the Quinn Chapel School. There, he also organized a successful effort on behalf of rural Black Kentuckians to reduce the amount of bond required to have a case heard in U.S. Circuit Court. He recalled, "The Ku-klux clans were murdering them and pillaging their property, and no redress could be obtained, as this large fee demanded made it impossible for them to have a hearing, for they were too poor to raise that amount." One of the men who "courteously received" Gibson's delegation and helped craft a reasonable solution to the bond problem was G. C. Wharton, the U.S. attorney for Kentucky.

In June 1870 Wharton joined Lincoln's former attorney general, James Speed, a Louisville native, in recommending Gibson as a railway mail agent to Absalom Markland. Railway mail agents sorted mail in specially designed railcars, and at regular stops they swapped incoming mail for the local postmaster's outgoing mail. The job required a high degree of literacy, physical dexterity, and an ability to learn complex rail schedules by heart. According to the U.S. Postal Service's official history, "By most accounts, Railway Mail Service clerks had the toughest job in the Post Office Department." In his recommendation letter to Markland, Wharton told of Gibson teaching "colored children" and "recruiting colored soldiers" and described him as "a man of intelligence and integrity." Although the letter did not explicitly say Gibson was Black, there is no doubt that Markland knew the color of the man's skin. Indeed, Gibson was such a well-known member of Louisville's Black community that Markland may have known of him even before he received the recommendation.[24]

Absalom Markland had grown up in Kentucky among enslaved people and the people who enslaved them, and he knew how desperately the latter had held on to the former, even after passage of the Thirteenth Amendment in January 1865. It was not until December of that year, when the requisite three-fourths of the United States ratified the amendment abolishing slavery, that slaveholding Kentuckians were finally forced to relinquish their human chattel. Markland would have known that Kentucky voted against ratification in February 1865, and he would have known that the six years from 1865 to 1871 had done little to make former slave masters tolerate Black persons in positions of equality—or even of dignified service. Like so many other Kentuckians, Markland knew that the "Bluegrass Klan" sought to terrorize free Black Kentuckians and their supporters, and yet he assigned Gibson to the route. The politically astute Gibson had no doubt what awaited him as the first Black route agent of the U.S. Post Office Department in the state where he had lived for years, and yet he accepted the position.[25]

Despite the potentially violent consequences, Markland and Gibson implemented the policy that Grant and Creswell had developed, and on July 11 Markland appointed Gibson to fill the vacant position of mail route agent on the railway mail route from Louisville to the small hamlet of Mount Vernon, which lay about one hundred miles southeast. According to Gibson, he

> served for eight months under very trying circumstances. The first and second day's trip was attended with great excitement. As the first negro mail agent in the State, I was equal to Barnum's animal show, for the people at every station gathered by hundreds, and climbed upon the [railroad] cars to get a view of the black animal who dared to invade their territory.
>
> At the end of the route, Mount Vernon, the people turned out to hang me. They followed me to the post-office and waited for me to enter the hotel across the way for lodgings, but I had made other arrangements and disappointed them.[26]

Gibson bravely continued his service on this route, though he was continually harassed and threatened by the KKK. Then, on January 21, 1871, Markland transferred Gibson to another route, a vastly more important one that ran from the state's largest city, Louisville, to its second-largest city, Lexington. Between those two cities—served by the same rail line—lies the capital of Kentucky, Frankfort. Gibson must have known that he would face hostility, if not violence, on the new route. Nevertheless, in line with Gibson's lifelong determination to "benefit his race," he courageously began his new job on Wednesday, January 25. In doing so, he became one of the most important but least recognized heroes of Reconstruction.

"The second day out [I was] attacked by three of the clan, at a lonely station, North Benson, between Frankfort and Lexington, a chosen day for the murderous purpose—snowing, raining, and hailing—the worst day of the year," Gibson wrote in 1897. Even today, the area is heavily forested and only sparsely inhabited. Four "large men" were on the platform when the train arrived. "At the station," Gibson wrote, "one jumped aboard of the mail coach and endeavored to throw me out, beating and bruising me considerably, but failed in his attempt. His two pals were waiting on the platform, with drawn pistols, to shoot me as I fell out, as they expected; but as God would have it, they missed their aim, and I was saved." Although there were "three coaches of passengers, conductor, and the train hands, no one came to my relief, and it was only the mercy of God that saved me. They riddled the car with bullets, but missed me."[27]

The report Gibson sent to Markland the day after the event provided more details. When he first arrived at the station, Gibson wrote, all had seemed quiet. He and the postmaster exchanged their mailbags, but when Gibson began to close the door of the car, "a large man" who had been standing on the platform stopped him. "He struck me a tremendous blow in the face . . . he tried to drag me out of the car, uttering at the same time, fierce epithets, such as 'We'll kill you! Come out! Come out!' I resisted as best I could, and while thus struggling with him, the train started, and he jumped out." Other witnesses reported that the men "hurrahed for Jeff Davis."[28]

The day after the attack, Markland assigned C. C. Green, an experienced white Louisville postal agent, to substitute temporarily for the bruised and shaken Gibson. Green then reported to Markland, "To my great surprise I found at nearly every depot crowds of excited men apparently waiting for the return of W. H. Gibson . . . but when informed that I had charge of the mail they retired . . . very much disappointed that there was no person there upon whom they could

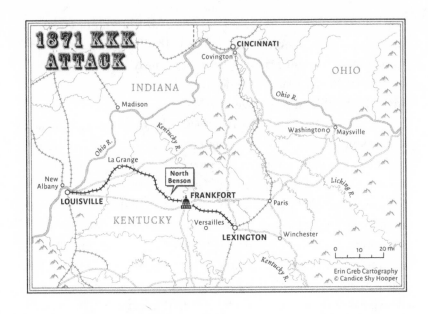

Map 2. 1871 KKK attack on the railway mail. The harassment and assault targeted William H. Gibson, a Black employee of the Post Office Department. Erin Greb Cartography.

wreak their vengeance." At another stop, when informed that the mail agent that day was white, a "very desperate man" who had boarded the train searching for Gibson also left "very disappointed." Green warned Markland that Gibson "could not have made another trip on the road and returned alive without protection from soldiers."[29]

So that is exactly what Markland arranged.

As Gibson recalled, "a squad of United States soldiers were dispatched from the fort to accompany me, and for three months I was escorted by the blue coats of Uncle Sam while I performed my duties. Many threats were made. . . . I feared a collision between the military and the mob that gathered at the stations for twitting [taunting] the soldiers for protecting a negro. I was convinced that under the pressure some one would be killed."[30]

Reports of the attack and of the subsequent daily company of ten armed military escorts for the mail agent echoed through the state. On January 31 Kentucky's Democratic governor, John White Stevenson, sent a strong message to the Democratic-dominated state Senate and House of Representatives, calling the attack an "open violation, both of the laws of the United States and of Kentucky." He further wrote, "You owe it to both Governments promptly to enact such laws as will tend to the capture of the offenders. And certainly prevent the recurrence of any attempt in the future by bad men upon any officer or agent of the Federal or State Government." But, as the *Louisville Courier* editorialized two months later about the attack on Gibson, "the legislature stood with a cigar in its mouth, and a champagne-glass in its hand, and would do nothing." Even after a KKK gang illegally breached the walls of the Kentucky state capitol and freed one of its members being held in temporary custody inside in a brazen act "perpetrated in the very center of the State, under the very noses of our government, . . . no measures [were] adopted for their suppression; not a single man brought to justice."[31]

Less than a year earlier, the last of the three great Reconstruction amendments to the U.S. Constitution had been ratified. The Fifteenth Amendment acknowledged Black persons' right to vote, joining the Thirteenth (banning slavery) and the Fourteenth (specifying that those born or naturalized in the United States were citizens, providing equal protection under the law to all citizens, and forbidding interference with government officials in the performance of their duties). In May 1870 and again in February 1871, the Republican-controlled Congress passed laws, called the First and Second Enforcement Acts, giving the federal government more power to compel compliance with the amendments. Despite the constitutional amendments and their enforcement acts, however, Black Americans continued to be targets of violence designed to deprive them of their votes, their property, their livelihoods, and often their lives.

Since 1868, committee hearings, field hearings, and testimony from victims read on the House and Senate floors had brought the brutality of the Klan to the attention of members of Congress on a daily basis. Tales of bloodshed at the hands of the KKK in North and South Carolina in particular were heard in Congress and read in newspapers around the country nearly every day. Northern Republican legislators' anger at reports of violence and lawlessness in the South was exceeded only by their outrage at their Democratic colleagues from the South who belittled or denied the same reports and refused to support measures to stop the violence. Southern Democrats often even claimed that those hiding under KKK robes were actually Republicans seeking to impugn Democrats with their violence. And yet, there was no federal legislative action to stop it. As Kentucky's legislative inaction had also proved, it was clear that southern states would not be easily convinced—or coerced—into enforcing civil rights for Black Americans.

But the former lieutenant general of the U.S. Army would display the same dogged determination in the battle against the Klan that he had in the war against the Confederacy. Even before he signed the Second Enforcement Act on February 28, 1871, Grant signaled to his cabinet that he was ready to use the strongest possible measures to deal with the racial violence. On Friday, February 24, about a month after the attack on Gibson, Secretary Fish recounted the day's cabinet meeting in his diary (abbreviations in the original):

> Prsdt mentions the violence which has been perpetratd on the Mail
> Route between Louisville & Lexington KY which passes through

Frankfort (State Capital). The Route Agent is a Colored man, who has been subjected to repeated violence—attempts to drag him from the Cars &c—for some time it has been necessary to send a ~~squad~~ guard of soldiers (10) on every train to protect it. He determines no longer to continue this protection—& gives instructions to Mr. Marshall (representing the P M-G) to discontinue the route under the provisions of the Act of Feb 28 1861.[32]

The Act of February 28, 1861, is a one-sentence law enacted in the bleak and turbulent days just before President Lincoln's inauguration, when six states had already seceded. It gave the postmaster general authority to discontinue any postal route when "the postal service cannot be safely maintained, or the post office revenues collected, or the postal laws maintained."[33]

One week after that cabinet meeting, on March 3, Markland implemented Grant's instructions. He notified Postmaster General Creswell in a telegram: "To prevent violence and bloodshed, the mails have been withdrawn from the Lexington road." As the *Daily Dispatch* (Richmond VA) reported, "So the train went out at the usual time this morning, but without the colored agent or his guard, or the mail for the people living along the line."[34]

The next day, Grant informed the Forty-Second Congress, which had convened that morning with the intention to adjourn right away until December (as was the usual practice), "that certain reasons existed why Congress should not yet adjourn. . . . Again, the President considered that the condition of affairs in the South demanded additional legislation," according to a Richmond newspaper. It further reported that Grant said "eleven Republicans had been murdered in one day" in one unnamed southern state, and "the mails had to be suspended between Frankfort and Louisville, Ky., because of Ku-klux outrages on a colored mail agent." In addition, the president "stated that he was quite powerless under the present laws to prevent this state of things, and required action of Congress." The article concluded by referring to a temporary committee that had been established in the Senate in January: "It is understood that the Select Committee of the Senate on the Alleged Outrages in the South [has] a bill nearly prepared to suppress them, which will be reported to the Senate next week, and pressed to a vote before an adjournment."[35]

Acceding to Grant's request, the majority Republican Congress did not adjourn. Instead, struggling to find things to occupy their time until the new bill was prepared for their deliberation, members of Congress considered a major appropriations bill and a host of small individual relief bills. They also took the floor of the House and Senate day after day to attack or excuse the Ku Klux Klan's ongoing reign of terror. Nearly three weeks later, no new bill was yet under active consideration. By March 23 Grant's impatience drove him to the Capitol to meet with Republican legislators in the President's Room, one of the most private and beautiful rooms in the building. The lawmakers could give him no assurance of quick action. So, to prod Congress into action, Grant requested paper, pen, and ink. There and then, he wrote a statement to be read aloud in both chambers. According to one of the members of Congress who was in the room, Grant penned these lines "without pause or correction, and as rapidly as his pen could fly over the paper," much as he had written his military orders during the war:

> A condition of affairs now exists in some States of the Union rendering life and property insecure and the carrying of the mails and the collection of the revenue dangerous. The proof that such a condition of affairs exists in some localities is now before the Senate. That the power to correct these evils is beyond the control of State authorities I do not doubt; that the power of the Executive of the United States, acting within the limits of the existing laws, is sufficient for present emergencies is not clear. Therefore, I urgently recommend such legislation as in the judgment of Congress shall effectually secure life, liberty, and property, and the enforcement of law in all parts of the United States. . . . There is no other subject upon which I would recommend legislation during the present session.[36]

Upon delivery of Grant's statement to the House and Senate, one after another southern representative rose to protest that nothing new had happened since Congress convened on March 4 to impel them to give the president additional powers. They were righteous and indignant and determined to impede any legislation giving the federal government new powers to enforce civil rights. Even members of Congress from Kentucky who knew about the attack on Gibson feigned ignorance. And then, Representative William Kelley of Pennsylvania—who had celebrated passage of the Thirteenth Amendment six years earlier with his former colleague, now Postmaster General Creswell—was recognized by the Speaker for remarks. He did not mince words. After swiftly reviewing a host of appalling actions committed by Klan members, Kelley thundered that his Democratic colleagues had encouraged the Klan by scornfully dismissing the seriousness of their terrible deeds. The transcript of the debate recorded this exchange:

> MR. KELLEY [of Pennsylvania]: They now enter your mail-cars to assassinate or scourge the officers of the Government.
>
> MR. BECK [of Kentucky]: Where was that done?
>
> MR. KELLEY [of Pennsylvania]: It was done in Kentucky.[37]

This was the tipping point leading to passage of one of the most important civil rights bills in the history of the nation: the Ku Klux Klan Act of 1871.

While unspeakable horrors in North and South Carolina had for years roused northern members of Congress to seek solutions, southern Democrats had felt free to dismiss and delay legislation on the subject. After all, they and their white supporters were not directly affected by the whipping of a Black woman, the lynching of a Black man, or the torching of a neighborhood filled with Black residents. Nor were southern Democratic representatives besieged by their constituents to have their taxes collected (in fact, difficulty in revenue collection was mentioned only two times during the congressional debate, both times by Republicans). But the realization that a major mail route could be terminated because a Black mail agent had been attacked—well, that shocked the southern legislators. Now, Democrats scrambled to engage in the debate over how to deal with the Ku Klux Klan's interference with the mail—and how to do so without granting new powers to the Republican president.

At the same time, Grant's message helped to unite and propel Republicans toward legislation. Within five days, Representative Samuel Shellabarger, a seasoned Republican from western Ohio, introduced H.R. 320, "To enforce the provisions of the fourteenth amendment to the Constitution of the United States, and for other purposes." It was swiftly reported from the Judiciary Committee for consideration by the full House of Representatives and then sent to the Senate for consideration.[38]

The actions of William Gibson, Absalom Markland, and John Creswell were quickly put under the microscope by southern members in both chambers. Their first avenue of attack was to question why Gibson was given the job at all. The second was an old refrain: it was a minor incident, blown out of proportion. But their overriding charge was that the whole episode had been a setup from the start, arranged by Grant and his minions to create an excuse for the president to grab tyrannical authority over the states.

In one typical exchange, Senator Garrett Davis (D-KY) asked why a Black man was put on any mail route in Kentucky when "it was utterly wrong to the people of Kentucky ... utterly revolting to their wishes, to their sense of propriety." He then answered his own question: "It was to play out the Radical [Republican] policy, to produce conflict and collision and bloodshed between the white and negro races." This policy, he claimed, would enable Grant and his supporters to usurp the power of the state. In the House, Representative Thomas Swann (D-MD) saw another purpose behind Grant's desire to focus on additional enforcement legislation: "He saw that his own star was waning. . . . He saw that his outrageous conduct in the San Domingo job was about to assume proportions. . . . He saw that there must be a diversion." The reason for placing Gibson in a position where he was sure to be attacked, according to Swann, was "to convert this Government from a civil into a military government, and further to ask that [Grant] be clothed with the power of a dictator."[39]

The nature of the attack on Gibson was downplayed and decried as a setup in newspapers as well as in Congress. "The negro mail carrier between Frankfort and Louisville says somebody 'threat-

"Our Continued Services Together"

ened him'—whether with a cowhide or a fine comb is not stated," according to a Democratic-leaning newspaper. "Hence the necessity for Congress . . . to protect the negro who wasn't hurt—only 'threatened.' . . . For this purpose was the 'threatened' negro expressly foisted on the Kentucky people." John White Stevenson, the former governor who had spoken out so strongly against the attack on Gibson in late January, was now Senator Stevenson, and he joined the Democratic chorus who argued that Gibson had been assigned that route to "provoke violence." Instead, Stevenson insisted, it had only resulted in a minor "rude assault" on Gibson that became "the flimsy pretext for punishing the Kentucky people by depriving them of the mails."[40]

Republican lawmakers, too, thoroughly examined Gibson's journey from his first mail route through the attack at North Benson and the subsequent military guard, attesting to his fine character and strong recommendations for the job. Markland's constant communication with Gibson and Creswell and the postmasters all along the Louisville-Lexington mail route was also explored. The record is filled with the numerous statements to Markland from postmasters in the area saying that Gibson could not safely be put back on the route without military protection. In addition, Creswell's staunch support of Black citizens and Grant's desire to protect people and government operations from Klan attacks were lauded by Republicans in the House and the Senate. Republicans argued that under the Constitution a Black man should be able to work as a mail agent in Kentucky as well as in New York.

In the broadest terms, debate over the bill was a battle between those who believed federal protection of the civil rights guaranteed in the Constitution was necessary in the absence of state protection and those who believed the bill gave unconstitutional, tyrannical powers to the chief executive. The *Congressional Globe* (predecessor to the *Congressional Record*) from March 23 through April 20, 1871, when H.R. 320 was finally approved, shows that three major questions surfaced again and again in the sixty pages devoted to the debate in the House and Senate: Does the continuing and unopposed violence against the Black population in the South warrant federal intervention? Does the proposed legislation give too much power to the president? In the absence of state action, did the attack on the Black mail agent in Kentucky warrant federal action? The first two questions have been explored in depth by historians studying the roots of the Ku Klux Klan Act of 1871. The last has not been previously discussed at all.

And yet there are no fewer than twenty pages of the *Congressional Globe* in which the Gibson attack is discussed, often in minute detail—roughly a third of the debate on the bill. No other single incident relating to the Klan with bearing on the legislation received more than a mention in the twenty-nine days between introduction and final passage of what was initially titled "An Act to Enforce the Provisions of the Fourteenth Amendment." One of the most important civil rights acts in U.S. history, it quickly became known as the Ku Klux Klan Act of 1871. The act made it a crime to conspire to deny persons equal protection under the law and to interfere with government officials in the course of their duties. It is still used today. Much has been written about the enactment of this law, by historians of Reconstruction and civil rights—and by Grant's biographers, who rightly point to it as one of his greatest accomplishments. However, the pivotal mail episode has never appeared as part of the story before, nor has the role of the courageous Black mail agent William Gibson.[41]

Before final passage of the bill, though, Gibson ended his brief, hazardous career with the Post Office Department. In early April, according to his account, "the soldiers were withdrawn from the train. Promises were made by the leading authorities of the State to provide protection, but I . . . had but little confidence in those promises, so I resigned." Gibson would not, could not, trust Kentucky officials to protect him and his family from Kentucky's Klan members. Nor would Markland trust another Black agent to the state's care. He assigned a white agent, William Van Pelt, to the route, and mail by rail resumed between Lexington and Louisville on April 15. In his diary, Fish noted with regret, "This will afford the claim of a triumph over the Govt to those in Kentucky who objected to the employment of a negro in the mail service."[42]

Five days later, the House and Senate voted final passage of the historic measure by a comfortable margin; both chambers had Republican majorities, and most Republicans fell in line with their president.

Notably, five "yes" votes in the House came from newly elected Black representatives. Grant, who had canceled a long-planned trip to California because he felt his absence from the capital "immediately after the enactment of the 'Ku-klux' bill, would not be proper," wasted no time in signing the measure. He returned to the Capitol on the day it passed, and as soon as the document was prepared for his signature, Grant signed it in the President's Room.[43]

But Grant was not satisfied with mere enactment of the historic law. He wanted to show he meant business. He issued a proclamation, prepared at his request by the attorney general, on May 3 that was then published throughout the country. In it, the president recounted the provisions of the law and declared his intention to use them when warranted. He put the deep South—and Kentucky and Tennessee—on notice. "I will not hesitate to exhaust the powers thus vested in the Executive whenever and wherever it shall become necessary to do so for the purpose of securing to all citizens of the United States the peaceful enjoyment of the rights guaranteed to them by the Constitution and laws," he proclaimed. Grant stood by his words, and the law was prosecuted with such vigor beginning that autumn that violence and terror attributed to the Klan noticeably abated during the rest of his presidency.[44]

The fall of 1871 saw a different kind of tragedy play out, this time in the northern part of the nation. The Great Chicago Fire, often blamed on Mrs. O'Leary's cow kicking over a lantern in her barn, began on the night of October 8, during a streak of searing temperatures and a record-setting drought. Though no definitive judgment upon the guilt of the cow has ever been rendered, most historians agree that a fire began in a shed on the O'Leary property and swiftly blazed through the unusually hot, dry, windy city. Most of Chicago's buildings were made of wood, but even those built of brick could not withstand the scorching temperatures, particularly once the city's water pumping system quickly failed.

Among the largest and most important structures destroyed was the massive U.S. Post Office and Custom House. A large, modern distribution hub for east-west mail routes, it handled more mail daily than any other city but New York. As the wall of flames approached, postal workers labored heroically to remove nearly one hundred tons of mail to safety. Although the building had been "designed to be fireproof," only the exterior walls survived the conflagration. Despite the extensive damage to the building and the city, postal workers established temporary post offices and processed mail distribution amid acres of smoking rubble. According to post office lore, not a letter was lost because of the fire.[45]

By October 10, when the worst of the fires were out, an accounting revealed that the flames had reduced more than three square miles of the city to ashes, killed more than three hundred people, and left homeless more than one hundred thousand. Assistance poured in from around the country. At the Post Office Department in Washington, employees agreed to have "one day's salary from each officer, clerk and other employe[e] for the month of October" subtracted from their pay and distributed "to the sufferers of the recent fire." Contributions beyond the salary deduction were noted from more than fifteen men at Post Office Department headquarters, including an additional $100 from Creswell and $25 from Markland. In all, they sent $2,400 to Chicago, or nearly $50,000 in today's currency.[46]

Markland had been called to Washington by Creswell because "in addition to his usual and ordinary duties," according to a news report on October 12, he "was to-day specially appointed by the Postmaster General inspector at large of post office buildings." In the wake of the Chicago fire, there was an understandably urgent emphasis on "the fitness of the post office buildings." Markland was tasked to determine if they were suitable and safe for employees and the public. By this time, however, Markland's "usual and ordinary duties" did not include being superintendent for Kentucky and Tennessee. As he wrote to a friend two years later, rather than supporting his efforts to defeat the Klan, Kentucky politicians, including "the leaders of the [state] republican party banded themselves together to rid the state" of Markland. The strong animosity on the part of Kentucky politicians had led to a different job in a different state.[47]

Shortly after passage of the Ku Klux Klan Act, he had been promoted to assistant superintendent of the Railway Mail Service, with headquarters in Indianapolis, Indiana. The additional inspector-

　　　　　"Our Continued Services Together"

general duties meant more money and more travel for Markland. Less than a week later, he was in Boston, no doubt inspecting postal facilities but also attending a dinner with Canadian and U.S. post-masters in honor of Creswell, arranged by "Postmaster Burt and the attachees of the Boston post-office." The Grants were in Boston, too, and it is more than likely that the Grants, Creswells, and Marklands traveled north from Washington together.[48]

The three men would have had much to celebrate in the passage of the Ku Klux Klan Act. From the beginning of the year, at the start of the new Congress, Grant had made it clear he wanted yet another law to compel compliance with the Reconstruction amendments—a third enforcement act. But this time he wanted one with teeth. In the aftermath of the Kentucky mail stoppage, he got one. Fish's diary and Grant's public statements show that Grant was well informed about the events surrounding the attack on Gibson. And though in the cabinet meeting the postmaster general told Grant (through his representative) that an 1861 law gave him the power to halt mail on the route, it is noteworthy that Fish documented that it was Grant who directed the mail be stopped.

In all the public discussion of the mail issue, however, neither Congress nor newspapers identified Markland or Creswell as the men who halted the mail. There is no mention of Grant's direct order, though he was often accused of being the "master" who orchestrated the entire chain of events from Gibson's initial hiring through the stopping of the mail. Nor is there any evidence that Grant and Creswell in Washington and Markland and Gibson in Kentucky engaged in a conspiracy to provoke violence that would lead to a mail stoppage, which would lead to passage of the law with the powers that Grant needed to address the Klan's violence. That seems far-fetched, except perhaps for the most robust conspiracy theorist. But Markland and Gibson knew what would happen when Gibson traveled the Louisville-Lexington route, and the law allowing stoppage of mail was conveniently at Grant's fingertips in that cabinet meeting, no doubt courtesy of the postmaster general's representative.

Even if no conspiracy had been crafted in the White House to create conditions necessary for passage of the law, two of the principal actors in the 1871 drama were soon rewarded for their outstanding service. As we know, Markland was promoted months after the law passed. Later that year, Gibson was "appointed a secret service agent by the United States Attorney" to find witnesses to a notorious Klan murder and convince them to testify. In 1872 Gibson traveled to the White House, where he was introduced to President Grant by his attorney general, Benjamin Bristow, a Kentucky native. Two years later, in 1874, he was appointed a federal gauger, an employee of the Internal Revenue Service who certifies and collects excise taxes on distilled spirits, one of the most important civil service jobs in Kentucky.[49]

Another of the principals in the drama also received attention from the White House. Not long after the attack on Gibson, officials identified the assailant as Simeon Cook, brother of the KKK leader in Shelby County, Kentucky (where North Benson is located), and charged him with the assault. Even before Cook was apprehended, a presidential pardon was sought on his behalf, as part of a proposed deal with the state's governor to "heal up the wounds in that part of the Country." But Grant, who issued more than 1,300 pardons during his eight-year tenure, refused to pardon Cook.[50]

The partnership of Grant and Markland—begun in those bleak, early days of a war whose end no one could predict—recognized from the outset the value of mail to the morale of the Union Army and thus to its success. For four years, Grant had trusted Markland to deliver his soldiers' mail swiftly and reliably—and trusted him, too, to handle the sensitive and sometimes difficult military-civilian relations between the army and the Post Office Department. The two men had worked together for years to ensure that letters between the home front and the front lines were delivered almost as regularly as was the mail in cities far removed from the battlefield. The smooth and often innovative operation of the mail service was one of Grant's most valuable contributions to his troops' welfare, as many veterans testified at their annual reunions. And in the wake of Lincoln's assassination, Grant called on Markland again, trusting him to find any mail that might reveal a larger plot against the U.S. government.

"Our Continued Services Together"

After the war, Grant chose Creswell as postmaster general and supported Creswell's determined hiring of Black postal employees. The president knew that real progress in bringing the formerly enslaved Black population into the mainstream of American society could only be made when they were put into positions that made white southerners uncomfortable. It is conjecture, to be sure, since we have no record of their meeting, but it is also reasonable to assume that when Grant met with Markland that day in April 1870 and asked him to take on the diminished role of assistant superintendent for Kentucky and Tennessee, they discussed the possibility of hiring Black mail agents in that territory. After all, he knew Markland was intimately familiar with Kentucky's politics and knew he could be trusted to manage the sensitive and volatile situation.

When the local Ku Klux Klan decided to inflict its racial vengeance on William Gibson, Grant recognized that an assault on a Black agent of the U.S. Post Office Department was an assault on the Constitution and on all Americans to whom it promised equal justice under the law. The president ordered the mail route stopped, and Markland stopped it. In his handwritten message to Congress, Grant presented the assault on the mail as one of three proofs that he needed more tools to enforce the Constitution's guarantees of civil rights. The other two offenses (threats to life and property, inability to collect revenue) were important, of course, though they had not previously acquired sufficient traction to prod lawmakers into action. But Grant knew that stopping the mail would make Kentucky—and the rest of the South—howl. He was right. And it did more—it energized his supporters. Shortly after that message, the Ku Klux Klan Act of 1871 became law.

When he gifted his saddle to Markland six years earlier, the president had expressed hope that he and his childhood friend would continue their service together. They did, and the partnership of Grant and Markland continues to benefit citizens of the United States today.

TEN

The "Colonel" Becomes a "General"

1872–84

A mong the many legacies of the Civil War were fraternal societies formed by former members of the armed forces at the end of the war. They held huge annual reunions, erected monuments to beloved dead comrades, and raised funds for members and their families in need. Mostly, however, they celebrated the close brotherhood they had gained at so dear a price. Foremost among the Union Army societies were those of the Army of the Tennessee, the Army of the Ohio, and the Army of the Cumberland. According to their rules, membership was limited to U.S. Army officers who had served in the respective armies. However, Absalom Markland was not only welcomed as a member of each society after the war and addressed as "Colonel" despite his lack of genuine military credentials, but the societies also elected him an officer on several occasions, and he actively participated in the reunions, along with Sherman, Grant, and Thomas.[1]

The Society of the Army of the Tennessee was the largest and most prominent of the fraternal societies that met annually in cities across the nation; more than eight hundred men had joined its ranks by 1873. It got its start even before the war officially ended. On April 14, 1865, three days before Sherman had his first discussion with Johnston outside Raleigh, North Carolina, several of his officers gathered in the vacant Senate chamber of the rebel capitol. Chaired by Gen. Francis Blair, the informal committee drafted a brief outline of an organization they envisioned "to keep alive and preserve that kindly and cordial feeling which has been one of the characteristics of this Army during its career in the service."[2]

At its first annual meeting, held in Cincinnati in 1866, the society formally adopted a charter that specified its membership to include "every officer who has served with honor in that Army," and it provided that "honorary members may be elected from those who have served with honor and distinction in any of the Armies of the United States." The charter also called upon the members to erect memorials to their fallen comrades and to take care of their survivors. Those who could not attend the annual meetings were "expected to write to the Corresponding Secretary of the Society, and impart such information in regard to themselves as they may desire, and which may be of interest to their brother officers." Lastly, upon invitation from the president or one of the several vice presidents, officers of the other armies could attend the Society of the Army of the Tennessee's reunions. Soon, veterans of the other armies began to organize similar fraternal leagues.[3]

In mid-1868 Sherman—as president of the Society of the Army of the Tennessee—called upon all the various army societies to meet in Chicago, with the hope that they would come together under one umbrella organization. The societies all joined in the "Grand Reunion," as it was called, in the city's opera house. There, the three most prominent military men of the day sat together on the dais—Lt. Gen. and now also President-Elect Ulysses S. Grant, Maj. Gen. William T. Sherman, and Maj. Gen. George Thomas. Sherman, the presiding officer, opened the meeting with eloquent but pointed remarks:

> Happily, my friends, you did not belong to that class of our people in whose very youth was planted the pernicious doctrine that the highest allegiance was due to the place of birth or of residence, and that a citizen should love a part of his country better than the whole. . . . You may search history in vain for a more flagrant violation of faith, a more causeless breach of a national compact than that which resulted in our civil war. . . . The volunteer soldier stepped upon the arena. . . . He has kept his oath, and we now behold again the good ship of State, full-rigged, once more on her course.[4]

The "Colonel" Becomes a "General"

The Grand Reunion proved to be a great success in every way except in uniting the army societies into one body. Sherman's own Society of the Army of the Tennessee passed a resolution to remain independent, and none of the others could be tempted to do otherwise.

The Society of the Army of the Tennessee returned to Cincinnati in 1871, where the call for a statue to memorialize John Rawlins, the late general and secretary of war, was met by Sherman with a plea for one "plain tablet" memorial in honor of all dead members of the society, to save time and money. "We are dying too fast," he declared. That proposal, too, was rejected, and a committee was directed to proceed with a design. A newspaper account of the reunion noted the presence of "Col. Markland," along with Generals Belknap, Sherman, Pope, Meade, and Lew Wallace.[5]

But even as Union Army veterans annually celebrated their victory, historian George Rable noted, "defeat produced a unity in the South that had never before existed, even during the halcyon days of the Confederacy." While the Grant administration would be successful in reining in the Ku Klux Klan during his tenure, white southerners became even bolder in organizing against hated "Yankee overlords." Slowly but surely, Democrats clawed back their political power. Violence continued in the ravaged southern states in myriad localized efforts to suppress Republican votes, even as the economy boomed in the northern and western parts of the country. Expansion of railroads and steamship lines, mining in the West, and financial centers in the East created the Gilded Age, when the glitter of wealthy industrial barons and their bejeweled wives obscured the grim hunger and poverty of the lower class.[6]

As the year 1872 opened, President Grant signed into law a bill creating Yellowstone National Park, the first national park in the United States—and arguably the first in the world. The presidential election loomed, and Philadelphia hosted the Republican nominating convention in June. A vocal minority of Republicans unhappy with Grant's pro–civil rights stance split away to form the Liberal Republican Party, nominating the irascible and often irrational newspaper publisher Horace Greeley as its candidate. The remaining mainstream

Republicans nominated Grant by acclamation for a second term as president. When the Democrats assembled for their convention later that year, the delegates decided that their best chance to defeat Grant lay in uniting with the Liberal Republicans, so the Democrats also nominated Greeley. To make the political situation even more unusual, Victoria Woodhull, a leading women's suffrage activist, announced her candidacy for the presidency, and—without prior consultation—added the famous Black orator and social reformer Frederick Douglass as her vice presidential candidate on the Equal Rights Party ticket.

That year the Society of the Army of the Tennessee met in Madison, Wisconsin, over the Fourth of July weekend. It was "a vaster and happier throng than the citizens have ever witnessed," according to the *Inter-Ocean* newspaper in Chicago, which received breaking news of the meeting by "Special Telegram." Its reporter also breathlessly engaged in celebrity spotting nineteenth-century style, which included an emphasis on phrenology, the now-discredited practice of deducing intelligence from the size and shape of one's head:

> The universal cry is for Sheridan. All desire to lay their eyes on "Little Phil," and searching for him many ludicrous blunders are committed. . . . Secretary [of War] Belknap attracts the attention of all. His fine and commanding presence, his immense head, indicative at once of a preponderance of intellect and great executive ability, commend him to the recognition of all. Other gentlemen are eagerly sought after—Gov. Noyes of Ohio, and Gen. Pope and Col. Markland, who during the war, had control of the entire mail facilities of this grand army. The latter, with his presence, commands recognition and by many is mistaken for the secretary of war.[7]

The society elected "Col. Markland" to be vice president of the organization that year, and he was recognized in the formal reply to one of the thirteen toasts that were annually made. The ninth toast of the banquet was "The Navy—the Army's other half," and in response, Brig. Gen. Manning Ferguson Force observed, "It was an amphibious life; it was hard to tell where land service ended and water service began. . . . We were blended with the navy." He spoke of cooperation in battles from Fort Henry to Fort Donelson to Vicksburg to Savannah and then recalled a favorite memory for all the men: "When Fort McAllister was taken, and the troops reached the sea, the navy was there, bearing Colonel Markland with our hoarded mails."[8]

August found Markland and other prominent men visiting Grant's political headquarters in the Fifth Avenue Hotel in New York, where early results from North Carolina's gubernatorial election gave the president's supporters reason to worry. When all the votes were counted, Republican candidate Tod Caldwell won by only 50.49 percent. But results of the November 5 national election confirmed Grant's continuing popularity. Grant won the popular vote in thirty-one of the thirty-seven states. Greeley's resounding defeat at the polls, just six days after his wife's death, was not the last insult that fate had in store for him that year. On November 29, before the Electoral College cast its votes, Greeley died. As a result, the electors pledged to Greeley cast their votes for four other presidential and eight vice presidential candidates, so in the end Greeley received only three Electoral College votes. Though the campaign had been an ugly one (cartoonist Thomas Nast portrayed Greeley shaking hands with John Wilkes Booth), Greeley's death was sincerely mourned, and many prominent men whom he had skewered in his newspaper attended his funeral, including Ulysses Grant.

Shortly after the election, the Society of the Army of the Cumberland met in Dayton, Ohio. One of the innovative features of that meeting was a trip to the National Asylum for Disabled Volunteer Soldiers, most often called the Dayton Soldiers Home. Opened in 1867, it was one of the first national soldiers homes, and it incorporated the most recent approaches to rehabilitation of disabled veterans. Located on 355 acres of rolling farmland, the home accommodated as many as seven thousand men in a year, providing medical aid in addition to food and lodging, as well as religious, intellectual, and recreational resources. Members of the society were quite affected by their visit with the disabled veterans that year, as recorded in the speeches given by many of them at the home, and they pledged to visit other soldiers homes when reunions were held in those cities.[9]

Markland was moved to do more for the veterans in Dayton. He mentioned to the home's manager, Lewis B. Gunckel, that "he had in his possession the saddle upon which General Grant had ridden during all the battles from Fort Henry, in Tennessee, to the surrender of Lee, at Appomattox, Virginia." Gunckel then suggested that the home was an excellent place for the saddle to be displayed, since the beautiful gardens and walking trails attracted visitors from all over the country. Accordingly, Markland sent the precious saddle—his most treasured memento of the war—from his home in Indianapolis in December 1872, with the proviso that it be returned to the Markland family if the home should "be abandoned or used for any other purpose than to care for soldiers."[10]

As the year 1873 opened, forty-eight-year-old Markland remained on the payroll of the Post Office Department as "assistant superintendent Railway Mail Service, and inspector of P.O. buildings." By the fall, however, he was seeking another government job, the post of sergeant at arms for the U.S. House of Representatives. In newspaper accounts of his candidacy, such as one in the *Nashville Union and American*, Markland was described as a "Grant man" who had been "prominently brought forward with an apparent concert of action by Western members and papers." His closeness to Grant did not prevent at least one Republican newspaper from editorializing against him, however. The *National Republican* in Washington DC, which held the lucrative contract for publishing the debates in Congress in the daily *Congressional Globe*, editorialized, "Markland relies on his record as a military mail agent to secure his election; but it has served him so long as a recommendation for office that it has become as worn and smells as bad as a professional beggar's certificate." This may have reflected the editor's desire to continue his friendship—and working relationship—with existing congressional staff. The article in the Nashville newspaper contained the same facts but omitted the editorializing.[11]

Markland traveled from Indianapolis in mid-October to participate in the annual meeting of the Society of the Army of the Tennessee, held that year in Toledo, Ohio, and it was deemed "a very successful affair." According to a local reporter, "The attendance was large," and among the prominent attendees were President Grant, Secretary of War Belknap, and Generals Sherman, Sheridan, John Logan, John Pope, and Oliver Howard. Sherman was reelected president of the society, and "Col. Markland" was elected one of twelve vice presidents.[12]

Shortly after he returned to Indianapolis, Markland attended a newsworthy gathering in that city. "Ex-Governor Pinchb[a]ck, of Louisiana, the colored gentleman who filled the gubernatorial chair in that State on Tuesday evening address[ed] his colored brethren," reported the *Fort Wayne Gazette*, "and one might say his white brethren also for he seems to have nearly as much claim to relationship with one race as the other[,] being a light mulatto." Pinckney Benton Stewart Pinchback was born free in Georgia to a formerly enslaved woman; she had been freed by the man who fathered Pinckney and nine other children by her. These mixed-race children were considered illegitimate under Georgia law (Maj. William Pinchback also had children with his white wife). Pinckney Pinchback received an education in Ohio, and at the outset of the Civil War he decided to fight for the Union. He became one of the very few Black commissioned officers but encountered enormous racism in the army, and in 1863 he resigned his commission.[13]

After the war, Pinchback pursued a career in politics as a Republican, becoming a state senator in Louisiana in 1868 and president pro tempore of the state Senate in 1871. In that position, he succeeded to the post of lieutenant governor when the incumbent died, but an even higher office awaited him in the wake of a heavily disputed election for governor, when his name was put forward. As historian George Rable has observed, "There are no means short of necromancy to determine who won the election of 1872 in Louisiana," and in the postelection maneuvering Pinchback ended up in the governor's chair, though for barely six weeks. He thus became the first elected Black governor of any state. Pinchback drew large crowds of prominent residents wherever he spoke, as in Indianapolis, where his purpose was "to disprove the impression sought to be made upon the people of the North, that the colored people of the South have made no progress since the war, and that they are improvident, idle and thievish." Among the white attendees mentioned in one article were the Indiana state treasurer, several members of the legislature, a judge, and Markland. Among the "prominent colored citizens" present were pastors of three churches and a doctor. Pinchback warned the Black members of the audience that "we cannot desert the Republican party, either now or any time."[14]

Elections within the halls of the U.S. Congress were complicated, too. What began as a three-way race for sergeant at arms of the House—between Markland, longtime incumbent Col. Nehemiah G. Ordway, and Col. D. W. Munn—acquired a fourth candidate in November. "Now comes the colored brother who wishes to bear off the laurels," reported the *Cincinnati Gazette*. Dr. R. A. Green from Bowling Green, Kentucky, "issued a circular to the members, setting forth that he thinks it about time the 800,000 colored voters of the country shall be recognized."[15]

As the contest heated up, Indiana newspapers took up Markland's banner, portraying him as a champion without regard to race. A lengthy article in the *Fort Wayne Daily Gazette* related Markland's pivotal role in the Gibson affair:

> When General Grant became President, without intimation or consultation, he assigned Colonel Markland to duty as Superintendent of the Railway Postal Service, with headquarters at Louisville, Ky. In this position he has proved as efficient as when in the army. He withheld the mail *six weeks* [original emphasis], because the people along the road between Louisville and Lexington sought to do violence to a colored route agent, "an official act," says the Indianapolis *Sun*, "which endeared him to all law and order loving people, displayed the energy and pluck of the man, and made his name familiar in all parts of the country."[16]

Even though Markland was "earnestly supported by the entire Indiana delegation," his candidacy for the sergeant at arms post was a losing effort. When the time came for votes to be cast, Markland "saw no chance of securing the nomination," and he graciously withdrew from the race in favor of Ordway, who emerged the winner by a large margin.[17]

Markland had always been a realist when it came to his career. He continually sought higher, more responsible positions but never burned any bridges along the way. In the face of certain defeat, he stepped aside, never offending those against whom he competed or from whom he sought assistance. Even in his aggressive effort to obtain a brevet rank in the army it appears he pulled back when it became clear he would not achieve his goal. In 1873 the opposition to his election as House sergeant at arms, based on the very action that the Indianapolis newspaper celebrated, became too great and too obvious for Markland to ignore. In a letter that year to Kentucky friend and businessman Luther Thustin, Markland pointedly noted that back in 1871, "I had the confidence & sympathy of good Republicans & law abiding democrats every where save in Ky," where he had been "soundly berated for his efforts" to stop the Klan. Markland had long been identified with Kentucky, but when that state's congressional delegation made its opposition to him known, Markland excelled at reading the handwriting on the wall, and he withdrew from the sergeant at arms election. Markland remained inspector of post office buildings and assistant superintendent of the Railway Mail Service for the Fourth Division.[18]

In December the Marklands joined President Grant and his daughter Nellie, along with Commanding General Sherman and his daughter Minnie, at the wedding of Arizona Territory delegate Richard McCormick to the daughter of Senator Allen G. Thurman of Ohio. This was the second time Martha and Absalom witnessed a wedding of McCormick. The Arizonan's first wife, Margaret, whom they had watched wed in 1865 before they all embarked on a trip to California, had died in childbirth two years later. McCormick's second wedding was "very quiet and informal" and "by no means crowded," and "the little circle who were present to give their congratulations were unanimous in saying they had never seen a prettier or more tasteful wedding."[19]

By the end of that year, the nation was in the throes of what is now known as the panic of 1873, which was to result in a depression that lasted for five years more. Sparked by a wave of speculative European investments in the U.S. railroad boom, European markets failed first, followed by those in the United States. Numerous bank failures, including the Freedman's Savings Bank, of which William Gibson was then a director, exacerbated the downward spiral in the U.S. economy, and rampant joblessness led to riots and labor strikes.[20]

When railroad workers went on strike in Indiana in late 1873, the newly elected governor, Thomas Hendricks, beseeched Markland to have the federal government "quell the disturbance," according to a local newspaper. Markland reportedly replied, "Governor, whenever you say you are unable to carry out the laws of the State, as the Executive thereof, and are powerless to enforce them, I will lay it before the [federal] government." After noting these comments, the reporter for the *Indianapolis News* concluded that "the Governor has been found perfectly able to hoe his own row now." During another rail strike, on the Erie Railroad around the same time, "passenger and freight cars were left on track nearby, but mail cars were allowed through."[21]

Later in 1874, Henry Van Ness Boynton, a retired brevet brigadier general, began exchanging letters with "General A. H. Markland" with regard to research for one of Markland's clients. Boynton had received the nation's highest award for valor, the Medal of Honor, for his actions in the Battle of Missionary Ridge, where he was severely wounded when "he led his regiment in the face of a severe fire from the enemy." After the war, he was a correspondent for the *Cincinnati Gazette*. Why Boynton would have addressed Markland as "General" is lost to history, but no doubt Markland's vanity was touched. None of Markland's replies have been found, but he did not discourage Boynton from using that title (or at least, not successfully), since the hero and veteran of the Union Army addressed Markland over a period of at least ten years as "My dear General."[22]

Boynton was then in Washington DC, where he could access government records for Markland, still in Indianapolis. Several of the Boynton letters discuss various War Department papers Markland wanted to use in his legal/lobbying work, but one of them reveals that Markland needed lobbying for himself. On July 24, 1874, Boynton wrote from Washington, "I suppose until the Post Office Department is running with a head again nothing can be done toward getting you

The "Colonel" Becomes a "General"

here." He continued, "When anything in my power can be accomplished, trust me, & I will do what I can." Apparently, Markland had sought Boynton's help in obtaining a post at postal headquarters, which was then under temporary management. After Creswell retired in June 1874, James W. Marshall, previously first assistant postmaster, was appointed acting postmaster general. He would remain in that position until Marshall Jewell, who was serving as minister to Russia, could return to take the top post at the Post Office Department as Grant wished. During that time, Markland's desire to return to Washington in a senior position in the Post Office Department was temporarily thwarted.[23]

When Jewell became postmaster general in August 1874, Markland's wish was permanently thwarted. The *National Republican* in Washington announced that Jewell had dismissed a number of clerks—seven male and thirteen female—and removed nine special agents. It also noted that "A. H. Markland has resigned as special agent, and W. F. Cox, of Ohio has been appointed a special agent." According to another newspaper, "Markland, who has been for 10 years special agent of the postoffice department in the west . . . applied to be stationed in Washington this winter, but was refused, and thereupon resigned." This was not the first time he resigned from the postal service, but it was the last time. Markland never again worked for the U.S. government.[24]

For thirteen years he had been known throughout the divided-then-reunited nation as a special agent of the U.S. Post Office Department. For four years, he had been the man who kept U.S. soldiers and their families in touch across the miles, in the service of war. Then he labored to restore regular mail service to the defeated states, in the service of peace. And when Grant asked him to take charge of the mail in Kentucky and Tennessee as the Klan's terror escalated, he stopped the mail, in the service of civil rights.

As the first civilian postal official to supervise mail for the U.S. Army, Markland's impact on military mail operations can still be seen today. All important aspects of military mail procedures must meet official U.S. Postal Service (USPS) standards, from the secure handling of mail to detailed attention to finances. Today, USPS postal inspectors, as the successors to special agents, are key to keeping mail "flowing to and from the military in times of conflict." The U.S. Postal Inspection Service provides the Military Postal Service and its contractors with security and information essential to their safe and secure operation. Postal platoon officers, the senior military postal officials in the field, and postal clerks are trained in USPS practices; the latter are responsible for stamps and money orders that remain in high demand by soldiers even in the age of email and electronic fund transfers.[25]

Today's military mail carries a high priority within the services' logistical operations, just as it did a century and a half ago. The amount of funding, training, and staff time the Defense Department devotes to postal operations is a testament to the importance of mail to military morale. And in a world of uniform uniforms, haircuts, housing, and chow, military mail is still one of the most customer service–oriented aspects of military life, just as it was in Markland's day.[26]

Markland's devotion to the department of the government that preceded the establishment of the government itself carried within it a deep understanding of the nation's need for news, the economy's need for information, the human need for communication. Being a special agent of the Post Office Department had never been just a job; it had always been a calling. Now, at the age of forty-nine, Absalom Markland put that calling aside forever.

Markland had already exceeded the life expectancy for a white male in the United States in the late 1870s, and it was at about this time that his health began failing. Indeed, it may have been for health reasons that Markland had sought a job in Congress or at Post Office Department headquarters instead of the peripatetic life of a special agent. The first evidence we have of his decline is in a letter he wrote seven years later to Gen. Andrew Hickenlooper, longtime corresponding secretary of the Society of the Army of the Tennessee:

Washington City, April 4, 1881

My dear Hickenlooper:

I am greatly disappointed that I can not be with you at the reunion of our Society on the 6th and 7th inst. I had intended to leave for

Cincinnati to-night, having procured my tickets for that purpose. I am an invalid, and we are in the midst of a snow storm, which will render it imprudent for me to take the risk of travel in my present condition. I am just recovering from a most aggravating catarrhal disease with which I have been afflicted for the past seven years, and am forbid by my physician from taking any chances in such weather. I especially regret not be[ing] with you at the coming meeting, because I have been unable to attend the meetings of late years for the reason given above. . . .

Very respectfully, your friend and obedient servant,

A. H. Markland,

Formerly Superintendent of Mails for the Armies of the U.S.[27]

The term "catarrh" has been used for more than one hundred years to describe a wide range of symptoms caused by infection of the mucous membranes of the nose, with associated problems involving the sinuses, throat, lungs, and ears. Chronic catarrh, which it seems Markland suffered over a period of many years, interfered with breathing and could lead to congestion of the lungs and even deafness.[28]

Despite his illness, the Marklands attended the wedding of General Sherman's daughter Maria, or "Minnie," as she was called, in the fall of 1874. The wedding was a high-society event in Washington, with more than 1,500 guests gathering in the grand St. Aloysius Catholic Church. A beautifully engraved invitation to the wedding ceremony and to the reception immediately afterward at the Shermans' home was delivered to Colonel and Mrs. Markland at the Hamilton House hotel in the city. Also included was one of Sherman's calling cards. On the reverse, the general penciled a note to "Dear Markland," expressing regret that he had missed seeing Markland earlier and asking him to arrange a meeting for the next Tuesday. "I wish it very much," Sherman wrote (emphasis in the original).[29]

By spring of the next year, the Marklands were settled back in Washington, where he resumed his practice of assisting clients seeking restitution from the U.S. government for use of their property during the war. In a letter to Secretary of War William W. Belknap, Markland sought records from the army relating to the confiscated property of a woman whom he described as "the sister of Genl [Charles] Rand of the U.S. Army & one of the most thoroughly . . . loyal citizens of St. Louis."[30]

A month later, Markland was one of a party of men ferried to Marshall Hall, the ancestral home of Chief Justice John Marshall, on the banks of the Potomac River across from Mount Vernon. Though abandoned by the family in the early 1800s, the picturesque vine-covered remnants of the house and its original 959-acre property were magnets for Washingtonians seeking to escape summer heat. Ferries carried tourists from Washington and Alexandria to Marshall Hall and Mount Vernon for a $1 toll. Markland's trip in late May garnered notice in the *National Republican* because it featured several prominent men, including the host, Gen. Alexander Hamilton Blake.[31]

A veteran of the Mexican War, Blake served as a cavalry commander under George McClellan in the Army of the Potomac and had fought in the Battle of Gettysburg. After the war, he served as cavalry commander at Fort Vancouver in Washington Territory, ultimately retiring to Washington DC in 1870. In Blake's retirement, according to the reporter, "when he undertakes to please his friends he is always in at the right time and right place." May 28, 1875, was the right time and Marshall Hall, the right place, for a special feast of planked shad, according to a reporter who may have imbibed some of the champagne before he wrote:

> They had scarcely landed when the shad, fat with roe, came up two by two, claiming the honor of being eaten on the happy occasion. . . . General Blake and all his friends know how to eat. They are all epicures, and on a plate, large enough for the purpose, a whole shad was placed before each one; then great glasses of champagne, lime juice and sugar; then a bowl of turtle soup and eggs, followed by champagne; then another shad, and round of lime juice, champagne and sugar. Men never had such appetites, and never enjoyed anything so much. . . . When they could eat no more, they joined hands round the table and sang, "Shad auld acquaintance be forgot?"[32]

Later that year, the same newspaper also recorded both Marklands' participation in the "first hop of the season at Willard's hotel." Apparently, his catarrh had not advanced enough to prevent his enjoying life with friends and family.[33]

There is no specific record of Markland's attendance at the ninth annual gathering of the Society of the Army of the Tennessee, held in Des Moines, Iowa, but even if his health had kept him from attending, he would have known about the speech that Grant gave there. Unlike his previous speeches, which rarely exceeded three sentences and were given very reluctantly, Grant prepared the 1875 speech as a tribute to free public education. In one of his most profound and prophetic statements, Grant told his former comrades, "If we are to have another contest in the near future of our national existence, I predict that the dividing line will not be Mason and Dixon's but between patriotism and intelligence on the one side, and superstition, ambition and ignorance on the other."[34]

Commanding General Sherman appointed Markland to the arrangements committee for the reunion of the Society of the Army of the Tennessee that met in Washington in October 1876. This was a historic meeting, since it was the occasion upon which the society's statue of beloved Gen. James McPherson, who was killed in the Atlanta campaign, was unveiled in the public square at K and Fifteenth Streets that bears his name. That same week, Markland was one among many well-known figures who attended a reception at the White House. Since Grant was not running for reelection in 1876, the *Alexandria Gazette* noted, "this reminder that the 'beginning of the end' of the pleasant receptions . . . has come is not pleasant food for reflection. . . . It is not possible for Mrs. Grant's successors there to make the house more pleasant to all than she has done."[35]

"Pleasant" was certainly not the word to be applied to the process or the outcome of the presidential election one month later. In fact, the election of 1876 remains one of the most controversial in U.S. history. When the Electoral College votes were counted, Democrat Samuel J. Tilden had 184 votes, and Republican candidate Rutherford B. Hayes had 165. Twenty votes were intractably in dispute due to irregularities in four states, so the election was thrown into the

House of Representatives, which established a bipartisan commission. After extended discussions that initially awarded all 20 disputed electoral votes to Hayes, the two parties finally agreed to what has become known as the Compromise of 1877.

In exchange for conceding the presidency to the Republicans, the Democrats succeeded in securing the removal of the last U.S. military forces from the last of the former Confederate states—South Carolina, Louisiana, and Florida—and requiring that a southern Democrat be appointed to Hayes's cabinet (David Keyes of Tennessee replaced Marshall Jewell as postmaster general). This compromise marked the end of Reconstruction as a federal policy. It opened the door for the rise of the Democratic Party and its virtually unopposed suppression of the Black population in the South.

Throughout the four fraught months between the election in November 1876 and the Compromise of 1877, hammered out in March of that year, Markland was among the political insiders who provided background information to Hayes, who had been an army general, and his supporters to aid their negotiating strategy. In one letter to Hayes in January, for example, Markland told him that there were twenty-six southern members of Congress who favored his inauguration. Martha Markland, who received a humorous and appreciative note from the president in response to her congratulations on his victory, was "among the ladies received by Mrs. Hayes" at the White House days after the inauguration, as one local newspaper reported. Former president Grant, who had campaigned eight years earlier with the simple plea, "Let us have peace," soon departed the country with his wife for a two-year trip around the world.[36]

The next year, Markland's help was sought by a man with whom he had spent time in the log cabin post office at Pittsburg Landing before the Battle of Shiloh. In 1878 President Hayes nominated former general Lew Wallace to the post of territorial governor of New Mexico. Shortly thereafter, Wallace telegraphed Markland for assistance. Wallace wrote that a "Ring" of men was working against him, one led by Stephen Elkins, an attorney in New Mexico and son-in-law of Senator Henry G. Davis of West Virginia. It is unknown what, if any, direct aid Markland provided, but in the end Wallace's nomination succeeded. It was while he was governor in Santa Fe that Wallace completed the work for which he is best known: the writing of *Ben Hur: A Tale of the Christ*.[37]

Veterans of the Army of the Cumberland had a "large and enthusiastic meeting" in Washington in late 1879 to formalize their society, and Markland was named to a committee to reorganize that entity. The minutes of the meeting also noted that "the orator designated at the last regular meeting of the society, Gen. Munderson, of Nebraska, notifies the society of his inability to be present, and the alternate, Gen. A. S. Williams, of Michigan, being dead, it devolved on the local committee to select an orator." Markland was among those who chose "Gen. Ben. H. Harrison, of Indiana" for that honor, the man who would become president of the United States ten years later.[38]

When the Society of the Army of the Tennessee met in Chicago in November 1879, the popularity of its most famous member was such that the headline on the front page of the *Chicago Daily Tribune* announcing his arrival did not even need to mention his name. Grant's appearance in Chicago two months after returning from his two-year world tour was cause for celebration by the entire city. Citizens lined the designated parade route beginning at daybreak on November 12, waiting more than five hours in the damp, chilly autumn air to pay their respects to the general, whose arrival by train at precisely 12:57 p.m. was noted in the newspaper. When the society's meeting convened that evening, General Sherman welcomed "our first commander, Ulysses S. Grant—[cheers]—who has been, like his namesake, wandering all around the world, and has at last come back to God's land. [Applause and laughter.]" Markland was present at that meeting, listed with other members of the society who paid their dues of $2 on November 12.[39]

The U.S. Census of 1880 reported Absalom and Martha living at 1342 K St., NW, Washington DC, which was the location of the Hamilton House hotel, which Mary J. Colley operated as a "fashionable boarding house." Its thirty-six residents and other Washingtonians frequented "hops" in its dancing hall, decorated with elaborate floral arrangements and three large chandeliers "festooned with smilax" (a colorful woody vine). It was "noted for the easy leather chairs in its lobby and the sophistication of its residents," according to a history of Washington, which added that "many members of Congress stayed there and thus it was reportedly the 'scene of much political gossip.'" It was the perfect place for the sociable Marklands. The census listed his occupation as "lawyer," but once again his and Martha's correct ages were not recorded. She was recorded as forty; she was forty-seven. He was listed as fifty years old; he was fifty-five. In January 1880 Markland was selected for jury duty on the DC Circuit Court and traveled to Lancaster, Pennsylvania, to consult with another lawyer.[40]

An April snowstorm in 1881 prevented the Marklands from attending the Society of the Army of the Tennessee reunion in Cincinnati, but Absalom was nonetheless prominently mentioned at the meeting when Col. Ozro J. Dodds of Ohio took the floor as the "regular orator" to reminisce with his comrades about the war. Dodds spoke about the army's pioneering use of the railroad and extolled the talented engineers and soldiers who designed and built massive bridges, including the 740-foot-long, 70-foot-high bridge over the Chattahoochee River near Atlanta, which they "put up in four and a half days."[41]

Dodds also lavished praise on the army for the "railroad fast mail service." He charged that some civilians "who were old enough to be in the army, but were not" claimed to have invented the system after the war, "but I maintain that the Army of the Tennessee gave birth to the railroad mail service." Furthermore, he said, "I mention this fact, not to pay a compliment to Markland, who we all love as a brother, and who was charged with the superintendence of that department of staff duty, but rather to draw a lesson from the war and recognize the services of enlisted men as mail messengers . . . and to trace this system . . . to its humble original in the Army of the Tennessee in the early days of the spring of 1862."

Dodds then spoke more generally about the mail service and its inestimable value to the army. Using the word "pathetic" in its nineteenth-century sense as "moving or affecting," he said, "I can recall no more pathetic picture in the experience of the war than the

The "Colonel" Becomes a "General"

delivery of the mail. How disappointed were those who received no letter; how generous those who did. They were passed from man to man of the same company, of the same neighborhood, of the same family, the same set, so that a single letter often did decimal duty." The Ohioan had witnessed death on the battlefield, and he lamented, "How many poor fellows perished with missives of encouragement, of love and affection, delivered under fire, some only half read, and some with seals unbroken in their clenched hands."

As the country geared up for the presidential election, according to the *Evening Star* (Washington DC), "Gen. A. H. Markland, of Indiana, who served at one time as third assistant Postmaster General, says that he feels confident that the republicans will carry Indiana." Although the reporter misstated both Markland's usual honorary military title and his previous postal office, Markland was correct in predicting that Indiana would vote for the Republican Party's former general, James A. Garfield, over the Democrats' former general, Winfield Scott Hancock. Garfield and his vice presidential candidate, Chester A. Arthur, prevailed, and they were sworn in on March 4, 1881.[42]

Nearly four months later, "Dear Colonel Markland" received a letter marked "Private & Confidential" from Kenneth Rayner, solicitor general of the Department of the Treasury, who was then a client of Markland. In three closely written pages, Rayner provided Markland detailed instructions on what to say to President Garfield in their forthcoming meeting. "You must pardon the anxiety I feel in regard to what is going on," he wrote. He reminded Markland,

Don't forget to call [President Garfield's] attention to . . .
   Don't forget to mention that while one man has made $100,000 in 4 years, I have not made one cent, beyond my salary.
   Had you not better suggest . . .
   Mention the fact, that I read to you a letter I have just received from [Senator John] Sherman . . .
   Please don't forget to say to him I now have written . . .[43]

After so many years of lobbying, it would not seem that Markland needed instructions on how to do it, but Rayner was in a situation that was the subject of national news, there were powerful people aligned against him, and he was understandably anxious about his future.

Before the Mexican War, Rayner had represented the district that included Raleigh, North Carolina, in the U.S. House of Representatives. In the presidential election year of 1848, Rayner came within one vote of besting Millard Fillmore in a canvass for vice president on presidential nominee Zachary Taylor's Whig Party ticket. When Taylor died of gastroenteritis in July 1850, Fillmore succeeded him as president, and Rayner was forever known as the man who missed the presidency by one vote. In April 1865, Rayner was one of several prominent Raleigh citizens who surrendered North Carolina's capital to General Sherman's troops to avoid bloodshed and destruction. President Grant made him solicitor general of the Treasury Department in 1877. In 1881 Rayner was seventy-three, and because he was "elderly" and had not actively campaigned for Garfield, he was a prime target for removal by several "Garfield men" who sought the solicitor general position for themselves. He would not leave without a fight.[44]

In choosing Markland to plead his case to the president, Rayner had selected one of the most well connected and prominent lawyer/lobbyists in Washington in the post–Civil War period. While he was not a kingmaker in the sense that he could make a man a president, Markland knew how to talk to powerful men to achieve a goal, and he knew many powerful men. From the time he wrote that first advertisement for his services as "General Collector and Travelling Agent" in 1845, his ability to win friends and influence people was obvious. He learned about the levers of government as a clerk in the Bureau of Pensions, as a correspondent in Congress, and as a civilian special agent in a vast military organization. Markland was known as a man of integrity, one who could be entrusted with secrets and special missions. He was a hard worker and a talented innovator as well.

Markland was not just smart, though; he was lucky, too. He hailed from Kentucky at the time that state became central to the nation's future. And he knew many Kentuckians (and many men from other states) who held vital posts in government before, during, and after the war. Indeed, his unique service during the war—when he was treated as a high-ranking officer even without military grade—gave him postwar entrée to social and political society that his wished-for brevet rank might have duplicated but likely would not have enhanced. In his nationwide travels on behalf of the postal service, he met and formed friendships with men in all walks of life. Doing favors for others came naturally to Markland. From the tenor of his reports about efforts he made on behalf of others—whether as paid counsel or not—it seems apparent that he enjoyed the work or, more precisely, that it did not seem like work to him. Markland was a man whose company others enjoyed, and personal chemistry is a valuable asset when seeking a favor. Like the best lobbyists, he left no evidence of powerful men acknowledging his intervention and granting his requests, but time and again, we find a request for his help, a report of a meeting he arranged, and a report of success.

On the day that Rayner wrote Markland about the forthcoming meeting with President Garfield, the elderly solicitor general was furious about a rumor circulating that Senator Sherman had said he was "failing physically and intellectually." Rayner told Markland that in a letter, Sherman "positively denie[d]" saying that, and "far from it, he told Presdt Garfield that he thought I ought to have some place that would pay me more money." Rayner continued in his letter to Markland, "My good friend, I regard it as a piece of good fortune, that you and I were brought to understand each other. There was a determined purpose, to enlist you in the crusade against me. But thank God! They are caught in the trap, that was set for me."[45]

The day after receipt of the letter, June 30, Markland saw Garfield at the White House. Whether Markland's was the deciding word or not, Rayner retained his position in the Garfield administration. The president reportedly responded with a heartfelt answer to a reporter's query about why he kept a "nondescript without any pull or party following" in the Treasury rather than appoint a "good Republican": "I am not going to remove him from a little place in the Treasury, whose duties he fully meets, an old man who came within a single vote of filling the place I fill and of being President of the United States."[46]

Two days after the meeting with Markland, a man often identified as a "disgruntled office seeker" shot Garfield as the president waited in the Baltimore and Potomac Railroad station to go to New Jersey. The injury from the bullet in his spine was serious, but—according to most biographers and contemporary medical experts—it was his doctors who killed him with the worst combination of nineteenth-century medical care available. Alexander Graham Bell offered to use his latest invention, an early form of metal detector, to locate the bullet still lodged in the president's body, but Garfield's doctor, who had probed the wound again and again with unsterilized fingers, dictated the area where Bell could use his equipment. The bullet was not detected in that tightly circumscribed area of the president's back (as Bell and others suspected it would not be), so the doctor told Bell to remove his equipment from the president's room. Although initially able to carry on some duties from his sickbed, Garfield suffered terribly for two and a half months before succumbing to infection from his wound on September 18.[47]

Presidents change, but lobbyists are forever. The next February found Markland visiting with the man who had been Garfield's vice president and was now President Chester A. Arthur. He met with the president at the White House together with the "national committee of the National Union League of America." Markland was then one-half of Kentucky's delegation to the league (John D. White was the other), which was endeavoring to assist the Republican Party's chances in the forthcoming elections. Markland retained his close ties to Kentucky, hoping to move it more toward the principles of the Republican Party, but with little success. Also in February 1882, one Kentucky newspaper wryly observed of their political efforts that White and Markland were "opposed to the revolt of the Unionists from the Confederate democracy of Kentucky."[48]

Nor had things changed in Kentucky's postal arena. In March a newspaper article headlined "Colored Route Agents" noted with approval the appointment of a "colored school teacher" to the position of mail route agent in Indiana on the Jeffersonville, Madison & Indianapolis Railroad. This Indiana newspaper then commented,

The "Colonel" Becomes a "General"

Kentucky has 35,000 colored voters, and not a colored route agent in the State. A few years ago a colored man of education was appointed, at the instance of Col. Markland, on one of the roads and was driven off by the Democrats, and last winter the man who assaulted the agent was nominated for door-keeper of the House of Representatives in Kentucky, because he had driven from the railroad a colored mail agent in the State. Democracy in any form is against the colored man holding office in Kentucky. In every other Southern State colored men are employed as route agents, and their work is found to be well done.[49]

Later in 1882, "Gen. Markland" received a letter from Secretary of War Robert Todd Lincoln, replying to Markland's "personal note . . . touching on the site of the statue of General Rawlins, and expressing [Markland's] desire for a change to a more favorable locality." It is fair to say that the statue of the loyal Union man John Rawlins, said to be cast from a Confederate cannon, was relocated more times in the nineteenth and twentieth centuries than that of any Confederate general in the twenty-first. First installed in 1874 in what is now Rawlins Park in Washington DC at the corner of Eighteenth and E Streets NW, it was temporarily moved in 1880 to Tenth and D Streets NW at the insistence of the Society of the Army of the Tennessee, which was unhappy about the poorly maintained and infrequently visited neighborhood of Rawlins Park. Secretary Lincoln told Markland that his authority over the statue had ended when it was first installed, claiming it would "require an Act of Congress" to authorize and pay for another change. But he reassured Markland that "the improvements about to be commenced in the vicinity of Rawlins' Square will . . . materially change its character, and make that square a prominent feature in an attractive part of the city."[50]

In fact, the bronze general moved three more times. Because a newspaper production facility was to be built at the Tenth Street site in the mid-1880s, the Rawlins statue was moved to Pennsylvania Avenue between Seventh and Ninth Streets NW. In 1886 it was forced to cross the street to make room for a "public bathroom."

There, because of "heavy foliage," according to an article in 1905, the statue was "seldom seen by either resident or tourist." Finally, construction of the National Archives building in 1931 required the bronze Rawlins's relocation to, amazingly enough, the original site in Rawlins Park, where it stands today. As Secretary Lincoln promised, the neighborhood improved greatly, owing to the addition of the Department of the Interior headquarters, the General Services Administration building, and the Federal Reserve building. The shady park became a favorite lunch spot for area workers, most of whom likely do not know who John Rawlins was. A small reflecting pool, flanked by stunning magnolia trees and inviting park benches, faces the memorial, one of the few non-equestrian Civil War statues in the city. Rawlins is depicted standing with one hand on his sword hilt and the other holding a pair of field glasses, as befits a man and a statue that were so often on the move.[51]

As Markland aged, his pen became even busier. He corresponded on a variety of topics with a wide range of people, including Secretary of the Treasury Benjamin Bristow, *New York Sun* editor Charles A. Dana, Secretary of the Interior Carl Schurz, and former Confederate president Jefferson Davis (who had been Markland's father's boss). In April, when Grant was briefly in Washington, Markland stopped by his hotel to leave a letter from a friend who was interested in investing in timber property along the future route of the Mexico Southern Railroad, of which Grant was then president. But "when I called with the letter," Markland wrote, "General and Mrs. Grant were out driving." According to Grant's written reply to Markland, "I am sorry I missed you, but . . . the Mexican road with which my name is connected is not commenced, nor is it likely to be soon," and he discouraged the proposed investment.[52]

In June 1884 Markland penned a lengthy letter to Col. Thomas Wentworth Higginson in response to a newspaper article in which Higginson was mentioned. The subject was the Republican presidential candidate, James G. Blaine (who was accused of selling his influence while in Congress), and Markland regretfully excoriated him. He also expressed hope that the Democratic Party would nominate a candidate "of the highest possible potential & personal char-

The "Colonel" Becomes a "General"

acter." As it happened, the Democratic nominee, Grover Cleveland, was initially regarded as a pillar of rectitude but was soon accused of—and didn't deny—fathering a child out of wedlock. The mudslinging by both candidates reached its merciful conclusion on Election Day, when Cleveland bested Blaine by less than one-third of 1 percent of the popular vote, which translated to an Electoral College win by thirty-seven votes. One of the interesting aspects of Markland's letter to Higginson is that Markland signed it with his usual, "Your Obt Svt, A. H. Markland." Nevertheless, Higginson's brief and swift (next day) reply was addressed to "Gen. A. H. Markland."[53]

It was at about this time—spring of 1884—that Markland's childhood friend Grant suffered two terrible reversals of fortune. The first was the loss of his actual fortune, when on May 4 the investment firm of Grant & Ward suddenly dissolved and both the investors' money and Ward disappeared. Ferdinand Ward had founded the firm several years earlier with Grant's son, Ulysses Jr. (known as Buck). Ward handled the business side of what he alone knew was actually a pyramid scheme, thus swindling Buck, his father, and many other prominent people who had invested because of the Grant name. On May 5 the *New York Sun*'s front page trumpeted the news of the swindle and asked in bold type, "Is Grant Guilty?" He was not guilty in any legal sense, but his sense of honor required that he make reparations to his friends. Even the sale of all the Grants' possessions could not repay friends whose money was lost. He and Julia were bankrupt, and the whole world knew it.

As cruel as that turn of fate was, the second reversal Grant suffered that spring would prove fatal. On June 2, when he and Julia were living in reduced circumstances at their cottage on the Jersey shore, Grant bit into a peach and cried out in pain. That pain was the first sign of the cancer that would kill him barely a year later. At first only a very few people knew he was ill; his family and doctors and Grant himself would not admit to any problems, even though his voice was hoarse and he was losing weight. In October he returned to New York City and saw the leading throat specialist, Dr. John Hancock Douglas. Dr. Douglas found several cancerous growths at the base of Grant's tongue and in his throat that by then were inoperable. By the end of October, the Grants knew he had little time left. Because he had neither a presidential nor a military pension, Grant had begun to write accounts of battles for *Century Magazine* in June for money. He would soon begin writing his memoirs, which Mark Twain's company would publish. Word of his illness and his writing spread that fall, bringing some of his old comrades (and even some old enemies) to his home in New York, ostensibly to provide details about battles and maneuvers for the memoirs but mostly to see their dear friend once again. Grant kept many away, especially early on, when he tried to hide his illness, but he admitted his closest friends and those whose recollections of the war he sought to supplement his own.

Markland was one of the friends whom Grant welcomed in New York that October. Though we do not know if Markland was then aware of the gravity of Grant's illness, on December 10, 1884, Markland sent perhaps the most heartfelt letter he ever wrote to Grant. In it he referenced that October visit and once again sought to force Grant to accept credit for the idea of the military mail service.

> Referring to the subject of mail facilities for the army during the war of the rebellion, about which we had a short conversation when I was at your house in October last I am positively certain that the suggestion for that service first came from you.... [On the boat to Fort Henry in February 1862, you] asked me if I thought it possible to keep the mails up with the army as it moved and promptly collect and forward such letters as the officers and soldiers might write.... I remember that you gave as a reason for desiring such "that the troops would be more happy and contented if they could hear frequently from home and the relatives & friends at the rear would give a great encouragement to the prosecution of the war."[54]

Markland continued with a detailed description of how, after that conversation, Grant tasked him to handle his soldiers' mail and how he was then "directed" by the Post Office Department "to remain with you for the purpose of looking after the Post office Department's interests within the lines of your command. Your command finally absorbed all others and thereby I took charge of all the mail arrange-

The "Colonel" Becomes a "General"

ments for the Army of the United States." Markland protested, "I did not suggest the army mail service. You did that. . . . This may appear like a small matter and yet it is not a small matter. Leaving out all consideration of its benefits in the time of war it demonstrated the practicability of the distribution and delivery of the mails under the most adverse circumstances and out of that demonstration grew the present rail way mail service of the country."

In closing, Markland wrote to his friend of more than forty years, "In a letter written by you to Benson J. Lossing, one of the historians of the war, you gave me the credit of suggesting that branch of Army service. I was not entitled to that credit and I am unwilling to accept it especially when I know so well to whom it belongs."

By January newspapers were reporting that Grant was ill, although it would be another two months before the *New York Times* carried this blunt and awful headline: "Sinking Into the Grave: Gen. Grant's Friends Give Up Hope, Dying From Cancer." From that point on, there was a nearly daily newspaper death watch, featuring reports from his doctors (who sought to manage the news of Grant's illness) and a host of reminiscences about Grant from anyone who would talk to reporters. On numerous occasions, Markland provided insights into Grant, all with one thing in common—they made Grant look like a paragon of virtue. Whether noting that Grant never swore (Rawlins did the swearing for him) or that Grant never whispered (he refused to say in secret what he would not say in public), Markland's brotherly love and worshipful admiration for Grant shone through everything he said. In March, Markland wrote to his brother-in-law Fletcher, "Poor Grant. He is proving the adage 'that the paths of glory lead to the grave.' As I think of his going away not to return, I have an almost unspeakable sorrow. He was my school boy friend, the friend of middle age and had we reached three score & ten we would still have been friends. . . . How glad he was to see Martha & myself last fall, saying from the fullness of his heart, 'It seems like old times to see you around again.'"[55]

He told Fletcher that he had just written a letter to Julia Grant, and he enclosed a copy of a letter he had received from Fred Grant, which said, "I'm sorry I can't give you any encouragement about father. For the last three days he has been free from pain, but that is all. He get[s] more feeble every day. Please remember me to Mrs. Markland." In April Ely Parker wrote to Markland in the same clear script he had written the surrender terms at Appomattox: "General Grant is almost gone. I am very, very sorry for him."[56]

The courage and determination that Grant had shown against Confederates and the Ku Klux Klan were on national display during the year-long race to finish his memoirs before the excruciatingly painful cancer claimed his life on July 23, 1885, at the age of sixty-three. But he managed to beat the deadline battle, submitting his final pages to Twain on July 19 and thus providing his beloved Julia with royalties of roughly $500,000 over the remainder of her life.

As Markland reminisced with friends and reporters before and after Grant's death, he may have thought back to the Maysville Academy, where he and Hiram Ulysses Grant participated in the Philomathean Society, and to that debate in 1832 he was assigned to judge. The topic had addressed an issue that frequently arose in the young republic: "*Resolved,* That America can boast of as great men as any other nation." Markland had fallen asleep during the debate, and when he awoke at its conclusion, he had nothing by which to judge the winning side except his thought that America was younger than other nations, so had less time in which to produce great men. As a result, he had given the win to the negative side. More than fifty years later, had he been asked the same question, Absalom Markland could have ruled in the affirmative from personal acquaintance with two of the United States'—and the world's—greatest men: Abraham Lincoln and Ulysses Grant.

ELEVEN

A Man in Search of Himself

1885–88

While Markland was a special agent of the Post Office Department, he traveled to places across the continent, from New York City to San Francisco and from New Orleans to Savannah, with countless trips between Louisville, Cairo, Memphis, Nashville, City Point, and Washington. His world shrank dramatically when he resigned his position in 1874.

It appears that afterward he and Martha traveled infrequently, mainly to army society meetings and to Concord, Massachusetts, to visit his sister Violinda and her husband, Fletcher. Markland's health was never good after 1874, when he wrote about having catarrh, the ailment that affected his ears, nose, and throat. We know from letters to Martha decades earlier that he had suffered from ear problems. As mentioned earlier, chronic catarrh can cause loss of hearing. In 1900, the first year that the U.S. Census tracked the causes of deafness, medical doctors attributed to catarrh nearly one-third of the approximately thirty-five thousand cases of adults who had lost hearing after the age of twenty. By 1883 fifty-eight-year-old Absalom Markland had entered the silent world of the deaf.[1]

Helen Keller, born in 1880 and left blind and deaf after an illness at the age of nineteen months, said of her two disabilities, "Being deaf is much worse than being sightless." More than a century earlier, the great British literary figure Samuel Johnson had called deafness "the most desperate of human calamities," since it robs deaf people and all those around them of the ability to communicate easily. Even the nineteenth century's explosion of inventions and "cures" for deafness barely improved the life of a deaf person, although Alexander Graham Bell (whose wife and mother were deaf) and Thomas Edison (who was deaf himself) were working on devices to improve hearing in the late 1800s.[2]

It is a ceaseless, tiring struggle to understand and communicate in a silent world. Various forms of sign language were taught in the late nineteenth century, mostly to children who were deaf from birth. For one who is "late-deafened"—whose loss of hearing occurs after acquiring language skills—there are additional challenges. A late-deafened person's ability to speak well often leads listeners to forget or even to disbelieve that the person cannot hear, creating additional stress. In addition, the person who loses hearing, especially if it happens gradually over time, undergoes a lengthy grieving process for that lost ability not unlike the five stages of grief over a death: denial, anger, bargaining, depression, and acceptance. Even today, late-acquired deafness can be an isolating and depressing experience.[3]

In the late 1800s, newspapers featured advertisements for a plethora of hearing devices and patent remedies. The former—often an ear trumpet in the guise of a cane or a lady's fan—provided little help except to those with mild hearing losses. The latter were ineffective and often harmful quack treatments, like the ones concocted from snakes that Chinese laborers brought to California during the gold rush, giving rise to the epithet "snake oil." Nearly forty years later, one of the most widely advertised cures for deafness was also marketed as an oil from China but not made from snakes: "Foo Choo's Balsam of Shark's Oil."[4]

We do not know if Markland experimented with any of these innovative offerings, but we do know he dealt with his deafness for the most part by removing himself from society, a cruel blow to one so sociable. By February 1885 he was being described as "leading a retired life." A later report said, "During recent years, deafness prevented him from enjoying general society." Perhaps in compensation for his auditory isolation, he ramped up his correspondence with a host of friends and even some bare acquaintances. He wrote numerous stories for publication, too, which he mailed to newspapers and magazines. The man on whom millions of Americans once depended

A Man in Search of Himself

to stay connected through the postal service became dependent on the mail himself for his primary means of communication with the world. In deafness, Markland found his voice as a writer.[5]

Markland particularly delighted in recounting stories of the war years that featured Grant and Sherman. He furnished laudatory tales of Grant to so many journalists after the former president's tragic death in July 1885 that Markland wrote to old friends from Maysville days, asking if they could provide him any new stories to supplement his own. This is the period of his life when Markland told the tales of newly commissioned Lieutenant General Grant's anonymity aboard the train from Culpeper Court House to Washington and of the singular pass across all military lines that Grant gave him in 1864. Markland provided a Pittsburgh newspaper with copies of two letters written in 1862 by Col. George Ihrie to Iowa senator James Harlan blasting Harlan for his remarks on the Senate floor "that Gen. Grant was in the habit of becoming intoxicated and was unfit to have the command of troops." Markland's tales of the quartermaster conned by the spurious "General Clark," the diplomatic kerfuffle arising from the pronunciation of "L Street," and his confession that he smoked the good cigars destined for Sherman in Savannah all appeared in newspapers in the 1880s. While Markland never wrote of Grant as less than dignified, he was willing to poke fun at Sherman.[6]

In fact, no wartime story of Markland's received wider publication than one with Sherman as the target of a joke. It was variously headlined "Old Tecumseh" or "The Old Flanker Flanked" in newspapers across the country. The *Omaha Daily Bee* revealed the story was "from the manuscript notes of Col. A. H. Markland, the head of the mail service during the war." To appreciate its humor, you need to know that in the nineteenth century, one of the most common medicines in use was "Seidlitz powder," which, when dissolved in water, had the bubbly appearance of Alka-Seltzer and the purgative effect of a strong laxative.[7]

It was while Sherman was visiting General Howard's headquarters tent in Goldsboro, North Carolina, in 1865 that Sherman "felt the need of a small draught of whisky to drive off the malarial effects of the climate on his system." Sherman knew, however, that Howard would have no whisky, due to his "rigid temperance proclivities." So, when the camp medical director, Dr. John Moore, came into the tent, Sherman "gave him the wink and said, 'Doctor, have you a Seidlitz powder in your quarters?'" Before the doctor could reply, Howard spoke up, saying, "General Sherman, it is not necessary to go to the doctor's quarters. I have plenty of Seidlitz powders here, and good ones, too. I will get you one." As Sherman protested that Howard should not trouble himself since the doctor's tent was nearby, he looked to the doctor for help. But Dr. Moore, "who was a great wag," saw an opportunity for mischief. He slyly told Sherman that he did not believe he had any Seidlitz powder in his tent. "By this time, General Howard had the powder all ready for use and handed the glass to General Sherman," according to Markland. "Rather than offend Howard by saying he meant whisky he drank the foaming stuff down to his disgust, to the satisfaction of General Howard and to the amusement of the staff officers."

Markland continued his active correspondence with Ely Parker, in which Grant was almost always the topic of conversation. In June 1885 Parker responded to a letter from Markland, who had apparently complained about an article by Grant's former staff officer Adam Badeau in the *Century Magazine*. In it Badeau not only skipped over the Maysville days in his description of Grant's early life but also failed to mention that Grant's given name was Hiram Ulysses, by which Markland first knew him. Parker wrote "that your old schoolmate of Maysville, Ky, was no other than the present grand hero, Genl Ulysses Simpson Grant, who himself says, in his yet unpublished memoirs, that he went to school at Maysville, Ky." Parker then wrote, "The change of name occurred, as I have gathered from camp conversations during the war, by the warrant of appointment to West Point, which was for Ulysses Simpson Grant instead of Hiram Ulysses Grant." Parker claimed Badeau "must have known all this, and why he ignored it in his article, I cannot imagine, unless it is that he will not condescend to dabble in seemingly small things and loves generalization." Parker closed his letter, written barely a month before Grant's death, with, "Your suggestion of the duty and responsibility devolving on those who have been closely connected with Gen. Grant, of preserving in some shape or form their recollections of him is an excellent one."[8]

Grant's death was followed by the nation's largest funeral procession to date and the temporary entombment of his body in a vault in New York's Riverside Park, to await determination of his final resting place and construction of his memorial. His only definitive instructions had been that Julia should be buried with him, but he did not say where. Grant's family and friends were besieged by reporters for insight and recommendations on the location for his interment, and cities around the country vied for the privilege of hosting the hero's remains. When asked by the *Evening Star* for his recommendation, Markland said, "After the death of Gen. McPherson, the news of which affected Gen. Grant very much, he said he supposed Gen. McPherson should be buried at West Point. He added, 'I would like to be buried at West Point myself, because it was there that I was fitted to command an army, and I will die a soldier.'" But West Point did not allow women to be buried there, so when pressed for another location, Markland said, "Galena [Illinois], by all means," and after that, he recommended Grant's final residence, the cabin on New York's Mount McGregor, where he died. After much discussion and debate over many sites, Grant's body was moved in 1897 into one of two identical red granite sarcophagi in the magnificent monument dedicated to him on Riverside Drive in New York City. When Julia died in 1902, her body was laid to rest next to his, as he had insisted.[9]

Markland also carried on an extensive correspondence with Charles A. Dana, who served as assistant secretary of war under Lincoln and who became publisher of the *New York Sun*. In many of his letters, Dana thanked Markland for furnishing war stories, which he eagerly published. For example, on January 6, 1887, Dana wrote that he was "very much obliged to you for that letter about Grant. It is very good and new, and does honor both to Grant and Rawlins. I expect to publish it on Sunday." On Sunday, January 9, the *Sun* did indeed carry Markland's firsthand account of how Grant was approached by the Democrats to run for president but eventually accepted the Republican nomination, which Rawlins had recommended. Some letters revealed Dana's own insights, as when he wrote to Markland later in January: "I know that your view of Rawlins's feeling in the first six months of 1869 (Grant's first year as president) is not exaggerated. 'If things are to go on this way,' he said to me one day in the time after the Cabinet had been installed, 'it would have been better if we had elected [Horatio] Seymour.'"[10]

In another series of letters touching on Rawlins, Markland wrote to Sherman in July 1887 to dispute Sherman's claim that John Rawlins was the "chief of staff" whom Grant claimed in his memoirs had opposed the March to the Sea. Markland said that he had been at Grant's City Point headquarters during the time the campaign was under discussion and that he did not hear any words of opposition from Rawlins. In a letter to Ely Parker on the same subject, Markland pointed the finger at Halleck, who had become effectively the first "chief of staff" of the army when Grant was promoted to lieutenant general over him in 1864. Parker replied that Markland's designation of Halleck as the chief of staff in question "is ingenious and generous, but I do not agree with you. . . . Rawlins is the man to whom Grant points, yet we will look in vain for any evidence to sustain the assertion." Parker concluded, "The shaft cannot be turned on Halleck, who was not Grant's Chief of Staff, who was not his friend, and who never gave him one iota more aid than the law and regulations compelled him to give."[11]

Perhaps the most interesting letter Markland wrote during this time was one to former Confederate president Jefferson Davis after President Grover Cleveland announced he would return Confederate battle flags that U.S. forces had captured. Cleveland agreed with a suggestion by Adj. Gen. R. F. Drum that it would be a "graceful act" of reconciliation to return the flags being stored by the War Department, and Cleveland issued the general's statement as an executive order. It created a firestorm in the ranks of the GAR and every other army society and was a topic of impassioned debate in newspapers all over the nation. Davis, who was then touring the South and appearing at numerous celebrations of Confederate heritage, was sought for his opinion on the subject. Newspapers reported that he opposed the flags' return as a sign of reconciliation, since he said former Confederates would never renounce their "principles," and he believed it would be merely an opportunity for each side to renew its disagreements with the other.[12]

Markland began his letter to Davis, "My dear Sir, Presuming on an acquaintance with you as a public man in the decade immediately preceding the year 1861," and went on to discuss the status of the captured battle flags, agreeing with Davis that Cleveland and his administration had made several mistakes in deciding to return the flags and that it was a subject best left alone. In the letter, Markland took a shot at Cleveland, the first man elected president in the postwar era not to have served in the military: "It is the fellows who were not in the war, and who were far removed from the danger line, who resurrect disturbing relics of the war." It is a lengthy letter, full of talk of reconciliation efforts and battle flag etiquette and errors by politicians North and South, but without a particular purpose other than perhaps to enable Markland to connect with his own past through the man who had employed his father so many years ago as a clerk in the War Department.[13]

The 1880s marked the publication of many Civil War memoirs as books, in magazines, and in newspapers, by famous and unknown participants alike. Their steady output kept Markland busy, since he took pains to correct the historical record at every opportunity. Whether he was disputing the name of the vessel that was Grant's headquarters boat during the Battle of Fort Donelson or was pushing back on tales of Grant's drunkenness aboard a steamboat to Nashville in 1862, Markland wrote detailed firsthand accounts to editors, publishers, and authors to set the record straight. He was even planning to dispute a passage about the Battle of Shiloh in Grant's memoirs, he wrote Fletcher, by writing "the story of the old log house at Pittsburg Landing." Markland contended, "It was my HdQtrs before and after the battle of Shiloh and has been the subject of as much misstatement as the battle itself." He continued, "Even Genl Grant could not tell the truth about it. He says it was under the hill when it was the only house on the hill."[14]

From nearly the beginning of the Civil War, when he wrote under the byline "Oily Buckshot," Markland told friends and reporters he was writing his war stories for publication. However, there is no evidence he ever collected them into a manuscript for a book. Markland humorously claimed that Sherman had discouraged him from "writing up the pleasantries of camp life," as a newspaper article in 1887 recorded. "Don't," Sherman told him, perhaps reflecting upon his own experiences after publishing his memoirs fifteen years earlier: "Some fellows you will have to leave out, and they will be certain to be disgusted. Some of the fellows you put in will not think they are well enough treated, and you will on the whole involve yourself in a mess of trouble and make no end of enemies." Sherman also returned the manuscript Markland had sent him earlier that year about Gen. John McClernand claiming credit for the victory at Arkansas Post in 1863. It was folded three times, with this endorsement:

Dear Markland—

I doubt if I should publish this. McClernand was a brave & patriotic officer, and is now very sensitive. If he claims the originating of the expedition which he [illegible] commanded I don't object—All I wanted was to cover that flank preparatory to the next movement on Vicksburg. This was done promptly & effectively and I care little who conceived the idea or planned the expedition. It is sufficient that it was done & well done. I have all the honor I covet.[15]

There is also no extant diary such as Markland mentioned to Charles Dana—at least, there is none available to the historian. Instead, Markland penned his war stories one at a time and forwarded them to various outlets, where they were welcomed and published, though there is no record he was ever paid for his writing. His opinions and insights and remembrances of the war were sought and valued even amid hundreds of offerings by more famous participants.[16]

But he wrote about more than the war, and some of his recollections unrelated to the war were compiled into a book that was published in his hometown. Published under the pseudonym "O.B.," Markland wrote a series of letters, ostensibly to his old friend John P. Phister, which were first published as letters to the editor in the

Maysville Republican newspaper and later published as *"O.B.'s" Reminiscences: Memories of Old Maysville between the years 1832 and 1848.* In sixteen letters written over ten months in 1883, Markland delved into his past, recalling vast numbers of people, places, and events in the bustling city of Maysville during his youth. Most of the stories were humorous, and most of them were true, but he deliberately fudged some details for comic effect and to obscure his identity. He warned the reader in his third letter, "My reminiscences partake of the unexpected. They are not chronological, alphabetical, or governed by any well-planned order of regularity. I fear they may not be strictly accurate in all details."[17]

Indeed, they were not. From the opening salutation in the letters to his childhood friend of roughly the same age ("Dr. John P. Phister—My Young Friend"), to references to his daughter and son-in-law (of which he had neither), to his claim to have seen the Sphinx in Egypt, Markland sprinkled falsehoods like fairy dust through his letters to keep readers of the *Maysville Republican* entertained and guessing about the author. Some of his tales of old Maysville seem like tall tales, until the reader visits Maysville and finds physical evidence for those memories.

The "O.B." series of letters was sparked in January 1883 by a report in the *New Maysville Republican* that the market house in the city was to be demolished. Nearly five hundred miles away in Washington DC, that news triggered Markland's vivid childhood memories of the building in the town that he loved. Indeed, his letters, when read together, evoke the magical realism of *Dandelion Wine*, Ray Bradbury's paean to his hometown of Waukegan, Illinois. In Letter #1 from Washington DC, "O.B." wrote,

> I read [about the market house's destruction] with feelings something akin to sorrow. Among my early recollections of Maysville, the market house always looms up as the most prominent feature. It was the playground of my boyhood days; under its roof I heard the first political speeches; in its primitive days it was the opera house of the city. . . . In it the magician performed his tricks. . . . In the time of pestilence in 1832, it was the morgue. . . . On Wednesday and Sun-

day mornings the people, regardless of age, sex or previous condition of servitude, met under its roof or on the pavements adjacent; they were not called sidewalks then.

The old market house was a huge wooden structure built in 1829 in the center of town on what was then called Main Cross Road but quickly was renamed Market Street. "Market days were grand days in Maysville," Markland recalled. "Through that old market house was the fashionable promenade of the city." In succeeding letters, he remembered Abijah Casto, whose grocery was just west of the market, and "Mathew Markland [who] kept a grocery on the east side of the market house." Without mentioning his relationship to Matthew, Markland observed that the man "was a 'squire who made decisions according to the equities."

Markland wrote about natural wonders, like the spectacular meteor shower of 1833. He also recalled natural disasters, such as the great flood of February 1832, when the Ohio River rose more than sixty feet above its banks. From the heights above Maysville, he wrote, the whole town watched "houses, barns, hay stacks, stock, and all the paraphernalia of a farm floating by without any means of saving them."

Maysville's destiny was written in the path that the bison pounded between Lexington and the Ohio River. Along with the Buffalo Trace, the other major physical feature of Maysville is the Ohio River, formed by the confluence of the Allegheny and Monongahela Rivers near Pittsburgh, Pennsylvania. It flows generally southwestward nearly one thousand miles to join the Mississippi at Cairo, Illinois; Maysville is roughly halfway along its journey. Flooding was an ever-present danger to the community.[18]

Maysville lies along a crescent-shaped bend in the river, where steep, wooded hills rise from a slender riparian plain just three city blocks deep. The turnpike to Lexington, which had a toll house just outside the city limits, winds sharply uphill, west from the city up and around the heights above Maysville before it stretches southwestward, following the original Buffalo Trace. From the river, one can walk easily only from Front Street to Second Street to Third Street before the ground rises sharply to Fourth Street (where the sidewalk becomes a steep, block-long staircase) and then again to Fifth, the last numbered street that can be accommodated by the terrain. The hills are so vertical that to an observer across the river, Maysville appeared like an "Italian hill town." The old part of the city is itself crescent-shaped. As one historian wrote, "Unlike other Ohio River towns, Maysville is not oriented to the four points of the compass but echoes the course of the adjacent river." In later years, the city expanded upon the ridge high above the city, but in Markland's day, the heart of the city was essentially five blocks wide and three blocks deep.[19]

Within that small area, Markland's memory summoned hundreds of colorful tales and details from the past. He recalled "our old African friend, Richard Craig," the town crier and auctioneer, who in his "fantastic dress . . . used to scour the town, bell in hand . . . ringing up lost children." He remembered that when Charles Williams became mayor, "he became a convert to the doctrine that incessant labor would destroy the strongest constitution." Markland observed that "by a rigid adherence to that doctrine he has been enabled to live to a green old age." Markland honored the stonecutter James Phillips of Market Street: "He carved all the tombstones for the city and neighborhood. I used to go there and read about blissful immortality, good husbands and wives, devoted fathers and mothers, dutiful children, etc. . . . I thought better of the world then than I do now."

Markland paid humorous tribute to Maysville's many hatmakers in Letter #3, including T. S. Thornly, William Tinker, Henry L. Davis, and John F. Mitchell. "In no city of the world were heavier and harder hats made than in Maysville," he declared. "I have often thought that if I had gone to school to Rand & Richeson [the Maysville Academy] and never worn any Maysville manufactured hats I would have been a factor in the finances of the world [but] no intellect, however gigantic, could flourish under such a hat." In the next letter, he reminisced about the cabinetmaker on Third and Limestone Streets, Andrew Mitchell. He pondered whether he and the hatmaker with the same surname were brothers, because "if Andrew's make of coffins were as solid as were the hats made by John F.[,] there may be some delay in the burial grounds round about Maysville on resurrection day."

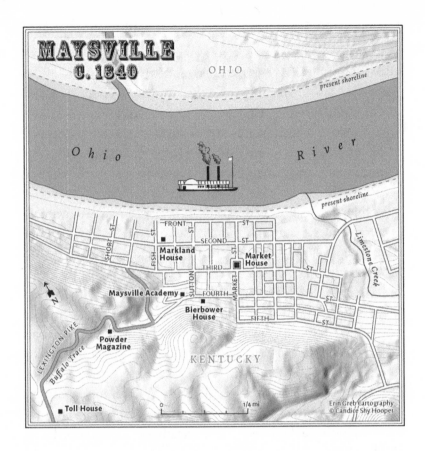

Map 3. Maysville, Kentucky, ca. 1840. Erin Greb Cartography.

But the most memorable figure in his letters was not a person. It was a cannon called "Old Tip," which Markland introduced in Letter #2. "Now that the market house . . . soon will be thundering down the track of ages, I will direct your attention to a different type of celebrity and one that was a factor in fun, politics, liberty and charity nearly fifty years ago," Markland began. In 1835 or 1836, he wrote, "two of the old Maysville boys" visited Pittsburgh and decided to buy a cannon from the city's armory because the weapon was "condemned and for sale for ninety dollars." It was a six-pounder (the weight of cannonball it shot), which was at the time deemed "a heavy gun." The young men bought the cannon and had it loaded onto the steamboat for Maysville, where it arrived about midnight. No matter what time a steamboat arrived, Markland recalled, "it was the custom at that time for all draymen and hotel porters in the city to be at the wharf."

The new artillerists soon found an individual whose master hired him out as a drayman (someone who drove a two-wheeled cart, called a dray) and with his help loaded the gun "with the muzzle towards the tail of the dray so that when the horse was taken out of the shafts the elevation would be about right." News of the cannon and rumors "that there would be music in the air" spread quickly through the night, and at least half a dozen young men joined the cannon on its trip from the river up Sutton Street, "then up the hill by the way of the pike," until they reached a small, level area not far from the Maysville Powder Magazine. The dray's traces were removed from the horse, the gun was pointed to the east, and the young amateur artillerists "loaded her to the brim and rammed it until exhausted with the work." A match was applied to a slow fuse, while the crew covered their ears and ducked under a ridge to hear the results of their industry in safety.

Fifty years on, in his shell of silence, the deaf Markland vividly recalled the moment:

> Great heavens, since the foundation of the world no such music had
> ever been heard in that section as that gun gave forth. . . . The recoil
> of the gun started the dray down the pike. The explosion frightened

the horse. We could hear the clatter of his feet and the jingle of his harness as he ran up the pike. He was found next day in Washington, having with great good judgment avoided all the tollgates. The drayman, who was a slave and belonged to Jim Artus, broke for Canada, and was never heard of about Maysville afterwards. The music of that gun soothed him on his weary way to the land of freedom.

The next day being market day, everyone learned the full details of the cannon's arrival and its "successful test," and it "was ever afterward, so far as I know, the pet of Maysville and Mason County."

Indeed it was. A carriagemaker volunteered his services to build a dedicated wagon for the gun, which made its appearance in parades and at town picnics over many years.[20] The same young men used it more than once to raise money "at the cannon's mouth" for favorite local charities by hauling the gun near enough homes to break glass, then pledging to move it if funds were donated to the benevolent cause. It was in the presidential campaign of 1840 that the cannon got its name. That contest pitted the hero of the Battle of Tippecanoe in 1811, William Henry Harrison, and his running mate, John Tyler—"Tippecanoe and Tyler, too!"—against Martin Van Buren. "Old Tip" was emblazoned on the side of the cannon's carriage, and it was stationed at the river end of Sutton Street as part of Harrison's "log cabin and hard cider campaign." Markland claimed that "it contributed its voice towards elevating the grand original 'Old Tip' to the presidential chair."

Originally labeled "condemned"—meaning surplus to the army's needs—the gun earned the negative connotation of the word, too, since "nearly every time it was used it did sad work," Markland recalled, and "some man's life or limb paid the forfeit." Nonetheless, it remained a fixture of Maysville, and "its hoarse bellowing reverberating through the hills" always gave him "a feeling of delight." Markland's memories of Old Tip sparked somber memories as well. This one is from Letter #2:

When war was abroad in the land[,] I used to think of that gun. . . . Who of the confederates that lay in the field of Shiloh after the first day's fight will ever forget the four minute guns fired from the U.S.

A Man in Search of Himself

gunboats lying in the Tennessee river . . . the pitiless rain was falling in torrents on the living, dead and dying. The belching of those great guns every four minutes and the frightful screeching of the shells as they shot up into the heavens and dropped into the camps was the essence of despair. I know how it was and knowing it can draw the line between "Old Tip" and the murderous guns of war.

In Letter #9, dated June 7, 1883, Markland returned to memories of the war, this time because he had traveled from Washington DC to Louisville and along the way "visited the scenes of my early days in the war." He recalled Fort Donelson, writing, "Oh! how bitter cold it was. How the snow hail and sleet did fall, and how illy prepared the soldiers were for this infliction of the elements." Grant's victory there "upset all the calculations of the confederacy, and especially did it run the city of Nashville wild." He remembered his days as postmaster at Nashville, when he encountered his old Maysville neighbor, the Reverend Dr. Edgar. "In fact, I remember ten thousand things intimately connected with war times in that state capital," but he cautioned, "I am not a historian of the war."

Markland used several tricks to hide the identity of "O.B." Letter #2, written from "Washington City" on January 30, 1883, closed with an outright lie. "I will say to you that I do not live here," wrote the Washington resident. "I am here by reason of the misfortunes of my son-in-law. He got elected to congress. I am sure he is sorry for it now." And the childless Markland threw more dust in the readers' eyes. "My daughter don't like the aristocratic flummery of society here." Sometimes he went to even greater lengths to obscure his association with "O.B." In a letter to Fletcher, Markland wrote that he had asked a friend to write his previous "O.B." letter and another friend to take it to Augusta, Kentucky, to mail it, thereby disguising both the handwriting and the postmark.[21]

So, what do the initials "O.B." signify? Because he mentions the "old boys of Maysville" several times, the logical conclusion would be that they stand for *Old Boy*. But there are important clues that lead to another conclusion. In Letter #1, dated January 18, 1883, "O.B." wrote, "In the magnificence and grandeur of old Maysville she was the first to erect beacon lights on the banks of the Ohio river for the benefit of commerce and navigation. Away back in 1834 or 1835, council directed that two large lamps or lanterns should be put up; one at the foot of Main Cross or Market street, the other at the foot of Sutton street, so that the steamboat pilots might be enabled to find the city on dark nights."

Two months earlier, a strikingly similar item appeared on the front page of the *Louisville Courier-Journal* under the byline "Oily Buckshot." Another clue appears in a letter he wrote to Fletcher: "Phister has not answered the letter I wrote him from this city over my river name." Oily Buckshot was his river name—that is, his steamboat crew name—in the 1840s. While he was reminiscing about his childhood in Maysville, he was also reliving another part of his past, his steamboat days.[22]

Although Markland never lived in Maysville after he left in 1848, the "O.B." letters are proof of the city's lifelong hold on him. He may not have always accurately recorded its people, places, and events, but they were deeply etched in his memory. His desire to reconnect with them is evident in every line of the seventy-five single-spaced typeset pages published as the collection of his letters—and in the promise of a "second volume, which we hope to have serially [published] during the winter," but which, alas, never appeared.[23]

Markland also reminisced about Abraham Lincoln at the request of Allen Thorndyke Rice, publisher of the *North American Review*, who collected and edited *Reminiscences of Abraham Lincoln by the Distinguished Men of His Time*, published in 1886. The thirty-three distinguished men included Ulysses S. Grant (Fred Grant submitted several anecdotes his father had excised from his *Memoirs*), former secretary of state Elihu Washburne, orator and activist Frederick Douglass, abolitionist Henry Ward Beecher, poet and humanitarian Walt Whitman, Gen. Benjamin F. Butler, former member of the House of Representatives William Kelley, and Absalom Markland, who spoke of how he first met Lincoln "shortly after his inauguration," recalling,

A few weeks after the occupation of Paducah, Kentucky, I went to that section of the State as a Government officer, and from that time until the close of the war I was in the lines of the United States Army. I returned to Washington at monthly intervals and always called on Mr. Lincoln at such times. . . . I was one of the officers of the government who came east with General Grant in March, 1864, [and] from that time until December, 1864, when I left to join General Sherman with the mails for his army when it came out to the sea, there was scarcely a week I did not see him.[24]

From his vantage point, Markland refuted the notion that the strong personalities in the president's cabinet had controlled Lincoln. "My observation was quite to the contrary. He was the master spirit of his administration." As president, Markland wrote, Lincoln "always had the courage to do the proper thing at the proper time." Like Markland, Lincoln was "favored with a fund of humor and sense of the ridiculous . . . but as President he used those gifts, if they may be called gifts, for a worthy and laudable purpose. When oppressed with care and anxiety, beset with importunities he could not grant, humor was to him a relief, and encouragement to his despondent listener." He recounted the story of how Lincoln ingeniously resolved the disagreement between Stanton and Blair over the handling of Grant's mail in the East and how Lincoln asked Markland to carry his message "God bless him and God bless his army" to Sherman at Savannah. Abraham Lincoln was a man of "unselfish patriotism and unyielding integrity," Markland concluded.[25]

Markland was not the only one of his peers who was reminiscing about his past as he grew older. Sherman, five years older than Markland, had published his memoirs in 1875 and reflected on the war in annual letters he and Markland exchanged around the winter holidays. Markland wrote Fletcher that he valued Sherman's 1885 letter because of "the very beautiful language in which he refers to the identity of Martha & myself with the war." In January 1886, Sherman wrote from St. Louis: "Though twenty years have intervened the memories of the war come back with the vividness of yesterday. Especially such as you recall, when you were always connected with the branch of service which united us with our homes & friends."[26]

In late December 1885 the Shermans were living in the Fifth Avenue Hotel in New York City, where the general penned another heartfelt letter to Markland, who was living at the Clarendon Hotel in Washington DC. Sherman hoped Markland would

> continue many years to receive the assurance of the love of the many thousands to whom you carried comfort & solace in the days of the war. What you say of the early events at Paducah & Arkansas Post are known to but few of the living and now that John Logan is gone we are all reminded that the Civil War will soon be as much in the past the Revolutionary War. . . . You were a witness of many most interesting events, and your testimony should be carefully worded for present or future publication.[27]

Sherman not only acknowledged Markland's wartime service to the army but also recognized his continuing influence within the military family. In late 1886 he sought Markland's assistance in stopping the spread of a false report regarding one of Sherman's speeches. Markland had apparently heard that Sherman blamed the continuing delays in compiling and publishing the official "war records" on Capt. Robert N. Scott, who was laboring to manage that daunting task. Sherman wrote that he "did not know that my remarks at the Union League were reported." He wanted Markland "and all your friends to understand that I don't blame Scott for the dilatory publishing of the War Records." Instead, Sherman placed the blame on the government for not "providing the means from the first." And he added, "Now I fear the Government, having passed into the hands of those who opposed the war, these Records may never reach completion." The monumental project, *The War of the Rebellion: A Compilation of the Official Records of the Union and Confederate Armies*, was finally completed in 1901.[28]

In 1887 Markland responded to an invitation from Crocker's Iowa Brigade, composed of officers and soldiers who "served with honor" in the brigade during the war, to attend its fourth reunion on September 21–22 in Davenport, Iowa. He vowed that he and his wife would be there, "barring the contingencies of physical disability," to see again many of the "officers and men I knew personally in the years of the war."[29]

A Man in Search of Himself

Shortly after accepting that invitation, Markland regretfully declined one from the Society of the Army of the Tennessee because its annual meeting in Detroit was too close in time to the Crocker's Brigade meeting, and "'tho I am yet young, too much travel vexes me." The letter was addressed to Gen. O. M. Poe, in his capacity as head of the local organizing committee, and Markland continued, "I have in my mind, as I write, those young officers and genial fellows, Buell and Reese, who used to ring the cow bell that good fellows might come and enjoy the hospitality of their quarters in Savannah." He recalled, "You and I and some other fellows lived a quiet life in family quarters on Bull Street." And in an aside, he wrote, "We tried prohibition in the army, but some how or other it failed, as it will fail wherever good fellows meet, and even General Howard's head-quarters was not a dreary waste."[30]

Even as Markland maintained an extensive correspondence, he also continued to serve as attorney and counselor to a few friends and clients. In 1885 Markland took the time to write a letter of rec- . ommendation to President Grover Cleveland on behalf of Gen. Don Carlos Buell. Buell was seeking a government position in Washington DC, and Markland praised Buell as "among the very able men now in private life in this country. . . . He would fill any office of trust with credit." Buell was, in fact, appointed to serve as a government pension agent that year and held that position for four years, until his health declined. When "Colonel" Markland penned that letter to help General Buell, he may have recalled the many generals who had praised him and supported him for government positions over the years. In 1887 Markland prepared two documents comprising eight pages of closely written legal arguments in support of Charles H. Page, an unsuccessful Democratic candidate for the House of Representatives in 1884, but there is no record of a formal legal appeal. And in late 1887, Markland's old friend Alex Boteler, who was then a pardons clerk in the Department of Justice, reported to him there was no news on the status of a legal action he and Boteler were pursuing with regard to a coaling station in Hawaii.[31]

As Markland reminisced about the places and people of his past, his thoughts turned inward, sparked by a trip he and Martha took in

1885 to Winchester, Kentucky, where he was born. After they returned home, he wrote a chatty five-page letter to Fletcher, declaring, "I am more interested in working out the history of my grandfather [Absalom] Hanks than I have ever been." But he made little progress until the following year, when the monumental Nicolay and Hay biography of Lincoln was published serially in the *Century Illustrated Magazine*. The first installment, containing a genealogy of the sixteenth president, emphasized the Lincoln family's close relationship with Daniel Boone and related Thomas Lincoln's marriage to Nancy Hanks. Markland told Fletcher that reading it once again prompted him to reflect upon his own family's heritage, and Markland explored that subject in lengthy letters to his twice-brother-in-law and lifelong best friend. He focused on what seemed to him more than mere coincidence: his mother's maiden name was Hanks, as was Lincoln's. Both of their families were originally from Virginia, and Kentucky loomed large in their lives. Were they related?[32]

At first blush, it seems strange that this question had not occurred to Markland earlier. After all, he had visited often with Lincoln before and during the war—why had the question of a possible family relationship not been raised? Of course his meetings with Lincoln before the war were political gatherings with other men, and in that situation private conversations would have been difficult. During the war their meetings were focused on mail and war matters—serious business that may not have lent itself to personal musings by Markland. And it is quite possible that at that point Markland did not know Abraham Lincoln's mother's maiden name. Lincoln had come from the back of a large pack of candidates to win the Republican nomination in 1860, and the presidential election in that fraught autumn focused much more on national issues of slavery and secession than on details of the candidates' personal lives.

But why did Lincoln not comment on Markland's middle name when they met? It is highly unlikely that Lincoln ever knew Absalom's middle name—or even his first name—unless Markland made a point of telling Lincoln his full name aloud. Like so many men of his time, Markland was referred to by his initials in official correspondence, and he signed personal letters (including those written to Martha) with his initials. Similarly, close friends referred to him as "Markland" or "Colonel" in their letters or speeches. "A. H. Markland" is the name on the documents that Lincoln endorsed in 1861 to give Markland a post in the War Department. Indeed, of the hundreds of contemporaneous documents to, from, and about Markland that were located for this biography, exactly zero feature all three names. One uses a name and an initial: the misspelled newspaper advertisement for "Absolem H. Markland" as a traveling agent in 1845. The rest all use "A. H. Markland."[33]

Even if we put aside the question of why Markland and Lincoln had not compared their "Hanks" lineages in the 1860s, it still may seem odd that the ever-curious Markland waited such a long time to think about his family's history. But there are several reasons he may have delayed his investigation into his past.

Youth is the time to look to the future, not the past, especially if one is a self-made man fully occupied in the business of making a living or surviving a war. Retirement brings with it the gift of time, time to develop an interest and explore the past. A survey of one thousand genealogists done in 2020 found that their average age was 56.7 years. Of the total, 0.2 percent were less than 30 years old and only 4.4 percent under the age of 40. The survey sponsor concluded, "There is a very specific and close relation between age and the interest for one's own family history." At 60 years old, Markland fit the profile of today's genealogist.[34]

Markland may also have felt hesitant about digging into his past earlier in his life because he knew it would arouse painful memories of his father's disappearance and apparent suicide in 1855, as well as his later disability. When Matthew Markland, the Maysville justice and town elder who had known Ulysses Grant's uncle Peter and Daniel Boone's cousin Jacob, surrendered to his demons and disappeared on that Sunday morning in Washington DC, Absalom was left to pick up the pieces for himself, his siblings, and his father. That had to have been arduous. In a chatty letter to Fletcher thirty years later, after a lengthy discussion of his maternal grandfather, Absalom Hanks ("a man of powerful size and great influence"), Markland wrote that he learned in Winchester that "Father is said to have been the highest liver and best entertainer in the county in his day." Then Markland observed, "The stories & mysteries of family life & doings are not told until too late." He concluded, "May be it is well," thus turning—as he often did—to ponder the darker side of life.[35]

Or Markland may have postponed thinking of his past because he wished to avoid confronting an aspect of both Matthew Markland's and Absalom Hanks's lives that was antithetical to his own. His father and grandfather had enslaved men, women, and children. In a letter to Markland, James Flanagan, one of the men in Winchester who was the source of much information for Markland in the 1880s, recalled that "at his death in 1829, [Absalom] Hanks was the owner of between 50 & 60 Negroes of all ages and sexes." It appears that Flanagan's memory was faulty with respect to the number of enslaved persons in Absalom Hanks's household, as well as the precise year of the man's death, since an inventory of Hanks's slaves in 1828, stating to whom they were "allocated" in his will, listed ten males and six females and their monetary value at that time. Two were allocated to Matthew Markland—"Dick (Hanks) (Markland), $425," and "Daniel (Hanks) (Markland), a man subject to rheumatism, $350." Matthew may have had more already or may have added to that number afterward, since twelve years later the 1840 census listed Matthew Markland of Maysville, Kentucky, as part of a household of six "Free White Persons" forty-nine years old or younger and four "Slaves" between the ages of fifty-four and ten.[36]

Although his maternal grandfather and his father had enslaved people, Absalom never did. His familial regard for those men may have been the reason that in one "O.B." letter he included the time-worn apologia of enslavers and their sympathizers: "I may say that the slaves [of Maysville] were well treated." But that familial regard did not persuade him to remain the Democrat he had been in the years just before the war or to speak in support of slavery. He changed parties to support Lincoln's election in 1860, and he never looked back. Markland worked with Lincoln and Grant to free those held as slaves when that became the war's aim, and he later worked with Grant to enlarge opportunities and enforce civil rights for Black Americans. He appointed William Gibson to a high federal government position, albeit one that both knew held danger for Gibson, and then sent in the troops to protect him and the mail that was Gibson's responsibility. The question is certainly not exclusive to Markland, but it bears asking: What would make a child in a household—and in a town—with enslaved men, women, and children grow to be a man who worked to free them?[37]

Individuals and events in his childhood could have led him to think differently about Black people than had his father and grandfather and to believe freedom was a basic human right and ownership of human beings a moral wrong. The Maysville Academy he and Grant attended was across the street from the Bierbower house, part of the Underground Railroad system in a town known as a last stop before crossing the Ohio River to freedom. The school building was within two blocks of the site of a Baptist church established by Elisha Green, an enslaved man. A block from the academy was the house built by Grant's uncle Peter, president of one of the first abolitionist societies in Kentucky (established in Maysville around 1817), and it was in this house where Grant boarded with his widowed aunt. One historian of Hiram Ulysses Grant's time in Maysville wrote, "Atypical neighbors surrounded the Maysville Academy on every side, suggesting antislavery minds and hearts intentionally perched together in this high corner of Kentucky." In addition, Markland attended Augusta College, which was shuttered soon after he graduated because of the vocal antislavery stance of its teachers.[38]

Markland's swift action to protect railway mail agent William Gibson with a squad of soldiers after the KKK attack in 1871 speaks volumes about his dedication to the Fourteenth Amendment, particularly as Democratic Kentucky state and federal officials decried his actions and dismissed the seriousness of the KKK's terror. He was proud of what he did then and was later bitterly disappointed that his fellow Kentuckians were destroying the civil rights gains Grant and Creswell, as well as William Gibson and Markland himself, had fought to achieve. While Markland may have been embarrassed by his slaveholding ancestors, his own life was not blemished in that regard. His heroes were champions of freedom in his lifetime: Grant and Lincoln.

Markland's efforts to trace his lineage were ultimately unsuccessful, as were the author's. So, like the subject of this biography, the reader will arrive at the end of the man's life without knowing for sure whether Absalom Hanks Markland was related to the man he most admired: Abraham Lincoln, martyred president and son of Nancy Hanks.[39]

The question of whether Lincoln was a blood relative was not the only puzzle about himself that Markland sought to solve in his lifetime. The first question confronted him as a young man in Maysville, and it was not about his past. It was about what kind of man he would be. He answered that puzzle in his untiring efforts at self-improvement and in service to his country throughout his life. Like so many men of the early nineteenth century (Lincoln, Grant, and Sherman, for example), Markland tried many jobs—teacher, steamboatman, lawyer, landlord, delivery agent, government clerk—before the tragedy of the Civil War created an environment in which his many skills and his virtues of hard work, integrity, and ingenuity could be deployed on a national scale for the most valuable possible cause: saving the Union.

From the first, Markland seemed made for the job of special agent of the Post Office Department: he not only performed the duties in the job description but also created a new model of a special agent and modernized the system of delivering priceless mail to troops in the field. Early on, he aligned himself with the cause of preserving the United States and with those who believed in freeing the enslaved, and he devoted himself to keeping their memories alive. Markland's search for himself found its answer in his service to his country.

Away from the battlefront, he was a loyal friend, a caring husband, a gossipy raconteur, and a prolific correspondent with some of the most famous—and infamous—men of his day. Markland wielded his pen as a weapon in his battle against the isolation of deafness. As 1887 ended, "in the midst of adversity and physical limitation, [Markland] seems to have found an expansiveness, creativity, and humor" in his reminiscences and letters and counsel. The biggest event of the next year was what is still known as the Great Blizzard of 1888, one of the worst blizzards in U.S. history. Following a week of mild weather, a "white hurricane" slammed into the East Coast on March 12, dropping up to fifty-eight inches of snow, killing more than four hundred people, and isolating cities when streets, railroad tracks, and telegraph lines were covered or downed by wind-driven drifts that reached more than thirty feet high. Though Washington was on the extreme southern end of the blizzard, it was paralyzed by the ferocity of what has been called "the blizzard of the century."[40]

The day before the brutal and unexpected storm hit, Markland wrote Julia Grant and her son Fred. Like Ely Parker and a host of Grant's friends at that time, Markland offered to assist them in beating back a legal challenge by Grant's former staff officer Adam Badeau, who claimed coauthorship of the *Personal Memoirs of Ulysses S. Grant* and demanded some of the royalties. Markland recalled the visit he and Martha made to the Grants in October 1884, when he learned of the general's intention to write his memoirs. "I am astounded by the correspondence of Genl Badeau [which had been published in many newspapers].... To those who are at all acquainted with the Generals style of writing the book is evidence that it was his work." Fred Grant replied, "I thank you for the interest you have taken in the Badeau matter. I did have some dread of a newspaper discussion as to the authorship of my father's book, but have no fear of the courts.... Please present my highest regards to Mrs. Markland." Markland never stopped trying to be of service to the man who had given him the chance to be part of something much larger than himself—part of saving the Union.[41]

The war to reunite the United States had been over for more than twenty years, but its battles lived on as entertainment and education in numerous venues throughout the country. One of the most successful means of bringing the Civil War to life then was as a panorama, or cyclorama—a 360-degree sound, light, and visual portrayal of an important battle. Cycloramas that immersed the viewers in the clashes at Gettysburg, Atlanta, and Missionary Ridge were great successes, as was the panorama of the Battle of Shiloh, which opened in Chicago in 1885. Painted by French artist Théophile Poilpot, who never set foot in the United States, the painting spanned more than four hundred feet by fifty feet, included more than two thousand individual soldiers' faces based on their *carte de visite* photographs, and was exhibited in an enormous circular building designed and built especially for its exposition. By the spring of 1888, the panorama had been moved to a newly constructed building on the National Mall in Washington DC. The "Amusements" column of a local newspaper advertised it as "open daily from 9am to 10pm, on 15th St., two blocks south of U.S. Treasury building." There, thousands of visitors every day—often Union Army veterans bringing their families or their comrades—relived the glorious victory, after viewing gruesomely authentic details of the famous battle. There is no evidence that Markland visited the Shiloh panorama, but it seems likely that he would have, since we know that Shiloh was on his mind in the spring of 1888.[42]

On April 5, 1888, the eve of the anniversary of the Battle of Shiloh, Markland wrote a letter to seventy-year-old Fletcher at his home in Concord, Massachusetts. It is the most reflective and wide-ranging of his letters to his brother-in-law:

> This night twenty six years ago the army of Genl Grant lay at Pittsburg Landing all unconscious of danger. . . . I think of the days when battles went on and the horrors of war were on every side. . . . The actors who were immediately about one at that time have nearly all gone off the stage of life. . . . They played parts in the battle scene and afterward toiled in the paths of peace. . . . I may have been only a super[intendent] among them but I played my part to the best advantage and got as much credit for it as the manner of my play deserved.[43]

The man whose face had been mistaken for Grant's twenty-six years earlier wrote Fletcher that he now looked like Prussian leader Otto von Bismarck, according to fellow residents of the Clarendon Hotel "who have seen and know him." Then he turned to the weather, as so many correspondents do, and waxed lyrical. "We have had a few days of splendid weather" followed by heavy rain, he wrote. "But it has been the rain of spring time . . . that makes the grass grow, the leaves come out and the flowers open. . . . The coming and going of the Seasons are among the great wonders of God's universe." He philosophized, "In youth there is not much thought of the wonder and in age there is but little else to think about."

But he was, in fact, thinking about something else. He was thinking about death. "The death columns in our city papers tell of those who were in society for the last time in the past winter months. . . . Martha has just come home from enquiring after my old army friend John H. King, who is now at death's door and physicians say he must pass on in a short time." King and his wife, who had stayed in the Marklands' home in Washington while the Marklands traveled to California so many years ago, came to Washington for the winter season, according to Markland, and they had a good time until "the March blizzard caught him and laid him up with a cold which culminated in pneumonia a few days ago." King had commanded troops at the Battle of Shiloh, was "a credit to the Service, a gentleman, and friend. His family are good people. But all that won't stop his going in at the door which is forever closed against return."

Nor did Markland's creditable war service, his integrity, or his honor stop him from following King through that same door for the same reason. On May 24 a Washington newspaper carried this item on the front page: "Colonel A. H. Markland, who has been ill at the Clarendon Hotel for the past two weeks, is slowly sinking and his death may be expected at any time."[44]

Early the next morning—one of those glorious spring mornings he had rhapsodized about, when the nation's capital is a living rainbow of azaleas and tulips and wisteria and while the panorama of the Battle of Shiloh was still drawing visitors—Absalom Hanks Markland died of pneumonia. His beloved Martha and his best friend, Fletcher, who had hastened from Concord, were by his side. Absalom was sixty-three.

Hundreds of newspapers across the country carried notices of Markland's death over the following weeks, often on their front pages. Most of the death notices were short, referencing his service in the war and friendship with Grant, but lengthy obituaries ran in a number of major city newspapers. "[Colonel Markland] was known throughout the armies that Gen. Grant commanded as the originator and manager of the army mail system under which letters were often collected and delivered under fire," the *New York Times* reported. "Before Sherman's point of reaching the coast was known to the public Gen. Markland, with tons upon tons of mail . . . was on his way down the coast to meet the men who were marching through Georgia," stated the *Buffalo Morning Express*. "His reminiscences of the exciting scenes and events of [the war] period have furnished material for a good many newspaper sketches," reported the *Evening Star*. The *Courier-Journal* in Louisville headlined his obituary "An Old and Prominent Kentuckian Passes Away at Washington." Gen. Henry Van Ness Boynton wrote a moving tribute to Markland that was widely reprinted. He praised Colonel Markland's organization of the field postmasters, who "kept lines of march and company places in view, and when the column halted its mails were seldom long delayed." Boynton continued, "Both regular camps and bivouacs gleamed ever with lights of home. It was no unusual matter to have letters distributed along the very lines of battle, and even among the skirmishers. There are few who had experience at the front who have not witnessed this."[45]

The authoritative *Appleton's Annual Cyclopaedia and Register of Important Events of the Year 1888* contained a lengthy homage to Markland and his handling of the military mail, noting that "few, even to-day, can appreciate the immense amount of detailed work, the executive ability, and the personal dangers involved in the task."[46]

Many other newspapers and magazines also lauded Markland's remarkable service in keeping the front lines connected to the home front and delivering mail while under fire. Markland was mourned and remembered in communities from Oregon to New York and in many southern cities he had served, like Memphis and Nashville, by those who sent letters and those who received them during those long, terrible war years.

Perhaps the most eloquent of those who recalled Absalom Markland was his friend William Tecumseh Sherman. The general sent Martha, "to whom my heart goes out in condolence and sympathy," a beautiful letter recalling her husband's vital wartime service. "At Memphis, Vicksburg, Nashville, and especially at Savannah he seemed to anticipate our movements and arrived almost to a day with us, bearing the precious mails carefully assorted and promptly distributed," he wrote, adding,

> At all our army meetings since he has been a constant attendant & much welcome guest, generally attended by his faithful wife whose face and form were always associated with the memories of our own distant homes. May heaven's cherished blessings attend you in the time left you alone in this selfish world, and be assured that as long as a single man of the Army of the Tennessee remains, you will have a friend and admirer. Count me as one during my short remainder.[47]

"The colonel during our war was always a messenger of joy to us," Sherman told her, "for we knew he was the bearer of news from Home."

Epilogue

1889–Today

A year after Markland's death, the Society of the Army of the Tennessee published a lengthy obituary in its annual report of the organization's gathering and activities. "While he reported to the [Post Office] Department at Washington," it said, "he also had full military authority as a member of General Grant's staff, and, under the great power of such a position, he was, for all practical purposes, Post-Master General for army mails." The obituary concluded with a warm, personal tribute from "the boys" to the man they knew and loved: "He will be remembered by the boys as a man of commanding presence, great physical strength, but with as gentle a spirit and kindly disposed heart as that of any woman. He was a devoted husband, a true friend, a zealous patriot, and a soldier citizen in every sense worthy of the confidence reposed in him by all with whom he came in contact."[1]

Absalom H. Markland occupies a unique place in American history. At the beginning of the Civil War, at the request of his childhood friend, Ulysses S. Grant, he created a highly efficient military mail system, parts of which survive today. Throughout the war, he was almost always the first civilian representative of the U.S. government to enter major cities when the Union Army reclaimed them from the Confederacy, bringing with him priceless mailbags that brought both letters and improved morale to the troops. He followed Grant and his armies from Fort Henry in 1862 to City Point in 1865, and he arrived in Savannah—ahead of Sherman and his army at the end of their historic march—with twenty tons of mail. Markland also met regularly with President Lincoln during the war, and he carried important messages between Lincoln and Generals Grant and Sherman at crucial points during the nation's perilous fight for survival.

When the Ku Klux Klan waged its savage reign of terror and intimidation after the Civil War, his decisive action proved to be the tipping point in securing the executive powers President Grant needed to combat the Klan. Although no record of even an honorary U.S. Army commission exists, General Grant called Markland "Colonel," and because he did, the army and most civilians did, too, for the rest of his life. For decades, Colonel Markland made national news wherever he went. Hundreds of newspapers throughout the continental United States reported his movements and his actions during and after the war.

The Civil War looms large in our past; if our national timeline were reduced to one day, it would be both our worst and our finest hour. The Civil War is also studied with great passion in the present, as we wrestle with the unfinished business of the war and the reconstruction that followed. One of the reasons we can grapple with that history is because we have a rich trove of tangible, firsthand accounts with which we can explore the people, places, and events of that time. We are fortunate that so many Americans of that era wrote letters describing their hopes, their hates, their lives, their loves, and their struggles. And we are fortunate that so many of those letters were saved.

This is an aspect of the Civil War that makes it qualitatively different from earlier and later U.S. wars. At the beginning of our nation, the postal service was in its infancy, and relatively few who fought in the Revolutionary War were literate, so fewer firsthand accounts exist from which to draw. In later wars, censorship made letter writing more problematic and less revealing. Today's wars are fought in the era of email and social media—ephemeral messaging that may vaporize with the senders' and recipients' deaths, leaving little to no lasting record of their ordeals. Americans owe a huge debt to those who wrote and saved and later archived the many millions of letters written in the last half of the nineteenth century; that correspondence is the foundation of so much of the scholarship that we can all study.

We also owe a great debt to those who delivered that mail.

One-time postmaster Lincoln and Generals Grant and Sherman knew the value of mail to the success of their armies against the Confederacy. That made getting mail to the soldiers a priority, and Markland made it happen. Shortly after that war was won, Grant saw that fighting the poisonous residue of the Confederacy—the Ku Klux Klan—required that the mail be stopped. Markland made that happen, too.

And yet . . . Markland is all but invisible now, even as books about the Civil War and Reconstruction proliferate. Many biographies of Lincoln, Sherman, and Grant include a footnote about Markland, but his important, sometimes daily, interaction with them—especially with Grant during and after the war—has so far escaped notice.

One place, however, positions Markland front and center: the Smithsonian Institution's National Postal Museum website. A portion of General Howard's letter to Markland just after the war is at the top of the page devoted to the Postal Inspection Service—successor to the special agent division. It is a tribute to that service's importance to military mail and recognizes the value of news from home in every war ever fought: "You well know how anxiously the officers and soldiers of the Army watch and wait for letters from home, and the receipt of them is the greatest pleasure they enjoy, and when a long period has elapsed and there is no mail, no news from home, a feeling of despondency and gloom seems to settle on all."[2]

Absalom Hanks Markland carried more than letters in the mail he delivered under fire. He carried soldiers' hopes and the nation's future.

Acknowledgments

In the best of times, properly thanking the many people who help an author take a book from concept to completion is a daunting task. Against the backdrop of a worldwide pandemic, writing acknowledgments takes on a different cast entirely. Every person I asked for assistance over the past three years—whether longtime friend, eminent historian whom I barely knew, or archivist in a distant library—readily provided information and advice. In doing so, they also threw a lifeline from their confined worlds to mine. Such generosity amid chaos and death linked my life in the twenty-first century to Absalom Markland's in the nineteenth. As I wrote his story, nearly as many Americans had died of COVID as died in the Civil War. That made writing this book almost an experience in time travel. Every person mentioned in these acknowledgments—and those whom I assuredly have mistakenly omitted—will, I hope, recognize that my gratitude is not just for the words they sent, spoke, tweeted, or zoomed but also for making me feel we were comrades in the battle to keep history relevant to the future of our nation.

Archives and archivists, libraries and librarians are the mainstay of any effort to learn about a forgotten hero. My thanks go to Dr. Tom Kanon, since retired from the Tennessee State Library and Archives; Jennie Cole and Hannah Costelle, Filson Historical Society; Jayne Ptolemy, William L. Clements Library, University of Michigan; Cayla Broseus, Teton County Library, Jackson, Wyoming; Amy McCoy Glover, Ohio History Connection; the staff of Emmett D. Chisum Special Collections, University of Wyoming Libraries; Dr.

Christopher A. Schnell and Kaleb Jacobs, Abraham Lincoln Presidential Library and Museum; Elizabeth Dunn, recently retired from the David Rubenstein Library, Duke University; Dara Flinn, Fondren Library, Rice University; Dr. Ryan Semmes, Ulysses S. Grant Presidential Library; Graham Greer, Newberry Library; Patrick Kerwin and Loretta Deaver, Library of Congress Manuscript Division; Jennifer Laredo, U.S. Army Heritage and Education Center; Justine Kessler, Historical Society of Pennsylvania; Nicole Grady, University of the Pacific Special Collections and Archives; and Toni Vanover and Mary Knight Vickers, Johann Fust Community Library. This project was my first foray into the postal world, one inhabited by passionate and generous experts, and I am especially grateful to Scott Tiffney at the American Philatelic Research Library, who responded so helpfully to a number of inquiries. Heartfelt thanks go to Cay Chamness and Sue Ellen Grannis of the Kentucky Gateway Museum Center in Maysville, who provided hours of personal assistance and the priceless 1885 photo of Markland that brought me to tears. And I greatly appreciate Weldon Svoboda and Marissa Lindsey, among others, at the U.S. Army Quartermaster Museum, who took the time to photograph for this book the priceless Grimsley saddle that Grant gave to Markland.

I am indebted to longtime friend Rob Wallace for introducing me to John Nau III, a true hero of every Civil War scholar. John graciously put me in contact with Sally Anne Schmidt, curator of the Nau Civil War Collection, who introduced me to priceless Civil War letters, including those by and about U.S. Colored Troops. Dr. Barbara Gannon generously spent hours with me on the phone at the height of the pandemic as I tried to untangle Markland's military/civilian titles and understand post–Civil War veterans' organizations. Once again, Tom Tate's artillery expertise was invaluable, as was Dr. Eric Michael Burke's superb knowledge of the Army of the Ohio. And I learned important aspects of my story from Charles Spearman at Shiloh National Military Park; Dr. Minoa Uffelman; Lt. Col. Casey Doss (U.S. Army, Ret.); Martha Beltran (Captain, U.S. Army Adjutant General Corps, 1996–2004); Dr. Megan Kate Nelson; Doyl Fritz; Dr. Ronald H. Spector; and Dr. Hope Harrison.

Valuable research assistance and/or advice were provided by Certified Genealogist LaBrenda Garrett-Nelson; Dr. Rebecca Brenner Graham; Dr. Michele Krowl, Civil War and Reconstruction specialist, Library of Congress; researcher Katherine Morton; Bobbie Marquis; Dr. Kelly Mezurek; Dr. Holly Pinheiro; filmmaker Trent Shy; and the Society for Military History Facebook Group.

The experts who generously read my draft manuscript and provided valuable comments—but are not responsible for any errors—deserve more than my sincerest thanks. Perhaps a bottle of Old Pogue bourbon? Richard McMurry's many corrections were valuable, as was his tour of the Dalton, Georgia, railroad tunnel that Absalom admired, and Richard provided both even as his monumental biography of Joseph Eggleston Johnston was in its final pre-publication stage; Dr. Brooks Simpson pointed out deficiencies that led to important revisions in the manuscript; Dr. Steven Woodworth volunteered his considerable expertise about the Army of the Tennessee and the Civil War in general in the midst of an incredibly demanding schedule; Roger Lewis asked keen questions; and Evan Laney found errors everyone else had missed. Once again, Matthild and Jim Morton not only provided corrections to the manuscript but also twigged me to key bits of history that I had overlooked.

My literary agent, Cheryl Pientka of Nancy Yost Literary Agency, negotiated the contract for the book just before the pandemic descended, and I have thanked her every day for giving me the gift of Markland's company over the past two years. And I am grateful beyond words to Tom Swanson, editor at Potomac Books, who appreciated Markland's story in proposal form and shepherded it to production with enthusiasm, encouragement, excellence, and humor. Tom led me to Erin Greb, cartographer extraordinaire. The Potomac Books/University of Nebraska Press team deserve all my thanks for polishing and publishing my manuscript and for the brilliant cover design. Maureen C. Bemko performed magic as copyeditor for this CMS-challenged writer, and Susan Certo provided the excellent index.

This has been my second opportunity to work with independent book editor Rosemary Ahern. What a gift she has; what a gift she is!

It is hard to overstate how helpful Rosemary has been in bringing Markland back to life. She came to know him at least as well I did, and I believe it was Markland's spirit that led an abandoned kitten to follow her home—from the post office!

People and organizations from every part of the country inspired and encouraged me throughout the process, including Dr. Peter Veru, Dr. Rebecca DeWolf, along with my terrific book clubs in Florida, Washington DC, and Wyoming. Thanks to Rae Forker Evans, Nancy Dorn and Will Ris, David Fierrero, Alice Gorman, Kendall and Joseph Hartman, Terry Saban, Gwendolyn Fulcher Young, Frannie and Gordon Burns, and Nancy and David Donovan. Very special thanks for their valuable support and advice go to Linda Fairstein and Pia Lindstrom, dear friends whom I admire greatly. And I'm always indebted to the Shy Kids—my siblings Linda Shy Moats, Melody Shy Bobisuthi, and Richard Shy.

My research road trip to the amazingly well preserved city of Maysville in April 2021 enabled me to see Markland's hometown through nineteenth- and twenty-first-century eyes. Thank you, Lacey Holleran, the county's dynamic tourism director, who opened many doors; Marti and Mike Insko, who hosted, fed, and educated me at their exquisite Moon River B & B; Kentucky Gateway Museum Center executive director C. J. Hunter IV; and Marla Toncray, exhibits curator at the center and its Old Pogue Experience (she has the best job in town). I am also deeply indebted to Glen Bishop, founder of the National Underground Railroad Museum, who graciously opened the Bierbower House on a snowy April afternoon. With his colleagues Donna Jacobson and Crystal Marshall, he gave me a master class in the dynamics of slavery and freedom in the region.

For more than a decade, I have been fortunate to have the friendship of acclaimed writer Lucinda Dixon Sullivan, who has generously encouraged my efforts at prose and poetry. With this book, she became my muse. A native of Versailles, Kentucky, Lucinda guided me through the thickets of that state's complicated Civil War and Reconstruction history, and she provided me with invaluable literary advice in her close reading of the manuscript.

Again, and always, my husband, Lindsay, deserves more thanks than the word limit on this book will allow. From my earliest tentative notion about writing Markland's story through the final sprint to submit it to the publisher, Lindsay's enthusiasm and support for the project have never flagged. He is the ideal reader—smart, well read, and intolerant of sloppy thinking and sloppy writing. I am grateful for the time he has taken to listen to my thoughts about the book, to read my manuscript, and to critique both ruthlessly. It has been a joy to write about a man of intelligence, integrity, resourcefulness, generosity, and humor while living with one. As I write this, I can see through my window the snow-capped Teton Range of Wyoming, the state where Lindsay's family homesteaded and where he was born and raised. I'm a long, long way from the Pacific islands where I was born and raised, but I'm home. As Absalom wrote to Martha, I say to Lindsay: "Home is where you are."

Notes

Abbreviations

AHM	Absalom Hanks Markland
DFB	Daniel Fletcher Barker
Filson	Filson Historical Society
LoC	Library of Congress
MSM	Martha Simms Markland
NARA	National Archives
OR	*Official Records* (formal title: *The War of the Rebellion: A Compilation of the Official Records of the Union and Confederate Armies*)
PMUSG	*Personal Memoirs of Ulysses S. Grant*
PUSG	*Papers of Ulysses S. Grant*
TSLA	Tennessee State Library and Archives
USG	Ulysses S. Grant
WTS	William Tecumseh Sherman

Prologue

1. Quoted in J. Grant, *Personal Memoirs of Julia Dent Grant*, 156.

2. Swanson, *Manhunt*, 113; Freeman, *Boys in White*, 258.

3. T. S. Bowers, Assistant Adjutant-General, to Col. A. H. Markland, April 17, 1865, copy in Absalom H. Markland (hereafter AHM) Papers, LoC.

1. A Boy of the Buffalo Trace

1. Details of Absalom Markland's family history in this chapter are from the Papers of Matthew Markland and Absalom Hanks Markland, Filson (hereafter Markland Papers, Filson). Matthew was also spelled "Mathew" at times, and Maysville was originally called Limestone, Kentucky. Wood, "Limestone."

2. From *The Writings of Caleb Atwater* quoted in "Maysville," Kentucky Atlas and Gazetteer, accessed March 28, 2022, https://www.kyatlas.com/ky-maysville.html.

3. Dickinson, *Stories of Achievement*, 2:159–61; "Maysville," Kentucky Atlas and Gazetteer.

4. Mary Augusta Rogers, "Old Kentucky Towns," *New York Times*, October 5, 1986; National Underground Museum, Maysville, Kentucky, accessed March 28, 2022, http://www.cityofmaysville.com/contact/national-underground-railroad-museum/.

5. Matthew Markland Sr. was also elected by the city council "to preside with the mayor." Resolution of April 6, 1839, vol. A-2, 312, Hixson Papers, Kentucky Gateway Museum Center and Genealogical Library.

6. Dickinson, *Stories of Achievement*, 2:159.

7. Dickinson, *Stories of Achievement*, 2:159–61.

8. [Markland], *"O.B.'s" Reminiscences*, Letter #10.

9. Quotations from Garland, *Ulysses S. Grant, His Life and Character*, 18–19.

10. Grant, *Personal Memoirs of Ulysses S. Grant* (1885 ed.), 25 (hereafter PMUSG; all citations are to the 1885 edition unless indicated otherwise).

11. [Markland], *"O.B.'s" Reminiscences*, 17.

12. "The History of Augusta," City of Augusta, Kentucky, accessed March 28, 2022, https://www.augustaky.com/history-of-augusta.

13. *Public Ledger* (Memphis TN), November 14, 1873; Rice, *Reminiscences of Abraham Lincoln*, 629.

14. *Morning Courier and American Democrat* (Louisville KY), January 15, 1845.

15. Kentucky Historical Society, "Kentucky Marriages and Obituaries."

16. Absalom Markland items (thumbnail images of individual items), New York Signatures Historical Manuscripts Auction, Heritage Auctions, April 2011, https://historical.ha.com/itm/autographs/-absalom-h-markland-silver-congressional-presentation-goblets-and-archive-/a/6054-34247.s?ic4=GalleryView-ShortDescription-071515 (hereafter Markland items, Heritage Auctions).

17. U.S. Senate, *Message of the President of the United States Communicating the Report of the Secretary of the Interior and the Secretary of War*, 125, 126, accessed May 1, 2022, at University of Oklahoma College of Law Digital Commons, https://digitalcommons.law.ou.edu/cgi/viewcontent.cgi?article=1941&context=indianserialset.

18. U.S. Senate, *Message of the President Communicating the Report of the Secretary of the Interior and the Secretary of War*, 125, 126, 137, 155, 157, 158. It does not appear that all the gold was distributed to that delegation.

19. U.S. House of Representatives, *Letter from the Secretary of the Interior Transmitting a List of Clerks*, 9; *Daily Republic*, August 27, 1851.

20. *Baltimore Sun*, September 24, 1844; "An Old Organization," *Evening Star* (Washington DC), February 26, 1898.

21. AHM to Martha Simms Markland (hereafter MSM), September 17, 1852, Absolom [sic] Hanks Markland Papers, 1821–88, Tennessee State Library and Archives (hereafter TSLA).

22. Tunnel Hill Heritage Center & Museum, accessed April 30, 2022, https://www.civilwarrailroadtunnel.com.

23. M. W. Grand Lodge, *Proceedings of the M. W. Grand Lodge of Free and Accepted Masons*, 50; *Fayetteville* (NC) *Semi-Weekly Observer*, January 4, 1853.

24. Hunter, *Washington and Georgetown Directory*.

25. "Classification of Clerks in the War Department, July 1st, 1853," *Baltimore Sun*, July 6, 1853.

26. Hunter, *Washington and Georgetown Directory*, 65.

27. *Evening Star*, September 8, 1855.

28. *Daily American Organ* (Washington DC), September 10, 1855.

29. Among the many newspapers that reported on Matthew Markland were the *New York Daily Times*, September 10, 1855; *Spirit of the Times* (Ironton OH), September 25, 1855; *Louisville Daily Courier*, September 15, 1855; and *Nashville True Whig*, September 15, 1855.

30. *Louisville Daily Courier*, September 15, 1855.

31. Charles Thomas to Jefferson Davis, September 10, 1855, Papers of Jefferson Davis Documents and Reference Collection 1815–2015, MS 638, Woodson Research Center, Fondren Library, Rice University.

32. AHM to MSM, October 15, 1861, Absolom [*sic*] Hanks Markland Papers, TSLA.

33. "Gene Is Linked to Susceptibility to Depression," *New York Times*, July 18, 2003.

34. Dorman, *Virginia Revolutionary Pension Applications*, 61.

35. *Richmond Dispatch*, October 1, 1856.

36. M. W. Grand Lodge, *Proceedings of the M. W. Grand Lodge of Free and Accepted Masons*, 74.

2. A Man in Search of a Mission

1. More information on this bloody era can be found in Foner, *Free Soil, Free Labor, Free Men*; and in Etcheson, *Bleeding Kansas*.

2. *Washington (DC) Union*, May 17, 1856.

3. *Evening Star* (Washington DC), November 11, 1856; *Washington Union*, November 14, 1856.

4. *Evening Star*, May 14, 1857; "Died," *Weekly American* (Washington DC), November 25, 1857; *Evening Star*, August 13, 1859.

5. Rice, *Reminiscences of Abraham Lincoln*, 628.

6. "The Press Gallery in 1860," *Evening Star*, December 16, 1902; *Louisville Daily Courier*, April 1, 1859; speech of U.S. Rep. John Shanks, *Appendix to the Congressional Globe*, April 1, 1871, 143.

7. Rice, *Reminiscences of Abraham Lincoln*, 315.

8. Rice, *Reminiscences of Abraham Lincoln*, 315.

9. Chester, "Inside Ft. Sumter," 66.

10. Rice, *Reminiscences of Abraham Lincoln*, 318. Although the town of Cairo is named for the Egyptian capital city, locals pronounce it "KAY-ro."

11. Joshua Speed quote from Burlingame, *With Lincoln in the White House*, 1:20, cited in Hooper, *Lincoln's Generals' Wives*, 51; Abraham Lincoln to Orville H. Browning, September, 22, 1861, in Basler, *Collected Works of Abraham Lincoln*, 532.

12. *Daily Louisville Democrat*, July 13 and August 6, 1861, for example.

13. AHM to Abraham Lincoln, September 1, 1861 (copy), Fold3 Military Records of Ancestry.com, accessed May 3, 2022, https://www.fold3.com/image/299743236.

14. Endorsements appended to AHM to Abraham Lincoln, September 1, 1861 (copy), Fold3 Military Records of Ancestry.com, https://www.fold3.com/image/299743371.

15. Lincoln endorsement appended to AHM to Abraham Lincoln, September 1, 1861 (copy), Fold3 Military Records of Ancestry.com, https://www.fold3.com/image/299743371; Abraham Lincoln to Simon Cameron appended to AHM to Abraham Lincoln, September 1, 1861 (copy), Fold3 Military Records of Ancestry.com, https://www.fold3.com/image/299743194. In the nineteenth-century dictionary definition, "consistently" meant "consistent with a person's beliefs."

3. Absalom Markland, Special Agent

1. U.S. Department of the Interior, *Register of Officers and Agents*, 448.

2. U.S. Department of the Interior, *Register of Officers and Agents*, 448.

3. U. S. Grant (hereafter USG) to John Charles Frémont, September 6, 1861, in U.S. War Department, *War of the Rebellion*, ser. 1, vol. 4, 197. (This source, which some authors refer to as the *Official Records [of the Union and Confederate Armies]*, will be cited hereafter as simply OR, plus series, volume, part number [if any], and page numbers.)

4. "Federal Occupation of Paducah, September 5, 1861" (text of marker located at 100 Broadway in Paducah), City of Paducah, accessed March 30, 2022, http://paducahky.gov /~paducahky/sites/default/files/FederalOccupationofPaducahMarker.pdf.

5. Abraham Lincoln to Orville Browning, September 22, 1861, in Basler, *Collected Works of Abraham Lincoln*, 532; Markland statement and related Lincoln comment in Rice, *Reminiscences of Abraham Lincoln*, 322.

6. AHM to MSM, October 9–11, 1861, Absolom [*sic*] Hanks Markland Papers, TSLA.

7. Jaronski, "Absalom Markland, U.S. Grant's Postmaster," 24; Markland quoted in Brown, *Life of Ulysses Simpson Grant*, 330.

8. Hooper, *Lincoln's Generals' Wives*, 295.

9. Hooper, *Lincoln's Generals' Wives*, 308, 309.

10. AHM to MSM, October 9, 10, 11, 14, 15, 16, 18, 1861, Absolom [*sic*] Hanks Markland Papers, TSLA.

11. AHM to MSM, October 10, 11, 24, 1861, Absolom [*sic*] Hanks Markland Papers, TSLA.

12. AHM to MSM, November 2, 1861, Absolom [*sic*] Hanks Markland Papers, TSLA.

13. Hecht, "Union Military Mail Service," 238.

14. Hecht, "Union Military Mail Service," 228; Davis, *Deep Waters of the Proud*, 87.

15. Anderson, "Postal System Development during the Civil War."

16. "Adversity Covers," National Postal Museum, Smithsonian Institution, accessed March 30, 2022, https://postalmuseum.si.edu/exhibition/a-nation-divided/adversity-covers.

17. "Mail Call: History of America's Military Mail," National Postal Museum, Smithsonian Institution, accessed March 30, 2022, https://postalmuseum.si.edu/mailcall/index.html.

18. American Tract Society, "Mail Call," 61.

19. Sharland, *Knapsack Notes*, 57.

20. Quoted in E. Smith, *Incidents of the United States Christian Commission*, 105.

21. Whitman, *Memoranda during the War*, 9; Alcott, *Hospital Sketches*, 38.

22. Quoted in Zach Klitzman, "Women of the Civil War," President Lincoln's Cottage, August 2017, https://www.lincolncottage.org/women-of-the-civil-war/.

23. Mowris, *History of the One Hundred and Seventeenth Regiment, N.Y. Volunteers*, 71.

24. Hanson, *Historical Sketch of the Old Sixth Regiment of Massachusetts Volunteers*, 153.

25. Alicia Zuberbier, "Women and Nostalgia during the American Civil War: Cursed as a Cause, Blessed as a Cure" (2012), accessed at Kappa Omicron Nu, March 30, 2022, https://www.kon.org/urc/v11/zuberbier.html.

26. AHM to MSM, November 2, 1861, Absolom [*sic*] Hanks Markland Papers, TSLA.

27. Rice, *Reminiscences of Abraham Lincoln*, 324.

28. U. S. Grant, *Papers of Ulysses S. Grant* (hereafter PUSG), 17:589.

29. AHM to MSM, January 17, 1862, Absolom [*sic*] Hanks Markland Papers, TSLA.

30. Simpson, *Ulysses S. Grant*, 109–13; Frederick Grant quoted in Polk, "General Polk and the Battle of Belmont," 359.

31. *PMUSG*, 1:292.

32. Quoted in Brown, *Life of Ulysses Simpson Grant*, 331.

33. USG to Benson Lossing, July 30, 1866, in Lossing, *Pictorial History of the Civil War*, 224n1.

34. *OR*, ser. 1, vol. 7, 586.

4. "An Honored & Favored Man"

1. U.S. Post Office, *Annual Reports of the Postmaster General* (1898), exhibit A, 216–21, accessed at Google Books, May 6, 2022, https://www.google.com/books/edition/Annual_Report_of_the_Postmaster_General/uDLVAAAAMAAJ?hl=en&gbpv=1&bsq=Markland.

2. *Chicago Tribune*, February 12, 1862, dateline February 9.

3. H. Porter, *Campaigning with Grant*, 242.

4. *OR*, ser. 1, vol. 7, 609.

5. "U.S. Grant's Original Notification to Union Headquarters That He Has Arrived at Fort Donelson . . . ," The Raab Collection: Catalog 68, October 6, 2011, 8, 9, https://issuu.com/raabcollection/docs/-catalog-68.

6. *Louisville Daily Journal*, February 14, 1861.

7. Quoted in Woodworth, *Nothing but Victory*, 115.

8. *PMUSG*, 1:311.

9. O. H. Ross, "First Mail Carrier," *National Tribune*, May 10, 1888, 10; *Philadelphia Inquirer*, March 11, 1862; Hecht, "Union Military Mail Service," 238, 239; "Memoranda on the Civil War," 779; *Buffalo (NY) Morning Express*, February 20, 1862.

10. Peter Doherty, "A Valentine's Day History Lesson," *Greeting Card Association Card Talk Blog*, February 9, 2017, https://www.greetingcard.org/a-valentines-day-history-lesson/.

11. Meg Groeling, "Roses Have Thorns, Violets Proliferate," *Emerging Civil War Blog*, February 13, 2019, https://emergingcivilwar.com/2019/02/13/roses-have-thorns-violets-proliferate-vinegar-valentines-during-the-civil-war/.

12. AHM to MSM, February 18, 1862, Absolom [*sic*] Hanks Markland Papers, TSLA.

13. John Kasson to AHM, February 20, 1862, *OR*, ser. 1, vol. 10, pt. 2, 7.

14. Kasson to AHM, February 20, 1862, *OR*, ser. 1, vol. 10, pt. 2, 7–9.

15. AHM to MSM, February 21, 1862, Absolom [*sic*] Hanks Markland Papers, TSLA.

16. AHM to MSM, February 21, 1862, Absolom [*sic*] Hanks Markland Papers, TSLA.

17. *Chicago Tribune*, February 18, 1862.

18. Report from *Nashville Banner* printed in *Detroit Free Press*, March 14, 1862; *The Sun* (New York), January 30, 1887; *The Press* (Philadelphia PA), March 1, 1862.

19. *Philadelphia Inquirer*, March 11, 1862; *Nashville Banner* article reprinted in *Detroit Free Press*, March 14, 1862; *Evansville (IN) Daily Journal*, March 8, 1862; *New York Times*, March 22, 1862.

20. Gallagher, *How the Post Office Created America*, 150, 151; Trudeau, *Southern Storm*, 51.

21. Gallagher, *How the Post Office Created America*, 151; Columbia Historical Society, *Records*, 145.

22. Columbia Historical Society, *Records*, 148.

23. Corbett, *Orphans Preferred*, 5, 120–22; Markland quote from U.S. Post Office, *Letter from the Postmaster General*, 1, 2. This was later disputed, as discussed in this letter from the postmaster general to the U.S. Senate.

24. "The United States Postal Service: An American History" (Publication 100), 22, USPS, 2020, https://about.usps.com/publications/pub100.pdf.

25. *Philadelphia Inquirer*, March 11, 1862.

26. *Philadelphia Inquirer*, March 11, 1862.

27. *Mobile Advertiser and Register*, March 12, 1862; *Philadelphia Inquirer*, March 11, 1862.

28. *Chicago Tribune*, April 17, 1862.

29. OR, ser. 1, vol. 7, 672 (Markland's assignment to handle mail for the Army of the Ohio); Fitch, *Annals of the Army of the Cumberland*, 313; OR, ser. 1, vol. 10, pt. 2, 3.

30. Fitch, *Annals of the Army of the Cumberland*, 314, 315; Army of the Ohio, battle order, AHM Papers, LoC; Hecht, "Union Military Mail Service," 240.

31. AHM obituary, *New York Times*, May 26, 1888.

32. *Letters from the Forty-Fourth Regiment M.V.M. . . . by "Corporal,"* 48; Norton, *Army Letters, 1861–1865*, 76; Gage, *From Vicksburg to Raleigh*, 52; Blessington, *Campaigns of Walker's Texas Division*, 44.

33. AHM to MSM, March 3, 1862, Absolom [*sic*] Hanks Markland Papers, TSLA.

34. See, variously, Kelsey, "Ulysses S. Grant"; "False Portraits of U.S. Grant," *Antique Prints Blog*, February 2012, https://antiqueprintsblog.blogspot.com/2012/02/false-portraits -of-us-grant.html; Barber, *U.S. Grant, the Man and the Image*, 18, 19; Harris, *Blue & Gray in Black & White*, 261.

35. *Chicago Journal* quoted in *Border Sentinel* (Mound City KS), April 20, 1866.

36. MOLLUS Mass Photograph Collection, vol. 69, 3442, U.S. Army Heritage and Education Center.

37. *PMUSG*, 1:326, 327.

38. Woodworth, *Nothing but Victory*, 188.

39. O. H. Ross, "First Mail Carrier," *National Tribune*, May 10, 1888; *Evansville Daily Journal*, May 31, 1862; Wallace, *Lew Wallace*, 1:453; Livermore, *My Story of the War*, 141.

40. AHM to Daniel Fletcher Barker (hereafter DFB), April 5, 1888, Absolom [*sic*] Hanks Markland Papers, TSLA.

41. *Evansville Daily Journal*, May 31, 1862.

42. *Steuben Republican* (Angola IN), June 7, 1862, dateline Cairo, June 2.

43. *Chicago Tribune*, June 10, 1862, dateline Cairo, June 9; "[Memphis] 1862 Post Office," Historical Marker Database, last revised June 16, 2016, https://www.hmdb.org/m.asp?m =84464.

44. OR, ser. 1, vol. 17, pt. 2, 7.

45. AHM to MSM, June 20, 1862, Absolom [*sic*] Hanks Markland Papers, TSLA.

46. "Military camps are no place for ladies," wrote Sherman to his wife. William Tecumseh Sherman (hereafter WTS) to Ellen Sherman, August 10, 1862, CSHR 1/147, William T. Sherman Family Papers, University of Notre Dame Archives; Hooper, *Lincoln's Generals' Wives*, 8.

47. AHM to MSM, June 20, 1862, Absolom [*sic*] Hanks Markland Papers, TSLA.

48. AHM to Andrew Johnson, June 21, 1862, Southern History, June 21, 2013, http://www.southernhistory.co/2013/06/6212013-tennessee-civil-war-notes-first.html; Col. J. B. Fry to AHM, June 19, 1862, Absolom [*sic*] Hanks Markland Papers, TSLA.

49. *Memphis Avalanche* quoted in the *Nashville Daily Union*, July 3, 1862.

50. AHM to MSM, July 8, 1862, Absolom [*sic*] Hanks Markland Papers, TSLA.

51. Bruesch, "Disasters and Epidemics of a River Town"; LaPointe, "Military Hospitals in Memphis," 332.

52. AHM to MSM, July 8, 10, 1862, Absolom [*sic*] Hanks Markland Papers, TSLA; *Nashville Daily Union*, July 18, 1862.

53. "Sampson Simms," Find a Grave, accessed April 1, 2022, https://www.findagrave.com/memorial/60862310/sampson-simms.

54. "Of Justice and Conscience," in T. Parker, *Ten Sermons of Religion*, 84, 85.

55. *PMUSG*, 1:368.

5. "The Flood of Letters"

1. Abraham Lincoln to Albert G. Hodges, April 4, 1864, Speeches and Writings, Abraham Lincoln Online, http://www.abrahamlincolnonline.org/lincoln/speeches/hodges.htm.

2. Benjamin Stevenson to his sister quoted in McPherson, *For Cause and Comrades*, 23; Samuel Storrow quoted in Manning, *What This Cruel War Is Over*, 101.

3. Manning, *What This Cruel War Is Over*, 36, 85 (quote), 120 (second quote).

4. Manning, *What This Cruel War Is Over*, 89.

5. Manning, *What This Cruel War Is Over*, 45.

6. *New York Times*, October 4, 1862 (dateline October 3); William L. Kelly, assistant postmaster at Louisville, to AHM, November 4, 1862, AHM Papers, LoC; request to Grant in *PUSG*, 6:156; Quartermaster to AHM, November 1, 1862, National Postal Museum, Smithsonian Institution, https://postalmuseum.si.edu/object/npm_2003.2004.82; Livermore, *My Story of the War*, 141.

7. George W. McLellan to AHM, November 8, 1862, AHM Papers, LoC.

8. Grant quoted in Lossing, *Pictorial History of the Civil War*, 225n1; *Newark (OH) True American*, July 18, 1862; "Mail Service and the Civil War," USPS, accessed May 6, 2022, https://about.usps.com/news/national-releases/2012/pr12_civil-war-mail-history.pdf.

9. *PUSG*, 6:446; R. K. Scott to AHM, November 6, 1862, AHM Papers, LoC.

10. Anderson, "Postal System Development during the Civil War"; "Mail Service and the Civil War," USPS, accessed May 6, 2022, https://about.usps.com/news/national-releases/2012/pr12_civil-war-mail-history.pdf.

11. Confederate States of America, *Report of the Postmaster General*, prepared by John H. Reagan, November 27, 1861, 11–12, 16 (quote), accessed at HathiTrust, https://babel.hathitrust.org/cgi/pt?id=dul1.ark:/13960/t5r79583x&view=1up&seq=2&skin=2021; Wiley, *Life of Johnny Reb*, 7.

12. Grimes, *Absalom Grimes, Confederate Mail Runner*, 2–37. All quotes within this discussion are from Grimes's book. For the video and the children's eBook, see Barnes Bradshaw, "Life and Times of Absalom Grimes," May 29, 2013, https://www.youtube.com/watch?v=3zUU2KEdHBU; and Tracey A. Fern, *Grimes and the Grapevine* (Cricket Media, 2018).

13. *St. Louis Post-Dispatch*, May 19, 2017; *Memphis Bulletin*, June 6, 1863.

14. *Ralls County (MO) Record* (Grimes obituary), March 31, 1911, accessed at "Gratiot Street Prison," Civil War St. Louis, http://www.civilwarstlouis.com/Gratiot/Grimesobit .htm; "Absalom Carlisle Grimes," Find a Grave, accessed April 2, 2022, https://www .findagrave.com/memorial/19196135/absalom-carlisle-grimes.

15. Absalom Markland, "A Chapter in War History" (unpublished, 1887), Markland Papers, Filson.

16. Copy of General Order No. 8, AHM Papers, LoC. See also Marszalek, *Sherman's Other War*, 131–63.

17. Both quotes from Richardson, *Secret Service, the Field, the Dungeon, and the Escape*, 317.

18. Richardson, *Secret Service, the Field, the Dungeon, and the Escape*, 317; Marszalek, *Sherman's Other War*, 152; Rees, *Foot-Prints of a Letter-Carrier*, 322–23. Instead, the president referred the matter to Grant, who backed up Sherman's order, forbidding Knox to gain entry to his camps.

19. AHM to Gov. Andrew Johnson, January 19, 1863, Image 969, Andrew Johnson Papers, LoC; AHM to MSM, June 22, 1863, Absolom [*sic*] Hanks Markland Papers, TSLA. Matthew rejoined his regiment and was mustered out at the end of the war. "Roster of the Twenty Second Regiment, Kentucky Infantry," Carter County, Kentucky, Genealogy & History Research Website, accessed April 2, 2022, https://kycarter.com/military/22nd.htm.

20. Markland, "Chapter in War History," Markland Papers, Filson. Unless otherwise noted, all quotes in this discussion of Arkansas Post are from this document.

21. Copy of McClernand's Special Orders No. 13, January 6, 1863, AHM Papers, LoC. Buell had been relieved of command of the Army of the Ohio in October, and with McClernand's arrival, Sherman had become a corps commander in the Army of the Mississippi. Markland, "Chapter in War History," Markland Papers, Filson.

22. Copy of McClernand's aide's order, January 8, 1863, AHM Papers, LoC.

23. Grant, *Personal Memoirs of Ulysses S. Grant* (2017 annotated ed.), 304, 305, 305n14.

24. Markland, "Chapter in War History," Markland Papers, Filson; *PMUSG*, 1:440–42.

25. Lincoln quoted in Admiral Porter, *Incidents and Anecdotes of the Civil War*, 95, 96; J. Grant, *Personal Memoirs*, 111.

26. Doyl Fritz, email to author, June 13, 2021, quoting the diary of his great-great-grandfather, Cpl. John Newton Prentice.

27. Robert Gist to A. N. Zevely, March 23, 1863, AHM Papers, LoC; AHM to Robert Gist, March 27, 1863, AHM Papers, LoC; *Louisville Daily Democrat*, October 5, 1862.

28. AHM to MSM, June 22, 1863, Absolom [*sic*] Hanks Markland Papers, TSLA.

29. AHM to John G. Nicolay, April 12, 1863, Abraham Lincoln Papers, LoC.

30. AHM to Nicolay, April 12, 1863 (includes Meigs's note).

31. Receipt from Postmaster of Memphis to AHM, June 1, 1863, AHM Papers, LoC; *OR*, ser. 1, vol. 24, pt. 3, 448–49.

32. "Black Soldiers in the U.S. Military during the Civil War," National Archives, last reviewed September 1, 2017, https://www.archives.gov/education/lessons/blacks-civil-war.

33. Capt. Robert Wilkinson to his father, in J. D. Smith, *Black Soldiers in Blue*, 97.

34. Rice letters included in F. W. Diggs to G. William Rosencrans, September 10, 1864, D-296, 1864, Letters Received, series 2593, Department of the Missouri, U.S. Army Continental Commands, Record Group 393, pt. 1, National Archives. Private Rice survived the illness that had landed him in the Benton Barracks Hospital, and he was reunited with his

wife and most of his formerly enslaved children in St. Louis in September 1864. After the war, the remaining two daughters rejoined the family. Rice became a minister and served Black congregations in Kansas, Missouri, New Mexico, and Colorado. He died in Colorado Springs in 1907.

35. George Washington to Abraham Lincoln, December 4, 1864, W-953, 1864, Letters Received, series 360, U.S. Colored Troops Division, Adjutant General's Office, Record Group 94, National Archives.

36. Harmon quoted in Redkey, *Grand Army of Black Men*, 35, 36.

37. Jane Welcome to Abraham Lincoln, November 21, 1864, W-934, 1864, Letters Received, series 360, U.S. Colored Troops Division, Adjutant General's Office, Record Group 94, National Archives, accessed at Freedmen and Southern Society Project, last revised February 4, 2022, http://www.freedmen.umd.edu/JWelcome.html.

38. AHM to MSM, June 22, 1863, Absolom [*sic*] Hanks Markland Papers, TSLA.

39. Abraham Lincoln to USG, July 13, 1863, and Abraham Lincoln to James Conkling, August 26, 1863, both quoted in Hooper, *Lincoln's Generals' Wives*, 320.

40. *Detroit Free Press*, July 9, 1863; copy of Bingham's order of July 6, 1863, AHM Papers, LoC.

41. *Semi-Weekly Wisconsin* (Milwaukee), July 14, 1863; *Free Press* (Beaufort SC), July 18, 1863; R. K. Scott to AHM, July 22, 1863, AHM Papers, LoC.

42. R. K. Scott to AHM, July 22, 1863, AHM Papers, LoC; USG to Francis J. Herron, July 24, 1863, *PUSG*, 9:113; *New York Herald*, August 15, 1863.

43. *Harper's Weekly*, July 25, 1863, 465, 478.

44. Copy of Grant's General Orders No. 49, July 30, 1863, AHM Papers, LoC; "Civil War Postal History of Vicksburg, Mississippi," Civil War Philatelic Society, accessed April 3, 2022, https://www.civilwarphilatelicsociety.org/resources/books/civil-war-postal-history-of-vicksburg-mississippi/#US-Occupation; OR, ser. 1, vol. 34, pt. 3, 585–86.

45. AHM to Andrew Hickenlooper, September 8, 1885, in *Report of the Proceedings of the Reunions of the Society of the Army of the Tennessee*, 1885, 166–67, accessed at HathiTrust, https://babel.hathitrust.org/cgi/pt?id=uc1.$b541288&view=1up&seq=176&skin=2021&q1=Pleasant%20Ridge,%20Hamilton%20O.%20September%201885.

46. AHM to MSM, August 24, 1863, Absolom [*sic*] Hanks Markland Papers, TSLA.

47. AHM to MSM, August 25, 1863, Absolom [*sic*] Hanks Markland Papers, TSLA.

48. AHM to MSM, September 17, 1863, Absolom [*sic*] Hanks Markland Papers, TSLA.

49. Sherman quoted in Dieck, *Life and Public Services of General U.S. Grant*, 256; Grant quoted in Burr, *Life and Deeds of General Ulysses S. Grant*, 411.

50. Burr, *Life and Deeds of General Ulysses S. Grant*, 410.

51. Reports touting Markland for Mississippi military governor appeared in the *Daily Milwaukee News*, October [n.d.], 1863; *Pittsburgh Daily Commercial*, October 26, 1863; *Cleveland Daily Leader*, October 23, 1863; and *Nashville Daily Union*, October 25, 1863 (quote).

52. Copy of Maj. Gen. George H. Thomas to Postmaster General Montgomery Blair, October 11, 1863, AHM Papers, LoC.

53. *National Republican* (Washington DC), October 28, 29, 1863.

54. *Courier Journal* (Louisville), February 7, 1886. Quotations in subsequent paragraphs on this incident are from this source.

55. Burr, *Life and Deeds of General Ulysses S. Grant*, 410.

56. Honorable Order of Kentucky Colonels, https://www.kycolonels.org.

57. Marcellus Mundy to Thomas Bramlette, November 17, 1863, in Civil War Governors of Kentucky, http://discovery.civilwargovernors.org/document/KYR-0001-002 -0005. The militia commander was not replaced.

58. Markland's honorary commission as a colonel in the Kentucky militia, November 18, 1863, Absolom [*sic*] Hanks Markland Papers, TSLA.

59. Hecht, "Union Military Mail Service," 238; Notes from postmasters to AHM regarding locks and keys and mailbags, December 1863, AHM Papers, LoC; Copy of George W. McLellan to John M. G. Parker (New Orleans), December 14, 1863, AHM Papers, LoC. One example of the "judgement and discretion" phrase appears in George W. McLellan to AHM, December 29, 1863, AHM Papers, LoC.

6. "Twenty Tons of Mail"

1. Livermore, *My Story of the War*, 140–41.

2. AHM to MSM, March 3, 1862, Absolom [*sic*] Hanks Markland Papers, TSLA.

3. *New York Times*, May 26, 1885; Boynton quoted in *Indianapolis Journal*, May 27, 1888.

4. Rees, *Foot-Prints of a Letter-Carrier*, 322–23.

5. "Engine" quote from Herndon, *Herndon's Lincoln*, 2:375. Frederick Douglass began giving lectures on the subject of "self-made men" as early as 1859. See his essay "Self-Made Men," in Blassinghame and McKivigan, *Frederick Douglass Papers*, ser. 1, 4:545–75.

6. Hooper, *Lincoln's Generals' Wives*, 177.

7. *PUSG*, 10:518. Markland had, in fact, requested a favor of someone "since the rebellion"—in the fall of 1861 he had asked President Lincoln for a position as paymaster.

8. Special Orders No. 9, January 14, 1864 (copy); instructions quoted in T. S. Bowers to AHM, January 14, 1864; and in George W. McLellan to AHM, January 22, 1864, all in AHM Papers, LoC.

9. George W. McLellan to AHM, January 22, 1864; R. W. Allen to AHM, January 27, 1864, both in AHM Papers, LoC.

10. George W. McLellan to John Parker (Esq.), April 9, 1864, AHM Papers, LoC.

11. *PMUSG*, 2:119.

12. Rice, *Reminiscences of Abraham Lincoln*, 325.

13. Some Virginia towns that are also county seats include "court house" in their names, examples being Culpeper Court House, Spotsylvania Court House, and Appomattox Court House.

14. *New Ulm (MN) Review*, May 8, 1885.

15. *Evansville Daily Journal*, May 21, 1864; *Evening Star*, May 16, 1864.

16. "From the Front," *National Republican* (Washington DC), May 20, 1864.

17. "From the Front," *National Republican*, May 20, 1864. Among the newspapers reprinting this article was the *Hartford Courant*, May 23, 1864.

18. Markland comment from Rice, *Reminiscences of Abraham Lincoln*, 327.

19. Blair letter in Rice, *Reminiscences of Abraham Lincoln*, 328. "Blair's dislike for Stanton bordered on hatred . . . when he wanted anything in the War Department, he was more likely to come to an old friend like [Charles Dana] than go to Secretary Stanton. Stanton, too, rather preferred that." Dana, *Recollections of the Civil War*, 157.

20. Markland comment from Rice, *Reminiscences of Abraham Lincoln*, 328–29.

21. Hooper, *Lincoln's Generals' Wives*, 341. When Julia arrived, they lived in a cabin.

22. Copy of Special Orders No. 39, AHM Papers, LoC.

23. "Army Mails," *Soldiers' Journal*, July 13, 1864.

24. Lossing, *Pictorial History of the Civil War*, 2:224.

25. Lossing, *Pictorial History of the Civil War*, 2:224, 225.

26. Marks, *Peninsula Campaign in Virginia*, 50, 51.

27. Hammond, *Army Chaplain's Manual*, 75–77.

28. All quotes, including Grant's letter, from Lossing, *Pictorial History of the Civil War*, 2:224n1.

29. J. Grant, *Personal Memoirs*, 132; Ulysses S. Grant–ordered pass for Mrs. A. H. Markland, Markland items, Heritage Auctions; Hooper, *Lincoln's Generals' Wives*, 324.

30. A. H. Markland, narrative of military mail plan for Sherman's March to the Sea, ca. 1864, AHM Papers, LoC.

31. *St. Louis Globe-Democrat*, August 2, 1886.

32. George W. McLellan to AHM, June 21, 1864, AHM Papers, LoC.

33. *Evening Star*, July 25, 1885.

34. S. Cooper to Gen. J. E. Johnston, July 17, 1864, OR, ser. 1, vol. 38, pt. 5, 885; telegraphed text reported in *New York Times*, September 5, 1864.

35. Abraham Lincoln blind memorandum, August 23, 1864, LoC, https://www.loc.gov/resource/mal.4359700/?sp=1.

36. *New York Tribune*, September 6, 1864.

37. AHM to Montgomery Blair, September 14, 1864, Abraham Lincoln Papers, LoC.

38. Postscript to AHM to Blair, September 14, 1864.

39. Montgomery Blair to John G. Nicolay, September 14, 1864, Abraham Lincoln Papers, LoC; John G. Nicolay to Horace Greeley, September 15, 1864, in Burlingame, *With Lincoln in the White House*, 159–60.

40. Holzer, *Lincoln and the Power of the Press*, 530.

41. Goodwin, *Team of Rivals*, 658, 659.

42. W. Dennison to USG, October 31, 1864, *PUSG*, 12:379.

43. USG to W. Dennison, November 4, 1864, *PUSG*, 12:380.

44. WTS to USG, November 6, 1864, in Simpson and Berlin, *Sherman's Civil War*, 751.

45. Sherman, *Memoirs*, 2:408.

46. Sherman, *Memoirs*, 2:166–68.

47. Sherman, *Memoirs*, 2:179; Trudeau, *Southern Storm*, 76.

48. A. H. Markland, narrative of military mail plan for Sherman's March to the Sea, ca. 1864, AHM Papers, LoC.

49. Col. Horace Porter to AHM, November 24, 1864, contained in A. H. Markland, narrative of military mail plan for Sherman's March to the Sea, ca.1864, AHM Papers, LoC.

50. A. H. Markland, telegram to Nashville postmaster, 9:30 p.m., November 27, 1864, AHM Papers, LoC.

51. The ten thousand figure is cited in Catton, *Never Call Retreat*, 415, 416. The nineteen thousand figure is cited in Drago, "How Sherman's March through Georgia Affected the Slaves," 363.

52. A. H. Markland, narrative of military mail plan for Sherman's March to the Sea, ca. 1864, AHM Papers, LoC.

53. Sandburg, *Lincoln*, 627; Johnson, "March to the Sea," 333; Trudeau, *Southern Storm*, 465, 466; Hurst, *Journal-History of the Seventy-Third Ohio Volunteer Infantry*, 163; Sherman, *Memoirs*, 2:204.

54. Extract from Grant's Special Orders No. 142, with original endorsement, AHM Papers, LoC; *PMUSG*, 2:271.

55. The date of Markland's visit comes from Dennison to Lincoln, December 5, 1864, Abraham Lincoln Papers, LoC; Markland recollection in Rice, *Reminiscences of Abraham Lincoln*, 324–27.

56. Rice, *Reminiscences of Abraham Lincoln*, 327; *Omaha Daily Bee*, April 7, 1885.

57. Sherman, *Memoirs*, 2:218.

58. *Pittsburgh (PA) Daily Commercial*, December 23, 1864.

59. *Evening Star*, December 20, 1864; *Evansville Daily Journal*, December 28, 1864.

60. *OR*, ser. 1, vol. 44, 796, 765.

61. Sherman, *Memoirs*, 2:228.

62. *Savannah Republican* reports quoted in *New York Times*, January 5, 1865.

7. "Trains Have Stopped Running"

1. WTS to Col. and Mrs. Markland, Savannah, January 3, 1865, James S. Schoff Civil War Collection, William L. Clements Library, University of Michigan.

2. Gen. Green B. Raum, "With the Western Army: Occupation of Savannah," *National Tribune* (Washington DC), June 18, 1903.

3. Quartermaster's note of January 5, 1865, AHM Papers, LoC; *Harper's Weekly*, January 29, 1865, 56.

4. "Congressional Smokers," *Wood County Reporter* (Grand Rapids WI), April 23, 1885. Quotations in subsequent paragraphs referencing this episode are from this source.

5. Thomas Velk and Terence M. Hines, "The United States Post Office Domestic Postal Money Order System in the 19th Century," January 2009, https://www.researchgate.net/publication/46475194_The_United_States_Post_Office_Domestic_Postal_Money_Order_System_In_The_19th_Century_A_Nascent_Banking_System.

6. Regarding Nashville, AHM to USG, December 23, 1863, Folder 351, Box 20, Series 3, USG Presidential Library Archives; regarding Chattanooga, *Louisville Daily Courier*, December 11, 1863; USG to W. Dennison, January 4, 1865, *PUSG*, 13:221.

7. D. Parker, *Chautauqua Boy*, 27.

8. Sherman, *Memoirs*, 2:249.

9. *Buffalo (NY) Commercial*, January 16, 1865; A. N. Zevely to AHM, January 23, 1865, AHM Papers, LoC.

10. *Harper's Weekly*, January 28, 1865, 50.

11. A. H. Markland to Dennison, January 23, 1865, Publication Number M1064, File M1627, 2–4, National Archives (hereafter NARA), accessed at Fold3 Military Records of Ancestry.com, https://www.fold3.com/image/305207987. Quotations in subsequent paragraphs are from this source unless indicated otherwise.

12. Copy of WTS to Hon. E. M. Stanton, January 14, 1865, enclosure to AHM, Publication Number M619, File M82, NARA, accessed at Fold3 Military Records of Ancestry.com, https://www.fold3.com/image/301035857?terms=markland,war,us,civil,h,a.

13. Brigadier general is the grade above colonel and below major general.

14. "Brevet Generals," American Civil War High Command, accessed April 5, 2022, https://americancivilwarhighcommand.com/commanders/brevet-generals/.

15. WTS to Hon. E. M. Stanton, January 14, 1865, Publication Number M619, File M82, NARA, accessed at Fold3 Military Records of Ancestry.com, https://www.fold3.com/image/301035853.

16. Publication Number M1064, File M1626, 4, 5, NARA, accessed at Fold3 Military Records of Ancestry.com, https://www.fold3.com/image/305207980; also File M1627, NARA, accessed at Fold3 Military Records of Ancestry.com, https://www.fold3.com/image/305207984.

17. Publication Number M1064, File M1626, 4, 5. The topmost endorsement and the first one on the Dennison letter are, in fact, currently misfiled within the National Archives in a folder relating to a John A. Miller, who was seeking appointment as a paymaster in the army at the same time.

18. U.S. Post Office, *Annual Reports of the Postmaster General* (1898), exhibit A, 216–21, accessed at Google Books, May 6, 2022, https://www.google.com/books/edition/Annual_Report_of_the_Postmaster_General/uDLVAAAAMAAJ?hl=en&gbpv=1&bsq=Markland.

19. Special agents of the Post Office Department received $1,600 per year plus $2 per diem. Hecht, "Union Military Mail Service," 238. If he had been given a colonel's salary (a brevet did not include a salary increase), he would have received $2,544 per year; as a special agent of the Post Office Department, he would have received $2,330 at the most (calculating the maximum 365 days of work). "Military Pay," American Battlefield Trust, accessed April 5, 2022, https://www.battlefields.org/learn/articles/military-pay; Hecht, "Union Military Mail Service," 238.

20. Publication Number M619, File M1423, NARA, accessed at Fold3 Military Records of Ancestry.com, https://www.fold3.com/image/299742961.

21. Varina Davis quoted in Furgurson, *Ashes of Glory*, 288.

22. "The Mail from Sherman's Army," dateline February 4, 1865, *London Illustrated News* 46, no. 1300 (1865): 118.

23. *Charleston (SC) Daily Courier*, February 22, 1865. The Union-controlled editions of the newspaper in 1865 were labeled "new series, vol. 1, nos. 4–228."

24. Long with Long, *Civil War Day by Day*, 648; *Charleston Daily Courier*, March 20, 1865.

25. *Charleston Daily Courier*, March 20, 1865; *Fort Wayne (IN) Daily Gazette*, November 2, 1873, quoting Lossing, *Pictorial History of the Civil War*.

26. Copy of Sherman's Goldsboro "circular," AHM Papers, LoC.

27. OR, ser. 1, vol. 47, pt. 2, 971.

28. Sherman, *Memoirs*, 2:322–24, which includes the March 22 letter from Grant.

29. Sherman, *Memoirs*, 2:324–32.

30. AHM to Gen. Andrew Hickenlooper, September 8, 1885, in *Report of the Proceedings of the Reunions of the Society of the Army of the Tennessee, 1885*, 169, accessed at HathiTrust, https://babel.hathitrust.org/cgi/pt?id=uc1.$b541288&view=1up&seq=176&skin=2021&q1=Pleasant%20Ridge,%20Hamilton%20O.%20September%201885.

31. Furgurson, *Ashes of Glory*, 313–20 (Lee quote, 320).

32. Quoted in D. Parker, *Chautauqua Boy*, 54, 55.

33. Chief quartermaster, Army of the Tennessee, note to AHM, April 4, 1865, AHM Papers, LoC; AHM, telegram to WTS, April 6, 1865, Publication number P2282, Catalog ID 1236976, NARA; AHM, telegram to WTS, April 6, 1865, OR, ser. 1, vol. 47, pt. 3, 120; copy of Sherman's Special Field Orders No. 55, April 6, 1865, AHM Papers, LoC.

34. WTS to AHM, April 7, 1865; and AHM to WTS, April 7, 1865, both in OR, ser. 1, vol. 47, pt. 3, 120, 121; Nichols, *Story of the Great March*, 286.

35. *PMUSG*, 2:479.

36. Marklands' travel pass, AHM Papers, LoC; description of Grant from Catton, *Stillness at Appomattox*, 380.

37. Sherman, *Memoirs*, 2:346, 347.

38. *New York Times*, April 14, 1865; *Evening Star*, April 15, 1865.

39. *Evening Star*, April 15, 1865; *Alexandria (VA) Gazette*, April 27, 1865; *Alexandria Gazette*, April 26, 1865.

40. Quoted in Morris, *Memorial Record of the Nation's Tribute to Abraham Lincoln*, 137.

41. This episode is described in Kauffman, *American Brutus*, 248, 249.

42. War Department telegram to Agent, Military Railroad, Alexandria, 12:20 a.m., April 15, 1865, OR, ser. 1, pt. 2, 773; Freeman, *Boys in White*, 258.

43. Copy of Grant's order to examine all mail destined for Richmond, April 17, 1865, AHM Papers, LoC.

8. "A Mark of Friendship and Esteem"

1. As late as April 24, Secretary of War Stanton issued a statement saying that "this department has information that the President's murder was organized in Canada and approved in Richmond." *Alexandria Gazette*, April 25, 1865.

2. Sherman, *Memoirs*, 1:349.

3. Sherman, *Memoirs*, 2:353.

4. *New York Times*, April 24, 1865; Marszalek, *Sherman*, 353; Hooper, *Lincoln's Generals' Wives*, 233.

5. AHM to Hickenlooper, September 8, 1885, in *Report of the Proceedings of the Reunions of the Society of the Army of the Tennessee*, 1885, 170.

6. AHM to Hickenlooper, September 8, 1885, in *Report of the Proceedings of the Reunions of the Society of the Army of the Tennessee*, 1885, 170.

7. AHM to Hickenlooper, September 8, 1885, in *Report of the Proceedings of the Reunions of the Society of the Army of the Tennessee*, 1885, 170 (original emphasis).

8. J. E. Smith, *Grant*, 416.

9. Grant to Markland, May 19, 1865, in "General Grant's Saddle," Quartermaster Department in the Civil War, https://qmcivilwar.wordpress.com/grants-saddle/.

10. Dowdall, *From Cincinnati to the Colorado Ranger*, 65; *Daily Press* (Newport News VA), December 5, 1965.

11. USG to W. Dennison, May 9, 1865; and Post Office Department to AHM, May 17, 1865, both in Markland items, Heritage Auctions.

12. *Charleston Daily Courier*, May 15, 1865; copy of order from E. W. Smith to AHM, May 1, 1865, AHM Papers, LoC.

13. *Pittsburgh Press*, February 3, 1888. The minister's name was Frederick Bruce, not Edward Bruce, as this article reported.

14. *Evening Star*, May 17, 1865, 2nd ed. Dr. Mudd and the other three "lifers" were pardoned by President Johnson just before he left office in 1869.

15. O. O. Howard to AHM, May 22, 1865, OR, ser. 1, vol. 47, pt. 3, 555, 556. The historically Black university founded in 1867 in Washington DC bears Howard's name.

16. *New York Herald*, June 30, 1865.

17. *New York Herald*, October 2, 1865.

18. Free travel pass for Mr. and Mrs. Markland, October 31, 1865, Markland Papers, Filson; F. F. Low to AHM, November 14, 1865, University of the Pacific Archives; *Evening Star*, November 13, 1865; *Daily Mountaineer* (The Dalles OR), December 5, 1865.

19. G. W. McLellan to AHM, December 23, 1865, Markland Papers, Filson; *Daily Mountaineer*, January 17, 1866; Ancestry.com passenger lists, accessed April 7, 2022, https://www.ancestry.com/search/categories/img_passlists/?name=a.+h._Markland&arrival=1866-1-19&keyword=Henry+Chauncey.

20. *Cincinnati Enquirer*, March 17, 1866.

21. USG to AHM, April 11, 1866, Folder 44, Box 107, Series 3, Collection: Ulysses S. Grant, USG Presidential Library Archives.

22. *Cleveland Daily Leader*, April 12, 1866; *Daily Ohio Statesman* (Columbus), May 19, 1866.

23. *Buffalo Commercial*, June 18, 1866.

24. Gordon-Reed, *Andrew Johnson*, 79–85.

25. Quote from "a constituent of Elihu Washburne," who was a member of Congress from Illinois, in Gordon-Reed, *Andrew Johnson*, 12.

26. Georgia was readmitted in 1868, but because it then expelled nearly thirty Black members of its legislature, Congress reimposed federal military management until 1870, when Georgia successfully petitioned for readmittance.

27. Henry Mars, "Kentucky Freedman to the Secretary of War," May 14, 1866, Freedmen and Southern Society Project, http://www.freedmen.umd.edu/Mars.html.

28. One of the best books on Reconstruction is Brooks D. Simpson's *The Reconstruction Presidents*.

29. P. Samuel Tate petition, PUSG, 17:583, 583; AHM's Paducah claim, PUSG, 17:589; P. G. T. Beauregard to AHM, February 10, 1867, Folder 162, Box 36, Series 3, Collection: Ulysses S. Grant, USG Presidential Library Archives.

30. Williams, *P. G. T. Beauregard*, 78.

31. Williams, *P. G. T. Beauregard*, 260.

32. *Detroit Free Press*, December 21, 1866; *National Republican* (Washington DC), December 24, 1866; "[Absalom H. Markland] Silver Congressional Presentation Goblets," sold April 8, 2011, Markland items, Heritage Auctions.

33. A "Copperhead" was a Northern Democrat who opposed the war and was often accused of Southern sympathies.

34. *Daily Empire* (Dayton OH), August 20, 1866; A. H. Markland, "How General Grant Was Persuaded to Accept a Nomination for the Presidency," *Indianapolis Journal*, January 12, 1887, reprinted from the *New York Sun*; "In Cleveland, Ohio, the Democratic-Aligned Soldiers and Sailors Union, Holds Its First Annual Convention," House Divided: The Civil War Search Engine at Dickinson College, accessed April 7, 2022, http://hd.housedivided.dickinson.edu/node/45653.

35. Markland, "How General Grant Was Persuaded to Accept a Nomination for the Presidency," *Indianapolis Journal*, January 12, 1887.

36. Johnson returned to Tennessee, but he continued to pursue a political career. He was elected to the U.S. Senate, taking office in 1875, but he died at the age of sixty-six after suffering a stroke later that year.

37. Simpson, *Let Us Have Peace*, 146.

9. "Our Continued Services Together"

1. *New York Sun*, December 12, 1868; *National Republican* (Washington DC), December 14, 1868.

2. McFeely, *Grant, a Biography*, 290; Calhoun, *Presidency of Ulysses S. Grant*, 70.

3. Calhoun, *Presidency of Ulysses S. Grant*, 74.

4. Calhoun, *Presidency of Ulysses S. Grant*, 74.

5. Alexander R. Boteler to AHM, November 23, 1885, Papers of Alexander Boteler, David M. Rubenstein Rare Book and Manuscript Library, Duke University (original emphasis). All quotations in the discussion of Markland's meeting with Grant about Santo Domingo are from this source.

6. Osborne and Bombaro, *Forgotten Abolitionist*; Abraham Lincoln to J. A. J. Creswell, March 7 and 14, 1864, Abraham Lincoln Papers, LoC. The descriptions of Creswell as "burly" and "debonair" come from Osborne, *Forgotten Abolitionist*, 53; and J. E. Smith, *Grant*, 469, respectively.

7. John A. J. Creswell, *Congressional Globe*, January 5, 1865. His speech was widely reprinted.

8. *New York Tribune*, January 6, 1865; Martin, *New Administration*, 138–49; *Harper's Weekly*, February 18, 1865, 1.

9. Osborne, *Forgotten Abolitionist*, 53–55.

10. Osborne, *Forgotten Abolitionist*, 53–55. Congress later reinstituted franking but on a limited basis.

11. Osborne, *Forgotten Abolitionist*, 54.

12. U.S. Senate, *Journal of the Executive Proceedings of the Senate of the U.S.*, vol. 19, April 16, 1869, 192.

13. *Memphis Daily Appeal*, April 19, 1869; *Baltimore Sun*, April 19, 1869; *Cincinnati Enquirer*, April 23, 1869.

14. Briggs, *Olivia Letters*, 121.

15. *Daily Standard* (Raleigh NC), May 8, 1869; *Times-Picayune* (New Orleans LA), May 8, 1869; *National Republican*, May 8, 1869.

16. *St. Louis Globe-Democrat*, August 2, 1885.

17. *Clarion-Ledger* (Jackson MS), May 20, 1869. See also *Annual Report of the Postmaster General* (1869), 14, 15, at Philatelic Frajola, accessed April 8, 2022, https://www.rfrajola.com/PMG/1869PMG.pdf.

18. "The Civil War: Side 1," Historical Obelisks, Freedom Park, University of Louisville, accessed April 8, 2022, https://louisville.edu/freedompark/historical-obelisks/the-civil-war; "Population by Counties, 1790–1870: Table II, State of Kentucky" (census publication), accessed April 8, 2022, https://www2.census.gov/library/publications/decennial/1870/population/1870a-07.pdf.

19. *National Republican* (Washington DC), May 5, June 25, 1869; *Evening Star*, February 8, 12, 1870 (original emphasis).

20. *Buffalo Morning Express*, August 10, 1869; *Daily Milwaukee News*, October 22, 1869.

21. *Tennessean* (Nashville), November 21, 1869; *Memphis Daily Appeal*, August 28, 1869.

22. Rable, *But There Was No Peace*, 106, 107.

23. Gibson, *History of the United Brothers of Friendship*, pt. 2, 3–84. All Gibson quotes not otherwise identified are from this biography.

24. G. C. Wharton to AHM, June 20, 1870, *Congressional Globe*, U.S. Senate, 42nd Cong., 1st sess., March 23, 1871, 238; U.S. Postal Service official history, USPS, accessed May 11, 2022, https://about.usps.com/who/profile/history/pdf/mail-by-rail.pdf.

25. Kentucky did not vote to ratify the Thirteenth Amendment until 1976.

26. Gibson, *History of the United Brothers of Friendship*, pt. 2, 53–54.

27. Gibson, *History of the United Brothers of Friendship*, pt. 2, 54.

28. W. H. Gibson to AHM, January 27, 1871, *Appendix to the Congressional Globe*, April 3, 1871, 145; *Daily Evening Express* (Lancaster PA), March 9, 1871.

29. C. C. Green to AHM, undated, in *Appendix to the Congressional Globe*, April 3, 1871, 145.

30. Gibson, *History of the United Brothers of Friendship*, pt. 2, 55. It was actually one month, rather than three, that the military protected Gibson.

31. Gov. John Stevenson to the Kentucky Senate and House of Representatives, January 31, 1871, *Congressional Globe*, March 23, 1871, 239; *Louisville Courier*, March 24, 1871, quoted in *Congressional Globe*, April 3, 1871, 146.

32. Diary entry of Hamilton Fish, February 24, 1871, Hamilton Fish Papers, LoC.

33. Act of February 28, 1861, in Digest of Bills, *U.S. Statutes at Large*, 36th Cong., 2nd sess., chap. 61, 177–78, accessed at https://www.loc.gov/item/llsl-v12/.

34. AHM to John A. J. Creswell, March 3, 1871, *Congressional Globe*, March 23, 1871, 239; *Daily Dispatch* (Richmond VA), March 10, 1871. Eventually, mail between Frankfort and Lexington was carried by stagecoach, but that route was longer and much slower.

35. *Daily Dispatch* (Richmond VA), March 10, 1871.

36. Quoted in Calhoun, *Presidency of Ulysses S. Grant*, 317. An anti-Klan bill introduced in the House earlier by Representative Benjamin Butler (R-MA) did not gather support enough to pass.

37. *Congressional Globe*, March 23, 1871, 247.

38. *New York Tribune*, March 24, 1871.

39. *Congressional Globe*, March 31, 1871, 347, 362.

40. *Brooklyn (NY) Daily Eagle*, March 8, 1871. The *Eagle* was a Democratic newspaper from its inception in 1841; its distribution was suspended during the Civil War. *Congressional Globe*, March 30, 1871, 95.

41. "St. Louis Prosecutor Invokes 'Ku Klux Klan Act' in Lawsuit," Associated Press, January 15, 2020; "Capitol Police Officers Sue Trump, Right-Wing Groups over Jan. 6," *The Hill*, August 26, 2021.

42. Gibson, *History of the United Brothers of Friendship*, pt. 2, 55; *Hickman (KY) Courier*, April 15, 1871; diary entry of Hamilton Fish, April 4, 1871, Hamilton Fish Papers, LoC. The draft order for the resumption of mail service was read in the cabinet meeting that day. Railway agent Gibson co-founded the United Brothers of Friendship in 1876, which

became a highly successful national Black fraternal and charitable organization. He helped to establish the Colored Orphans Home and the Colored Cemetery in Louisville, was a trustee of Wilberforce University, and was active in many musical societies. He died in 1906 at the age of seventy-six.

43. Diary entry of Hamilton Fish, April 4, 1871, Hamilton Fish Papers, LoC; *Philadelphia Public Ledger*, April 21, 1871, *PUSG*, 21:251.

44. *PUSG*, 21:337; Rable, *But There Was No Peace*, 106–8.

45. Old Chicago Main Post Office Building, Chicago Landmark Designation Report, December 2017, https://www.chicago.gov/content/dam/city/depts/zlup/Historic_Preservation/Publications/Old_Chicago_Main_Post_Office_Bldg.pdf.

46. *Evening Star* (Washington DC), October 11, 1871.

47. *Wheeling (WV) Daily Intelligencer*, October 12, 1871; *Selma (AL) Morning Times*, October 12, 1871; AHM to Luther Thayer Thustin, August 27, 1873, Papers of Luther Thayer Thustin, Filson.

48. *Burlington (VT) Free Press*, October 17, 1871.

49. "Well-Known Negro Succumbs to Death," *Louisville Courier-Journal*, June 4, 1906, 2; Gibson, *History of the United Brothers of Friendship*, pt. 2, 75. As a gauger, Gibson held keys to padlocks on all distillery warehouses in the state.

50. *PUSG*, 22:437; P. S. Ruckman Jr., "Federal Executive Clemency in United States, 1789–1995: A Preliminary Report," accessed April 11, 2022, https://web.archive.org/web/20110326045557/http://ednet.rvc.cc.il.us/~PeterR/Papers/paper3.htm. Most of Grant's 1,332 pardons went to former Confederates and Confederate sympathizers.

10. The "Colonel" Becomes a "General"

1. The Grand Army of the Republic (GAR) was different from the individual army societies. It was an activist group that, among other things, lobbied for pensions for its members. It required proof of military service from the War or Navy Department to join. It also welcomed former U.S. Colored Troops. At its height, the GAR had more than four hundred thousand members (Markland was not among them). Confederate veterans also formed fraternal societies.

2. *Report of the Proceedings of the Society of the Army of the Tennessee*, 1873, 407, 408, 97, 98, accessed at HathiTrust, https://babel.hathitrust.org/cgi/pt?id=chi.100981037&view=1up&seq=109&skin=2021&q1=%22Seventh%20Annual%20Meeting%22. In 1873 the society's recording secretary lamented that only about one hundred of the society's approximately eight hundred members had paid their dues. *Report of the Proceedings of the Society of the Army of the Tennessee*, 1873, 100, accessed at HathiTrust, https://babel.hathitrust.org/cgi/pt?id=chi.100981037&view=1up&seq=110&skin=2021&q1=%22Seventh%20Annual%20Meeting%22.

3. *Report of the Proceedings of the Society of the Army of the Tennessee*, 1866, 6, accessed at HathiTrust, https://babel.hathitrust.org/cgi/pt?id=mdp.39015069385238&view=1up&seq=3&skin=2021.

4. *The Army Reunion with Reports of the Meetings of the Societies of the Army of the Cumberland, the Army of the Tennessee, the Army of the Ohio, and the Army of Georgia* (Chicago, 1869), 18–19, accessed at HathiTrust, https://babel.hathitrust.org/cgi/pt?id=mdp.39015069385238&view=1up&seq=3&skin=2021.

5. *Daily State Journal* (Alexandria VA), April 7, 1871.

6. Rable, *But There Was No Peace*, 188.

7. *Inter-Ocean* (Chicago IL), July 5, 1872.

8. *Report of the Proceedings of the Society of the Army of the Tennessee*, 1872, 283, accessed at HathiTrust, https://babel.hathitrust.org/cgi/pt?id=uc1.$b541285&view=1up&seq=293&skin=2021&q1=hoarded%20mails.

9. "History of the Soldier's [*sic*] Home," Soldiers Home of Dayton, Ohio, last updated July 27, 2018, http://www.carolynjburns.com/soldiers/.

10. *Indianapolis Journal*, December 12, 1872.

11. U.S. House of Representatives, *Papers Relating to Postal Railway-Car Service*, 38; *Nashville Union and American*, October 17, 1873; *National Republican* (Washington DC), October 21, 1873.

12. *Tiffin (OH) Tribune*, October 23, 1873.

13. *Fort Wayne Daily Gazette*, November 2, 1873.

14. Rable, *But There Was No Peace*, 123; *New Orleans Republican*, October 26, 1873, reprinted from the *Indianapolis Journal*, October 22, 1873.

15. *Cincinnati Gazette* quoted in *Nashville Union and American*, November 26, 1873.

16. *Fort Wayne Daily Gazette*, November 2, 1873.

17. *Chicago Daily Tribune*, December 1, 1873.

18. AHM to Luther Thayer Thustin, August 27, 1873, Papers of Luther Thayer Thustin, Filson.

19. *Arizona Sentinel* (Yuma), December 20, 1873.

20. Mixon, "Crisis of 1873."

21. *Indianapolis News*, January 5, 1874; Gutman, "Trouble on the Railroads," 220.

22. "Henry Van Ness Boynton," Congressional Medal of Honor Society, accessed April 12, 2022, https://www.cmohs.org/recipients/henry-v-boynton; miscellaneous correspondence from Boynton to AHM, 1872 to ca. 1884, Papers of Henry Van Ness Boynton, Ohio History Connection.

23. Boynton to AHM, July 24, 1874, Papers of Henry Van Ness Boynton, Ohio History Connection.

24. *National Republican* (Washington DC), September 30, 1874; *Quad-City Times* (Davenport IA), October 2, 1874.

25. "Military Mail Service," National Postal Museum, Smithsonian Institution, accessed April 12, 2022, https://postalmuseum.si.edu/exhibition/behind-the-badge-postal-inspection-service-duties-and-history-history/military-mail.

26. Lt. Col. Casey Doss (U.S. Army, Ret.) and Martha Beltran (Captain, U.S. Army Adjutant General Corps, 1996–2004), Zoom discussion with author, September 8, 2021.

27. Hacker, "Decennial Life Tables for the White Population"; AHM to Hickenlooper, April 4, 1881, in *Report of the Proceedings of the Society of the Army of the Tennessee*, 1881, 27–28, accessed at HathiTrust, https://babel.hathitrust.org/cgi/pt?id=uc1.$b541287&view=1up&seq=7&skin=2021.

28. Williamson, *Observations on Nasal Catarrh and Catarrhal Deafness*, 3–7.

29. WTS calling card enclosed in wedding invitation sent to AHM, fall 1874, Markland Papers, Filson.

30. AHM to W. M. Belknap, April 27, 1875, NARA, accessed at Fold3 Military Records of Ancestry.com, https://www.fold3.com/image/299139603.

31. *National Republican* (Washington DC), May 29, 1875.

32. *National Republican* (Washington DC), May 29, 1875.

33. *National Republican* (Washington DC), December 22, 1875.

34. "Speech of General Grant," *Report of the Proceedings of the Society of the Army of the Tennessee*, 1875, 384, accessed at HathiTrust, https://babel.hathitrust.org/cgi/pt?id=ucl. $b541285&view=1up&seq=394&skin=2021&q1=Speech%20of%General%20Grant.

35. *Intelligencer Journal* (Lancaster PA), July 18, 1876; *Chicago Tribune*, August 29, 1876; *Alexandria Gazette*, October 26, 1876.

36. AHM to R. B. Hayes, January 5, 1877, quoted in Alexander, "Persistent Whiggery in the Confederate South," 325n58; R. B. Hayes to MSM, June 20, 1876, Markland items, Heritage Auctions; *National Republican* (Washington DC), March 14, 1877; Simpson, *Let Us Have Peace*, 146.

37. Theisen, "Public Career of General Lew Wallace," 282.

38. *Evening Star* (Washington DC), October 10, 1879.

39. *Chicago Daily Tribune*, November 13, 1879; *Report of the Proceedings of the Society of the Army of the Tennessee*, 1879, 328, 329, 407, https://www.google.com/books/edition /Report_of_the_Proceedings_of_the_Society/8cX-Sk9vKlYC?hl=en&gbpv=1.

40. "Our Story," Hamilton Hotel, accessed May 30, 2022, https://www.hamiltonhoteldc .com/about/our-story; "Streets of Washington," January 23, 2010, https://www .streetsofwashington.com/2010/01/hamilton-hotel.html; U.S. Census, 1880, accessed at Ancestry.com, https://www.ancestry.com/imageviewer/collections/6742/images/4240114 -00699?backlabel=ReturnSearchResults&queryId=68a7f4a243851477d9c4fa002e33ac2c &pId=26900229; *Washington Law Reporter*, January 1880, 2; *Intelligencer Journal* (Lancaster PA), January 19, 1880.

41. *Report of the Proceedings of the Society of the Army of the Tennessee*, 1871, 105, 106, accessed at HathiTrust, https://babel.hathitrust.org/cgi/pt?id=mdp.39015070227304& view=1up&seq=113&skin=2021&q1=put%20up. Quotations from Dodds in subsequent paragraphs are from this source.

42. *Evening Star*, August 28, 1880.

43. Kenneth Rayner to AHM, June 29, 1882, Absolom [*sic*] Hanks Markland Papers, TSLA. Rayner is often misspelled Raynor.

44. John R. Jordan Jr., "Kenneth Rayner, 1808–1884," Documenting the American South, accessed April 12, 2022, https://docsouth.unc.edu/nc/rayner/bio.html; "Rayner, Kenneth," History, Art & Archives, U.S. House of Representatives, accessed April 12, 2022, https://history.house.gov/People/Listing/R/RAYNER,-Kenneth-(r000087)/.

45. Kenneth Rayner to AHM, June 29, 1882.

46. *Evening Star*, June 30, 1881; Garfield comments to *Louisville Courier* quoted in *Progressive Farmer* (Winston-Salem NC), November 27, 1900.

47. Candice Millard's *Destiny of the Republic* is a masterpiece of medical and political history on the shooting of Garfield and its aftermath.

48. *The Critic* (Washington DC), February 8, 1882; *Semi-Weekly Interior Journal* (Stanford KY), February 10, 1882.

49. *Princeton (IN) Clarion-Leader*, March 2, 1882.

50. Robert Todd Lincoln to AHM, October 4, 1882, Lincoln Collection, Lincoln Financial Foundation.

51. "Statues in Out-of-the-Way Places," *Sunday Star* (Washington DC), June 11, 1905; "General John A. Rawlins (sculpture)," Art Inventories Catalog, Smithsonian Institution Research Information System, accessed April 13, 2022, https://siris-artinventories.si.edu /ipac20/ipac.jsp?&profile=all&source=~!siartinventories&uri=full=3100001~!19546 ~!0#focus.

52. Markland comment in *Washington Evening Star*, August 1, 1885; USG to AHM, April 8, 1884, *PUSG*, 31:131.

53. AHM to Col. T. W. Higginson, June 9, 1884; Higginson to AHM, June 10, 1884, both in Markland Papers, Filson. Higginson is best remembered as Emily Dickinson's mentor and coeditor of her first two books of poetry.

54. AHM to USG, December 10, 1884, *PUSG*, 31:233, 234. The quotations in the next two paragraphs are from this source.

55. *New York Times*, March 1, 1885; *St. Louis Globe-Dispatch*, August 2, 1885; AHM to DFB, March 30, 1885, Absolom [*sic*] Hanks Markland Papers, TSLA.

56. Frederick Grant to AHM, March 22, 1885, EAC Gallery, Lot #71, Spring 2013, https:// www.liveauctioneers.com/auctioneer/393/eac-gallery/; Ely S. Parker to AHM, April 10, 1885, Ely S. Parker Papers, American Philosophical Society.

11. A Man in Search of Himself

1. Ear problems discussed in AHM to MSM, October 10, 11, 16, 18, 1861, Absolom [*sic*] Hanks Markland Papers, TSLA; Alexander Graham Bell, "The Deaf" (report drawn from the 1900 census), accessed April 20, 2022, https://www2.census.gov/library/publications /decennial/1900/blind-and-deaf/blind-and-deaf-part-4.pdf; *Indianapolis Journal*, May 27, 1888.

2. Helen Keller quote, November 1, 1950, Helen Keller Archive, American Foundation for the Blind, https://www.afb.org/HelenKellerArchive?a=d&d=A-HK02-B229-F02-007 &e=-------en-20--1--txt--------1-2-1-undefined-3--------------0-1; "Captives of Silence," *New York Times*, August 8, 1975.

3. Lohmiller, "Emotional Issues of Dealing with a Hearing Loss," 2, 3.

4. *Cashocton Clarion* (Mechanicsville MD), July 26, 1883.

5. *New York Times*, February 16, 1885, May 26, 1888.

6. AHM, draft letter to John P. Phister, MD, 1885, Absolom [*sic*] Hanks Markland Papers, TSLA; "Grant as Commander," *Pittsburgh Press*, February 9, 1888.

7. "Old Tecumseh," *Omaha Daily Bee*, April 7, 1885. The quotations in the subsequent paragraph are from this source.

8. Ely S. Parker to AHM, June 18, 1885, Ely S. Parker Papers, American Philosophical Society.

9. *Evening Star* quoted in *Wahpeton (ND) Times*, July 30, 1885.

10. Charles A. Dana to AHM, January 6 and 29, 1887, Papers of Charles A. Dana, New York Public Library; *New York Sun*, January 9, 1887.

11. AHM to WTS, July 18, 1887, Abraham Lincoln Presidential Library and Museum; Ely S. Parker to AHM, July 21, 1884, https://www.nps.gov/apco/learn/education/upload /APCO-3415-and-3416-Parker-Lettersfeb16.pdf.

12. *New York Times*, July 1, 1887.

13. AHM to Jefferson A. Davis, July 1, 1887, in Dunbar, *Jefferson Davis, Constitutionalist*, 571, 572.

14. "Memoranda on the Civil War," 779 (see also the "Memoranda on the Civil War" feature in *Century Illustrated Magazine* 30 [1885]: 150); *New York Sun*, January 30, 1887; AHM to DFB, December 24, 1885, Absolom [*sic*] Hanks Markland Papers, TSLA. In fact, Grant's first reference to the log house is correct (PMUSG, 2:345), but he misstates the location on his second mention of it (PMUSG, 2:349).

15. *Courier-Journal* (Louisville), November 19, 1887; WTS to AHM, January 3, 1887, Markland Papers, Filson.

16. Charles Dana to AHM, June 25, 1886, Papers of Charles A. Dana, New York Public Library.

17. [Markland], *"O.B.'s" Reminiscences*, 18. All subsequent quotes in the discussion of Markland's "O.B." letters are from this source but will not be identified by page number.

18. In 1937 the Ohio River crested at 75.6 feet, damaged most of the city's infrastructure, and spurred the town to action. In 1950, with the aid of the Army Corps of Engineers, the city built a vast concrete floodwall engineered to protect it from floodwaters up to 79 feet deep.

19. Federal Writers' Project of the Works Progress Administration for the State of Kentucky, University of Kentucky, *Kentucky*; "Maysville Downtown Historic District," National Register of Historic Places Inventory, 1962, accessed at NP Gallery Digital Asset Management System, https://npgallery.nps.gov/.

20. During the Civil War, "Old Tip" was buried to prevent it from being stolen by either army. It was later turned upside down and anchored in front of the New York Store on Second Street to keep horses and wagons off the sidewalk, according to the *Cincinnati Enquirer*, September 21, 1968. Today, it sits proudly next to the Mason County clerk's office.

21. AHM to DFB, March 23, 1885, Absolom [*sic*] Hanks Markland Papers, TSLA. Markland was ultimately unsuccessful in hiding his identity. In the Kentucky Gateway Museum and Genealogical Library in Maysville and in the Kentucky Historical Society in Frankfort, *"O.B.'s" Reminiscences* are filed under Markland's name.

22. *Louisville Courier-Journal*, October 29, 1882; AHM to DFB, November 25, 1885, Absolom [*sic*] Hanks Markland Papers, TSLA.

23. "O.B. has played his last card and left its mystery with Phister," commented Markland. AHM to DFB, November 25, 1885, Absolom [*sic*] Hanks Markland Papers, TSLA.

24. AHM in Rice, *Reminiscences of Abraham Lincoln*, 324, 325.

25. AHM in Rice, *Reminiscences of Abraham Lincoln*, 326–29.

26. AHM to DFB, December 25, 1885, Absolom [*sic*] Hanks Markland Papers, TSLA; WTS to AHM, January 4, 1886, Markland items, Heritage Auctions.

27. WTS to AHM, December 27, 1886, Heritage Auctions, https://historical.ha.com /itm/autographs/william-t-sherman-autograph-letters-3-signed-all-are-signed-w-t-sherman -and-were-written-between-q/a/6054-34253.s?ic4=GalleryView-Thumbnail-071515.

28. WTS to AHM, November 23, 1886, Abraham Lincoln Presidential Library and Museum.

29. Crocker's Iowa Brigade, *Proceedings of Crocker's Iowa Brigade at the Fourth Reunion*, 36.

30. AHM to O. M. Poe, September 1, 1887, *Report of the Proceedings of the Society of the Army of the Tennessee at the Twentieth Meeting*, 1887, 26, accessed at HathiTrust, https://

babel.hathitrust.org/cgi/pt/search?id=mdp.39015071545787&q1=A.+H.+Markland&
sz=25&start=1&sort=seq&h1=true.

31. AHM to President Grover Cleveland, April 28, 1885, Absolom [*sic*] Hanks Mark-land Papers, TSLA; two documents supporting Charles H. Page, 1885, AHM Papers, LoC; A. R. Boteler to AHM, November 21, 1887, Papers of Alexander Boteler, David Rubenstein Library, Duke University.

32. AHM to DFB, November 21, 1885; and AHM to DFB, December 9, 1886, both in Absolom [*sic*] Hanks Markland Papers, TSLA.

33. For example, William Tecumseh Sherman also signed letters to his brothers and wife "W. T. Sherman" or "Sherman."

34. "The Genealogist: A Unique Survey," InstaRestoration, accessed April 14, 2020, https://www.instarestoration.com/blog/the-genealogist-a-unique-survey.

35. AHM to DFB, November 24, 1885, Absolom [*sic*] Hanks Markland Papers, TSLA.

36. James Flanagan to AHM, November 11, 1885, Markland Papers, Filson; inventory in Comstock, *Before Abolition*, 306; U.S. Census, 1840, accessed at Ancestry.com, https://www.ancestry.com/discoveryui-content/view/2114302:8057?tid=&pid=&queryId=a779226b1a964ff0fe7f1b929cba53bc&_phsrc=KgN2&_phstart=successSource.

37. [Markland], *"O.B.'s" Reminiscences*, Letter #10.

38. Corum, *Ulysses Underground*, 138, 140, citing a local Maysville family history. Peter Grant died seven years before Hiram Ulysses boarded with Peter's widow and his cousins.

39. The author's plan to obtain a professional genealogical study to determine whether Markland was related to Lincoln was thwarted by the COVID-19 pandemic, which shut-tered essential genealogical archives during the researching of this biography.

40. Larry Margasak, "The Blizzard of 1888" (blog post), *O Say Can You See?* (National Museum of American History), March 9, 2016, https://americanhistory.si.edu/blog/blizzard-1888.

41. AHM to Julia Grant, March 19, 1888, PUSG, 31:281; Frederick Grant to AHM, April 11, 1888, EAC Gallery, Lot #71, Spring 2013. In the end, Badeau received $10,000, pursuant to the contract he signed before Grant's death, and he disavowed coauthorship of the memoirs.

42. Suzanne Wray, "A Tale of Two Cycloramas," National Park Service, 2018, https://www.nps.gov/articles/000/a-tale-of-two-cycloramas.htm; *Evening Star*, May 19, 1888. While the panoramas of Gettysburg and Atlanta have been restored and are open to visi-tors today, the one of Shiloh disappeared after its exhibition in Washington.

43. AHM to DFB, April 5, 1888, Absolom [*sic*] Hanks Markland Papers, TSLA. This is the last extant letter between the two men that is available to historians. Note that Mark-land says he was "only a super[intendent]" and did not say he was "only a colonel." Quotes in subsequent paragraphs are from this April 5, 1888, letter by Markland.

44. *The Critic* (Washington DC), May 24, 1888.

45. *New York Times*, May 26, 1888; *Buffalo (NY) Morning Express*, May 28, 1888; *Evening Star*, May 25, 1888; *Courier-Journal*, May 26, 1888; *Indianapolis Journal*, May 27, 1888.

46. *Appleton's Annual Cyclopaedia and Register of Important Events of the Year 1888*, 645.

47. WTS to MSM, May 31, 1888, Heritage Auctions, https://historical.ha.com/itm/autographs/william-t-sherman-autograph-letters-3-signed-all-are-signed-w-t-sherman-and-were-written-between-q/a/6054-34253.s?ic4=GalleryView-Thumbnail-071515. The quotes in the final paragraph of the chapter are also from this source. Described as "as an

elegant lady of this city," Martha arranged for her husband's funeral at St. John's Episcopal Church, across Lafayette Square from the White House, and his interment in Oak Hill Cemetery, where her mother and father were buried. Later in the summer of 1888, fifty-year-old Martha became seriously ill and moved from the Clarendon Hotel to the "sanitarium of Dr. Johnson," where she died on December 6. In a testament to the devoted friends she and Markland had made through his army contacts and to her family's stature in the community, her pallbearers included Surgeon General John Moore (of the Seidlitz powders anecdote), Gen. Alexander R. Boteler, Gen. Henry Van Ness Boynton, and Henry A. Willard (proprietor of Willard's Hotel).

Epilogue

1. *Report of the Proceedings of the Society of the Army of the Tennessee*, 1888, 179, 180, accessed at HathiTrust, https://babel.hathitrust.org/cgi/pt?id=nyp.33433079009563& view=1up&seq=192&skin=2021&q1=kindly%20disposed%20heart.

2. "Military Mail Service," Behind the Badge: The U.S. Postal Inspection Service, National Postal Museum, Smithsonian Institution, accessed April 14, 2022, https://postalmuseum.si .edu/exhibition/behind-the-badge-postal-inspection-service-duties-and-history-history /military-mail. A quote from General Howard's letter is also etched on the entrance to the museum's Civil War exhibit.

Bibliography

Archives and Manuscript Materials

Abraham Lincoln Presidential Library and Museum, Springfield IL

American Foundation for the Blind, New York NY
 Helen Keller Archive

American Philatelic Research Library, Bellefonte PA

American Philosophical Society, Philadelphia PA
 Ely S. Parker Papers

David M. Rubenstein Rare Book and Manuscript Library, Duke University, Durham NC
 Papers of Alexander Boteler

Filson Historical Society, Louisville KY
 Papers of Luther Thayer Thustin
 Papers of Matthew Markland and Absalom Hanks Markland

Kentucky Gateway Museum Center and Genealogical Library, Maysville KY
 Absalom Markland Papers
 Hixson Papers

Kentucky Historical Society, Martin F. Schmidt Research Library, Frankfort KY

Library of Congress, Washington DC
 Abraham Lincoln Papers
 Absalom H. Markland Papers
 Andrew Johnson Papers
 Charles A. Dana Papers
 Hamilton Fish Papers

Lincoln Financial Foundation, Fort Wayne IN
 The Lincoln Collection

National Archives, Washington DC
 Letters Received, Department of the Missouri, U.S. Army Continental Commands, Record Group 393, pt. 1
 Letters Received, U.S. Colored Troops Division, Adjutant General's Office, Record Group 94
 Letters Received by the Adjutant General, 1861–1870

Nau Civil War Collection, Houston TX

New York Public Library, New York NY
  Papers of Charles A. Dana
Ohio History Connection, Columbus OH
  Papers of Henry Van Ness Boynton
Tennessee State Library and Archives, Nashville TN
  Absolom [*sic*] Hanks Markland Papers, 1821–88
Ulysses S. Grant Presidential Library Archives, Mississippi State MS
University of Notre Dame Archives, Notre Dame IN
  William T. Sherman Family Papers
University of the Pacific Archives, Stockton CA
University of Wyoming Libraries, Emmett D. Chisum Special Collections, Laramie WY
U.S. Army Heritage and Education Center, Carlisle PA
  MOLLUS Mass Photograph Collection
William L. Clements Library, University of Michigan, Ann Arbor MI
  James S. Schoff Civil War Collection
Woodson Research Center, Fondren Library, Rice University, Houston TX
  Papers of Jefferson Davis Documents and Reference Collection, 1815–2015

Published Works

Alcott, Louisa May. *Hospital Sketches*. Boston, 1863.

Alexander, Thomas B. "Persistent Whiggery in the Confederate South, 1860–1877." *Journal of Southern History* 27, no. 3 (1961): 305–29.

American Tract Society. "Mail Call." In *The Family Christian Almanac for 1864*. New York, 1864.

Anderson, John. "Postal System Development during the Civil War." Paper presented at the Conference of the Association for Education in Journalism and Mass Communication, San Francisco CA, August 2006.

Appleton's Annual Cyclopaedia and Register of Important Events of the Year 1888. New York: D. Appleton, 1891.

Barber, James G. *U.S. Grant, the Man and the Image*. Washington DC: National Portrait Gallery, Smithsonian Institution, in association with Southern Illinois University Press, 1985.

Basler, Roy P., ed. *Collected Works of Abraham Lincoln, 1809–1865*. Springfield IL: Abraham Lincoln Association, 1953.

Blassinghame, John, and John McKivigan, eds. *The Frederick Douglass Papers*. Series 1, Speeches, Debates, and Interviews. Vol. 4, 1864–80. New Haven CT: Yale University Press, 1999.

Blessington, Joseph P. *The Campaigns of Walker's Texas Division*. New York, 1875.

Briggs, Emily Edson. *The Olivia Letters: Being Some History of Washington City for Forty Years as Told by the Letters of a Newspaper Correspondent*. New York: Neale, 1906.

Brown, Emma Elizabeth. *Life of Ulysses Simpson Grant*. Boston, 1885.

Bruesch, S. R. "The Disasters and Epidemics of a River Town: Memphis, Tennessee, 1819–1879." *Bulletin of the Medical Library* 40, no. 3 (1952): 288–305.

Burlingame, Michael. *With Lincoln in the White House*. Carbondale: Southern Illinois University Press, 2000.

Burr, Frank A. *Life and Deeds of General Ulysses S. Grant*. Battle Creek MI, 1885.

Calhoun, Charles W. *The Presidency of Ulysses S. Grant*. Lawrence: University Press of Kansas, 2017.

Catton, Bruce. *Never Call Retreat*. London: Phoenix Press, 1965.

———. *A Stillness at Appomattox*. New York: Doubleday, 1954.

Chester, James. "Inside Ft. Sumter." In *Battles and Leaders of the Civil War*, vol. 1, edited by Robert Johnson Underwood and Clarence Clough Buel. New York, 1887.

Columbia Historical Society. *Records of the Columbia Historical Society*. Vol. 13. Washington DC, 1910.

Comstock, Lyndon. *Before Abolition: African Americans in Early Clark County, Ky*. N.p.: Create Space Independent Publishing Platform, 2017.

Corbett, Christopher. *Orphans Preferred: The Twisted Truth and Lasting Legend of the Pony Express*. New York: Broadway Books, 2003.

Corum, G. L. *Ulysses Underground: The Unexplored Roots of U.S. Grant and the Underground Railroad*. West Union OH: Riveting History, 2015.

Crocker's Iowa Brigade. *Proceedings of Crocker's Iowa Brigade at the Fourth Reunion*. Davenport IA, 1888.

Dana, Charles A. *Recollections of the Civil War*. New York, 1898.

Davis, William C. *The Deep Waters of the Proud*. Garden City NY: Doubleday, 1982.

Dickinson, Asa Don, ed. *Stories of Achievement*. 6 vols. New York: Doubleday, Page, 1916.

Dieck, Herman. *Life and Public Services of General U.S. Grant*. Philadelphia, 1885.

Dorman, John Frederick, ed. *Virginia Revolutionary Pension Applications*. Vol. 1. Washington DC, 1958. https://babel.hathitrust.org/cgi/pt?id=mdp.39015010864596&view=1up&seq=1.

Dowdall, Denise M. *From Cincinnati to the Colorado Ranger: The Horsemanship of Ulysses S. Grant*. Dublin, Ireland: historyeye, 2012.

Drago, Edmund L. "How Sherman's March through Georgia Affected the Slaves." *Georgia Historical Quarterly* 57, no. 3 (1973): 361–75.

Dunbar, Rowland. *Jefferson Davis, Constitutionalist*. Jackson: Mississippi Department of Archives and History, 1923.

Etcheson, Nicole. *Bleeding Kansas: Contested Liberty in the Civil War Era*. Lawrence: University Press of Kansas, 2004.

Federal Writers' Project of the Works Progress Administration for the State of Kentucky, University of Kentucky. *Kentucky: A Guide to the Bluegrass State*. New York: Harcourt Brace, 1939.

Fitch, John. *Annals of the Army of the Cumberland*. Philadelphia, 1864.

Foner, Eric. *Free Soil, Free Labor, Free Men: The Ideology of the Republican Party before the Civil War*. New York: Oxford University Press, 1970.

Freeman, Julia Susan Wheelock. *The Boys in White: The Experience of a Hospital Agent in and around Washington*. New York, 1870.

Furgurson, Ernest B. *Ashes of Glory: Richmond at War*. New York: Knopf, 1996.

Gage, Moses D. *From Vicksburg to Raleigh*. Chicago: Clarke & Co., 1865.

Gallagher, Winifred. *How the Post Office Created America*. New York: Penguin, 2016.

Garland, Hamlin. *Ulysses S. Grant, His Life and Character*. New York, 1898.

Gibson, William H., Sr. *History of the United Brothers of Friendship and Sisters of the Mysterious Ten*. Louisville KY, 1897.

Goodwin, Doris Kearns. *Team of Rivals.* New York: Simon and Schuster, 2005.

Gordon-Reed, Annette. *Andrew Johnson.* New York: Times Books, 2011.

Grant, Julia Dent. *Personal Memoirs of Julia Dent Grant.* New York: Putnam, 1975.

Grant, Ulysses S. *Papers of Ulysses S. Grant.* 32 vols. Carbondale: Southern Illinois University Press, 1967–2012.

———. *Personal Memoirs of Ulysses S. Grant.* 2 vols. New York, 1885.

———. *Personal Memoirs of Ulysses S. Grant: The Complete Annotated Edition.* Edited by John Marszalek. Cambridge MA: Belknap Press, 2017.

Grimes, Absalom. *Absalom Grimes, Confederate Mail Runner.* Edited by Milo M. Quaife. New Haven: Yale University Press, 1926.

Gutman, Herbert G. "Trouble on the Railroads 1873–1874: Prelude to the 1877 Crisis?" *Labor History* 2, no. 2 (1961): 215–35. https://doi.org/10.1080/00236566108583874.

Hacker, David J. "Decennial Life Tables for the White Population of the United States, 1790–1900." *Historical Methods* 43, no. 2 (2010): 45–79. https://www.ncbi.nlm.nih.gov/pmc/articles/PMC2885717/.

Hammond, Rev. J. Pinkney. *The Army Chaplain's Manual.* Philadelphia, 1863.

Hanson, John Wesley. *Historical Sketch of the Old Sixth Regiment of Massachusetts Volunteers.* Boston, 1866.

Harris, Brayton. *Blue & Gray in Black & White.* Washington DC: Brassey's, 1999.

Hecht, Arthur. "Union Military Mail Service." *Filson Club History Quarterly* 37, no. 3 (1963): 227–48.

Herndon, William H. *Herndon's Lincoln: The True Story of a Great Life; The History and Personal Recollections of Abraham Lincoln.* Vol. 2. Springfield IL: Herndon's Lincoln Publishing Company, 1921.

Holzer, Harold. *Lincoln and the Power of the Press.* New York: Simon and Schuster, 2014.

Hooper, Candice Shy. *Lincoln's Generals' Wives: Four Women Who Influenced the Civil War—for Better and for Worse.* Kent OH: Kent State University Press, 2016.

Hunter, Alfred. *Washington and Georgetown Directory: Strangers' Guide-Book for Washington.* Washington DC: Kirkwood and McGill, 1853.

Hurst, Samuel H. *Journal-History of the Seventy-Third Ohio Volunteer Infantry.* Chillicothe OH, 1866.

Jaronski, Stefan T. "Absalom Markland, U.S. Grant's Postmaster." *La Posta,* March 2008.

Johnson, W. C. "The March to the Sea." In GAR *War Papers: Papers Read before Fred C. Jones Post, No. 401, Department of Ohio,* 1:309–36. Cincinnati, 1891.

Kauffman, Michael W. *American Brutus: John Wilkes Booth and the Lincoln Conspiracies.* New York: Random House Trade Paperbacks, 2004.

Kelsey, Marie. "Ulysses S. Grant: Portrait of an Unknown Soldier." *Grant Network Newsletter,* Fall 2001.

Kentucky Historical Society. "Kentucky Marriages and Obituaries." *Register of Kentucky State Historical Society* 40, no. 132 (October 1942).

LaPointe, Patricia M. "Military Hospitals in Memphis, 1861–1865." *Tennessee Historical Quarterly* 42, no. 4 (1983): 325–42.

Letters from the Forty-Fourth Regiment M.V.M. . . . by "Corporal." Boston, 1863.

Livermore, Mary A. *My Story of the War.* Hartford CT: A. D. Worthington, 1890.

Lohmiller, Erika. "Emotional Issues of Dealing with a Hearing Loss." Paper presented at meeting of the Association of Late Deafened Adults (ALDAcon), St. Louis MO, 2006. https://alda.org/wp-content/uploads/2019/09/SelfAdvocate-Lohmiller.pdf.

Long, E. B., with Barbara Long. *The Civil War Day by Day*. New York: Da Capo Press, 1985.

Lossing, Benson John. *Pictorial History of the Civil War*. Vol. 2. Hartford CT, 1868.

Manning, Chandra. *What This Cruel War Is Over*. New York: Knopf, 2007.

[Markland, A. H.]. *"O.B.'s" Reminiscences: Memories of Old Maysville between the Years 1832 and 1848*. Maysville KY, 1883.

Marks, Rev. J. J. *The Peninsula Campaign in Virginia or Incidents and Scenes on the Battle-Fields and in Richmond*. Philadelphia, 1864.

Marszalek, John. *Sherman: A Soldier's Passion for Order*. New York: Free Press, 1993.

————. *Sherman's Other War*. Kent OH: Kent State University Press, 1991.

Martin, Edward Winslow. *The New Administration; containing Complete and Authentic Biographies of Grant and his Cabinet*. New York: George S. Wilcox, 1869.

McFeely, William S. *Grant, a Biography*. New York: Norton, 1981.

McPherson, James M. *For Cause and Comrades: Why Men Fought in the Civil War*. New York: Oxford University Press, 1997.

"Memoranda on the Civil War." *Century Illustrated Monthly Magazine* 29 (March 1885): 777–79.

Millard, Candice. *The Destiny of the Republic: A Tale of Madness, Medicine and the Murder of a President*. New York: Anchor Books, 2012.

Mixon, Scott. "The Crisis of 1873." *Journal of Economic History* 68, no. 3 (2008): 722–57. https://doi.org/10.1017/S0022050708000624.

Morris, B. F., ed. *Memorial Record of the Nation's Tribute to Abraham Lincoln*. Washington DC, 1865.

Mowris, J. A. *A History of the One Hundred and Seventeenth Regiment, N.Y. Volunteers*. Hartford CT, 1866.

M. W. Grand Lodge. *Proceedings of the M. W. Grand Lodge of Free and Accepted Masons of the District of Columbia, 1850–1862*. Washington DC, 1861.

Nichols, George Ward. *The Story of the Great March: From the Diary of a Staff Officer*. New York, 1866.

Nicolay, John G., and John Hay. "Abraham Lincoln: A History." *Century Illustrated Magazine* 33, no. 1 (November 1, 1886).

Norton, O. W. *Army Letters, 1861–1865*. Chicago: O. L. Deming, 1903.

Osborne, John M., and Christine Bombaro. *Forgotten Abolitionist: John A. J. Creswell of Maryland*. Carlisle PA: House Divided Project at Dickinson College, 2015. https://www.smashwords.com/books/view/585258.

Parker, David B. *A Chautauqua Boy in '61 and Afterward*. Boston: Small, Maynard, 1912.

Parker, Rev. Theodore. *Ten Sermons of Religion*. Boston, 1853.

Polk, William. "General Polk and the Battle of Belmont." In *Battles and Leaders of the Civil War*, vol. 1, edited by Robert Johnson Underwood and Clarence Clough Buel. New York, 1887.

Porter, Admiral [David Dixon]. *Incidents and Anecdotes of the Civil War*. New York, 1886.

Porter, Horace. *Campaigning with Grant*. Edited by Wayne C. Temple. Bloomington IN: First-Rate Publishers, 1961.

Rable, George. *But There Was No Peace*. Athens: University of Georgia Press, 2007.

Redkey, Edwin S., ed. *A Grand Army of Black Men*. New York: Cambridge University Press, 1993.

Rees, James. *Foot-Prints of a Letter-Carrier*. Philadelphia, 1866. https://www.gutenberg.org /files/47190/47190-h/47190-h.htm.

Rice, Allan Thorndike, ed. *Reminiscences of Abraham Lincoln by Distinguished Men of His Times*. New York, 1885.

Richardson, Albert D. *The Secret Service, the Field, the Dungeon, and the Escape*. Hartford CT, 1865.

Sandburg, Carl. *Lincoln: The Prairie Years and the War Years*. New York: Harcourt, 1964.

Sharland, George. *Knapsack Notes of Gen. Sherman's Grand Campaign*. Springfield IL, 1865.

Sherman, William T. *Memoirs of General William T. Sherman*. 2 vols. 4th ed. New York, 1891.

Simpson, Brooks D. *Let Us Have Peace*. Chapel Hill: University of North Carolina Press, 1991.

———. *The Reconstruction Presidents*. Lawrence: University Press of Kansas, 1998.

———. *Ulysses S. Grant: Triumph over Adversity, 1822–1865*. New York: Houghton Mifflin, 2000.

Simpson, Brooks D., and Jean V. Berlin, eds. *Sherman's Civil War*. Chapel Hill: University of North Carolina Press, 1999.

Smith, Edward Parmalee. *Incidents of the United States Christian Commission*. Philadelphia, 1869.

Smith, Jean Edward. *Grant*. New York: Simon and Schuster, 2001.

Smith, John David. *Black Soldiers in Blue: African American Troops in the Civil War Era*. Chapel Hill: University of North Carolina Press, 2002.

Swanson, James. *Manhunt: The 12-Day Chase for Lincoln's Killer*. New York: William Morrow, 2006.

Theisen, Lee Scott. "The Public Career of General Lew Wallace, 1845–1905." PhD diss., University of Arizona, 1973.

Trudeau, Noah Andre. *Southern Storm: Sherman's March to the Sea*. New York: Harper, 2008.

U.S. Department of the Interior. *Register of Officers and Agents*. Washington DC, 1862. https://www.google.com/books/edition/Official_Register_of_the_United_States /UoMhAAAAMAAJ?hl=en&gbpv=1.

U.S. House of Representatives. *Letter from the Secretary of the Interior Transmitting a List of Clerks*. U.S. House Exec. Doc. No. 110, May 3, 1852, 32nd Congress, 1st session.

———. *Papers Relating to Postal Railway-Car Service*. House of Representatives Misc. Doc. No. 280, 43rd Congress, 1st session. Washington DC, 1874.

U.S. Post Office. *Annual Reports of the Postmaster General* (1898). U.S. House of Representatives Doc. No. 4, 55th Congress. Washington DC, 1898.

———. *Letter from the Postmaster General*. U.S. Senate Exec. Doc. No. 140, 50th Congress. Washington DC, 1888.

U.S. Senate. *Journal of the Executive Proceedings of the Senate of the U.S.* Vol. 19. Washington DC, 1869.

———. *Message of the President of the United States Communicating the Report of the Secretary of the Interior and the Secretary of War*. U.S. Senate Ex. Doc. No. 49, May 23, 1850, 31st Congress, 1st session. Washington DC, 1850.

U.S. War Department. *The War of the Rebellion: A Compilation of the Official Records of the Union and Confederate Armies*. Washington DC, 1880–1901.

Virdi, Jaipreet. *Hearing Happiness: Deafness Cures in History*. Chicago: University of Chicago Press, 2020.

Wallace, Lew. *Lew Wallace: An Autobiography*. 2 vols. New York: Harper & Brothers, 1906.

Whitman, Walt. *Memoranda during the War*. Camden NJ, 1876.

Wiley, Bell Irwin. *The Life of Johnny Reb*. Baton Rouge: Louisiana State University Press, 1943.

Williams, T. Harry. *P. G. T. Beauregard: Napoleon in Gray*. 1955. Baton Rouge: LSU Press, 1995.

Williamson, A. N., MD. *Observations on Nasal Catarrh and Catarrhal Deafness*. New York, 1877.

Wood, Eleanor Duncan. "Limestone, a Gateway of Pioneer Kentucky." *Register of Kentucky State Historical Society* 28, no. 83 (April 1930): 151–54.

Woodworth, Stephen. *Nothing but Victory: The Army of the Tennessee, 1861–1865*. New York: Knopf, 2005.

Index

Page numbers in italics refer to maps.

Absalom Grimes, Confederate Mail Runner (Grimes), 78

Act of February 28, 1861, 193

Adams, Henry, 107, 174

Adjutant General's Office (AGO) files, 142–43

"adversity covers," 37–38

African Americans. *See* Black Americans

Agen, James, 40

Alabama, 26, 167

Alcott, Louisa May, 39

Alexandria Gazette, 219

Allen, Robert W., 111

amalgamation, 74

ambition, 109

amnesty for former Confederates, 166–67, 169, 170

annexation: of Santo Domingo, 175–77; of Texas, 11

Antietam, Battle of, 70

anti–Ku Klux Klan congressional bills, 193–99

Appleton's Annual Cyclopaedia and Register of Important Events of the Year 1888, 260

"Application of the Colored People of Shelbyville," 168

Arkansas, 26, 167

Arkansas Post, 84–86, 240

Armstrong, George, 163

Army Chaplain's Manual (Hammond), 119

army mail service. *See* mail service, army

Army of the Cumberland, 103

Army of the Mississippi, 69, 87, 208n21

Army of the Ohio, 58–59, 62, 69, 103, 208n21. *See also* Society of the Army of the Ohio

Army of the Potomac, 89, 93, 103, 112–13, 114, 117–18

Army of the Tennessee, 54, 58, 69, 103, 161, 222. *See also* Society of the Army of the Tennessee

Arthur, Chester A., 223, 226

Atlanta GA, 112, 121–22, 125–26, 127, 257, 295n42

Augusta College, 9, 255

Averasboro, Battle of, 147

"Awaiting Audience at the White House" (Briggs), 181

Badeau, Adam, 236, 257, 295n41

Báez Méndez, Ramón Buenaventura, 176

Baltimore MD, 127–28, 163

Baltimore Sun, 180

Banks, Nathaniel, 82, 95

Barker, Daniel Fletcher: about, 20, 70, 97, 259; Absalom Markland letters to, 64, 231, 239, 247–49, 252, 258–59, 295n43

Barker, Rebecca Markland, 6, 20, 70

Barker, Violinda Markland, 97, 233

Battle of Antietam, 70

Battle of Atlanta, 121–22, 257, 295n42

Battle of Averasboro, 147

Battle of Bentonville, 147

Battle of Chancellorsville, 89

Battle of Chickamauga, 99, 100

Battle of Chickasaw Bayou, 82–83

Battle of Cold Harbor, 115
Battle of Fort Wagner, 90, 92
Battle of Gettysburg, 93–94, 257, 295n42
Battle of Lookout Mountain, 100, 103, 170
Battle of Milliken's Bend, 90
Battle of Missionary Ridge, 100, 103, 214, 257
Battle of Olustee, 90
Battle of Shiloh, 63–64, 71, 169, 239, 257–58, 259, 295n42
Battle of Vicksburg, 81–83, 84, 86–87, 89–90, 92–95
Battles of Bull Run, 28, 70, 155
Beauregard, Pierre Gustave Toutant, 168–70
Beecher, Henry Ward, 248
Belknap, William W., 207, 208, 211, 217–18
Bell, Alexander Graham, 226, 234
Bell, John, 26
Ben Hur (Wallace), 221
Bentonville, Battle of, 147
Bierbower family and house, 6, 255, 270
Bingham, J. D., 94
Black Americans: Absalom Markland and, 254–55; free population of, 183; KKK and, 185, 187–89, 191–93, 203; as postal employees, 179, 226–27; relocation of, 175, 177; and right to vote, 167, 191; as soldiers, 90–92, 280n34; in Tennessee, 183
Black Codes, 167–68
Black Hawk (ship), 82, 85
Blaine, James G., 184, 228–29
Blair, Francis Preston, 11, 205–6
Blair, Montgomery: about, 31; Absalom Markland and, 123–24; accomplishments of, 55–56, 138; Edwin Stanton feud with, 115–16, 124, 143–44, 282n19; mail stoppage by, 36, 52; resignation of, 124; Ulysses Grant and, 120–21
Blake, Alexander Hamilton, 218
Blue Wing (ship), 85
bonds for case hearings, 187
Boone, Daniel, 5, 252
Booth, John Wilkes, 2, 152, 157, 161, 209
Bostick, Absalom, 22
Boteler, Alexander R., 176–77, 251, 296n47
Bowen, Sam, 78
Bowers, Thomas S., 3, 110–11

Boynton, Henry Van Ness, 106, 214–15, 260, 296n47
Bradbury, Ray, 241
Bramlette, Thomas E., 101
Breckinridge, John C., 24, 26, 27
brevet promotions, 142–45, 285n19
Briggs, Emily Edson, 180–81, 184
Briggs, Joseph, 55
Bristow, Benjamin, 202, 228
Brooks, Preston, 25
Brown, George T., 170, 171–72
Bruce, Frederick, 161
Buchanan, James, 23, 24, 25–26
Buckner, Simon Bolivar, 50
Buell, Don Carlos, 54, 58, 68, 86, 251, 280n21
Buffalo Commercial, 139
Buffalo Morning Express, 260
Buffalo Trace, 5, 242
Bull Run, Battles of, 28, 70, 155
Bureau of Pensions, 12, 13–14
Bureau of Refugees, Freedmen, and Abandoned Lands, 162, 167, 168, 187
Burr, Frank A., 101
Burton, Allan A., 29
Butler, Benjamin F., 181, 248

Cairo IL, 28, 33–34, 44, 66, 86, 97, 165, 275n10
Cairo post office, 33, 76
Caldwell, Tod, 209
California, 163–64
California Steam Navigation Company, 163
Cameron, Simon, 29, 31
Caribbean islands, 175–77
Casey, John C., 13
Casto, Abijah, 242
catarrh, 217, 233
censorship, 58, 81, 83–84, 264
Century Illustrated Magazine, 252
Century Magazine, 230, 236
Chancellorsville, Battle of, 89
chaplains, 80, 118–19
Charleston Courier, 147
Charleston SC, 27, 146–47
Chattanooga TN, 100, 102, 111, 129, 138, 162, 185
Chauncey (ship), 164
Chicago Daily Tribune, 221

Chicago IL, 199–200, 257

Chicago Journal, 61

Chicago Tribune, 48, 58, 65

Chickamauga, Battle of, 99, 100

Chickasaw Bayou, 82–83, 84, 93

cholera, 68–69

cigars, 136–37, 235

Cincinnati City Council, 164

Cincinnati Enquirer, 180

Cincinnati Gazette, 212, 214

City Point Post Office, 138–39

City Point VA, 117, 119–20, 123–24, 138–39, 146, 148, 156

civil unrest, 170–71

Civil War, ending of, 145–46, 148–49, 151–52

Clarksville TN, 54–55

Clay, Cassius, 27

Clemens, Samuel L., 78

Cleveland, Grover, 229, 238–39, 251

Cleveland Soldiers' and Sailors' Convention, 180

Cohen, Solomon, 140, 143

Cold Harbor, Battle of, 115

Colley, Mary J., 221

Colored Troops, U.S., 90, 92, 183, 290n1

Columbia SC, 146

Committee on Invalid Pensions, 25

Committee on the Conduct of the War, 158, 170

Compromise of 1877, 220

Confederacy: Abraham Lincoln and, 27, 73, 155–56; Atlanta and, 121; Battles of Bull Run and, 70; Civil War end and, 145–46, 151, 156–59, 166–68; constitution of, 37; Corinth and, 62, 64–65; Democratic Party and, 26–27; discarded mailbags of, 51; Fort Donelson and, 43, 51; Fort Henry and, 48, 50; Kentucky and, 27–28, 31–32; Nashville and, 53–54, 57; nonmilitary terms of surrender of, 156–58; postal service of, 36–37, 57, 76–77; return of battle flags of, 238–39; Savannah and, 131; Sherman's march and, 146, 147; surrenders of, 43, 50, 54, 93, 146, 151–52, 155–58; value of slaves to, 73, 75; Vicksburg campaign and, 82, 87, 90, 92–93

Confederate Post Office, 36–37, 57, 76–77

Confederate states: reentry of, to Union, 167, 287n26; secession of, 26–27

Congressional Directory, 25

Congressional Globe, 197–98, 210

Constitutional Union party, 26

Cook, Simeon, 202

Copperheads, 26–27, 171, 287n33

Corinth MS, 62–63, 64, 65, 87

Correspondents Gallery, 25

corruption, 17, 36, 88–89, 163, 165

counterfeit bonds and paper money, 11, 179

"covers," 37–38

Craig, Richard, 243

Crater (Petersburg VA), 90–91

Crescent (ship), 95

Creswell, Hannah, 179, 184

Creswell, John A. J.: about, 177–79, 200, 215; Black postal employees and, 203; KKK Act and, 195, 196, 197; mail stoppage and, 201; social events and, 184, 201; special agent reorganization by, 182

Crocker's Iowa Brigade, 250

cycloramas, 257–58, 295n42

Daily Dispatch (Richmond VA), 193

Daily Mountaineer (The Dalles OR), 164

Daily Republic, 13, 14

Dana, Charles A., 174, 228, 237–38

Dandelion Wine (Bradbury), 241

Danville TN, 48

Davis, Garrett, 196

Davis, Henry G., 220

Davis, Henry L., 243

Davis, Henry T., 123–24

Davis, Jefferson: Abraham Lincoln's death and, 155, 156; Absalom Markland and, 228, 238–39; Civil War end and, 149, 157, 169; Confederate Post Office and, 37; strategy of, 82, 121

Davis, Varina, 145

Davis, William C., 36

Dayton, L. M., 148

Dayton Soldiers Home, 209–10

Dead Letter Office, 60

deafness, 233–35, 256

Democratic Party: Absalom Markland and, 24, 26; election of 1856 and, 23–24; election of 1860 and, 26; election of 1864 and,

Democratic Party (*cont.*)
116; election of 1872 and, 208; election of
1876 and, 219–20; election of 1880 and,
223; election of 1884 and, 228–29; KKK
Act and, 195, 197; postwar power gain of,
207; secession and, 26–27
Dennison, William, 116, 125, 138, 140–42,
160, 163, 164
Dent, Frederick, 173, 181
Department of the Interior, 12, 228
depression, 20
depression of 1873–78, 213–14
Detroit Free Press, 94, 170
disease, 68–69. *See also specific diseases*
Dodds, Ozro J., 222
Dominica. *See* Santo Domingo
Douglas, John Hancock, 229–30
Douglas, Stephen A., 26
Douglass, Frederick, 109, 186, 208, 248,
282n5
Drum, R. F., 238
Dumbarton Avenue Methodist Church, 14
Dunn, William K., 130, 136–37
Dwight, William, 90

Edison, Thomas, 234
elections, presidential: of 1840, 246; of
1848, 224; of 1856, 23–24; of 1860, 26; of
1864, 116, 122–24, 126–27; of 1868, 171,
237–38; of 1872, 207–8, 209; of 1876, 219–
20; of 1880, 223; of 1884, 228–29
Elkins, Stephen, 220
emancipation order in Missouri, 28
Emancipation Proclamation, 69, 70, 73, 74–
75, 90
emergency use of private and public property, 163, 164. *See also* land reclamation
Emerson, Ralph Waldo, 107
Enforcement Acts, 192–93, 201
envelopes, 37–38
Equal Rights Party, 208
Erie Railroad, 214
Evening Star (Washington DC): Absalom
Markland in, 113, 180, 223, 260; election
of 1856 in, 24; Matthew Markland in, 18;
Ulysses Grant burial in, 237
express companies, private, 56, 77, 138

Fabens, Joseph Warren, 175
Fayetteville NC, 147
federal intervention, 164, 197–98
Fifteenth Amendment, 191
Fifty-Fifth Massachusetts Regiment, 90, 186
Fifty-Fourth Massachusetts Infantry, 90
Fillmore, Millard, 23, 24, 224
Fish, Hamilton, 174–75, 177, 192–93, 198, 201
Fisk, Clinton, 39
Five Forks VA, 149
Flag (ship), 128
Flanagan, James, 254
Flanner, F. W., 76
"flood of letters," 75–77
floods, 242, 294n18
Florida, 13, 26, 90, 167, 220
Floyd, John, 49–50
Foote, Andrew, 43
Force, Manning Ferguson, 208–9
Forest Queen (ship), 82, 84
Fort Donelson, 42, 43, 47–51, 53, 119, 247
Fort Henry, 42–43, 48, 50
Fort Hindman, 84–86, 240
Fort McAllister, 128, 209
Fort Pillow, 90–91
Fortress Monroe, 119–20
Fort Sumter, 27, 73, 146
Fort Wagner, Battle of, 90, 92
Fort Wayne Daily Gazette, 212
Fort Wayne Gazette, 211
Forty-Second Congress, 193–99
Fourteenth Amendment, 191–92, 196, 198,
255
franking privilege, 179, 288n10
Franklin, Benjamin, 12
fraternal societies, 185, 205–7, 238, 290n1
Free and Accepted Masons, 16, 21
Freedmans' Savings Bank, 214
Freedmen's Bureau, 162, 167, 168, 187
Freeman, Julia Wheelock, 154
Frémont, John Charles, 23, 24, 28, 116, 122,
126
Fry, J. B., 68
Fulton (ship), 128–29, 132

GAR. *See* Grand Army of the Republic
(GAR)

Garfield, James A., 223, 224, 225–26
genealogy, 252–53
"general collectors and travelling agents,"
    9–10, 15, 17
Georgia, 16, 26, 128, 211, 287n26. *See also specific cities*
Gettysburg, Battle of, 93–94, 257, 295n42
Gibson, William H., 186–91, 196–98, 201–2,
    214, 254–55, 289n42, 290n49
Gilded Age, 207
Gist, R. C., 88
Glymont, 184
Goldsboro NC, 147, 148–49, 151
Goodloe, William Clinton, 27
Graham, George Washington "Wash," 96
Grand Army of the Republic (GAR), 238,
    290n1
Grand Reunion, 206–7
Grant, Fred, 61, 112, 231–32, 248, 257
Grant, Jesse, 98–99
Grant, Julia: Abraham Lincoln's death and,
    1, 152; Absalom Markland and, 34–35,
    257; death of, 237; field visits of, 66–67,
    93, 119–20, 151; husband's beard and, 34,
    42; husband's death and, 231, 232, 237; at
    social events, 179
Grant, Peter, 253, 255, 295n38
Grant, Ulysses "Buck," Jr., 229
Grant, Ulysses S.: about, 11, 12, 236; Abraham Lincoln's death and, 1–3, 152–54;
    Absalom Markland during war and, 33–
    34, 95, 99, 114, 119, 202; Absalom Markland postwar and, 41–42, 159–60, 231–32;
    Absalom Markland writings on, 114, 235;
    Andrew Johnson and, 173–74; appearance
    and personality of, 34, 42, 48–49, 60–61,
    95; Arkansas Post and, 86–87; army mail
    service and, 2–3, 43–45, 76; bankruptcy
    of, 229; Black mail agents and, 203; cabinet choices of, 174–75, 177, 178–79, 224;
    Chattanooga and, 100; chiefs of staff
    for, 238; childhood of, 7, 8, 255, 295n38;
    Civil War end and, 149, 151, 158–59; Fort
    Donelson and, 47–50; Fort Henry and,
    34, 42–43; fraternal societies and, 206,
    221; illness and death of, 179, 229–30, 231–
    32, 237; injury of, 98; KKK Act and, 196–

97, 199, 201; and lieutenant general of
    the army position, 103, 109–10, 112, 173;
    Mexico Southern Railroad and, 228;
    Money Post Office and, 137–38; Overland
    Campaign of, 114–15, 116–17; Paducah
    and, 32–33, 41–42; pardons from, 202,
    290n50; Peter Hudson and, 164–65; post-
    presidency travel of, 220; as president
    elect, 173, 176–77; presidential elections
    of, 171, 172, 207–8, 209, 237–38; promo-
    tions of, 53, 103, 109, 112–13; public edu-
    cation and, 219; racial violence and, 192,
    193–94, 203; Santo Domingo and, 175–77;
    as secretary of war, 171; train anonymity
    incident of, 113, 235; "Unconditional Sur-
    render" Grant moniker of, 50; Vicksburg
    and, 81–82, 87, 89–90, 92–94; William
    Dennison and, 158; William Sherman's
    march and, 126, 130; William Sherman's
    surrender terms and, 156–57
Grant, William, 61
Grant & Ward, 229
Gratiot Prison, 80, 81
Great Blizzard of 1888, 256–57
Great Chicago Fire, 199–200
Greeley, Horace, 122–23, 124, 207–8, 209
Green, C. C., 189–91
Green, Charles R., 131
Green, Elisha, 255
Green, R. A., 212
Grimes, Absalom, 77–81
Grimsley saddle, 159–60, 210
Gunckel, Lewis B., 210

Haiti, 175
Haldeman, Walter Newman, 7, 9, 10
Halleck, Henry W., 42–43, 62–65, 69, 103,
    109, 238
Hamilton House, 217, 221–22
Hamlin, Hannibal, 166
Hammond, Jonathan Pinkney, 119
Hancock, Winfield Scott, 223
Hanks, Absalom, 252, 253–54
Hanks, Nancy, 252, 256
Hanks family lineages, 252–53
Hanson, John Wesley, 40
Hardee, William J., 131

Harlan, James, 235
Harmon, Henry S., 92
Harper's Weekly, 60–62, 68, 95, 136, 139–40, 178
Harrison, Ben H., 221
Harrison, William Henry, 246
hatmakers, 243
Hayes, Rutherford B., 170, 219–20
hearing devices, 234
hearing loss, 233–35, 256
Hendricks, Thomas, 214
Henry von Phul (ship), 86, 93
Herron, Francis, 95
Hickenlooper, Andrew, 216
Higginson, Thomas Wentworth, 228, 229, 293n53
Hispaniola, 175–77
Holt, Joseph, 27
Holzer, Harold, 124
Hood, John Bell, 121, 125, 126
Hooker, Joseph, 89
Hop at Willard's hotel, 17, 184, 219
hops, 17, 184, 219, 221
"house divided," 6
House of Representatives, U.S., 11, 25, 196, 210, 219–20
Howard, Oliver Otis: about, 161, 287n15; Absalom Markland and, 158, 161, 162; Freedmen's Bureau and, 162, 167; National Postal Museum and, 265, 296n2; New Orleans excursion and, 170; Seidlitz powder story and, 235–36; Society of the Army of the Tennessee and, 211
Howland, Esther, 51
H.R. 320, 196–99
Hudson, Peter, 165
Hurst, Samuel H., 129

Ihrie, George, 235
illiteracy, 38–39
Illustrated London News, 146
Indianapolis News, 214
Indian Head MD, 184
Indian Removal Act, 12
Ingalls, Rufus, 117
Inter-Ocean, 208
Island City (ship), 129

Jackson, Andrew, 11, 12
Jewell, Marshall, 215, 220
Jewett, Joshua H., 25
Johnson, Andrew: about, 166; Blacks and, 166, 167; Hispaniola and, 175; impeachment trial of, 171–72; pardons and amnesty from, 167, 168, 170, 173, 287n14; post-presidency, 288n36; Reconstruction and, 171; states' reentry to Union and, 167; Ulysses Grant and, 171, 173–74; as vice president, 153
Johnson, Benjamin, 95, 97, 98
Johnson, Samuel, 233
Johnston, Albert Sidney, 49, 62–63
Johnston, Joseph Eggleston: Bentonville and, 147; replacement of, 121; surrender of, 152, 155–56, 157, 169; Vicksburg and, 93
Jones, Charles, 154

Kansas-Nebraska Act, 23
Kasson, John, 52–53, 54, 56, 66
Keller, Helen, 233
Kelley, William D., 178, 195, 248
Kentucky: about, 5, 6, 101, 183; Abraham Lincoln and, 27–28, 32, 33; Black soldiers and, 90; Confederacy and, 27–28, 31–32; election of 1856 and, 24; KKK in, 185; neutrality of, 26, 27–28, 31–33; postwar, 183, 184, 226–27; ridding of Absalom Markland from, 200; Thirteenth Amendment and, 188, 286n25. *See also specific cities*
"Kentucky Colonels," 101–2
Kentucky Democratic Association of Washington City, 24
Keyes, David, 220
King, John H., 259
Kirkwood and McGill, 18
Know-Nothing Party, 23–24, 26
Knox, Thomas W., 83–84, 280n18
Ku Klux Klan, 185, 187–89, 190, 191–94, 203
Ku Klux Klan Act of 1871, 193–99, 201–2, 203

labor strikes, 214
Laffoon, Ruby, 101
land reclamation, 162, 167, 168, 169–70, 217–18

Lee, Robert E., 70, 92, 93, 113, 115, 149, 151

Lellyet, John, 63

L'Enfant, Pierre, 161

letters: from Black civilians, 92; Civil War "flood" of, 75–77; from George Thomas, 99; importance of, in war, 37–40, 60, 222–23, 265; of nineteenth century, 15–16, 264; from soldiers, 40, 73–75, 76, 91–92, 105, 132, 139–40, 146; for soldiers in Sherman's march, 127–29; volume of, 40, 58, 75–76. *See also* letters of Absalom Markland

"Letters from Sherman's Army," 139–40

letters of Absalom Markland: to Abraham Lincoln, 28–29; to Andrew Hickenlooper, 216–17; to Charles Dana, 237; to Ely Parker, 236; to Fletcher Barker, 64, 231, 239, 247–49, 252, 258–59, 295n43; to Jefferson Davis, 238–39; to John Nicolay, 88–89; to John Phister, 240–41; *"O.B.'s" Reminiscences*, 241–48; to Ulysses Grant, 110, 230–31; to wife of personal nature, 15–16, 35, 42, 98; to wife on war, 52; to wife on work, 33–34, 35–36, 53, 60, 66, 88, 97; to William Dennison, 140–42; to William Sherman, 238

Liberal Republican Party, 207–8

Lincoln, Abraham: Absalom Grimes and, 80; Absalom Markland and, 27–30, 33, 41, 116, 130–31, 248–49, 252–53, 256; biography of, by Nicolay and Hay, 252; censorship of, 81; childhood of, 166; Civil War end and, 148–49, 156, 158, 166–67; Civil War start and, 27; death of, 1–3, 152–54, 155–56, 286n1; elections and, 26, 116, 122, 126; and Emancipation Proclamation, 69, 70, 74–75; John Creswell and, 177; John McClernand and, 84; Kentucky and, 27–28, 32, 33; postmaster general position and, 124–25; and Proclamation of Amnesty and Reconstruction, 166–67; trial of conspirators in assassination of, 161–62; Ulysses Grant and, 53, 103, 112, 116–17; Vicksburg and, 87, 93–94; William Sherman and, 131

Lincoln, Mary Todd, 39–40, 114

Lincoln, Robert Todd, 227

Lincoln, Thomas, 252

literacy, 38–39

Little Women (Alcott), 39

Livermore, Mary, 105

Lookout Mountain, Battle of, 100, 103, 170

Lossing, Benson J., 44, 118, 119, 231

Louisiana, 26, 167, 211, 220. *See also* specific cities

Louisiana Native Guards, 90

Louisville & Nashville Railroad, 127

Louisville Courier, 9, 19, 25, 33, 101, 191

Louisville Courier-Journal, 7, 248, 260

Louisville Democrat, 33, 88

Louisville ky, 6, 67, 75–76, 183, 193

Low, Frederick F., 163

loyalty oaths, 52, 78, 167, 168

MacFeely, Robert, 97

mail: cash sent through, 138; city delivery of, 55–56, 78, 79–80; collection boxes for, 56; halting of, 36, 52, 201, 203, 215; home delivery of, 55–56; international, 56, 163–64; morale and, 38, 105, 202, 216; privileged access of transports of, 111; robberies, 138; runners, 77; sorting of, 56–57, 59, 187; unclaimed, 87–88; volume of, 40, 58, 75–76

mail distribution, army: Absalom Markland and, 89, 106; by chaplains, 118–19; Confederate, 77; to Sherman's march soldiers, 129–30, 132, 140–41; Ulysses Grant's orders on, 59, 96

mail routes: Cairo to New Orleans, 165; to China, 163–64; discontinuation of, 193, 195, 201, 203; Louisville to Lexington, 188–93, 190, 197–98, 201, 212, 289n34, 289n42; Louisville to Mount Vernon, 188; Nashville to Knoxville, 111

mail service, army: about, 216; Absalom Markland and, 47, 89; Don Carlos Buell's army and, 58; establishment of, 43–45; halting of, 36, 52, 193, 195, 201, 203, 215; idea credit for, 44, 230–31; mail sorting and, 56–57, 59, 187; transportation and, 37, 56, 75, 86, 111, 128–29. *See also* mail distribution, army; mail routes

malaria, 69

March to the Sea, 125–27, 128, 161, 238

Markland, Absalom Hanks: as aid to the governor of Kentucky, 101; appearance, character, and personality of, 11–12, 34, 106–7, 108–9, 224–25; as assistant superintendent for Kentucky and Tennessee, 203; as assistant superintendent of Railway Mail Service, 200, 210, 213; birth and childhood of, 5, 6–9; brevet request of, 142–45, 285n19; and British diplomat incident, 161, 235; in California, 163–64; as a career realist, 213; "Colonel" moniker of, 2, 47, 48, 85, 107, 145, 205, 264; death of, 259–61, 263; death preoccupation of, 16, 21, 259; education of, 6–8, 9; and "General Clark" prank, 100–101, 235; "General" moniker of, 147, 181, 214, 229; as general superintendent of steamboat mail transportation, 163–65; health of, 68–69, 216–17, 233, 234–35; as honorary colonel, 102; as journalist, 9, 25, 88; legal practice of, 14–15, 16–17, 20–21, 165, 168, 169, 217–18, 251; life overview of, 256, 263–64, 265; lineage of, 252–56, 295n39; lobbying of, 165, 168, 182, 214–15, 223–25, 226; as mail supervisor of all army mail, 109–10, 115–16, 117, 120–21; marriage of, 14; "Oily Buckshot" moniker of, 9, 25, 28, 29, 33, 88, 240, 248; in Oregon, 164; and paymaster to the army position, 28–30, 88–89, 145; per diem for, 160; as self-made man, 106, 109; and sergeant at arms for the U.S. House of Representatives position, 210, 212, 213; social events attended by, 184–85, 217–19; as special agent of the U.S. Post Office, 31, 33, 36, 41–42, 215, 233, 256; steamboat days of, 9, 163–65, 248; as superintendent of the Third District of the Fourth Division, 182–84; and third assistant postmaster general position, 179–82, 185, 186; young adult occupations of, 9–11, 13–15, 16–17, 20–21. See also letters of Absalom Markland

Markland, Absalom Hanks as writer, 235–49, 256; Abraham Lincoln and, 248–49; journalism and, 9, 25, 88; "O.B.'s" Reminiscences, 240–48; Ulysses Grant and, 236–37; war stories of, 235–36, 237–38, 239–40, 247. See also letters of Absalom Markland

Markland, Adelia Ann, 6
Markland, Margaret, 6, 11
Markland, Martha Simms: about, 14, 17, 70, 222, 295n47; and death of husband, 259, 260–61, 295n47; failure of, to write to husband, 34–35, 41; Green Raum on, 135–36; with husband during travel, 151, 163, 164, 170; with husband in the field, 93, 95, 109, 120, 132; moving of, 66–67; Rutherford Hayes and, 220; social events and, 184, 213. See also letters of Absalom Markland

Markland, Matthew, Jr., 6, 28, 84, 242, 280n19
Markland, Matthew, Sr.: about, 5, 6, 253–54, 274n5; disappearance of, 18–20, 253; mental illness of, 20; Office of Indian Affairs and, 12–13; Office of Quartermaster General and, 17–18, 19–20
Markland, Rebecca, 6, 20, 70
Markland, Violinda, 6, 97, 233
Markland/Howard house, 161
Marks, James Junius, 118
Mars, Henry, 168
Marshall, James W., 215
Marshall, John, 218
Marshall Hall, 218
Maryland, 177–78, 184
Maysville Academy, 6–8, 255
Maysville KY, 5–6, 241–48, 244, 273n1, 294n18, 294n20
Maysville Republican, 8, 241
McClellan, George Brinton, 69, 70, 116, 124, 126
McClellan saddle, 159
McClernand, John, 84–87, 240
McClernand, Minerva, 93
McCormick, Richard, 163, 213
McLean, Wilmer, 151
McLellan, George W., 150
McPherson, James, 96, 219, 237
Meade, George Gordon, 93–94, 112–13, 114, 207
Meade, Margaretta, 120
Meigs, Montgomery, 89
melancholia, 20
memoirs: Absalom Markland's corrections on, 239; of Ulysses Grant, 48–49, 230, 232,

238–39, 248, 257, 294n14, 295n41; of William Sherman, 249

memorials, 206, 207, 219, 227–28, 237

Memphis and Charleston Railroad, 66

Memphis Avalanche, 68

Memphis Bulletin, 79–80

Memphis Post Office, 68, 85, 87–88

Memphis TN, 65–66, 67–69, 86, 87–88, 171, 183, 185

Military Division of the Mississippi, 103, 110, 111, 112

military mail service. *See* mail service, army

Military Postal Service, 138, 216

Milliken's Bend, Battle of, 90

miscegenation, 74

Missionary Ridge, Battle of, 100, 103, 214, 257

Mississippi, 26, 99, 100, 101, 167. *See also specific cities*

Mississippi River, 66, 82, 85, 89–90, 94, 95, 112, 242

Mississippi valley mail service reorganization, 165

Missouri, 26, 28, 78, 90

Mitchell, Andrew, 243

Mitchell, John F., 243

mixed-race children, 74, 211

money orders, postal, 137–39, 216

Money Post Office, 137–39

Moore, John, 236, 296n47

Morehead City NC, 147

Morning Courier and American Democrat (Louisville KY), 9–11

Mount Vernon, 188, 218

Mowris, James A., 40

"Mrs. President Grant's Tuesday reception," 184

Mudd, Samuel, 162, 287n14

mud season, 114

Mundy, Marcellus, 102

Munn, D. W., 212

Nashville Banner, 54

Nashville Daily Union, 69, 99

Nashville TN, 53–54, 57–59, 62, 67, 138, 185, 247

Nashville Union and American, 210

Nast, Thomas, 209

National Asylum for Disabled Volunteer Soldiers, 209–10

National Postal Museum, 265, 296n2

National Republican (Washington DC), 181, 210, 215, 218

National Union League of America, 226

National Union Party, 116, 123

Native Americans, 12–13

Nelson, Thomas Hill, 7

Nelson, William H. "Bull," 7, 27, 54

New Bern NC, 147, 148, 151

New Maysville Republican, 241

New Orleans LA, 95, 111–12, 165, 170–71

New Orleans post office, 111–12

newspapers, 81, 82–84, 122–24, 126–27, 143. *See also specific newspapers*

New Uncle Sam (ship), 43

New York Herald, 83, 101, 163

New York Sun, 229, 237

New York Times, 106, 123, 152, 157, 231, 259–60

New York Tribune, 122–23, 178

New York World, 124

Nichols, George Ward, 151

Nicolay, John J., 88–89, 123, 124, 252

North Benson KY, 189

North Carolina, 26, 139, 147, 167, 185. *See also specific cities*

Oak Hill Cemetery, 25, 70, 296n47

"O.B." identification and significance, 247–48, 294n21

"O.B.'s" Reminiscences (Markland), 241–48, 254

Ocean Steamer (ship), 95

Office of Indian Affairs, 12–13

Office of the Quartermaster General, 17

Ogeechee River, 128

Ohio River, 5, 6, 242, 294n18

"Old Tip" (cannon), 245–47, 294n20

"Olivia." *See* Briggs, Emily Edson

Olustee, Battle of, 90

Omaha Daily Bee, 235

Ordway, Nehemiah G., 212

Oregon, 164

Ossabaw Sound, 128

Overland Campaign, 114–15, 116–17

"pacific campaign," 27–28

Pacific Coast Steamship Line, 164

Paducah KY, 11, 32–33, 41–42

Page, Charles H., 251

panic of 1873, 213–14

panoramas, 257–58, 295n42

pardons for former Confederates, 167, 168, 169, 173, 202, 287n14, 290n50

Parker, David B., 138–39, 149–50

Parker, Ely S., 151, 173, 184, 232, 236–37, 238

Parker, Theodore, 70–71

Parks, William, 163

passes to all points within Union Armies' lines, 121, 235

Peabody Education Fund, 174–75

Pemberton, John C., 92, 93

penny postcards, 179

pensions, 13–15, 17, 21, 25, 290n1

Pentalpha Lodge, 16, 21

Personal Memoirs of Ulysses S. Grant (Grant), 48–49, 230, 232, 238–39, 248, 257, 294n14, 295n41

Petersburg VA, 91, 115, 117, 137, 145, 149

Peyton, Samuel, 25

Philadelphia Inquirer, 57

Phillips, James, 243

Philomathean Society, 7–8, 232

Phister, Elijah, 7

Phister, John P., 7, 240–41, 248, 294n23

photographs: of Absalom Markland, 61–62; of Ulysses Grant, 60–62, 95

phrenology, 208

Pickett, George, 149

Pierce, Franklin, 23

Pillow, Gideon, 32, 49–50

Pinchback, Pinckney Benton Stewart, 211–12

Pittsburg Landing, 63–64, 239

Poe, O. M., 251

Poilpot, Théophile, 257–58

Polk, Leonidas, 32

Pony Express, 56

popular sovereignty, 23, 26

Porter, David Dixon, 82, 85, 86, 148

Porter, Horace, 49, 120, 127–28

Port Hudson LA, 90

postage rates, 56, 64, 76–77

postage stamps. *See* stamps, postage

postal clerks of USPS, 216

Postal Inspection Service, U.S., 216, 265

postal platoon officers of U.S. Army, 216

postal routes. *See* mail routes

postcards, penny, 179

postmaster general position, 31, 36–37, 55–56, 125, 177, 178–79, 193, 215

Post Office Department. *See* U.S. Post Office Department

post office openings, postwar, 160–61

Powell, Mary Rebecca, 21

Prentice, John Newton, 87

presidential elections. *See* elections, presidential

Presidential Reconstruction, 162, 166–68, 171, 174, 191, 220

Price, Sterling, 80

printing, 37

private express companies, 56, 77, 102

Proclamation of Amnesty and Reconstruction, 166–67

Provisional Constitution of the Confederacy, 37

public education, 219

Rable, George, 207, 211

racism, 90, 166, 167–68, 183, 211

Radical Democracy Party, 116

railroad companies, postwar, 163

railroad tunnel (Dalton GA), 16, 269

rail strikes, 214

rail system of the South, 77

Railway Mail Service, 56–57, 185, 187, *190,* 200–201, 210, 222, 231

Raleigh NC, 151–52, 155, 157, 224

Rand, Jacob, 6

Raum, Green B., 135–36

Rawlins, John, 174, 176, 207, 227–28, 237–38

Rawlins Park, 227–28

Raymond, Henry Jarvis, 123, 124

Rayner, Kenneth, 223–24, 225

Reagan, John H., 36–37, 76–77

Reconstruction, 162, 166–68, 171, 174, 191, 220

regimental postmasters, 118–19

Reilly, William M., 113

Reminiscences of Abraham Lincoln by the Distinguished Men of His Time (Rice), 248–49

Republican Party: Absalom Markland and, 180, 200; Blacks and, 212; election of 1856 and, 23–24; election of 1860 and, 26; election of 1864 and, 116; election of 1868 and, 171, 172; election of 1872 and, 207–8; election of 1876 and, 219–20; election of 1880 and, 223; election of 1884 and, 228; KKK Act and, 195–96, 197, 198; and states' reentry to Union, 167

Republic of Texas, 11

Reynolds, Belle, 93

the Rialto, 120

Rice, Allen Thorndyke, 248

Rice, Spotswood, 91, 280n34

Richardson, Albert D., 83

Richardson, John A., 17

Richeson, E. M., 7

Richeson, John Brett, 6, 8

Richmond Post Office, 149–50, 154

Richmond VA, 2–3, 69, 115, 127, 149–50, 154

the Ridge, 20, 97

right to vote, 169, 170, 191

riots, 170–71

River Queen (ship), 148

Riverside Park, 237

Ross, Orlando H., 102

Russell, Henry A., 110

saddle gift, 159–60, 210

Sandburg, Carl, 129

Santo Domingo, 175–77

Savannah GA, 128–29, 130–32, 136–37, 139–41

Savannah Post Office, 132–33, 140–41, 146

Savannah Republican, 132–33

Schurz, Carl, 228

Scott, Robert N., 250

secession, 26–27

The Secret Service, the Field, the Dungeon, and the Escape (Richardson), 83

Seidlitz powder, 235–36

Select Committee of the Senate on the Alleged Outrages in the South, 193–94

Seminoles, 12–13

Seward, William Henry, 56, 69, 175

Seymour, Horatio, 172, 238

Sharland, George, 38

Shellabarger, Samuel, 196

Sheridan, Philip, 149, 208, 211

Sherman, John, 149, 225

Sherman, Maria "Minnie," 184, 213, 217

Sherman, William Tecumseh: Abraham Lincoln and, 131; Absalom Markland and, 82, 141–42, 143, 217, 240, 249–50, 260–61; Arkansas Post and, 84–86, 280n21; Atlanta and, 121–22; Battle of Shiloh and, 63; Carolinas and, 132, 139, 146, 147; Civil War end and, 148–49, 155–58; family visits and, 66–67, 98–99, 278n46; as lieutenant general, 173; mail and, 129–30, 150; march of, 125–27, 128, 161, 238; memoirs of, 249; newspapers and, 81; Pierre Beauregard and, 168–69; postwar, 172, 184; promotion of, 112; Raleigh and, 151–52; Savannah and, 131, 135, 136–37; Seidlitz powder incident and, 235–36; Society of the Army of the Tennessee and, 206, 211, 219, 221; Vicksburg and, 82

Sherman, Willy, 99

Shiloh, Battle of, 63–64, 71, 169, 239, 257–58, 259, 295n42

Simms, Harriet, 17, 25

Simms, Sampson, 14, 24–25, 35, 70

Sixth Massachusetts Volunteers, 40

Slack, James R., 67–68

slave auctions, 6, 186

slavery: abolishment of, 178, 187–88, 285n25; Absalom Markland and, 73, 254–55; Civil War end and, 73, 75; Confederate Army value of, 73, 75; elections and, 23; Freemasons and, 21; Hanks/Markland family and, 254; states' Union reentry and, 167; Transcendentalists and, 107

slave states, 11, 26, 73

smallpox, 68–69

Society of the Army of the Cumberland, 205, 209–10, 221

Society of the Army of the Ohio, 205

Society of the Army of the Tennessee: about, 205–6; Absalom Markland and, 185, 208–9, 216–17, 222, 251, 263; General Rawlins statue and, 227–28; reunions of, 208–9, 210–11, 219, 221, 222; Ulysses Grant and, 219, 221; William Sherman and, 206–7

Soldiers' and Sailors' Convention, 171, 180

Soldiers' Journal, 117

South Carolina, 26, 139, 146, 167, 185, 192, 220. *See also specific cities*

special agent(s) of the U.S. Post Office: about, 31, 36, 76, 285n19; Absalom Markland as, 31, 33, 36, 41–42, 215, 233, 256; in early days of Civil War, 41; reorganization of, 182

Special Orders No. 1, 44–45

Special Orders No. 39, 117

Special Orders No. 55, 150

Special Orders No. 142, 130

Special Orders No. 217, 96

Speed, James, 27, 187

Speed, John J., 27, 42

Speed, Joshua, 27, 28, 42

stamp collecting, 37

stamps, postage: canceling of, 146; cost of, 56, 58, 64, 76–77; printing of, 37; sale of, 55, 57, 58, 64, 76, 132, 139; scarcity of, 40, 59

Stanton, Edwin, Jr., 149, 170

Stanton, Edwin, Sr.: Abraham Lincoln's death and, 2, 153, 154; Absalom Markland's petition and, 142–43; Confederacy's surrender terms and, 157; Montgomery Blair's feud with, 115–16, 124, 143–44, 282n19; postwar, 168, 171

steamboats, 9, 51, 95–96, 163, 165

Stevenson, John White, 191, 197

St. Louis Hotel, 170

Stowe, Harriet Beecher, 6

suffrage, Black, 169, 170, 191

Sumner, Charles, 25, 174

Surrat, Mary, 162

Swann, Thomas, 196

Tate, Samuel, 168

Taylor, Zachary, 224

Tennessee, 26, 42–43, 47–51, 183, 185. *See also specific cities*

Tennessee Staatszeitung, 165

Terrell, William Henry Harrison, 181

Texas, 11, 26

Thirteenth Amendment, 178, 187–88, 289n25

Thomas, Charles, 19–20

Thomas, George H., 99, 125, 126, 141, 173, 206

Thoreau, Henry David, 107

Thornly, T. S., 243

Thurman, Allen G., 213

Thurman, Margaret, 213

Thustin, Luther, 213

Tigress (ship), 84, 86

Tilden, Samuel J., 219

Tilghman, Lloyd, 43

Tinker, William, 243

Todd, C. S. S., 88

tracking army personnel, 58–59

Transcendentalists, 107

Tyler, John, 246

typhoid, 68–69, 98, 99

Uncle Tom's Cabin (Stowe), 6

Underground Railroad, 6, 255

Union Army: Black soldiers in, 90–92, 280n34; dismantling of, 158–59; tracking personnel of, 58–59. *See also* mail service, army

Union Navy, 43, 90, 128, 208–9

United Brothers of Friendship, 186, 289n42

universal postage rates, 56

Universal Postal Union, 56

unrest, civil, 170–71

U.S. Colored Troops, 90, 92, 183, 290n1

U.S. House of Representatives, 11, 25, 196, 210, 219–20

U.S. Military Academy at West Point, 8, 168, 237

U.S. Navy, 43, 90, 128, 208–9

U.S. Postal Inspection Service, 216, 265

U.S. Postal Service (usps), 57, 187, 215–16

U.S. Post Office and Custom House (Chicago), 199–200

U.S. Post Office Department: about, 12, 36–37; Absalom Markland and, 52–53, 94–95, 102–3, 144, 160–61, 165–66, 214–16; Blacks and, 179, 188, 203; Great Chicago Fire and, 200; John Creswell and, 179; under Montgomery Blair, 55–57, 138; Railway Mail Service and, 56–57, 185, 187, 190, 200–201, 210, 222, 231; third assistant postmaster general nominations and, 179–82; transportation companies and, 163; Ulysses Grant and, 214–15, 230; Union Army and, 110–11. *See also* mail service, army usps. *See* U.S. Postal Service (usps)

Vail, Mrs. Marion Wall, 79–80
valentines, 51
Van Pelt, William, 198
Vicksburg ms, 81–83, 84, 86–87, 89–90, 92–96, 103
Vicksburg post office, 94–96, 97–98
Virginia, 5, 26, 114, 282n13. *See also specific cities*

Wade, Benjamin, 170
Wadsworth, William Henry, 7
Wallace, Lew, 63–64, 207, 220–21
"The War, and What I Saw of It" (Markland), 88
Ward, Ferdinand, 229
War Department: Abraham Lincoln's death and, 2, 153–54; Absalom Markland's pursuit of paymaster position in, 28–30, 88–89, 145; Matthew Markland and, 17; Stanton-Blair feud and, 115–16, 282n19; Ulysses Grant and, 158, 171
The War of the Rebellion, 250
war records, 250
Washburne, Elihu, 174, 248, 287n25
Washington, George (slave), 91–92

Washington and Georgetown Directory (Hunter), 18
Washington Common Council, 24–25
Washington Union, 24
Welcome, Jane, 92
West Point, 8, 168, 237
Wharton, G. C., 187
W. H. Brown (ship), 54
White, John D., 226
Whitman, Walt, 39, 248
Whitney, James, 163
Willard, Henry A., 296n47
Willard Hotel, 17, 153, 184, 219, 231, 296n47
Williams, Charles, 243
Winchester ky, 5
winter of 1863–64, 105
wives, military, 66–67, 93, 119–20
women: of Absalom Grimes's "grapevine," 78, 79–80; in the field, 66–67, 93, 119–20, 278n46
Woodhull, Victoria, 208
wood scarcity, 136

XI Corps, 100

yellow fever, 69, 98
Yellowstone National Park, 207